La Terra Fortunata

OTHER BOOKS BY FRED PLOTKIN

Recipes from Paradise: Life and Food on the Italian Riviera

Italy for the Gourmet Traveler

Opera 101: A Complete Guide to Learning and Loving Opera

The Authentic Pasta Book

Italy Today: The Beautiful Cookbook (with Lorenza De' Medici)

La Terra Fortunata

THE SPLENDID FOOD AND WINE

OF FRIULI-VENEZIA GIULIA

Fred Plotkin

Broadway Books ❧ New York

Library of Congress Cataloging-in-Publication Data
Plotkin, Fred.
La terra fortunata : the splendid food and wine of Friuli-Venezia Giulia / by Fred Plotkin.—1st ed.
            p.   cm.
Includes bibliographical references and index.
1. Cookery, Italian—Northern style.
2. Cookery—Italy—Friuli-Venezia Giulia.   I. Title.
TX723.P5925 2001
641.5945´39—dc21   00-060845

FIRST EDITION

Book design by Pei Loi Koay
Map illustration by Jeffrey L. Ward
Food photography by Dennis Gottlieb

ISBN 0-7679-0611-X

01 02 03 04 05 10 9 8 7 6 5 4 3 2 1

For

Mark Anderson,

Laura De Angelis,

and their Silvia

Contents

Acknowledgments

Wine comes in at the mouth,
And love comes in at the eye.

—WILLIAM BUTLER YEATS

Writing this book was an act of love, and a reminder to me of the love that so many people showered on me as *La Terra Fortunata* slowly came to be. Love came to me not only by the eye but through many other means. By the time the manuscript was delivered to my publisher, I had been a frequent visitor and sometime resident in Friuli-Venezia Giulia for twenty-five years. It would be impossible for me to list every person who made a meaningful contribution to my knowledge of this complex and wonderful little region. What I know about it came slowly, with layer coming on top of layer, and new doors with new insights opening all the time. Each person I spoke with added to the whole. Yet there are some people in Friuli-Venezia Giulia, New York, London, and many other places on five continents (for such a small place, this region casts a very wide net) who were instrumental in the genesis of this book, and they deserve my special gratitude.

At the Doubleday Broadway Publishing Group, Judith Kern, the editor who acquired this book, was as patient as she is wise and warm. She had the wisdom and courage to believe in a book about Friuli-Venezia Giulia when others hesitated to create a work about an unknown place.

Jennifer Josephy and I have enjoyed something rare in modern publishing: an ongoing relationship between editor and author. After collaborating on *Italy for the Gourmet Traveler* and *Recipes from Paradise: Life and Food on the Italian Riviera*, I was happy that, when she came to my current publisher, she inherited this book. It is a pleasure to work with her. Thanks, too, to Anne Resnik for much invaluable assistance.

Thanks particularly to Mario Pulice, Creative Director at Doubleday Broadway, who lavished such care and time on the design of the cover of this book. Also, Dennis Gottlieb and Jim Ong did splendid work on the food photographs for this book, as did A. J. Battifarano and Amy Lord with the food styling for those pictures. My appreciation goes to Barb Fritz for the prop styling. Thanks also to Bruce Feiler, who took the portrait on the jacket, and to Catherine Pollock. Warm appreciation to Pei Loi Koay, the designer of this book. Much appreciation to Tammy Blake, also at Doubleday Broadway, who is responsible, through her fine publicity work, for bringing this book about a magnificent but little-known place to a wider audience. Thanks also to Rebecca Holland and the rest of my publisher's production department.

David Black is the Friuli-Venezia Giulia of agents, and it is no secret what I think of that place. Thanks to him and everyone in his office—Susan Raihofer, Gary Morris, Joy Tutela, Leigh Ann Eliseo—I am *un autore fortunato.*

I have been immeasurably assisted, counseled, encouraged, and steadied by Fern Berman, whose contributions to my work and life know no limits. Aside from her incomparable professional talents, she is also the perfect friend. Thanks also to Robin Insley and everyone else at Fern Berman Communications.

Carol Field, Corby Kummer, Lynne Rossetto Kasper, Nancy Harmon Jenkins, and Joyce Goldstein are so much more than colleagues. They are the mirror that makes clear to me what I should do in my work.

Every man needs his muse, and mine is Cara De Silva. Hers were the eyes and ears for whom this book was written, and I now add it to her pedestal.

Special thanks to Arthur Schwartz for his knowledge and humor and for his encouragement in writing about a region that turned out to be the home of his ancestors.

I traveled with Edward Behr through Friuli-Venezia Giulia in 1992 as he conducted research for a special issue of his superb newsletter, *The Art of Eating,* called "In the Vineyards of Friuli." While my role was as translator and guide to the region, I benefited from Ed's persistent and incisive questioning of wine producers to deepen my own knowledge of this region's extraordinary and diverse oenological scene.

Robert Draper has come to love Friuli-Venezia Giulia as much as I do, and we had a great trip of discovery together. My thanks to him. Carole Lalli, Erica Marcus, Rick Kot, and David Cashion were editors of earlier books who have become friends and continue to give me wonderful guidance and ideas. Michalene Busico of *The New York Times* commissioned a story about the region that helped focus my ideas fruitfully, and I thank her. Joan Bloom of Hill & Knowlton in New York so ably represents Trieste in the United States and has been helpful to me in infinite ways.

I was fortunate to have my mother and my late father travel with me in Friuli-Venezia Giulia on different occasions. They enchanted everyone they met, which made for many sweet moments.

Steven Jenkins is one of a kind, combining fire in the belly with gold in the heart. He and Sid Grabill, Valerie Blenman, John Rossi, and Robert Graham of Fairway Market devote their all to providing the finest foods to New Yorkers, including this one. Some of the dishes in this book were first presented in cooking classes at the store. The proceeds from these classes went to Citymeals-on-Wheels, and I thank Fairway for the chance to help. Thanks to Rob Kaufelt of Murray's Cheese Shop for his advocacy of artisanal cheeses. Brothers Tasso and Taki of the Mani Market in New York have been the most caring of local food sellers, always available with ingredients for recipe testing and an encouraging thumbs-up.

Lidia Bastianich and her son, Joseph, represent Friuli-Venezia Giulia so wonderfully in restaurants, books, wine making, television programs, tours of Italy, and all of their other endeavors. They are also special ambassadors of the best of New York to the rest of the nation and to Italy. They have always been most encouraging of my work, and I am grateful to them.

Peter Hoffman of Savoy restaurant in New York created a superb meal of the foods and wine of Friuli-Venezia Giulia and welcomed me to speak about the region to his clients. He is a special friend.

Michael Romano and Danny Meyer of the Union Square Cafe in New York have been wonderful friends to me and paragons of running a great restaurant. Danny has been a key supporter of the wines of Friuli-Venezia Giulia, and Michael is a person for whom superlative words always seem inadequate. There is no one like him.

Tony and Marisa May of San Domenico restaurant in New York welcome all Italians to their door as they try to find their way in the New World. They have been great supporters both of Friuli-Venezia Giulia and of my work.

Charles Draghi of Marcuccio's Restaurant produced a magnificent meal of the foods and wines of the region on a blizzardy night in Boston despite having casts on both arms. He has my great admiration. Thanks to Nancy Civetta, who so ably organizes the Boston Cooks! Dine Around, and to Annie Copps, Vita Juan, and Francie King, just because. And to Oldways Preservation & Exchange Trust of Cambridge, Massachusetts, for its devotion to discovering and safeguarding traditions of food culture through documentation and education.

Alice Waters of Chez Panisse restaurant in Berkeley, California, has done so much to promote the nurturing of farmers and suppliers who give us clean, delicious, and healthful food. Her approach is wholly in keeping with that of *La Terra Fortunata*. She has also been a marvelous advocate for the white wines of Friuli-Venezia Giulia. Great thanks to dear Glenn McCoy, who led me to markets and restaurants in San Francisco in search of foods of Friuli-Venezia Giulia and Istria. Thanks, too, to Andy Beckstoffer of Beckstoffer Vineyards in the Napa Valley, who gave me an extensive education in his outstanding vineyards about grape growing in that part of the world. His knowledge and responses to my many queries helped me juxtapose the choices and outlook of California growers with those I have come to know in Europe.

Un vivo ringraziamento to Fabrizio Camastra and Maria Woodley of the Italian Trade Commission in New York. Both have been very supportive, especially as I began to study prosciutto di San Daniele. Marta Marie Lotti of Alitalia in New York does Italy and her employer proud. Mary Kay Hartley, Antonia Imperoli, Eugenio Magnani, and Roberto Talignani of the Italian National Tourist Office in New York have offered continuing generous help and friendship, for which I am grateful. Patrick Martins, Carmen Wallace, and Carlo Petrini of the Slow Food movement, of which I am an ardent supporter, have done a phenomenal amount for the food and wine of Friuli-Venezia Giulia, and I have benefited from that.

Special thanks to Margherita Uras, who was always on the lookout for articles, books, and ideas that would help me in my research. Ellen Schenone and Gian Guido D'Amico are Ligurian friends who made several valuable introductions for me in Trieste.

I thank the 1,200,000 citizens of Friuli-Venezia Giulia, but especially the following: Dr. Roberto Antonione, Presidente della Giunta Regionale, who works daily to safeguard that which is so special about his land. Giulio Colomba generously shares his love and knowledge of the food and wine of his region with me and everyone he encounters. He is one of my oracles. In the years I worked on this book, I came to realize that I would not truly know or understand Friuli-Venezia Giulia unless I visited the émigré communities around the world as well. Mario Toros, President of Friuli nel Mondo, connected me with far-flung communities and was essential to my research.

The irrepressible Dr. Andrea Cecchini of ERSA (Ente Regionale per la Promozione dell'Agricoltura del Friuli-Venezia Giulia) took me to remote and special places in the region, zooming down the autostrada at a velocity that would exhaust a cheetah. He is a most enthusiastic and winning representative of his region. The Nonino family, with their high spirits and incomparable grappa and distillates, have given me great happiness and knowledge.

Grazie infinite to Elena Cozzi, Dr. Francesco Ciani, Rino Coradazzi, Carlo Zuccolo of the Consorzio del Prosciutto di San Daniele, and to Cesare Gallo, all of whom helped teach me about that divine ham. Sonia, Paola, and Vladimir Dukcevich of Principe Prosciutto helped me discover the special role of pork in the food and life of Trieste. Thanks to everyone at the consortium of producers of Montasio cheese. My warmest thanks and respect to Dr. Ernesto Illy, who is the Triestine God of Coffee, and to Myra Fiori of Illy USA, each of whom keeps my cup brimming.

Thanks to the tourist offices in Trieste, Udine, Gorizia, Pordenone, Cividale, Tarvisio, and Arta Terme. Special appreciation to Paolo de Gavardo, director of the Azienda di Promozione Turistica di Trieste. Also, a particular acknowledgment to the regional tourist office, which is based in Trieste.

Dr. Enrico Bertossi, president of the Chamber of Commerce in Udine and leader of the Made in Friuli initiative, has helped many of my colleagues discover the best of his region. Also Giovanni Masarotti and Luciano Snidar of Promosedia, the group that brings Friulian chair-making to the world and assures that everyone has a fine place to sit. They too have helped many Americans discover not only their products but their whole region.

In Tarvisio, Gabriele Massarutto of Senza Confini, Claudio Tognoni of the Consorzio Servizi Turistici del Tarvisiano e di Sella Nevea, and Giampaolo (Gianni) Macorotti, head of Associazione Italiana Sommeliers for FVG, have all been incomparably generous and dedicated in helping me discover their corner of the region. All of them are marvelous representatives of the place where Germanic, Slavic, and Latin Europe converge and are ambassadors for peace and tolerance. Alessandro Pennezzato has been a splendid teacher to me about the northern part of Friuli-Venezia Giulia, and a great friend.

Marco Grusovin in Gorizia patiently taught me about the history of Judaism in his city, and I also specially thank all the representatives of the Jewish community in Trieste who so generously shared their heritage and history with me. Peter and Anna Garassich taught me a lot about the baking tradition in Trieste, and enabled several of my colleagues to learn as well. Thanks also to Maria Brandmayr and Antonella Adamo, both of whom were constant companions in my discovering Trieste. Also, Fabio Malusà kept me informed on all things Triestine, and patiently corrected me as I slowly learned the town's dialect.

My darling friend Alessandra Dorigo, who has been so much a part of this book, only later revealed her skills as one of the region's best bakers. Walter and Patrizia Filiputti fed my mind, spirit, heart, and stomach in equal measure. I love them both. Cynthia Marie Zach, Lorenzo Dante Ferro, and daughter Carolina opened my eyes and nostrils to new worlds, and have been dear friends as well.

Patrizia Stekar, Marina Danieli, and Elda Felluga, three magnificent women, have contributed immeasurably to my knowledge about their region. In rereading this manuscript, I often heard their voices and saw their beautiful faces. All produce superb wine and marvelous food and are great nurturers in their own ways. Thanks also to Alvaro Pecorari and his family, all of whom have my greatest admiration. Similarly, Josko and Loredana Sirk and their family and chef Stefano Fermanelli, all of La Subida in Cormons, have educated me (and fed me) tirelessly. Josko is an irreplaceable treasure for his land.

Claudio Magris shared his precious insights with me about the region's zeitgeist, intellectual fervor, and discontents, and helped me cut through much that was stereotypical or wrong to reach the elusive essence of what Friuli-Venezia Giulia means. Giovanni Leghissa and Tatiana Silla, Triestine transplants in Vienna, helped me understand the powerful and subtle connections between those two cities.

I traveled extensively in former Hapsburg lands while conducting research for this book. It was important for me to understand the subtle differences in food preparations, spices, wines, and other products. Many of these have the same or similar names, like strudel or Tocai, but are profoundly different. Many people and organizations helped me learn, so that I could put to rest the countless misconceptions that exist about a large zone that falls under the charming but highly inaccurate name of Mitteleuropa.

Gabriele Wolf and Sigrid Pichler of the Austrian National Tourist Office in New York have been there since the start of this project and have helped in so many ways to contrast Austria's great heritage with that of Friuli-Venezia Giulia. Thanks also to Eva Draxler of the Vienna Tourist Authority. Manfred Stallmajer, general manager of the Hotel Das Triest in Vienna, maintains an outpost of Trieste in Austria. In Vienna, Herwig Gasser, chief baker at the Cafe Querfeld, Harald Fargel, instructor at the Gastgewerbefachschule, and Siegfried Dörre of the Café Restaurant Schottenring, all gave me private lessons in Viennese cooking and baking, enabling me to learn the classics and then compare them with their Friulian counterparts.

Thanks to Chris Lazarus of A. J. Lazarus Associates, in New York, who opened many doors to me in Hungary for conducting important research. Dr. István Meggyes, director general, Hungarian Tourist Board in Budapest, and Balazs Szucs, director, Hungarian Tourist Board in New York, also provided valuable assistance. Katalin Till was my outstanding guide and translator in Budapest and around Hungary and is an ideal representative of her marvelous country. Special thanks to Dominique Arangoits of Disznókó winery in Tokaj in Hungary for educating me about Tokaj wines and making me see, once and for all, that wines with a similar name in Hungary, Friuli-Venezia Giulia, and Alsace are entirely different.

Thanks also to the national tourist offices and information agencies of the Czech Republic, Slovakia, Croatia, and, especially, Slovenia, all of whom patiently explained things to me that clarified my research and then sent me to the right places in their nations to acquire firsthand knowledge and documentation. Early travel to visit the wine country in Argentina to discover the large and important Friulian émigré community there permitted me to see firsthand the way people there maintain powerful roots and traditions even on the other side of the world. Countless people in Canada and Australia filled similar functions for me in those countries, where vibrant communities from Friuli and Venezia Giulia have made important contributions.

I also visited communities from Friuli-Venezia Giulia in places as disparate as Los Angeles, San Francisco, Montreal, Paris, Berlin, and London, all of which keep home fires burning in faraway places. It was fascinating to me to discover how language and food persist and change when old ways meet new ones.

People and work in London have played an essential part in the character of this book. Mary Bruton of the Abner Stein Literary Agency has been an advocate for this and all of my books and becomes more dear to me all the time. So too is Laura Morris, who has been there since the beginning. Claudia Roden gave me first-person insight about being an Egyptian girl with a nanny from Gorizia, an important chapter of social and political history that is little known. Anna del Conte had a Friulian nanny in Milan and filled in many gaps in my knowledge. She and Philippa Davenport were travel partners nonpareil on a trip to the region. Thanks also to Rosemary Stark, Simon Parkes and everyone at the Food Programme of the BBC, Rose Gray and Ruth Rogers of the River Cafe, and to the Baillie Family.

I spent endless weeks and many happy hours at three institutions—the London Library, the British Library, and the Imperial War Museum—learning the intricacies of a vast range of topics that relate to Friuli-Venezia Giulia, from James Joyce to agrarian issues in the Roman Empire to the spice trade and, above all, the complicated and tragic stories of too much bloodshed and senseless loss of life, from the Punic Wars to the disintegration of the former Yugoslavia. The staffs at the libraries and museum were unfailingly generous with their time and efforts, and I am deeply grateful to them.

Above all, Rosa Bosco (formerly Rosetta Dorigo), more than anyone else, exemplifies everything I adore about Friuli-Venezia Giulia. This book is really for her. *Mandi!*

La Terra Fortunata

Introduction:
La Terra Fortunata

What wondrous life is this I lead!
Ripe apples drop about my head;
The luscious clusters of the vine
Upon my mouth do crush their wine;
The nectarine and curious peach,
Into my hands themselves do reach;
Stumbling on melons, as I pass,
Insnar'd with flow'rs, I fall on grass.

—ANDREW MARVELL

There is a place, at the very geographic center of Europe, that is home to one of the most refined food and wine cultures in the world. Follow all of your senses and let me lead you there.

Hemingway, Joyce, D'Annunzio, Rilke, and Pasolini all lived in this place, and yet it is nearly unknown in the United States, and even in much of Europe. It has been occupied by Julius Caesar (for whom it was named), Celts, Attila the Hun, Charlemagne, Hungarians, Venetians, Napoleon (who brought French grapes), Hapsburgs, Yugoslavia, and, ultimately, by Italy. It suffered some of the heaviest damage in Europe during two world wars. Much of it was leveled in 1976 by earthquakes. Yet, its people rise again and again, roll up their sleeves, plant food and vines, and plan for a better life.

This special place, called Friuli-Venezia Giulia, is the northeasternmost of Italy's twenty regions. It is easy to say that it is between Venice and Vienna, but that only gives you the most general notion of what it is about. This is a very small area, only 3,029 square miles (7,844 square kilometers). Compare this to the second and third smallest American states: Delaware (2,057 square miles) and Connecticut (5,009 square miles). Or to Puerto Rico (3,435), Corsica (3,352), and Crete (3,217). Yet its capital, Trieste, is Italy's most cosmopolitan city. Rome may have foreign embassies and *la dolce vita,* and Milan is Euroglitzy, but Trieste (218,000 inhabitants) is something more. It is the only Italian city where Catholics, Jews, Moslems, Protestants, and the Greek and Serbian Orthodox communities do not simply coexist peacefully, but create a magnificently complex society. It should not surprise you that James Joyce lived here for more than fifteen years.

But this region is so much more than Trieste. Tiny though it is (the fourth smallest of Italy's twenty regions), Friuli-Venezia Giulia has virtually every type of terrain except desert. It is 43 percent mountains, 19 percent hills, and 38 percent plains, but that only begins to tell the story. Think of it in bands that run east to west. The northernmost zone, known as Carnia, is part of the alpine chain of central Europe and was a finalist to host the 2006 winter Olympics. Its greatest natural resource is lumber. Nearby are the laghi di Fusine, pure deep-water lakes hemmed in by mountains that bring fjords to mind.

Throughout the area, dairy cattle graze and provide milk for superb cheeses. Gustav Mahler, who spent much time in this zone, wrote that cow bells are "the last greeting from earth to penetrate the remote solitude of the mountain peaks." Carnia is the custodian of an ancient heritage and the last bastion of an agricultural civilization that is little known elsewhere. One of my objectives in this book is to document and preserve many of those traditions that are about to disappear. The last survivors of this vanishing world are past seventy, and you will meet some of them in these pages.

Below Carnia are pre-alpine foothills that are swept by north-south winds (from Alps to sea) and winds from Italy's Veneto region to the west and the nation of Slovenia to the east. Smack in the middle of all of this ventilation is the town of San Daniele, the only place that makes a prosciutto that can match (and perhaps exceed) the famous one from Parma. The sweet mountain air and the salty breezes from the south air-dry the ham perfectly.

South of the foothills are several hilly zones that are idyllically beautiful and are the place where some of the world's best wine is produced. Many experts agree that Italy has three great food regions (Emilia-Romagna, Friuli-Venezia Giulia, and Liguria, with Sicily a close fourth) and three great wine regions (Friuli-Venezia Giulia, Piedmont, and Tuscany). So this is the only region in Italy where food and wine are at the same high level.

The Nose Knows

Deep in the Bassa Friulana, in the town of Gradiscutta di Varmo, lives a Friulian original, a master perfumer named Lorenzo Dante Ferro. Along with his American wife Cynthia, daughter Carolina, and brother Luciano and sister-in-law Silvia, he maintains a centuries-old tradition. Lorenzo is one of this region's trailblazing originals, safeguarding a tradition while finding relevance for it in the twenty-first century.

Although I have a highly developed sense of smell, Lorenzo's understanding of its impact changed how I approached Friuli-Venezia Giulia and all food and wine. Now, I smell everything before and as I taste it, and let flavors in my mouth reach my palate, so that my nose is suffused with more fragrances of food and drink. By incorporating my nose in the process, I taste things more slowly and fully. I discovered that this is how many people in the region eat, too.

Walking with Lorenzo in the fields and streams of his land is like an outing with a bloodhound. Every leaf, twig, flower, animal, and handful of water bears a fragrance that he can identify and describe. Each has meaning and an association, though he observes that most people do not use their olfactory abilities much at all. "We are missing a language of fragrance," he tells me. "We recognize colors. We have a codification of musical sounds. There is an extremely emotional element in the olfactory—it was our first sense. When we did yet not see or hear, we could still smell. A baby does not have language. Yet a newborn knows the smell of its mother's milk. We are prepared from that moment to face our lives through the emotion of olfactory sensation. Our noses can discern three thousand different scent notes, but how can we express them in words?"

When Venice was the center of the perfume industry in the Renaissance and later, this zone was its laboratory. Scents of flowers and plants were blended with local fruit plus spices that arrived on merchant ships. The master perfumers of Venice and the Bassa Friulana became famous through Europe. Their products were exported in beautiful glass bottles made in Murano. One local perfumer, Farina, found his way to Cologne in Germany, creating a fragrance based on Friulian traditions that is now called cologne, or eau de cologne.

Lorenzo believes in the dictum, "tell me what you eat and I will tell you who you are." By this, he does not suggest one necessarily adopts the smells of one's dinner. Rather, that certain foods appeal to certain peoples based on climate or tradition. So smells of wheat, cinnamon, and butter often appeal to northerners; herbal scents are favored by those who live near coasts; and fragrances based on oil or citrus are preferred by people who live in Mediterranean zones.

Spice preferences are even more distinct. "Cumin is like the smell of the body. In the Middle East, it is meaningful and elemental. In more northern societies, this is associated with body odor."

Without telling Lorenzo the name of this book or any of its ideas, I asked him what components he would use in a perfume called Friuli-Venezia Giulia. Without hesitation, he pulled out one he made called "Tiare," which is Friulian for "land." It was woody and aromatic, with notes of grass and flowers. It smelled like the local fields, yet not quite. He then pulled out a bottle called "Lebkuchen," which contains notes of cinnamon and butter. He said this evokes Carnia and parts of Gorizia and Trieste. By combining Tiare with a bit of Lebkuchen, he created a fragrance that really reminds one of the region: woody and grassy, rich in fresh herbs, with notes of cinnamon and butter. It was very beguiling, if a little strong in its original state. But on repeated sampling, one could understand how these notes of land and hearth were really very typical. I never told him the title of this book, so I am doubly impressed that he selected his fragrances that evoke the region I know.

The lesson from him—and me—is that when you go to a new place, especially Friuli-Venezia Giulia, fire up your nostrils, and you will add many dimensions to your ability to learn about and create memories of a newly encountered land. ❦

People here have a boundless knowledge of how food and wines interact and, while in most of Italy you have one local red and white wine, in Friuli-Venezia Giulia, there is by far the largest range of grapes of any Italian region. There is little dispute that Italy's best white wines are here, as are some of its top reds (especially the rare Pignolo). You will discover these wines and their producers as you journey through these pages.

In the center of the vast wine production zone is Udine (pop. 95,000), which is the unofficial capital of the Friulian part of the region. Trieste is the hub of "Giulian" culture. At the eastern end of the Collio wine zone, at the Slovenian border, is Gorizia (pop. 37,000), which has elements of Friuli and Venezia Giulia and a character all its own. In the far western part of the region is Pordenone (pop. 49,000), where one breathes air that is both Friulian and Venetian. Nearby is the famous NATO base at Aviano, which gives a strong American and European flavor to this tucked-away part of Italy.

Administratively, Friuli-Venezia Giulia has four provinces, named for their principal cities. Trieste (abbreviation TS) is the capital of both the region and of Italy's smallest province, barely larger than the city itself. Gorizia (GO) is the capital of another tiny province that probably has more superb wine per acre than any other in Italy. Pordenone (PN) has alps, hills, plains, and sea. Udine (UD) is the most diverse, occupying more than 60 percent of the region and ranging from Carnia to the sea. Learn the four abbreviations and, as you read descriptions in this book, you will have a much better sense about the region and its many subzones and cultures.

South of the wine country is a stunning plain as flat as Kansas with soil just as rich. Stalks of corn stand tall and strong as far as the eye can see, providing the region with flour to make its staple food, polenta. I am always struck by the silence of this zone, called the Bassa Friulana, and enthralled by the many secrets it reveals only on close examination. Here, where the land is so fertile, is a profusion of plants, herbs, flowers, and trees that are recognizable and intimately known by local people, who tell stories about them as if they were relatives. Nowhere in Italy (or anywhere else) have I ever seen such an intense relationship between people and land. The only thing that comes close is the connection between Ligurians and the sea.

South of the Bassa Friulana is a network of canals, marshes, lagoons, and bird sanctuaries at the northern end of the Adriatic Sea. Here are ports, world-class shipbuilding (in Monfalcone), gorgeous beaches (in Lignano), and important fishing towns, especially Grado. Under the Austrian Empire, Grado was the preferred seaside resort of the Hapsburg nobles and the Austrian bourgeoisie. The city's ancient nucleus of buildings in the Venetian style and its beautiful lagoon surroundings combine with sandy beaches, a clean sea, and abundant fish and seafood to make it an ideal summer place.

Until 1914 Grado was an island in the midst of a lagoon teeming with fish. A road was then constructed to connect Grado with the mainland. This isolation had made it somewhat exclusive, and those who arrived came for a prolonged stay. The town also had spas and a thermal station, which in 1892 was officially added to the list of Austria's foremost places to go to take a cure (everything that received official designation from the imperial family had added glamour and value). In that year, 1,000 visitors arrived, notable for that time. The sand was said to cure rheumatism and arthritis, and the sea and setting were thought to calm nerves. In years after, until the fall of the empire, Grado had its golden age.

Near Grado is Aquileia, which I will tell you about later. The final zone is a singular area called Carso. Its name, which means karst in English or German, suggests the stubborn soil of red rocks that require tenacity and intelligence on the part of the people who live there to grow food. Carso is also idyllic in its beauty, combining a lovely inland with a rocky coastline with coves and inlets, bringing to mind the Italian Riviera. It is also the site of the world's largest grotto and the city of Trieste, the true melting pot of Italy.

Few cities in Europe (perhaps only London, Paris, Berlin, Vienna, and maybe Moscow) can claim so much diversity and blending of cultures. Elsewhere in Italy there are cities and provinces where Italian peoples were under foreign domination (Greeks, Moors, Spanish, French, Normans, Germans, Austrians, to name a few). In these places, some foods, words, traditions, and DNA were absorbed into the local fabric, but the character of the place did not change significantly. In Friuli and most of Venezia Giulia, there were ancient peoples who came under outside control (Romans, Huns, Venetians, Austrians, and Slavs, among others) but through it all sought to retain their historic identity. They found, in the land and what it said to them, much of that identity.

Trieste is a separate matter in every sense of that phrase. The way current international boundaries are drawn, Trieste is but a few kilometers from three nations (Italy, to which it technically belongs but feels apart from; Slovenia; and Croatia). This area was inhabited and already a port well before the Romans arrived, in 46 B.C.

As Tergeste, it was a city of Roman foundation, and there are numerous traces of this era, including an outdoor amphitheater smack in the center of the modern city, near the Teatro Verdi, the Stock Exchange, and the port. The underpinnings of the people and their language are Latinate, although much has been added to the pot through the centuries. This area, and south through Istria, Croatia, Montenegro, and Albania, was Roman Illyria, setting for Shakespeare's *Twelfth Night*.

Through the centuries people arrived in Trieste from elsewhere: Friuli, Carinthia, Dalmatia, Styria, Istria, Slovenia, Serbia, Bosnia, Macedonia, Greece (including many Jews from Corfu), Venice, Bohemia, Moravia, Slovakia, Vienna, Hungary, Albania, Morocco, Tunisia, Egypt, Lebanon, Turkey, Armenia, England, Scotland, Ireland, France, Spain, Poland, Germany, Switzerland, Lombardy, Liguria, Emilia-Romagna, Marche, and Tuscany.

Almost all of these groups sustained their own ethnic communities but formed part of a great mosaic, much like twentieth-century New York City. Trieste was, and is, an open and tolerant town that provides a provocative example of peaceful coexistence in a part of the world that has been pulled apart by ethnic, racial, and religious conflicts that date back hundreds of years.

At first, all of these peoples arrived casually, randomly, following their stars and their fortune. Later, people came to insert themselves in communities of their own background and to find work. In many cases, then as now, people came to Trieste seeking the freedom to live and be what they could not be at home. Immigration increased significantly around 1770, when the city was well established as the principal port for the Austrian Empire, which was under the domain of Maria Theresa of the Hapsburg family.

Trieste was the New York of Europe for two centuries, from about 1715 to 1915. The chief reason for this was the city's long association with Vienna, dating more or less formally back to 1382. It was the chief port of the Hapsburg Empire, which by 1866 came to be known as Austria-Hungary and encompassed terrain from Italy and the Balkans in the south, to Romania and Moldova in the east, to Poland and Moravia in the north, and the Tyrol in the west. The population of the empire was 50 million people at the start of the twentieth century, and Vienna was its capital. The next cities in size and importance were Budapest, Prague, and Trieste.

As the principal port for this empire, Trieste was the place of entry and exit for peoples, products, and ideas. Venice, its glorious rival to the west, had a different agenda. Its total land holdings and population were nothing compared to Austria's. Venice's principal territories (Veneto, Trentino, most of Friuli, Istria, and part of Venezia Giulia) were in its hinterland, and most of that would be ceded to Austria with the fall of the Venetian Empire in 1797. It was the capital of a republic that produced war and commerce and art and genius, but was in a long period of decline as Trieste ascended. By about 1770, Trieste had become the most important port in the northern Adriatic.

Trieste had a fate different from Venice's. It was never the capital of an empire, and was far enough from its own capital, Vienna, that it enjoyed great freedom. Because Austria was interested in having a major port, it lavished money, thought, and care on Trieste. On June 2, 1717, an edict was issued making Trieste a free port, where the absence of duties on goods and services created a favorable environment for commerce.

As Trieste grew, its medieval walls were knocked down around 1750. A city center was built with streets and avenues that cross at rational 90-degree angles, as the urban planning ideas of the Enlightenment would have it. In this regard, central Trieste would be a cousin of Lisbon (rebuilt after the 1755 earthquake) and New York, the emerging metropolis of the New World.

The architectural style for Trieste's growth, along with much of the funding, came from Vienna. The grand buildings built in the nineteenth century would recall some of those on Vienna's Ringstrasse and Hofburg. A large part of the center of Trieste is called the Borgo Teresiano, named for Maria Theresa (born 1717), the worldly and reform-minded monarch who ruled the empire from 1740 until her death forty years later.

Maria Theresa's interest was always more practical than personal. She never set foot in Trieste because she was too busy overseeing her vast domain. Under her watch, many institutions of modern European government were born, including the state bureaucracy and a sense of a relationship between the citizen and government. This was in some ways a constitutional monarchy, but one based more on effective administration than that seen in Britain, Denmark, and certainly Spain and France.

Of course, the relationship between those who govern and those who are governed would be the defining factor in European history for the next two centuries while the United States was engaged in its ongoing experiment with democracy. Europe would see reinterpretation, revolution, liberalization, suppression, totalitarianism, liberation, the breaking down of borders, disintegration, and unification from 1789 to 2000.

One of Maria Theresa's chief reforms was the separation of administrative and judicial powers. This worked especially well in the major cities, but also made inroads all over the realm. The fact that her empire was a multinational one encompassing many languages, religions, cultures, and traditions was remarkable. Yet it must be quickly underlined that while the structure of the empire enabled some people to live better than they had, the benefits of *Austria Felix* were limited mostly to the mercantile and upper classes. Under the empire, all people were governed, but they were not necessarily free.

And in this lay the appeal of Trieste. Far enough from the center of power, enjoying much freedom and autonomy, and placed in a setting of considerable beauty, Trieste represented promise to the poor, the powerless, and the oppressed.

By 1755, fifteen years into the reign of Maria Theresa, Trieste was already a booming economic center. The Mercantile Exchange (Borsa) was opened, and the city had consulates from the Ottoman Empire, Venice, the Vatican, Denmark and Norway, France, Spain, England, Russia, and the Kingdom of the Two Sicilies (Sicily and Campania). It is interesting to note that despite the fact that Trieste has lost most of the power and influence it enjoyed in the past, the legacy of internationalism persists to this day. In the year 2000, the city had consulates from twenty-nine nations, which is quite unusual for a town of 200,000 souls that is the capital of Italy's fourth smallest region.

Between 1755 and 1780 (the year Maria Theresa died), Trieste saw the arrivals of many new residents and a whole range of products. Jews came from Veneto, Ancona, Livorno, Corfu, and Central Europe. In 1758, there were 221 Jews; by 1800, there were 900. They enjoyed relative freedom compared with most of Europe. The Jewish population grew to several thousand in the nineteenth and early twentieth centuries. Most of Trieste's Jews were exterminated by the Nazis in World War II. You can, and should, visit the Risiera di San Sabba, a concentration camp in the southern part of Trieste, and vow never to forget or let such things happen again. Now there are about 600 Jews, most quite elderly. Trieste has one of the two largest synagogues in Europe (along with Budapest), and I was privileged to be trained in Jewish Triestine cooking by members of the community.

Armenians, another people subject to endless persecution, found a welcome in Trieste. Some of them specialized in printing and publishing, and in 1773 an Armenian-owned plant opened where they produced works in Italian, German, French, Latin, Armenian, and Greek.

Maria Theresa decided that for Trieste to be a competitive maritime city, it would need a naval academy to rival those in Hamburg, Livorno, Genoa, and Barcelona. At her behest, it was established, and with that came instruction in navigation and shipbuilding. This latter profession took place in Trieste for a long time, and in recent years it has moved slightly north to Monfalcone, where some of the world's most luxurious passenger ships have been built, including those of the Disney Cruise Line.

As the chief port of entry of products destined to points throughout the empire (as well as those that the empire would export), Trieste also became a vibrant site for small and large industry. This began in the 1750s and continued until the fall of the empire in 1918. Among the goods that passed through were cotton, wool, silk, tobacco, wheat, fish and seafood, coffee, spices, lemons, sugar, salt, tea, cheese, olive and vegetable oils, dried fruit, incense, glass, iron, wood, petroleum, coal, and oils from plants and flowers.

With these products, many local industries sprang up: food packing, retailing, furniture and apparel manufacturing, perfumery, papermaking, coffee roasting, distilling of liqueurs among them. Trieste became one of the world centers of the spice trade. One local specialty was the production of playing cards suitable for games in Venice, Istria, and elsewhere in the empire.

The early nineteenth century saw some reversals. Leadership of the empire between 1780 and 1805 was not as steady as under Maria Theresa. In 1805, Napoleon conquered Friuli and Venezia Giulia and held much of them until 1813. Austria reclaimed them when the borders of Europe were redrawn at the Congress of Vienna in 1815. For the next forty years Trieste was prosperous but did not always receive the attention from Vienna it previously enjoyed. The port facilities and warehouses were not always kept competitive with the best of Hamburg, Barcelona, and Genoa. However, it also was not under the thumb of the capital, which was to its advantage.

When Udine and most of Friuli were returned to Italy in 1866 as the Italian Republic was being formed, Austria took renewed interest in keeping Trieste. The city would receive an economic boost from the opening of the Suez Canal in 1869, which brought products from Africa and Asia (including spices and coffee) more quickly to Europe. Soon after, Austria constructed two important rail routes to transport passengers and goods from Trieste to points throughout the empire.

One train went to Gorizia, Cormons, Udine, and then up to Villach. It was this train that began to distribute more international flavors to Venezia Giulia and Friuli and would have an important influence on the cooking of these areas. From Villach, some trains went to Salzburg, Innsbruck, Munich, Nuremberg, and beyond. Other trains went to Prague, Bratislava, and, especially, Vienna. The other rail route began in Trieste and went to Ljubljana and then straight to Vienna. One train on this route left Trieste each evening full of fish and seafood that would be in the markets of Vienna the following morning. From Ljubljana, other trains would go to Budapest and points east.

Of course, trains travel in two directions, so products from all over middle Europe arrived in Trieste, making the city much more worldly. Much wood that went north came back as furniture and musical instruments. Homes of the middle and upper classes almost always had an upright piano, usually a Bösendorfer from Vienna. Many artisans in Trieste produced violins, violas, cellos, basses, guitars, and mandolins that were widely exported.

The end of the nineteenth century saw the rise of large entrepreneurial, financial, and insurance institutions, including Cosulich, Lloyd Triestino, Adriatica di Navigazione, Riunione Adriatica di Sicurtà, and Assicurazioni Generali. A wealthy class collected art and fostered creativity throughout the city. There are now many small museums and collections, most famously the Revoltella, that house these works.

Even today, the city overflows with cafés and pastry shops, and with them comes the culture of intellectual debate, cabaret, performance art, and spontaneous music making and all-night chess matches. The people of Trieste have a very open sexuality, much more candid and varied than in the rest of Italy. Some men in Trieste say that the city is governed by *una ginocrazia,* a "gynocracy," which is not a lamentation on their part but rather an acknowledgment of a fact. This is a place where women have long enjoyed a degree of sexual freedom and autonomy and where the dynamic of relations between men and women is more balanced. It is also the city in Italy where psychoanalysis gained a foothold, thanks to Edoardo Weiss, Freud's first Italian disciple.

After World War I, Trieste became part of Italy and suffered terribly under Fascism. Its multiculturalism and openness did not please Mussolini, who sought to Italianize everyone and everything, and in so doing relentlessly persecuted the city's minorities. Like all of Europe, Trieste was devastated by World War II, especially its Jewish population. In the closing days of the war, the city became a strategic prize as Tito's Yugoslavian armies and the Allies (led by New Zealand) raced to claim it. Tito got there first and seized it.

A man born in Trieste in 1900 would have been conscripted into the Austrian army, then become an Italian in 1918, a Yugoslavian at the end of World War II, and would not return to being Italian again until 1954. Gorizia and a small part of the Carso also were returned to Italy in exchange for large parts of Istria, thanks to an agreement signed in London on October 5, 1954. The Allies entered Trieste on September 26, 1954, to prepare for an onslaught of Istrian refugees in a scene that presaged the wars in the former Yugoslavia in the 1990s. Between 1961 and 1989, Berlin was the northern end of the Iron Curtain and Trieste its southernmost point. I conducted research on this book during the 1990s and was not far from the scenes of battle next door. New waves of refugees arrived, and Friuli-Venezia Giulia gave them succor.

Echoes of War

The NATO allies' declaration of war on Serbia in March 1999 as an action to defend Kosovo had particular impact on Friuli-Venezia Giulia. The region borders what is now referred to locally as ex–Yugoslavia, specifically the now-independent republics of Slovenia and Croatia. So many people in the region, especially along the border that extends from Tarvisio to Cormons to Gorizia and down to Trieste, have family on "the other side." Trieste is filled with émigrés and refugees from all over southeastern Europe. While as Serbians, Croats, Slovenes, Bosnians, Montenegrans, and Kosovars they may have historically battled against one another, in Trieste they mostly coexist and, at times, form meaningful bonds.

People in this part of the world have long historical memories. Slights committed in the fourteenth century by one group against another are recalled as if they were yesterday. In the twentieth century, there were three major periods of war. World War I began in Sarajevo (Bosnia's capital) and brought an end to the Austro-Hungarian Empire. In World War II, Slovenia and Croatia were allied with the Nazis and Fascists, while Serbia fought bravely against these forces.

Under Tito, Yugoslavia was held together by force. In 1954, when the deal was struck to return Trieste to Italy in exchange for most of Istria, there was a migration of more than 350,000 people into Trieste as Istrians (many of Italian origin or sympathies) who were persecuted or feared for their lives fled. At the end of the century, Serbia's leadership sought to hold on to the republics and fought bloody wars (with horrible "ethnic cleansing") and hundreds of thousands of people died unnecessarily.

Since World War II, people in Friuli-Venezia Giulia have become accustomed to having Italian soldiers in the region. Because this region was at the border of the southern end of the Iron Curtain, the Italian government stationed many soldiers there. I have met men all over Italy who tell me how pleasant conscription was for them, only because they were made so welcome in this part of the country. Friulians welcomed soldiers into their homes and treated these boys with great affection and gratitude. More than a few men I have met from Sardinia and the rural south of Italy told me stories of losing their virginity in Trieste, where women have long been modern and independent. Unlike the typical story, in which money is transacted, in this part of the world it was an act of pleasure and (perhaps) generosity.

In the years I spent in Friuli-Venezia Giulia during the 1990s, there was always an unreal feeling: life was so good, people coexisted so well, peace was so prized. Yet in 1991 I stood in Stregna, Cormons, or Gorizia and could hear gun battles taking place five kilometers away in Slovenia. Later, in Trieste, I saw waves of refugees flood in from Croatia. Later still was the humanitarian disaster in Bosnia-Herzegovina, which most of the world shamelessly ignored.

Friulians and Giulians contributed generously to food and humanitarian missions throughout these years. Money was sent to relatives on "the other side," and children injured during these conflicts were brought over to the region for medical care and hugs. Wine makers in Cormons blended many international grapes to make the Vino della Pace, a wine of peace sent to world leaders as a metaphor of peaceful coexistence.

I spent April and May of 1999 in the region, just as the Kosovo conflict began. Italy covered itself in glory during that period as the principal coordinator of humanitarian aid. So well did the nation accomplish this task that it created a backlash after the war ended. Italians wanted to know why the nation was so able to muster food, shelter, medical care, child care, and schools as tent cities sprang up in refugee zones, yet was so inept at dealing with natural disasters at home. Friuli-Venezia Giulia, with its tradition of rolled-up sleeves and self-sufficiency, has always been able to look after its own. And it was one of the places that contributed most to the relief efforts throughout the 1990s to aid the people "on the other side."

The region also had two particularly delicate problems. The first, of course, was that many people who resided there had relatives in one faction or the other in the conflict across the border. The second was that the principal NATO air base in that part of Europe was in Aviano, not far from Pordenone in western Friuli. Here is a community of more than ten thousand Allied soldiers, most of them Americans. Relations between the Friulians and the soldiers have almost always been good. Sadly, the soldiers tend to keep to themselves and to the base, even though many Friulians have made efforts to extend hospitality.

During the Kosovo conflict, bombing missions took off each night from Aviano for Belgrade, Novi Sad, Pristina, and elsewhere. There would be a huge roar in the sky and a flash as the jets sped by. Then the same occurred when the craft returned hours later. I remember how tense sleep was, and how my friends in the region lived in unexpressed fear. If the war were to spread, this would be the place.

The week before I arrived, a friend who lives near Aviano wrote me a very telling letter:

25 March 1999

Dear Fred,

It's not always easy to be a direct witness when history is being made. When those planes take off in Aviano, I know there's not just an American going up but most likely a good friend of ours. . . . Last night, I heard the planes overhead before I saw it on CNN. As they were talking about and showing the base at Aviano, you really got more of the feel of the muscle, the incredible firepower and technological capability [there]. The pilots were calm and ready for their mission but the thought of any of them getting shot down is clearly disturbing. We know most of them so well, their wives and children, but they accept this as part of the job. They are serious and dedicated people. We've worked really hard during the past years to weave them into the community so they feel a part of it, and they do. The Italian people who know them obviously appreciate their efforts and know that we need them here in spite of the political ideals of the current maggioranza [the left-leaning government then in power in Rome].

The main thing that disturbs the locals is the fact that the war is so close by. It's hard to explain the accuracy of [military technology] to the old people in town who maybe fear a cruise missile on the loose. It's understandable that they worry when you consider that every so often they still might evacuate a town to detonate a bomb left over from World War II. People are also getting ready for the numerous refugees that will be coming into Italy, and I have to say Italians have always had a big heart when it comes to helping people. Though the attack is not popular they know it has to be done and that the Americans are the ones who can pull it off.

Then again there are always the contrasting scoops on the news. It is just amazing how Italian people get used to everything. Monday morning was Oscar day [the Academy Awards, at which Roberto Benigni's film about World War II won awards for best actor and best foreign film], *and yesterday was war day. Last night they showed the Serbs lining up for what might be their last loaf of bread till who knows how long. Today on TV, it's back to business as usual.*

Maybe people here take things in stride despite the fear we are feeling because they know that in the event something would go dreadfully wrong, there's survival power in living out here in the country where there will always be a chicken, always be an egg, always some polenta and radicchio and the experience of those who lived and survived before us to show us how.

This afternoon, the wife of our accountant told us that last night she went into the bedroom of their 7-year-old son and saw that he had packed 3 backpacks and lined them up by his door. When she asked him what those were for and what was in them, he replied, "Mamma, there is a war. If a bomb drops I am going to run and take all of my toys with me." She told him not to worry, that if a bomb fell they would probably all be dead and he wouldn't need any toys to play with. It might sound cruel, but here in Italy there is this unusual mix of a highly consumeristic society (heaven forbid a bomb on someone's new BMW!) coupled with this very fatalistic look at life and death at any age. When a church bell rings here at an odd hour, we know it means that someone has died. Our kids grow up with this. I do hope that it won't last long. 🍇

Look farther down a map, past Trieste and the fishing town of Muggia and you will see a zone called Istria. In ancient times it was part of Roman terrain when Trieste and Aquileia were the principal towns, along with places on the Istrian peninsula. Through the centuries, Istria was connected with Trieste by language and tradition, even at times when Istria was under Venice and Trieste under Austria. Since 1954 it belonged to Yugoslavia and, more recently, parts were in the nation of Slovenia, others in Croatia. Tiny bits of Istria have remained Italian.

Many Istrians feel and speak Italian, which is why 350,000 of them fled to Trieste when Yugoslavia took over. They then moved to New York, Los Angeles, Canada, Australia, and elsewhere, creating a new diaspora. One of these was a girl named Lidia Matticchio (later Bastianich), who would go on to become one of the pillars of the dissemination of the best of Italian food and wine culture in the United States through her restaurants, books, and television programs.

It is impossible to think of Friuli-Venezia Giulia without acknowledging nearby Istria. Politics, not culture or tradition, created the new border. This notion of borders is a key issue in the region. A man named Gabriele Massarutto, who lives in Tarvisio in northern Friuli, created an initiative in the 1990s that had important international significance. Friuli-Venezia Giulia is distinct because it is the point in Europe where three principal cultures converge. Just outside Massarutto's city of Tarvisio is the place where Latin Europe (Italy) meets Nordic/Germanic Europe (Austria) and Slavic Europe (Slovenia). The term "crossroads of Europe" is very overworked by chambers of commerce across the continent, but Tarvisio is, if not the crossroads, the point where Europe meets.

Massarutto understood the importance of this and created an initiative called *Senza Confini* (Without Borders) to ask people with warring ideologies and ancient hatreds to put them aside. To do this, he persuaded Austria and Slovenia to join Friuli-Venezia Giulia to make a joint bid for the 2006 winter Olympics. This would be the first time the games

Writers and Friuli-Venezia Giulia

While other regions of Italy have given us great painters or musicians, this one has been fertile soil for writers, both native and foreign. Rainer Maria Rilke experienced great happiness in Duino, just outside Trieste. Kafka was a visitor in 1913. Ernest Hemingway saw action during World War I and was badly injured. His book, *A Farewell to Arms,* is set in Friuli and the neighboring Veneto and is one of the most stirring evocations of what war really is about. His description of Gertrude Stein in *A Moveable Feast* as having "a Friulian face" was a compliment, despite our received image of Stein's appearance, because Hemingway was very taken with the region's formidable women. He returned later in his life, vacationing in a villa in the Bassa Friulana.

The most famous foreigner was probably James Joyce, who lived in Trieste. In *A Portrait of the Artist as a Young Man,* he wrote, "When the soul of a man is born in this country there are no nets flung at it to hold it back from flight." The words are Stephen Dedalus's, but it was James Joyce speaking of Ireland. The writer who created so many unforgettable images of his native land in his writing left home at age twenty (in 1902) and would live much of his life in exile, primarily in Trieste and Zurich. Joyce and his wife, Nora, arrived in Trieste in the autumn of 1904. Their son, Giorgio, and daughter, Lucia, were born there. They lived in Trieste until 1915, with trips to Dublin in 1909 and 1912. In his Trieste years he wrote *Chamber Music, Dubliners, A Portrait of the Artist as a Young Man,* and began *Ulysses* in 1914. After the war, the family moved back to Trieste before heading to Paris in 1920.

In the first decade of the twentieth century, Joyce was part of a circle of writers who lived in Trieste. Umberto Saba wrote of his hometown that "Trieste has a surly grace. If you please it, it is like a rough and voracious boy with absurd eyes and hands too large to give you the gift of a flower. Trieste is like love with jealousy."

Saba and Italo Svevo, who were in Trieste during the European Belle Epoque, rank among the greatest novelists Italy has produced. Giuseppe Ungaretti sang the praises of the Isonzo zone (home of great wine and dreadful war) in his poetry, even against the backdrop of the brutality of World War I. Other writers of Trieste during the first war include Scipio Sclapeter and Giani Stuparich, whose lives were brief but intense. In recent times there were Gillo Dorfles, a scholar and critic, and now Claudio Magris, perhaps Italy's foremost intellectual and scholar, even if Umberto Eco enjoys more fame abroad. Magris explores issues of frontiers, of national and personal identity, and the meaning of freedom in an individual and a society. There could be no more emblematic theme of

Trieste than that. His books, including *Microcosms* and *Danube,* should be required reading to understand the Europe of today.

Italy's foremost film critic, Tullio Kezich, is Triestine, and often evokes the city in his writing. Susana Tamaro, whose book *Va Dove Ti Porta Il Cuore* (Go Where Your Heart Leads You) was published only a few years ago and was an incomparable literary phenomenon in Italy and abroad, is from Trieste. By some estimates, it is the second or third best-selling book ever published in Italian, exceeded by Dante's *Divine Comedy* and perhaps Alessandro Manzoni's *I Promessi Sposi* (The Betrothed), which is regarded as the greatest novel in the Italian language. Tamaro's book is a somewhat sentimental story of a grandmother's advice for a granddaughter. It struck very deep chords among many Italian women, and made Tamaro rich and very famous.

Other parts of the region have also spoken to writers. Gradiscutta di Varmo in the Bassa Friulana attracted Sergio Maldini, who wrote *La Casa a Nord-Est,* a novel not only about a house but its inhabitants and their desires to fulfill themselves through its restoration. Grado's praises were sung by Biagio Marin, a poet who finds specialness in what to others are mundane elements of seaside resorts. He speaks of the "divine balance" with which Grado's "light, winds, and waves are orchestrated." Central Friuli found a voice in Ippolito Nieve, who saw beauty that eluded others. In Gorizia, there were Jews who flowered and died young, most famously Carlo Michelstaedter, who is unknown outside of his town but deserves recognition.

An extraordinary writer, one of Italy's finest, was Pier Paolo Pasolini. Born in Bologna of a Friulian mother from Casarsa, he felt intensely Friulian (and wrote in its language) even as he became a world-famous author, poet, and filmmaker based in Rome. 🍇

would be hosted by more than one country. Part of the underlying thought was to embrace the newly emerging nations of eastern Europe and to beat back extremist ideologies, including that of Jörg Haider, governor of the next-door Austrian province of Carinthia. This bid was a finalist for the games and, while it did not win, the *Senza Confini* concept took hold and now is expanding to commerce, culture, and other areas. As Massarutto told me, if God created land without borders, there is no good reason for man to create them.

What Massarutto raises is something fundamental and essential in the story of Friuli-Venezia Giulia. This is a place that has an ancient native people, but has known outside invasion and domination for all of its history. What became important here was identity, not ideology, which was a luxury the people could not afford. Identity came through language, land, common suffering, shared food and wine, and the realization that it was pointless to engage in civil conflict when, all around them, wars raged that were based on ancient ethnic and religious hatreds. That the mixed society of the region of Friuli-Venezia Giulia never had serious internal battles is remarkable.

This concept is best expressed by Claudio Magris, the great Triestine writer. "Ethnic purity, like all purities, is the result of a subtraction and it is as rigorous as subtraction is radical—true purity would be nothing." He went on: "Each identity is an aggregate, and there is little sense in dismantling it so as to reach the supposed indivisible atom. Identity is the product of a will."

The issue of identity in Friuli-Venezia Giulia is as old as the land itself. First, look at the name of the region. It is a joint name. Friuli refers to 80 percent of the land and 70 percent of the population. It covers the provinces of Udine and Pordenone and part of the province of Gorizia. Venezia Giulia, as a name, was coined in the late nineteenth century in Gorizia, but represents an ancient concept. Trieste, Grado, part of the zone of Aquileia, plus the eastern side of the Isonzo River, the Carso, and Gorizia constitute an area of a native population that fell under the sway of the Romans and many other peoples up to the Austrians in the nineteenth century and the Slavs in the twentieth so it is a mistake to refer to the whole region as Friuli, as is often done, because this denies the presence of everything that Venezia Giulia represents.

Friuli is separated from Venezia Giulia by a narrow stream called the Judrio River. You barely notice it as you drive over, but it is historically important. While all of this land was Roman, at various points in history the zones were divided. The word "Friuli" is a corruption of *Forum Iulii,* which means Julius' Forum, named for Julius Caesar. Ptolemy referred to Aquileia this way, and later the town of Cividale had the same name. Venezia Giulia roughly means "the Venice of Julius," but this is not accurate because this area was a flourishing civilization centuries before the birth of Venice.

The story of Friuli-Venezia Giulia is really the evolution of its people. In describing the way this special place evolved, we should always bear in mind that the peoples of what we now call Friuli-Venezia Giulia have always been there, welcoming friendly visitors and enduring hostile ones.

The western part of the region (roughly what we now call Friuli) was formed by glaciers in the Ice Age and gravelly sediment deposited by the Tagliamento River, the region's largest. The eastern part (generally, Venezia Giulia) was covered by the Adriatic Sea, so it is common even today to find maritime fossils in the wine zones near Gorizia. All of this activity in both areas created many terrains, soils, microclimates, and zones that would adapt distinctly to different forms of agriculture. In prehistoric times, dinosaurs roamed the land. Recently, the remains of "Antonio," the oldest dinosaur bones ever discovered in Europe, were found near Trieste.

The first people were hunters and cave dwellers. Some of the largest caves are in the Carso. These peoples made tools, first of stone, then of metal. Knife-making was important, and still is. The town of Maniago (PN) is the knife-and-blade capital of Europe. In the Bronze Age (2000 to 1000 B.C.), Friuli was densely populated with a people thought to be the Euganeans, a Ligurian tribe that occupied much of pre-alpine Northern Italy. From 1000 to 500 B.C. the Paleo-Veneti, Indo-Europeans who arrived from the east and came south over the Alps, occupied the area. It is believed that they gave geographic definition to the region, making the Livenza River the western border, the Carnia Alps the northern border, and the hills east of the Isonzo River the eastern border. Of course, the Adriatic Sea was the southern border.

These are borders in name only. This has always been an easily accessible zone of transit, and peoples would arrive for centuries to come. Even the Alps gave access. The area around Tarvisio is called the Canal di Ferro (the Iron Canal). Here one passes with relative ease through the mountains from Friuli to central Europe. The zone was full of iron, and during the Iron Age (the last millennium B.C.) it was very prized.

Around 500 B.C., peoples known as the Celts and the Carni arrived. The Celts dominated north-central Europe and occupied the south and central part of the region. They were a warrior people, but also very talented at land management. They were the ones who understood how to identify zones suitable for air-curing meats. This is how pigs began to be cured as prosciutto in the place we now call San Daniele. The Carni were a pacific people who occupied the mountain zone now called Carnia. On the other side of the mountains, in Austria, is a state called Carinthia and, to the east, in Slovenia, is the mountainous zone of Carniola. So when Gabriele Massarutto proposed an Olympics without borders, he was simply uniting the ancient lands of the Carni.

No matter who passed through Friuli-Venezia Giulia, the people of the land were, for the most part, the descendants of the Carni and the Celts. Other peoples settled in this area, and some of their words, traditions, and DNA were added to the mix. A period of real glory arrived with the Romans. They viewed the area under Celtic domination as key to their well-being and safety from northern peoples. In 186 B.C. the Romans seized a town that they would call Aquileia and made it their great city in northern Italy. By 169 B.C. it had a population of twenty thousand, including locals and Romans. It became a seat of enlightened, independent government, a strong military base, and a center of culture and commerce. Just nearby was its Adriatic port, enabling it to trade with much of the ancient world.

With Aquileia as its chief city, the Roman Empire built the roads that still serve Friuli-Venezia Giulia and beyond. The routes were meant to link the cities the Romans created or expanded. The Via Postumia, going from Aquileia to what is now Genoa, was finished in 148 B.C. The Via Annia (completed 128 B.C.) led to the Via Emilia and down to Rome. Other roads led to new Roman cities. A road south led to Tergeste (Trieste) and then Pola. Another, heading southeast, led to Tarasatica (Opatija). Going due east, a road reached Iulii Emona (Ljubljana). Heading north and then east, a road reached Forum Iulii (Cividale), then Santico (Villach), Virinum (Klagenfurt), and then Vidibona (Vienna). A road heading northwest led to Iulium Carnicum (Zuglio, in Carnia) and then Aguntum (Lienz). Going southwest, one reached Iulia Concordia (Portogruaro). All of these roads are still used today.

Before the Romans, the languages were of the Carni and the Celts. With the Romans, Latin was incorporated into local speech and the Friulian language began to evolve. The Romans created orderly agriculture and brought their skills in fermentation of food and drinks; wine production and exportation; and salting, curing, smoking, and roasting of meats, especially pork. Preservation of vegetables by fermentation became part of the local tradition, including *brovada* (turnips) and cabbage. Also sauces such as *savor* were used to preserve fish. Cereals, such as millet, were served hot in a mushy form. When polenta later became the standard, it was based on this older tradition. The Romans also brought glass-making, so that bottles would hold wine and chalices could be used to drink it.

The Roman era waned and Christianity arrived in A.D. 313. Again, Aquileia was distinct, in that the patriarchs continued the enlightened rule of the Romans. The early church here was a tolerant one, and the area continued to flourish. Outside invaders tried to conquer Aquileia and, in 452, Attila and his Huns arrived. Many Aquileians and their leaders fled to Grado and later to 118 inhospitable islands in the Adriatic, where they founded a city that would mirror the enlightened values of culture, commerce, and communal government: Venice. So add to the many accomplishments of Friuli-Venezia Giulia the fact that it is the mother of Venice.

Christianity stayed in Aquileia, but waned by 568. More people moved to Venice and the city began its astonishing development. In that year, the Lombards (or Longobards) arrived from the north and created their civilization in what they would call Cividale (previously, Forum Iulii). They remained until 776 and, though they were a warrior people, they also created in Cividale a model capital with outstanding ecclesiastical art, metalworking, and exquisite jewelry whose designs are still what many women wear today. All of this culture and sophistication spread to much of the region, and Lombard words entered the Friulian language. The Lombards allowed Christianity to continue and let Aquileia begin to regain its earlier traditions.

From 776 to 899 Charlemagne and the Carolingian kings dominated much of the region. The local characteristics of culture, language, and identity were submerged during this era. Charlemagne saw this as an area of military importance and built fortresses and castles. He also created the feudal system that subjugated much of the local population to servitude. Food would be served to masters, and Friulians had to learn how to survive on what remained. On this land, until his death in 814, Charlemagne would contend with the Slavs, Venetians, and Byzantines who coveted it. After his death, Cividale, then known as Civitas Austriae (Chief City of the Eastern Region) had a resurgence as a center of literature and visual arts.

Between 899 and 952, the region suffered relentless invasions by the Hungarians, who brought much destruction and created poverty in even the most developed zones. Many local people were enslaved and the region, which had pockets of high civilization, was in ruins. Between 952 and 1019 the region was prey to anyone who passed through, but some German nobles began to bring order and early seeds of revival. Some of their words entered the Friulian language, especially in Carnia.

Then, amazingly, in 1019, Aquileia rose again. Forward-thinking Christian patriarchs combined the best of church doctrine with a pragmatic approach to local needs to create the Patriarchate of Aquileia. They applied church rules as needed but were largely secular rulers. The patriarchs established peace treaties with nearby lands, nurtured agriculture, education, free thought, and the arts. After 1077, the Patriarchate spread from Aquileia to other parts of Friuli. However, some areas remained feudal under counts or dukes. Others were not worth consideration.

The result of this diversification was that towns began to acquire distinct identities, and it is now said that the modern region of Friuli-Venezia Giulia is made of a hundred ancient towns, duchies, and patriarchates.

In the early era of the patriarchs, a parliament was created that would be the oldest in continental Europe. Each town had citizen councils that worked in tandem with local governors. After 1251, Aquileia experienced a gentle decline, and Cividale became the region's center. Udine soon rose to challenge Cividale, and would later supersede it. Patriarchal government continued with greater or lesser effect until 1420. This period would represent a zenith of enlightenment in the Middle Ages and meant, once and for all, the establishment of a Friulian identity which would survive centuries of domination that would come when the region again fell into foreign hands.

An important aside is that Trieste went its own way during much of these years. It was geographically out of the mainstream, as warriors traversed the rest of the region, and remained a small seaport of Roman origin. Then, in 1382, it established a relationship with Vienna, becoming the point of entry by sea for the Austrian capital. This relationship would progress through the centuries with relative amity and, as described earlier, would blossom in 1717 when Trieste became a duty-free port.

In July of 1420, a Venetian representative arrived in Udine and effectively took control of many of the lands that were under the Patriarchate. Gorizia, which had been a more independent city under a count, also had to submit to Venice. The Venetians permitted patriarchal control to stay only in the towns of Aquileia, San Vito, and San Daniele, but the patriarchal state of Friuli had fallen. San Daniele managed to preserve relative independence in exchange for supplying hams to the Doges of Venice.

It is probably fair to say that Venice was not very good for Friuli. There was some beautiful civic architecture, especially in Udine and Gradisca, but otherwise Venice treated Friuli as a source of raw materials. Friulian lumber and stone built Venice and its grain, vegetables, hams, game, and wine abounded on Venetian tables while Friulians starved. The Venetians occupied Grado and feasted on the rich supply of seafood; they also arrived in Istria, bringing language and cuisine. Venetian dialect blended with that of Trieste, but the cities would be rivals as ports. Venetian words entered the Friulian language and the fork, which was invented in Venice, would sit next to Friulian knives.

Venice would be weakened by repeated wars with the Turks, conflicts with now-powerful Milan (whose people included Longobards who left Cividale centuries before). Between 1508 and 1523, Venice had numerous wars with the Hapsburg family for control of parts of Friuli and what is now called Venezia Giulia. In the end, key towns east of the Judrio River, including Cormons, Gradisca, Aquileia, and Gorizia were given to Austria and Venice kept the rest.

This regional division led to certain differences in character. Austria established schools, an administrative bureaucracy, and a relationship in which Vienna was mother and other towns were the child. This contrasted with Venice, which took so much more than it gave. Trieste continued to rise as Venice declined, and its commercial power was the key to Austrian dominance in the eighteenth century. When Venice finally fell in 1797, Napoleon Bonaparte was there to grab part of its lands. In a treaty signed at the Villa Manin in Codroipo (in the Bassa Friulana), France took Venice and some of Friuli, while Austria acquired much more terrain.

French culture brought language, certain cooking techniques, modern land management, and, especially, new grapes and wine-making traditions. When Napoleon's empire was parceled out at the Congress of Vienna in 1815, much of this territory went to Austria, as did the Veneto and Lombardy. But not for long. Nationalist sentiment was growing on the Italian peninsula and much of this zone broke free and joined Piedmont, Liguria,

Tuscany, Sardinia, and other areas to create the Republic of Italy. By 1866, only the lands east of the Judrio belonged to Austria, and those too would become Italian by 1918.

I took you on this express train through the millennia to quash certain stereotypes and assumptions most people have. The first is that Friuli-Venezia Giulia is a Germanic/Slavic region that is in Italy by an accident of history. As you can see, this is a region formed by many influences, but it is first and foremost the land of the people who lived there through endless misery and glory. The second is to show you that the language, culture, and food and wine traditions were both created and absorbed, but seldom imposed. Through it all, a regional identity was forged (with Trieste always being a distinct entity) that became essential to survival among a people who did not have the luxury of embracing ideology.

Note that when I discuss "Friuli-Venezia Giulia" in this book, I mean the whole region, and when I talk of Friuli or Venezia Giulia, I only mean those zones. Never do I say "Friuli" to mean the whole region, and I discourage you from doing so, even if many Italians do.

How does all of this relate to the region's splendid food and wine? This book is a biography of a people and their land using food and wine as the key. The food of Friuli-Venezia Giulia, like its people, is much more international than that of other regions of Italy. Although palpably and unmistakably Italian in its Roman roots and its preparations, it has stylistic influences and flavors from elsewhere. It is important to remember that its cooks make little effort to *be* international, but rather they work to express ideas and flavors that speak of their land.

*I*n his exhaustive, provocative, and heavily footnoted book, *The First World War* (1999), John Keegan observes that the Italian army launched "eleven costly and fruitless assaults on Austria's mountain borderland. The incidence of an offensive every three months, between May 1915 and August 1917, was higher than that demanded of the British or French armies on the Western Front and the contingencies more wearing; shellfire in the rocky terrain caused 70 percent more casualties per rounds expended than on the soft ground of France and Belgium." More than 100,000 people died in the zone around Gorizia during this war.

You can imagine that a place that has seen so much conquest and spilled blood would be precious to its people. They are stewards of their land and guard it carefully. It should not surprise you that the region always tops the list as the cleanest in Italy, with no polluted beaches and mostly pure lakes and rivers. This was the first Italian region to legislate and encourage organic farming. As of late 1998 there were 250 organic farms covering 732 hectares (1,809 acres). Grape-growing and wine-making practices are environmentally sound, with few if any added chemicals.

The soil here is sacred. In 1998, I spoke with a seventy-year-old man who is a former mayor, a businessman, and quite worldly, yet in love with his region. He told me, with misting eyes, that "when I go for a walk on the land and then come home, I almost feel guilty when I scrape the soles of my shoes."

In 1963, Friuli-Venezia Giulia, with its distinct history and culture, was granted special status as one of Italy's five autonomous regions (the others being Trentino-Alto Adige, Valle d'Aosta, Sicily, and Sardinia). Thus, the region could be more self-determining about expenditure, promotion, and identity. The Friulian language and Triestine dialect returned to schools next to Italian. The region looked to build its economy especially through the sale of furniture and wine.

The economic miracle here began in the 1960s, although there were setbacks and a higher number of bankruptcies and business failures than in the neighboring Veneto and other parts of northern Italy. Initially many industries required infusions of federal money to keep going. At first this money came directly from Rome, but when Friuli-Venezia Giulia became autonomous, the funds came from the government in Trieste. People in Friuli-Venezia Giulia were nearly unmatched in their capacity to work, but perhaps did not yet have the business acumen that was part of the mercantile heritage in Venice, Padua, Verona, Milan, Turin, and other cities.

When reversals came, people vowed to work harder. This was nothing new. The region had, per capita, more émigrés than any other in Italy. Unmarried women from Gorizia were sent to Egypt to be nannies and wet nurses to the children of the upper classes. Girls from elsewhere in the region became maids and cooks in homes in Milan. Many single men emigrated to jobs in construction and lumber trades in Canada. All the foremen on the construction of the Trans-Siberian railway—four thousand of them— were Friulian. Many buildings, public facilities, and infrastructure in North and South America, Europe, and Australia were built by Friulians. These people are natural builders. They say they suffer from *mal di matton,* or "brick sickness." What this means is an insatiable desire to build. With men gone, women ran businesses and farms on their own.

This propensity for work is best expressed by the notion of sleeve-rolling. The expression *rimboccare le maniche* (roll up one's sleeves) implies much more than the obvious. It is about a readiness and willingness to face any task, no matter how arduous or un-pleasant, because it is known that in the end life will be better for it. People here are proud to roll up their sleeves. In this context I once heard two women in a café in Cividale talking about their husbands. One said that no matter how much she had to do every day, she still found that her husband wanted something more. She said, "Even though he saw me work hard all day and knew I was tired, he still pleaded to make love with me."

"What did you do?" her friend asked.

"I rolled up my sleeves," came the response.

As recently as the 1960s, the region was exporting labor all over the world. Nowadays the region is looking for workers for factories and farms. According to the Banca d'Italia, 60 percent of the companies in the region looked for additional personnel in 1997. But of these, 70 percent reported that they had trouble finding new employees. Many workers are now immigrants to Friuli-Venezia Giulia from other nations, which is ironic when Italy has, at the same time, an unemployment rate that hovers between 10 percent and 12 percent.

The most extraordinary example of Friulian industry is the furniture business. After World War II, when people were starving, all they had was lumber and a chair-making tradition. Three small towns south of Udine (Manzano, San Giovanni al Natisone, and Corno di Rosazzo) came to be known as *Il Triangolo della Sedia,* or the "Chair Triangle." They now produce 40 percent of the world's chairs. The world's largest chair stands in the middle of this zone. At 20 meters (65 feet) high, and twenty times the original model, it is a typical nineteenth-century Friulian chair. It is a symbol of how far this place has come from extreme poverty to market dominance. Fifteen thousand persons live in these towns, and the factories employ fifteen thousand people from the surrounding areas.

By the mid-1970s the economy of Friuli-Venezia Giulia was doing well, when yet another immense tragedy struck. On May 6, 1976, I was in Venice, just a few days shy of my twentieth birthday. That evening one of the most devastating earthquakes in memory struck northeastern Italy, with its epicenter in the towns of Gemona and Venzone, north of Udine on the road to Carnia. These towns were destroyed, as was much of the region. Buildings collapsed many miles from the heart of the quake, industry came to a halt, vineyards were ruined, and many people died. The region was shell-shocked by the earthquake (*terremoto* in Italian and *orcolat* in Friulano).

In Venice, nearly 100 miles (155 km) away, the small island I was on shook mightily and bricks and marble crashed to the ground. As word spread of the quake and the damage that was done, I recalled the efforts of Americans a decade earlier who rushed to Florence, after the Arno had overflowed, to help clean the city and save precious art and books. I got on a train to Udine and found my way to Gemona, where I moved rocks, cleared rubble, salvaged people's property, and gave hugs.

Although I had already been to Trieste and elsewhere in Venezia Giulia, this was my first visit to the heart of Friuli. People were mystified that a young American would show up to help out in this unknown place. To me the most striking thing was that, despite the terrible tragedy this place had suffered, people were amazingly warm to me and apologetic that they could not offer the kind of hospitality they wanted to. It was this encounter with the people that has made me return to Friuli (and Venezia Giulia) so often. Italy is probably the most hospitable nation in the world, but perhaps the only Italians who can match Friuli-Venezia Giulia for this spontaneous warmth and openness are those from Emilia-Romagna.

Like most nations, Italy is notoriously slow and inefficient in the delivery of emergency services. You need only look at people in Campania and Umbria living in makeshift housing years after earthquakes to understand the impact of this. What stunned Italians is how the Friulians rolled up their sleeves and rebuilt by themselves without waiting for help. Despite severe damage, most of the region was up and running within months. Industries used the occasion to rebuild with modern machinery. Wineries invested in outstanding new grape stock, with the result that, by the early 1980s, many were producing spectacular wines.

A cooperative spirit emerged, with people helping one another. This contact created dialogue and changed the way people interacted. Where they might have been somewhat reserved with each other before, this event fostered communication and, more than any other occurrence in the region's long history, gave its citizens a sense of identity and ability. It was the turning point after which Friuli-Venezia Giulia shed once and for all its modest rusticity and took pride in its accomplishments.

The threat of earthquake is ever present, even though most buildings are fitted against that prospect. If you go to Venzone, north of Gemona, you will be startled by its beauty. Venzone had been designated a national monument, years before the quake, as an unspoiled walled town with lovely architecture. Just about every structure fell in the quake, but the citizens refused to erase their past. First they rebuilt every home as it was. Then in 1988 they collectively rebuilt the Cathedral of Sant'Andrea, numbering and replacing eight thousand stones. No attempt was made to hide that which was new nor to camouflage that which could not be saved. I asked a local friend why each stone was numbered. "Because," he answered undramatically, "when the church falls in another earthquake, we can put it up again."

The amazing capacity for recovery is, I believe, part of the regional character that honors individual achievement and self-realization on one hand and a sense of community on the other. This is best exemplified in the *osteria,* a combination wine bar and dining place. People in Friuli-Venezia Giulia use the *osteria* as a gathering place, a sort of tavern, where they may have wine and food, or just wine. They tend not to have an aperitif or cocktail, but a glass of wine, known locally as the *tajùt* (Tie-YOOT).

Men still enjoy cards and other games, along with animated conversation. Some young men, though thankfully not many, seem drawn to flashy but solitary video arcades, but most go to *osterie.* Women are welcome, too, and there is little sense of social pressure. Instead, it is a place of safety and serenity, where the people of the region have especially strong feelings of identity and well-being.

The *osteria* has similar institutions called the *frasca* in Friuli and the *osmizza* in Venezia Giulia. A place without class distinctions, the *osteria* is a spot where people from all walks of life share friendship and leave differences at the door. Historically, the *osteria* was also where all news and information could be found. And it still is today.

As central to Friulian identity as language and the *osteria* is the *fogolar.* This is a raised hearth, typically in the center of a room called the *čhase,* which means home. The rest of one's residence is called the *lûc,* which means building. In the past, the *fogolar* (whose name derives from the Latin for fire or flame) was the place where families cooked but also kept warm. They would sit around it telling stories and singing. Some families in Friuli were once so poor that they could not afford a *fogolar.* To stay warm they would gather in the barn with the cows, whose breath was a source of heat. The families would sit in a tight circle and the women would sew as they sang or told stories to children who dozed in their mothers' laps.

Most modern Friulian homes are built with a room with a *fogolar,* even if they also have modern kitchens that include a traditional wood-burning oven called a *spolert.* This is a room to receive guests and is intimately tied to the region's strong spirit of hospitality. The association of Fogolars Furlans is a worldwide organization of Friulians in Canada, Australia, Argentina, and many other countries. Wherever one goes in the world and finds a Friulian family, a *fogolar* will be there and people around it will be speaking in their historic language.

Mario Toros, president of the association and of the group called Friulians in the World insists on teaching the language locally, and sees to it that it is taught to communities abroad. He told me that "as long as there is the language, we are a people."

Friuliano (Furlan) evolved in the high Middle Ages from its Latin, Celtic, and Carnic roots. Spellings in it draw from French, German, and Spanish, but not Italian. The language has certain cadences that are German. For example, there is a long U sound (indicated in German with an umlaut) in Furlan that is distinct from anything heard in Italian.

Slavic languages have only had a minor impact on Furlan, yet many of them (especially Slovenian) are spoken by minorities in the region. Several people reminded me that Furlan was the language of people who lost battles of domination—the languages of the Venetians, Austrians, and Italians would prevail for most of the past thousand years—and Furlan exists as a form of solidarity and identity. Few people now have it as their mother tongue, but a sizable part of the Friulian population and some in Venezia Giulia still speak it.

Does identity still matter? A wine maker I know who lives just near the Slovenian border said to me, matter-of-factly, "My grandfather was Austrian, my father was Slovenian, and I, for now, am Italian." He said that if he were to ascribe a geographic identity to himself, then he would be "Friulian first, and also European, but it matters very little in the year 2000 what nation is technically my home. My land, family, and language tell me who I am."

Another wine maker friend, Alvaro Pecorari, works the land in the Isonzo wine zone. It is more difficult than some other zones, and he has to study soil, weather, wind, and talk to elders in the community as he tries to get the most from his land, and do it honor. One day years ago, he spent many hours telling me of the challenges that have been presented to him, not in a complaining way but with a sense of "rolled sleeves." At the end of this long conversation, he showed me his weathered hands caked with gray-brown dirt, gave me a shy smile, and said, *"Questa è la mia terra fortunata."* Suddenly, I knew what this book was about.

Some people, when I told them I was calling a book about Friuli-Venezia Giulia "the fortunate land" thought I was being ironic or even uncaring. Yet in nine years of research I came to realize that I was right. This land, which has been the scene of centuries of wars that have spilled untold amounts of blood, this land, which rumbles with earthquakes causing immense devastation, is nonetheless *una terra fortunata*. Friuli-Venezia Giulia is a fortunate land because of the people who live on it.

The Way to Eat in Friuli-Venezia Giulia

One cannot think well, love well, sleep well, if one has not dined well.

—VIRGINIA WOOLF

One of the core ideas in this book is the parity between wine and food in Friuli-Venezia Giulia. There is a good deal of dialogue between those who make wine and those who make food. People in this region have a knowledge that is second to none of the mysterious ways that flavors in food and wine combine to create something truly extraordinary in your mouth. This concept of parity is very important to fully enjoy the region's cuisine and wines. When you bear in mind that the food and wine of this region rank among the best in Italy, you quickly discover that Friuli-Venezia Giulia is not only a fortunate land, but also a secret treasure waiting to be discovered.

Italy has twenty regions, each with its own history, geography, politics, culture, languages and dialects, agriculture, cookery, and traditions. In most of Italy, regional wine is paired with regional food, in part because they come from the same soil, but also because when the regions were composed of autonomous duchies and city-states, each place needed to be self-sustaining and therefore food and drink were locally produced. This consequence of history has created the legacy of many splendid local and regional foods and wines throughout Italy, giving it a culinary heritage that is, I believe, unrivaled in the world.

When I ask Italians who are knowledgeable about food and wine to name the top three regions in each, many of them come up with the same names. The leaders in food are, alphabetically, Emilia-Romagna, Friuli-Venezia Giulia, and Liguria (with Sicily usually coming in fourth). Regions such as Tuscany and Campania (capital: Naples) have tasty food that is popular, although in the case of Tuscany, it is rather overrated. In the case of Campania, the food is really delicious but can only be appreciated in the region because the key ingredients are simply not as good elsewhere.

The runaway leaders in wine are Friuli-Venezia Giulia, Piedmont (Piemonte, in Italian), and Tuscany (with regions such as Trentino-Alto Adige, Veneto, Sardinia, Sicily, and others in a group that is several notches lower). So it is notable that only one region, Friuli-Venezia Giulia, figures in the top three in both food and wine.

In Emilia-Romagna and Liguria, the food is remarkable (look at Lynne Rossetto Kasper's *The Splendid Table* and my *Recipes from Paradise* to learn about these two regions), but even their best wines can seldom match the food in complexity and sophistication. Emilia-Romagna's rich opulent food is often served with big red wines from Tuscany, Piedmont, Lombardy, or Veneto, or sometimes a Sangiovese from Romagna. The more delicate Ligurian cuisine is consumed either with friendly local whites (Vermentino and Pigato) or with ones from Tuscany, Piedmont, Sardinia, Veneto, or Friuli-Venezia Giulia.

The wines of Tuscany are extraordinary, completely overwhelming a cuisine that is among the simplest in Italy. Many people think Tuscan food is great until they travel to other Italian regions. Tuscans consume large amounts of grilled, roasted, or stewed meats, plus lots of soup, bread, beans, spinach, and sheep's milk cheese, with thick olive oil covering just about everything. All of this is very tasty, but it is exceeded by many other regional cuisines in terms of complexity and interest. The marvelous Tuscan red wines (Chianti Classico, Brunello di Montalcino, Vino Nobile di Montepulciano, and the Supertuscan blends) are just too much for the region's humble foods.

The food of Piedmont is more interesting and varied, but uneven. There are superb appetizers and very good pasta and rice courses. But then the recipes become less interesting (second courses are usually braised or roasted meats) and desserts are limited, though the region has lots of good cheese and pears. Towering Piedmontese reds, such as Barolo and Barbaresco, are just too big for most foods, while less imposing (but still important) reds such as Dolcetto, Barbera, Grignolino, Carema, and others are typically the choices for dining.

Both Tuscany and Piedmont produce decent white wines (Vernaccia di San Gimignano, Gavi, Arneis), but they simply cannot compare with the luscious and fascinating whites of Friuli-Venezia Giulia. And while many Piedmontese and Tuscan reds are world famous, the best reds from Friuli-Venezia Giulia, though lesser known, are formidable indeed and more than hold their own in comparative tastings.

People who cook in Friuli-Venezia Giulia, whether in homes or restaurants, often tend to think in terms of what wine they will serve. In most Italian regions there usually is the local *vino rosso* and *vino bianco,* almost always tasty but intended to be all-purpose. Remember, most Tuscan reds derive from the Sangiovese grape and most Piedmontese reds are made with Nebbiolo. By contrast, Friuli-Venezia Giulia regularly uses Italy's broadest selection of grapes: about fifteen red and white wine grapes, and many more in smaller quantities. Even in regions with many grape varieties (such as Veneto, Campania, Puglia, and Sicily), local people tend to limit their choices to one red and one white for most purposes.

*F*or a long time, eating in Italy could be divided into two categories: the meals of the poor and those of everyone else. For the poor, the goal was to stave off hunger and whatever food was available was what was eaten. The received notion is that this was a phenomenon only of southern Italy, yet few places knew the level of misery and privation found in Friuli-Venezia Giulia and parts of the Veneto until about fifty years ago. In much of northeastern Italy, poor people lived on polenta and whatever they could flavor it with: herbs, cheese, onions, apples, gravy, bits of fish, or just butter and sugar.

People in Italy who were not poor ate in a more conventional way that became the norm in almost the whole country from about 1955 to 1990. This was a meal that included a *primo* (pasta, risotto, or soup) followed by a *secondo* (a small portion of protein) plus a *contorno* (a vegetable side dish). Dessert, in most cases, was a beautiful piece of fruit. On special occasions there might be a pudding or baked product. Wine was almost always consumed at this meal, along with mineral water. An espresso would conclude the meal. In a few regions (notably Piedmont, Emilia-Romagna, Puglia), antipasti (appetizers) were common at the start of some meals. In some regions (Friuli-Venezia Giulia, Lombardy, Tuscany, Sardinia), cheese appeared somewhere toward the end of the meal, often with the piece of fruit. The key thing about this meal is that families usually took it together, whether at home or in a trattoria.

In most restaurants and trattorias, people eat the preparations that are part of local tradition. It should also be noted that while chefs in trendy restaurants in Italy continue to attempt to create new dishes, most of the new dishes that find favor seem somewhat anchored in tradition.

In the 1990s, as Italian business practices became more aligned with those in Europe and North America, lunch hours shortened, yet workdays lengthened. Now more than 50 percent of Italian women work outside the home, so they cannot devote as much time to food preparation. It is no longer a given that grandparents will be near at hand, or that grandma will feel inclined to prepare food each night for three or four generations of family members. Italian children have become more independent, and often eat in school or with friends. Sad to say, fast food has made serious incursions in much of Italy.

So the multicourse meal of not too long ago may now be simply an appetizer followed by a pasta with a glass of wine, or perhaps a pasta followed by a salad. The portions might be larger than in the multicourse meal, and the whole repast will take less time than it used to. But the important thing to note is that even though Italians are eating less structured meals, they are not eating less well. Most of them still demand top-quality ingredients and want food preparation to be done with taste and care. Soups, pastas, main courses, vegetables, olive oil, and cheeses are still outstanding. Italian wine, always good, is now excellent in most of the country. And Italy still has the world's best coffee.

*N*ow that you understand how most of Italy eats, toss it away as you approach Friuli-Venezia Giulia. This is a place that has its own distinct traditions and, more than anywhere else in Italy, has a cuisine that is evolving. New ways of eating have penetrated this region more than any other.

The food of Friuli-Venezia Giulia, like its people, is much more international than that of most of the rest of Italy. Although palpably and unmistakably Italian in terms of the preparation of most dishes, it has stylistic influences from elsewhere. So the more prominent use of spices and many vegetable and fruit flavorings in some dishes draws from surrounding areas but also is particular to this place. The region's cooks make little effort to *be* international, but rather endeavor to express ideas and flavors that speak of their own fortunate land. It cannot be emphasized too strongly that it is a mistaken assumption that just because the region was long under foreign domination it therefore absorbed the ways of its occupiers. If anything, the people of Friuli-Venezia Giulia wanted to protect and exalt that which was innately theirs.

Because this part of Italy was so poor for so many centuries (with a few comfortable exceptions such as San Daniele and Trieste), polenta and a limited selection of other foods were the sum of the regional diet. These included milk, butter, cheese, fresh herbs that could be gathered, apples, pears, grapes, cherries, apricots, plums, beets, turnips, potatoes, horseradish, lard, eggs, vinegar, and grappa. In the hills, wild game could sometimes be caught. People near the seashore also had the fish and crustaceans they were able to catch. This may not sound like the promising foundations of a sophisticated cuisine, but local people did not think in those terms. Rather, they tried to be creative with what they had, so that there would be variety in their daily meals.

Spices also entered the parts of the region that were under Venice in the Renaissance and came to all of it when Trieste became a major port in the early eighteenth century. They lent a degree of subtlety that other Italian regional cuisines did not have. You need only look at the recipes for Risotto with Scallops, Zucchini Blossoms, and a Rainbow of Spices (page 230) or Cjarsòns (page 202) to understand the kind of impact spices had on the foods of this region, which no place in Italy could rival.

When people in Friuli-Venezia Giulia recount stories of *la miseria* to me, they are often about how a big pot of polenta would be made on Monday, a bit of which would be eaten hot that day and the rest would be allowed to cool for use throughout the week. It might be grilled, baked with cheese, or topped with butter and sugar as a treat. If a little piece of meat were available to make a gravy, that would be a special event. Polenta usually was a central part of all meals. Many people in Carnia and the Natisone Valleys told me that after the polenta was made, the pot would be covered with a cloth and hung from a high beam. This was not only to keep it from animals who might wander by, but also out of the reach of hungry children. The only significant alternatives to polenta-centered meals were those that had soup or some sort of stew.

Because it was customary (or, rather, inevitable) that one food or dish was the center-piece of most meals, when a certain degree of affluence came to the region in the last third of the twentieth century, eating habits in the region changed because the people were anxious to embrace variety. But cooks (mostly mothers) in the region were already adept at finding many ways to use whatever ingredients were available to them. So when they could afford a broader range of meats, fruits, vegetables, and grains, they applied their creativity and sense of experimentation to them to make a cuisine that is based in tradition but still evolves more than any other in Italy. Suddenly, many new food prepara-tions appeared in Friuli-Venezia Giulia. Older flavors and cooking methods of the region were used with new foods, and then paired with exquisite wines to make a grand repast.

*A*nother distinct thread in the culinary fabric of Friuli-Venezia Giulia is that of eating small dishes of food to wash down wine in an *osteria*. This practice is shared with Venice, although in most of the Veneto it is not as evolved as in Friuli. Udine is a paradise for this kind of eating. Little pieces of vegetables, fish, or spreads on toasted bread will come on a plate with your glass of wine. One *osteria* serves risotto at 7:30 P.M. to anyone who is present. This tradition of small dishes is also prominent in the towns of Venezia Giulia that were held by Venice, especially Gradisca d'Isonzo.

Gorizia and much of its province have a tradition known as *la merenda de piròn,* or "the fork snack." Workers who started their labors at dawn would be hungry by late morning, and this would be their sustenance before getting back to the job. They often worked until sundown and then went home for their principal meal of the day. Typically this snack was a little bowl of goulash or bread with prosciutto or salami. And, of course, a glass of wine.

The tradition of eating snacks or little meals has always been popular in Trieste, where this pause is known as a *rebechin*. Many historians think that the word came out of the Jewish community and relates to Rebecca. In all likelihood, the word comes from *ribeccare,* which means to "pick again" as might a bird, but it also means, more roughly, to stick something else in your beak.

The origin of the *rebechin* comes from the rhythms of life in Trieste's port. In most large port cities, food traditions spring up near the docks when carters and stevedores take a break and have a fast snack before returning to their work. This snack is intended specifically to stave off hunger and provide energy to manual laborers. In Genoa, for example, there are vendors at the docks who sell bowls of pesto-laced minestrone or stewed tripe. In Trieste, the classic dockside snack might be a little bowl of cinnamon-scented veal stew or *porcina* (cooked pork) with freshly grated horseradish served on a poppy seed bun.

The *rebechin* also became a tradition of office workers and shopkeepers throughout the city. It continues to this day, although snacks are smaller. For many it might be a *cappuccino triestino* and something sweet. But in the broader sense, a *rebechin* in Trieste may be had whenever one is hungry, and might be the above-mentioned items, or goulash, crab salad, fried sardines, or cooked cabbage. This is washed down with a glass of wine or, sometimes, a small beer.

*A*t the start of the twenty-first century, dining in Friuli-Venezia Giulia is radically different from that of twenty-five years earlier. Then, the mentality was still that of filling up to combat hunger, even though it was no longer a real threat. But as that generation moved on, the one that followed developed a new approach. "Humble" traditional ingredients are still prized, but other regional products that were once luxury items (seafood, game, foie gras, prosciutto) for very rare occasions are now part of daily eating.

The various historic components of alimentation in Friuli-Venezia Giulia have combined to create a new way to eat. The *rebechin, merenda de piròn,* and *osteria* food were often taken standing up with drinkable wine. Now, the trend in the region has been to adapt this tradition to create a seated meal of "small plates" of really good food (as opposed to that meant to fortify) paired with sensational wine. Cooks create an amalgam of the flavors of the past combined with new ingredients, often presented in faster preparations, and frequently in small portions. A meal of consequence in most of the region nowadays would be something similar to a tasting menu in a restaurant. Yet people also eat this way at home. There is a progression of vivid flavors and textures in small portions that match well with one or more wines.

Nowadays, a little dollop of hot polenta or a wedge of cooler polenta may appear on one or two of these courses. Polenta is no longer the stomach-filling staple meant to keep hunger at the door. Now it usually accompanies other foods or may come in a little portion topped with cheese or herbs or meat gravy. But for the people of the region, polenta remains an important symbol and a reminder of past privation and resilience, much as matzohs have such resonance for Jews. You are not being inauthentic if you create a Friulian meal without polenta, but you will never go wrong if you include it.

A cheese dish is also quite common as one of the courses. The most popular is crisp frico, which would come at the beginning of a meal. Soft runny frico might come later with a little white or yellow polenta. If a crisp frico has been formed into a flower or cup it may be the vessel that carries a small portion of salad or gnocchi.

*W*hat is the philosophy behind assembling a modern meal in Friuli-Venezia Giulia? Much of it relates to what sort of wine you want to serve. Sometimes, you will want to pour a different wine with each course or every second or third course. So the plates should be organized to pair with the wines as they appear. Within this structure, the dishes should probably go from lighter to more substantial, and from more delicate to more flavorful. Conversely, you could create a meal centered on a single wine that interests you, and every dish should go well with that wine and show its versatility.

So if you wish to build a meal around a Sauvignon Blanc, for example, you might think of foods that go well with it, such as asparagus, shrimp, eggs, and saffron. Part of the reason the region's dishes are so sophisticated is that cooks everywhere understand the interactions of food and wine. When I ask a farmer's wife who is whipping together an impromptu meal for me which wine she will serve, she will either say, "Based on the ingredients I am using, I think such-and-such a wine will be good," or "I wanted to serve a Refosco, so these are the foods I selected to go with it." The point is, they always seem to know. Never, in more than twenty-five years of visiting Friuli-Venezia Giulia, has anyone shrugged when I asked how to specifically pair food and wine.

You will see that just about every recipe in this book has a recommended wine (or, I should say, grape variety or blend). You will start to discover how certain flavor notes in wine match well with certain foods. For example, the somewhat vegetal aspect of Cabernet Franc seems to marry well with game and with aromatic spices such as clove. The somewhat astringent aspect of Pinot Grigio or Malvasia Istriana, plus an undercurrent of fruit, makes these wines congenial with shellfish and certain fragrant herbs.

One guideline you can use in planning a menu is to see which recipes have the same suggested wine and start from there. But there is another approach. In the region, where wine is quite affordable, they often serve a small glass of a different wine (or rather, a small portion in a larger glass so that the wine can be swirled) with each course. If you are making a meal for four or six persons, this is possible if you have a generous wine budget.

At the very least, consider having two wines at dinner, starting with the lighter one and proceeding to the more substantial one. In most of the world, this means beginning with white and proceeding to red. This is often done in Friuli-Venezia Giulia, too, but there is no hard-and-fast rule. You can serve two whites (Malvasia Istriana followed by Ribolla Gialla, for example), or two reds (Refosco followed by Pignolo or a big Merlot). Or you can even serve a lighter red to start with (such as Tazzelenghe) and then go on to a structured white blend from Collio or a big Chardonnay.

Whether you use wine or food as the point of departure in planning a menu, there are some guidelines. In a meal with more than one wine, use the lighter wine first. Therefore, first eat foods that go with that wine. If you are using the same wine throughout the meal, then plan the meal in a sequence that appeals to you. If there is a strong flavor in the meal, such as certain spices, leave them for later on so that the palate and taste buds are not dominated by that flavor too early. Another advantage to this is that after a few courses, the palate and taste buds often need some pronounced flavors to rouse them again.

How would you select which categories of recipes to be used as courses in these meals? You have much more freedom than in most of Italy, with its *primo/secondo/contorno/*dessert tradition. In Friuli-Venezia Giulia it is possible to have a meal, say, that has five small appetizers, one little *primo,* and a little *secondo.* Or you can take recipes that are for a *secondo* and serve small portions as an appetizer. You can create meals that are all fish or all meat or all vegetable. Or you may draw from many categories. Just remember to let wine be one of your guides.

Having small plates is often more appealing because one can tire of eating many mouthfuls of the same food, no matter how good it might be. Is it possible to have too much white asparagus or foie gras or chocolate? The sybarite in me says no, but the realist says yes, and he is correct. A dozen stalks of asparagus can make a nice centerpiece to a meal, but four can make a delectable course in a larger and more varied meal.

S ome advice about serving size for most of the recipes in this book: It is much more variable than in typical cookbooks. If something will be a main course, there will be fewer servings than if the dish is to be a "small plate" in a meal of five or more courses. If, for example, a recipe is for four to six servings, there might be enough food for four persons as a main course and six persons as an appetizer. And if you make a meal of several "small plates," then you might even get eight portions out of that recipe. Another pleasure of meals with several small courses is that you always feel you have room for another bite. And there will be a variety of taste sensations in a leisurely meal that will make for good conversation.

T here is another interesting practice in food preparation and presentation in Friuli-Venezia Giulia that one occasionally sees elsewhere, but not with the same consistency or degree of imagination. Very often, when you are served a dish in the region, a bit more of one (or occasionally more than one) of the ingredients will be sprinkled on the edge of the plate. It is a way of saying that this is a distinct flavor in the whole combination and bears revisiting. It is an invitation to dip a forkful of the food in to intensify and reinforce the sensation of that flavor and perhaps experience it more immediately with a sip of wine. The sensation when the ingredient is pressed into a fork is different than if the flavoring is cooked into the dish or put on top of the completed dish.

Some examples: A sauce for game that contains powdered nutmeg will be an amalgam of many flavors. By having a little more nutmeg on the side of the plate to dip hot meat into, the impact on the tongue is more vivid. Also, the blending of those two flavors with a sip of Cabernet Franc or Merlot will create stereophonic thrills in your mouth. If you finely grind some roasted coffee beans and sprinkle the powder near a piece of chocolate cake, the combination of the two flavors will be quite exciting. Or try poppy seeds with potato gnocchi. Or perhaps surround bread gnocchi with small amounts of dill, paprika, and caraway seeds.

You might ask why not put the ingredients on top, as cooks do elsewhere. The answer is that the diner then loses the element of choice as to whether to add the additional flavor component and the decision of how much should be added per mouthful. Grate fresh horseradish near prosciutto di San Daniele rather than on top and you will understand. Try serving a portion of pasta, risotto, or polenta with grated cheese around the border of the plate rather than on top of the food, so you can fold in cheese when and where you want to. You will find that the food tastes lighter than it would if you spooned cheese on top and let it melt in.

Here are some possible side garnishes that you can select if the ingredient is either in the recipe or is complementary (as in horseradish): spices in powdered form, especially cinnamon or paprika; poppy seeds; ground black pepper; whole pink peppercorns; dill leaves; chopped parsley or other fresh herbs; minced chive or scallion; caraway seeds; a little freshly grated horseradish; grated smoked ricotta or cheeses such as Montasio, Parmigiano-Reggiano, or Pecorino; cubed apple or pear and perhaps a few gratings of cheese; halved cherries or wine grapes or slivers of peach, plum, or apricot lightly tossed with grappa; chopped cucumber with dill on the side; finely ground coffee.

In studying a recipe, you will often decide which flavoring ingredient merits singling out for additional attention. Once you start using this method of presentation you will notice the intriguing added dimension it gives to dining and enjoyment of wine. I have drawn inspiration from this practice and apply it to many recipes I prepare that are not from Friuli-Venezia Giulia. And when a waiter in a New York restaurant approaches me now with his enormous pepper mill, I make him grind pepper *around* the food rather than on top of it.

A s you start to use this book, consider the recipes a point of departure for creating meals that have traditional or less traditional structure. And experiment with the marvelous wines of Friuli-Venezia Giulia to discover that they are probably the most food-friendly in the world. See which food and wine flavor interactions you can discover.

Remember that recipes are like sheet music, which is not really music, but the notation of music. Music is only real when it is played. Similarly, a recipe is a notation of how food might be prepared, but the variables that exist as you translate the recipe into food, using your senses and intuition and the ingredients and equipment available to you, will make your "performance" distinct, personal, and memorable. The only exception to this rule is baking, where you must follow directions very literally. So as you proceed to cook the exquisite dishes of Friuli-Venezia Giulia, consider these recipes as a careful rendering of a tradition and a way of eating, but it is up to you to make the music that is most beautiful to you.

The Flavors of the Land: Herbs, Spices, and Other Things to Savor

A fountain of gardens, a well of living waters,
and streams from Lebanon. Awake, O north wind;
and come, thou south; blow upon my garden,
that the spices thereof may flow out.

—THE SONG OF SOLOMON

In July 1999, I wrote an article for the *New York Times* about Friuli-Venezia Giulia, addressing a few of the countless things I find special and unique about this wonderful region. I was not involved in selecting the title of the article, and was surprised and pleased when I saw the morning paper: "Italy's Secret Garden." This amply says so much about the place in an elegant way. That Friuli-Venezia Giulia is still basically a secret is part of its allure. Here we are, at this late date, with a globalized world, yet this particular treasure is virtually unknown.

Although part of the region's land is unyielding, much of it is remarkably fertile. And its people are distinct in their ability not only to observe the land, but to listen to it. This intimacy means that the range of ingredients these people use in their kitchen is much greater than is typically assumed.

It is commonplace to say that the region consumes a lot of standard ingredients, such as pork, cheese, cabbage, beans, potatoes, beets, cornmeal, apples, and grapes, but that conjures an image that is only partially accurate. These foods are found in most of the world. What is different is how the people of Friuli-Venezia Giulia flavor them, using herbs, spices, vinegar, and wine to give them extraordinary subtlety. This may result in combinations such as cinnamon-flavored ricotta cheese as a pasta sauce; poppy seeds, feta cheese, lemon, carrots, and beans; dill, paprika, and caraway seeds in a cucumber sauce; ham cooked in vinegar; onions with cloves; polenta with ginger; or mussels with anise.

To understand what makes the cuisine of Friuli-Venezia Giulia so distinct, it is important first to know more about the herbs that grow in the *Terra Fortunata*. In years of living in and writing about Liguria, I felt that I had some idea about fresh herbs. Ligurian herbs have remarkably forward flavor and freshness, influenced in part by their proximity to the sea. The basil that grows near where I stay in Liguria is bracingly pungent and commands your attention. In Friuli-Venezia Giulia, herbs are more subtle and delicate, and seem to appear and disappear in a matter of days, only to be replaced by others. Almost every herb used in the cuisine of this region is fresh, except for the occasional dried oregano that one sees in Trieste and Gorizia.

The herbs in the plains of the Bassa Friulana are different from those in the hills of wine country or the Carso, and there are still different herbs high in the mountains of Carnia and the Val Canale. Take a woman from the mountains to the plains, and she may recognize certain plants by sight, but she will be startled because they have a different aroma and taste. This is because the weather and soil in which these herbs grew are not like those where she lives.

There are some recipes in this region that call for specific herbs, especially dill in the province of Gorizia or silene (called *sclopit* in Friulano) in the province of Udine. However, there are certain famous dishes in the region that are called *alle erbe* in Italian or *cu lis jàrbis* (or *jerbis*) in Friulano. This suggests that you gather as many fresh herbs as you can and mix them with delicate greens and leaves to give your recipe some character. The classic of this genre is Fertàe cu lis Jàrbis (Fresh Herb Frittata, page 144) in which egg is used to hold together herbs in an omelet that is bright green. Herbs are also central to gnocchi *alle erbe,* and as a filling for *cjarsòns* pasta.

A lovely event occurs in the Carnia town of Ravascletto on June 24, St. John's Day. The variety of herbs and edible flowers is thought to be at its peak on this day, so at dawn the women of the town go in the fields and collect more than twenty different plants, which collectively are called *Il Mac di San Zuan* (the vegetation of St. John). Special dishes are then prepared with this bounty, which is the concluding event of several days of observances of the summer solstice. Similar events happen more or less formally all over the region on many days of the year.

Friuli-Venezia Giulia is also the region of Italy that uses spices more than any other. It is typically said that Venice is the spice capital, but this is only partially correct. Through the centuries the Italian peninsula had three principal spice ports: Genoa, Venice, and Trieste. In Genoa, spices were specifically a commodity for trade and were not welcome in the dishes of the Ligurian kitchen. Genoese sailors complained of the strong smell of the spices, and were only too happy to be rid of them when they returned home.

Venice was a major importer of spices from the East. Certain flavors, especially cinnamon, appeared in Venetian dishes, while others were used for fragrances or trade. Because most of Friuli and parts of Venezia Giulia were under Venetian control from about 1420 until 1797, many of these spices came into these areas.

But it was Trieste that would play the crucial role. The story of Trieste is that it was the crucible where the spices and flavorings of Europe were blended with those of the rest of the world. In addition to the spices it imported from Asia and Africa to please local tastes, it was also the port of entry (and exit) for all the spices and flavorings used in the vast Austro-Hungarian empire. It is very important to underline that the city was also a port of exit for these flavors, so that Hungarian paprika or Polish caraway or Albanian wild fennel came to Trieste in addition to the black pepper, cinnamon, nutmeg, saffron, chocolate, coffee, and other exotic flavors from all over the world. Venice, which was basically an importer from spice-producing areas beyond Europe, could not compete with Trieste in terms of sheer variety.

A Visit with an Old Triestine Spice Seller

In English, the word *spry* is often used to describe old people who can look after themselves and have a twinkle in their eyes. I think this is a slightly dismissive term (by this definition, every old person I have met in Friuli-Venezia Giulia is spry). The Italian language has a much better one: *forte.* The first meaning of this word is strong, but when used to describe an old person, it gathers under its umbrella ideas such as sharp, self-sufficient, engaging, compelling, and admirable. *Una persona forte* is someone who not only gets by, but is involved with the world. Ernesto Illy, the patriarch of Trieste's coffee family, is famously *forte.* So is Livio Felluga, the great wine maker. And I have met several other men and numerous women in this region who are *forte.*

Which brings me to Hans Bauer, who is not only *forte* but also *dolce,* much like the paprika that is but one of the 350 herbs, spices, essential oils, and other flavorings that his family-owned firm, Bauer, has been importing since 1917. The company was founded in Trieste in 1884 under the reign of Austrian emperor Franz Josef. Hans's father arrived in Trieste in 1912 at age forty from Brno, Czechoslovakia, with his family and acquired the company soon after. He never learned Italian. In 1914 the father was called to fight in the Austrian army that would lose World War I. He returned to Trieste after the war and managed to revive his company.

Hans Bauer went to work in the company in 1927, at the age of seventeen. I met him more than seventy years later and found in him an oral history of twentieth-century Trieste that focused on the city's Jews. Hans had two brothers. The family owned one of the first cars in Trieste. In 1927, it collided with a streetcar and his mother and a brother were killed. "Every life is like a novel. Some are beautiful and some are not."

When he was not working for the family company, Hans liked to go mountain climbing. "I had literally hundreds of friends in the Club Alpino of Trieste. The secret police infiltrated the Club Alpino, and pulled almost all the Jews out. With the racial laws, pretty soon there were just three of us Jews left. I was connected to all of these people. You see, when you do climbing and are connected by a rope, you must all help and support one another. When the racial laws came, the rope was broken."

Jews were excluded from all aspects of life: schools, professions, sport organizations. In Trieste, separate schools were created for Jewish children.

He had a girlfriend during those years, but with the advent of racial laws in 1938, her fearful mother prevented the couple from seeing one another. He never married. "I live alone, but I only drink with friends. Solitary wine is sad wine."

He claims to have become younger as he aged. "When I was a boy, everyone called me Uncle Hans because I was so wise. After the war I said, 'Enough! I don't want to be wise anymore.'"

Thirty of Hans's relatives were captured and killed by the Nazis, and Hans was one of the few who survived by hiding in the country houses of sympathetic Italians. The Germans appropriated the Bauer spice company and later sold it to the British. The Bauers bought it back with what money they had. Hans had no doubt that this was the right thing to do: "When I opened the door again, I knew that this fragrance of spices was worth a million by itself.

"The spice business has changed a lot. When I began, Trieste was the center of the trade, and the only port of a great empire. We brought things from all over the world to sell in Italy, Vienna, Hungary, Czechoslovakia, and Germany. Now we have little contact with most of those places, because spices also come to Genoa, Hamburg, and, especially, Holland. So our business today is only for the Italian market."

One of his chief clients was Stock, a famous Trieste distillery that was sold to a German company in 1997. For decades, bottles of Stock liqueurs could be seen on shelves in just about every bar in Italy and much of Europe. Hans told me that, until recently, "Every bottle of Stock had a drop of Bauer in it."

He also used to have many local clients, even though the firm sells most of its products wholesale and not to the public. In the past, Italians had spice jars, each one with a different label. Back then they did not throw away the jars, but would buy small amounts of spices in paper (and later plastic) that would be poured into the empty jars. Hans decries the "new consumerism" that encourages people to throw away jars when they are empty. And he is correct.

During our visit, Hans pulled old books down from his shelf that contained drawings of plants. "That which is wonderful in the spice trade is that it is ancient. I have books from the sixteenth century that are still valid and still can teach us things." As he carefully fingered a book of plant drawings from 1856, he observed that "the greatest artist in the world is Mother Nature."

As he turned the pages of these books, yellowed pieces of paper placed as bookmarks decades ago served to reawaken memories as sweet, as bitter, as pungent, and as vivid as the spices he sells.

I asked Hans whether he used spices and herbs for medicinal reasons. "Only moderately," he replied. "Work is the greatest medicine there is. One does not have time to get sick. I have worked now for seventy-three years, ten hours a day, at double speed. So I think I have worked about three hundred years."

Most spice companies are now part of large multinational corporations. It is unclear whether a small family firm so animated by the knowledge and the passion of one man can continue after he is gone. A younger relative now runs much of the business while Hans Bauer, *forte* and *dolce,* provides the memory, the conscience, and the continuity in an era in which, he sadly observes, there is so little phosphorous (spark) in most people. "It is because they are alive but they have not lived." ❦

From Trieste grew three important spice trails that connected the city with the north. One went through the Carso and Gorizia and Ljubljana to Vienna, Budapest, and points east. Another went to Cormons, Udine, and north to Tolmezzo, and then through the Val

Canale to Tarvisio, and into Carinthia and Styria and then Vienna. The third trail followed the Trieste-Tolmezzo route and then went straight into Carnia and over the mountains to Salzburg, Prague, Munich, and all the way to Cologne.

As you have read, two of these roads connected Trieste and Vienna. The Austrian capital was not only an importer of products from the south, but a supplier of products from elsewhere in its empire that were then transported to the port of Trieste for export.

All along the spice roads of what is now Friuli-Venezia Giulia, flavorings "fell off the carts," as people now tell you with a grin, and found their way into local preparations. So I was not the least bit surprised when I met a woman in the small town of Tavagnacco, north of Udine, who flavors her white asparagus pasta sauce with saffron. If you look at the map and notice where the province of Pordenone is in the western part of Friuli-Venezia Giulia, far from the spice trails, you will understand why this is the part of the region that uses the least amount of spices in its cookery.

The traffic in these flavors had impact beyond cuisine in at least two important ways. The people of this region excelled in the use of herbs and, especially, spices for medicinal purposes. Itinerant men from Carnia known as *cramars* (or *kramars*) traveled all over Central Europe with wooden spice cabinets on their backs, selling their wares and offering prescriptions for different maladies. In many cases, they were the suppliers of raw materials to apothecaries from Geneva to Warsaw. What they did not sell by the end of their travels was brought home to Carnia, and entered the kitchens of the resourceful women of that area. Read more about the *cramars* on page 202.

The other business in which herbs and spices helped shape the region owes to the fact that Friulians (and nearby Venetians) were among the first to create perfumes from herbs and spices as opposed to flowers. It was a Friulian, Gian Maria Farina (usually known as Johann Maria Farina), who in 1792 created the Echtes Kolnisch Wasser 4711 fragrance that is still used today. Farina traveled to Cologne with his nose and his skills and took advantage of the fact that there were no copyright laws or patents when he created this fragrance. There already was what was known as Echtes Kolnisch Wasser or eau de cologne (created in 1714), which combines many of the fragrance elements that were well known in Friuli years before. It is probable that the formula for this was derived from older scents from Friuli and Venice. With their special relationship to the land, Friulians (especially from south of Udine) became master fragrance makers because they knew herbs and spices so thoroughly.

*W*hat follows is an exploration of some herbs, spices, bulbs, and particular plants that one might find in Friuli-Venezia Giulia, either in the ground or imported.

Remember that fresh herbs should be wiped with paper towels rather than washed in water, which would eliminate much of their fragrance. As for spices, they must be kept in airtight jars or containers and far from light. Whole spices last longer than those that have been ground and give off a much more vivid flavor when freshly ground. Use spices judiciously. The right amount can give extraordinary character to a dish, but too much can ruin it. Follow your own instincts, and check carefully before increasing the dose.

Allspice (Pimenta dioica)
In the pepper family, its aromatic fragrance is often a note in sausage. Whole berries are interesting in the steaming liquid for fish or vegetables. It also is a felicitous match with apples and apricots.

Angelica (Angelica archangelica)
The stems and leaves are eaten as one might eat celery, and they can flavor many dishes. It is aromatic, sweet, and can resemble anise.

Anise (Pimpinella anisum)
Sweet and fragrant and a bit peppery, it is the basic flavor for licorice but also appears with seafood, vegetables (especially cucumber), and fruit. You may use fresh leaves or the seeds.

Basil (Ocimum basilicum)
Basil is now so widespread that it is found in this region, too. It is not nearly as much at home here as in, say, Liguria, where it is the signature flavor and fragrance. A tisane made with basil is ideal for calming nerves.

Bay Leaf or Laurel Leaf (Laurus nobilis)
Roman heroes were given a crown of these leaves, and when they lived off their accomplishments, these were the laurels they rested upon. One leaf is usually sufficient for soups, stews, or sauces and should be removed before the food is served, as it should not be eaten.

Borage (Borago officinalis)
A very popular herb that sometimes has a slight cucumber taste about it. Borage frequently turns up in blends of fresh herbs in this region.

Burnet (Sanguisorba minor)
Light green in color, this herb has a flavor reminiscent of cucumber.

Rosazzo, birthplace of the Pignolo and Picolit grapes

(Photo by Walter Filiputti)

Arta Terme, in Carnia

(Photo by Fred Plotkin)

One of the Fusine lakes near Tarvisio

(Photo by Fred Plotkin)

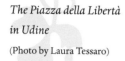

*The Piazza della Libertà
in Udine*

(Photo by Laura Tessaro)

The Basilica of Aquileia

(Photo by Laura Tessaro)

*A kitchen in
Capriva (Collio)*
(Photo by Fred Plotkin)

*A tray full of grappas
and spirits in Percoto*
(Photo by Fred Plotkin)

The Pirona pastry shop in Trieste, a favorite of James Joyce
(Photo by Fred Plotkin)

Trieste
(Photo by Fred Plotkin)

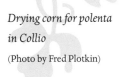

Drying corn for polenta in Collio

(Photo by Fred Plotkin)

Harvest time in Cormons

(Photo by Fred Plotkin)

Hillside in the Colli Orientali del Friuli (COF)

(Photo by Walter Filiputti)

Rocca Bernarda, in Premariacco (COF)

(Photo by Walter Filiputti)

Calendula *(Calendula officinalis)*

A flower which, when dried and pulverized, is often used as a substitute for expensive saffron to give foods a golden color. It is traditional to add ½ teaspoon to venison dishes. (When fresh, marigolds are used sparingly in herb mixtures to add color.)

Capers *(Capparis spinosa)*

These little flower buds are typically preserved in salt or brine. Many people believe that the very best capers come from the island of Salina, off the northern coast of Sicily. In the cuisine of Trieste, they are indispensable for making Liptauer cheese spread and also wind up in certain fish dishes.

Caraway *(Carum carvi)*

Caraway leaves and roots are sometimes used to flavor foods or appear in herb mixes. But most often, when we think of caraway, our mind goes immediately to caraway seeds, those wonderful, pungent, striped brown seeds that go into rye bread, combine with cabbage or potatoes, go into cheeses, or flavor pork. In Friuli-Venezia Giulia it is called *kummel.*

Cardamom Seed *(Elletaria cardamomum)*

Not a traditional flavor in most of the region, it has occasionally been a flavor in breads or combined with sugar in baking. It is also a popular new flavor for ice cream.

Cayenne *(Capsicum)*

This is a powder derived from grinding one or more types of dried red peppers, of which there are more than two hundred species. It can range in color from bright orange to dark red, and in spiciness from quite mild to rather hot. Its aroma is usually sweet. The difference between cayenne and paprika is that the former is drawn from many varieties of red peppers while the latter is derived from just a few, and therefore has distinct characteristics.

Celery *(Apium graveolens)*

Celery stalks are used to make soup or are minced to use in cooking. Their leaves are chopped and wind up in herb mixtures. Celery seed is an aromatic element in pickling and in herb mixes.

Chamomile *(Anthemis nobilis)*

Called *camomilla* in Italian, it is typically brewed as an infusion to be drunk in the evening to promote sleep. You can find it in almost every Italian coffee bar or pantry at home. Little bits of chamomile give floral flavor and fragrance to herb blends.

Chervil *(Anthriscus cerefolium)*
Delicious chopped over beets or eggplant or pureed with spinach.

Chives *(Allium schoenoprasum)*
Pencil-shaped tubular leaves from the onion family that give zingy freshness when minced and sprinkled over many foods. They are marvelous with eggs.

Cinnamon *(Cinnamomum zeylanicum)*
Psychological studies conducted on men and much circumstantial evidence all seem to indicate that no fragrance creates more of a sense of contentment, pleasure, warmth, and sensuality in them than cinnamon. Whether this is because cinnamon is a reminder of home and childhood or there is an actual biological trigger that makes men respond this way still needs to be determined. But I can attest to these sensations and suspect that this is part of why I am so drawn to the food of Friuli-Venezia Giulia. This is a signature flavor, especially when it appears atop fruit-filled gnocchi. The flavor, of course, is sweet and delicate, and best just when it is freshly ground from the stick (which is a piece of tree bark). Much of the cinnamon consumed in North America is really cassia *(Cinnamomum cassia blume),* much of which originates in China, Vietnam, and Java. Both cassia and the other variety (sometimes called true cinnamon and which is native to Sri Lanka) are sold as cinnamon, and you would probably have to develop a relationship with a spice seller to assure that you get one or the other variety.

Cloves *(Eugenia aromatica)*
This is the unopened flower of the clove tree. The word is probably derived from the French *clou,* or nail, because of the particular shape of this spice. The Italian word for nail is *chiodo,* and cloves are called *chiodi di garofano.* It is often mistakenly translated as "carnation nails," because *garofano* means carnation in Italian. But its secondary meaning is the clove tree, and that is the real meaning of *chiodi di garofano.* This is a strong, slightly musky flavor, so it is used in small quantities, famously in baked ham. But a particular use in this region is to flavor onions with clove.

Coriander Seed *(Coriandrum sativum)*
Coriander seed is often confused with its leafy relatives, coriander and cilantro. The seed

is referred to in Italian as *coriandolo,* and its delightful aroma and flavor of sage and lemon make it a pleasing addition to many traditional foods, including pork, apples, breads, and cookies. It also makes an interesting subtext when added to certain coffee blends.

Cress or Land Cress *(Lepidium sativum)*
Very good in herb butters, as well as with cauliflower, potatoes, and spinach.

Cumin *(Cuminum cyminum)*
Known as *comino* in Italy, this seed is often mistaken for caraway. But they are distinct. Cumin has a warm flavor, is aromatic, and should be used sparingly. It can be used in seed form or pounded into a powder. As cooks occasionally do in Friuli-Venezia Giulia, I like to add a little bit to rice that I serve as a side dish (but not to risotto).

Curry Powder
This is not one spice, but a blend of up to sixteen different spices. These might include cinnamon, ginger, turmeric, nutmeg, mustard seed, black pepper, cayenne, cardamom seed, and allspice. Curry powder is certainly not a traditional flavoring in Italian food, but it is becoming ever more popular. In Friuli-Venezia Giulia, curry might flavor risotto or buttered steamed carrots.

Dandelion Greens
Known in Italian as *tarassaco,* a popular green for risotto, omelets, or as a component in herb mixes.

Dill *(Anethum graveolens)*
Most Italians have never tasted dill and when I use the Italian word, *aneto,* they do not recognize it. In Friuli and, especially, Venezia Giulia, it is very well known, bringing its special perfume and pungency to many dishes, especially those with potatoes, cucumbers, soft cheese, or eggs. Only use the leaves; the stems are bitter. Dill seed may occasionally be sprinkled on crusts for fruit tarts and is an essential ingredient in pickling vegetables, such as cucumbers.

Fennel *(Foeniculum vulgare)*
Fennel is a delicious bulb with leaves. The fennel seed *(seme di finocchio)* is a popular flavoring in the region, especially in Trieste. Fennel seeds appear in breads (often in combination with yellow raisins).

Garlic *(Allium sativum)*
There are many varieties of garlic in the world. It is loved (and occasionally despised)
for its flavor and is universally acclaimed for its many medicinal properties. Naturally, it
can be found in Friuli-Venezia Giulia, but it does not enjoy the popularity of onions. It
does figure in a favorite Triestine sauce with shrimp that dresses pasta. In working with
garlic, always remove the green core, which gives off bitterness when cooked. Garlic
has numerous medicinal properties. It purifies blood, lowers blood pressure, and, when
pounded and mixed with a little oil, becomes an excellent salve on calluses and corns
on the feet.

Ginger *(Zingiber officinale)*
This is a root that is washed and then dried and used as a powder. The root can also be
ground, and fresher ginger can be shaved. It is both sweet and spicy and can tingle in the
mouth. It is a flavor that some people adore and others detest. Ginger varies a bit in flavor
and intensity depending on its origin. Most of what we see is Chinese or Japanese, and
there are others from India, Africa, and the Caribbean. My favorite comes from Jamaica.
Ginger finds its way into spice mixes used in Friulian baking, and I like it very much as a
flavoring in golden polenta. A teaspoon of grated fresh ginger stirred into a cup of hot
water is wonderful in treating a sore throat.

Hops *(Humulus lupulus)*
This plant is usually associated with brewing of beer; but in Friuli, it is also very popular
in risotto and other dishes calling for herbs or greens. The Italian word is *lupolo,* and in
Friulian, it is variously known as *urtiçons, urtizons, urtizzonòn, vidisòn,* or *bruscèndoli.* To
further add to confusion, *bruscandoli* (also called *bruscandoi*) are often called wild asparagus. This is not asparagus, but a green with a hint of asparagus in its complex flavor.

Horseradish *(Armoracia rusticana* or *Radicula armoracia)*
Called *rafano* in Italian, but *cren* or *kren* in Friuli-Venezia Giulia, this is one of those
flavors that sets this region apart from the rest of Italy. Horseradish is a classic flavor
here. It is marvelous when grated raw on ham baked in bread crust (a specialty from
Gorizia to Muggia) or on Trieste's magnificent buffet of pork products. Horseradish
flavors soups and sauces and is a perfect partner to boiled beef. This root appears
fresh in markets in late autumn and winter and can be kept in cold storage into spring.
For the rest of the year, it is preserved by storing it in apple cider vinegar or white
wine vinegar.

Hyssop *(Hyssopus officinalis)*

This is a member of the mint family and is often paired with berries. It also goes well with duck and pheasant.

Juniper Berries *(Juniperus communis)*

These are very popular in Friulian mountain cooking, especially with venison, rabbit, duck, and in meat broths. They are also delicious if used sparingly in sauerkraut cooked with white wine.

Lemon Balm or Balm *(Melissa officinalis)*

This is perhaps the favorite herb in Carnia, where it is called *melissa*. Its most notable characteristic is that it seems to combine flavors of lemon and mint, which has made it the preferred herb for treating sore throats and coughs. Although lamb is not a common meat in this region, I once had an extraordinary leg of lamb there that had been rubbed with *melissa* before being roasted.

Lovage *(Levisticum officinale)*

Lovage winds up often in herb mixes. Lovage seed is often used instead of fennel seed, aniseed, or celery seed.

Mace *(Myristica fragrans)*

Mace is a relative of nutmeg. It is derived from a scarlet-colored protective layer of the seed of a small orange-colored tropical fruit. The kernel of this seed becomes nutmeg. Mace is typically used as part of a spice mix in baking, and also is tasty in ground meat. You might add a touch of it to Cevapcici (Beef-Pork Patties, page 261). It also gives a wonderful subtext to mashed potatoes.

Marjoram *(Origanum marjorana)*

A lovely, delicate herb that appears sparingly on its own or in mixes, whether in eggs, with poultry, seafood, or all sorts of meats. As the name indicates, it is related to oregano (which is also called wild marjoram).

Mint *(Mentha)*

A popular family of herbs with an unmistakable flavor and fragrance. In fact, there are many herbs, including: apple mint *(Mentha guareolens),* curly mint *(Mentha spicata),* orange mint *(Mentha acquitica),* peppermint *(Mentha piperata),* and spearmint *(Mentha spicata)*. Mints are essential in herb frittatas and gnocchi and go well with carrots, potatoes, lamb, veal, fruit, fish, and many desserts. Mint is thought to stimulate the appetite before eating and aid digestion after.

Mustard Seed *(Brassica sinapis)*

Take thousands of these tiny seeds and combine with vinegar and other flavors and you have prepared mustard, usually just called mustard. In Italy it is called *senape* and, while it has become more popular with the unfortunate expansion of the fast food business, mustard has always been traditional in Friuli-Venezia Giulia to flavor pork products, sauerkraut, raw cabbage, and in salad dressings.

Nutmeg *(Myristica fragrans)*

This is the seed of the fruit of the nutmeg tree native to the Molucca Islands in Asia. It is now cultivated in places like Sri Lanka, Java, Sumatra, and Singapore, but also quite amply in Grenada in the Caribbean. I like to think of nutmeg as cinnamon for sophisticates. It has a more complex taste and fragrance than cinnamon, and they often are used together as a flavoring. It is frequently paired with ginger as well. A little bit goes a long way. In Italy one buys whole nutmeg and grates it with a tiny grater. In Friuli-Venezia Giulia, it is often used in preparations that contain fruit, and in creamy pasta sauces.

Onion *(Allium cepa)*

A universally recognized flavor and fragrance (or odor, to some). Onion is a bulb that descended from the lily family. There are many varieties of onions, from white to yellow to dark red, and from sweet to powerfully strong. Scallions are the tender young seedlings of onions that come before the bulb has formed.

Oregano *(Origanum vulgare)*

Also known as wild marjoram, oregano is most famous as a dried herb that lasts quite a while if stored in a cool, dry place. But fresh oregano is a pleasing herb with tomatoes and beans.

Paprika *(Capiscum annuum Linn)*

Paprika is as sweet as it is spicy, and it is a mistake to think of it strictly as a hot flavoring. While paprika can come from many areas, the classic one, and that which is used in Friuli-Venezia Giulia, comes from Hungary. It can be divided into three categories: *örlemény* (sweet), *rózsa* (rose), and *csípös* (hot). The variety typically used for recipes in this book is rose, but sweet is also acceptable. Hot paprika is delicious, of course, but makes more of a statement than is called for with the food in these pages.

Making Paprika in Hungary

In the interest of thorough research, and with the kind assistance of the Hungarian Tourist Authority, I journeyed in 1998 from Vienna to Hungary to immerse myself in the subject of paprika, first in Budapest, and then in Kalocsa, where I took part in the paprika harvest.

In Hungary women used to cook the peppers whole and then stored them for other seasons. In Kalocsa, there had always been a tradition of drying many foods for storage; around 1700 the idea came of drying peppers, which previously had been pickled. Once dried, the peppers were milled to make the powder that would change Hungarian cuisine and affect the cuisines of Austria, Serbia, Friuli-Venezia Giulia, and many other places. In the plains of Kalocsa, cattle for beef abounded, and the most traditional dish was braised beef with paprika powder. From this emerged the tradition of goulash and paprikás, to which other meats were later adapted.

Almost all Hungarian paprika comes from two towns: Szeged (whose product is mostly consumed in the country) and Kalocsa (whose product is mostly exported). There are three types of paprika, although all derive from the same red pepper variety. *Örlemény* is sweet and a crimson red. *Csípös* (also called *erös*) is sharp and pink. *Rózsa,* or rose, is somewhere between sweet and sharp in flavor and color. This last one is very popular in Trieste, the city that exported Hungarian paprika when it was the chief port of the Austro-Hungarian empire.

It might seem odd that the hottest, spiciest paprika is the one that is lightest in color. Hot paprika is milled with many of the white seeds (which are spicy) left in, while sweet paprika is milled only from a dried pepper from which all the seeds have been removed. As peppers are sorted after picking, seeds are extracted from the most beautiful ones for planting the next crop. So the choicest peppers often wind up being used in sweet paprika. You should note that in Hungarian, *paprika* is the word describing the red pepper as well as the powder derived when the pepper is dried and milled. By contrast, *paprikás* is a recipe (usually a slow-cooked dish) with paprika added.

The red pepper used in Hungary to make paprika powder was brought by the Turks in the 1540s. They got the pepper from the Arabs, who got it from the Spanish, who brought it from southern Mexico and Central America. In Hungary this pepper is called the *törökbors,* which means "Turkish pepper." Peppers for eating probably reached Trieste and Friuli-Venezia Giulia well before paprika powder arrived.

Turks were present in this part of Europe since at least 1456, the year of the Battle of Nándorfehérvár (now Belgrade in Serbia, but then a part of Hungary). In repeated battles the Turks were held off from taking over this area until 1526, when the Hungarians lost the Battle of Mohács. Among the food products that the Turks introduced to Hungary were phyllo dough (which would be used to make strudel and other pastries), coffee, cinnamon, poppy seeds (for consumption), and red peppers. These foods would later find their way to Vienna and, in short order, to Friuli-Venezia Giulia.

Another product that arrived in Hungary from Turkey was corn, whose meal could be used to make cereal. It was not often eaten in Hungary, but was sent elsewhere with success. It spread east to Transylvania (where the cereal is called *puliszica*) and Romania, where it is called *mamaliga*. It traveled south through Dalmatia and into Istria, Venezia Giulia, Friuli, and the Veneto. In these areas, cornmeal replaced millet, which had been used since ancient times to make a cereal called *pulentum*. And thus would polenta as we know it be born. It is worth noting that in northeastern Italy, cornmeal is called *grano-turco,* or "Turkish grain."

The Turks attempted to enter Vienna in 1683 and were repulsed, leaving behind the coffee and phyllo that would soon launch the cafés and bakeries for which Vienna is so renowned. As they retreated they fought the Hungarians again from 1686 to 1689, when they were finally defeated thanks in part to aid from a German kaiser who was a Hapsburg. From that point forward, Hungary looked west and was linked to the Hapsburgs until 1916. Periodically Hungary sought independence (with the help of Russia), but did not succeed. All through the centuries Hungarians used these Turkish peppers, but they did not start drying them as powder until sometime after 1700.

Each pepper must be selected when mature (a crimson red color is a good indicator), and all are picked by hand (machines would destroy them). To do this right, you must pull off the pepper from the stem so you do not tear its flesh. Once the peppers are picked, there are two methods for making the powder. The modern method is to bring the peppers to a factory, remove their tops by hand, and then examine each pepper individually. If it is considered "beautiful" (the word they invariably use), then the seeds are removed to plant next season and this pepper is selected to become sweet paprika. Rose paprika peppers will have a few seeds left in; for hot paprika, many seeds are left in the pepper. The peppers are then placed in a machine that dries them in 2 to 3 hours with dry heat, and then cuts them into small pieces. These are ground mechanically and become a powder to be put in little sacks if the spice will be used soon, or in tin or aluminum containers for longer storage. I recommend putting paprika in a dark jar and storing in a cool, dry, dark place (up to one year).

The traditional method is to sew batches of peppers together by their stems and hang them out of doors for 4 to 5 weeks in a place that is sunny but protected from rain. Some people prefer to hang them indoors for 6 weeks. Once the peppers are dried, stems are removed, each pepper is evaluated and seeds are discarded from some, and then the peppers are milled manually. In the past, the dried peppers were brought to the Danube, where rushing water powered the mills.

No one could definitively tell me whether the traditional or modern method is superior. I think the sweet pepper in the modern version more vibrant, while the hot pepper from the older method had a thrilling intensity. 🌶

Parsley (Petroselinum crispum)
Too often wasted as a garnish in restaurants, parsley imparts freshness (and vitamin C) to a dish. It is an essential ingredient in all herb mixes and sauces. You should use flat-leaf rather than curly parsley for recipes in this book.

Pepper, Black (Piper nigrum)
The most popular of all spices, it comes in small berries that are dried and called peppercorns. As they dry they become small and wrinkled, and range in color from brown to black. One needs about 500 peppercorns for 1 ounce / 28 g. There are more than one thousand species in the pepper family; for black pepper, the distinctions are typically geographic. There are varieties from India, Indonesia, Vietnam, Singapore, Malaysia, Madagascar, Brazil, and several islands in the Caribbean. Like all spices, it should be kept in a dark, dry place and only ground at the moment of use.

Pepper, White (Piper nigrum)
These are peppercorns that are picked when ripe (and light red in color) and peeled before drying. Some popular growing zones include Java, Singapore, Thailand, India, and, curiously, Livorno (in Tuscany). White pepper is milder than black.

Note that green peppercorns are derived from the same source, but undergo a light pickle before being dried, which changes their color and taste.

Poppy Seed *(Papaver rhoeas)*

This is the dried seed that is drawn from the annual poppy plant. Poppy seeds are immensely, uniquely popular in Friuli-Venezia Giulia, and little seen outside of northeastern Italy in Italian cookery. They are slate-colored rather than real black, and (to answer a perennial question) the seeds have no narcotic properties. You can enjoy the flavor of the whole seed, which is a little dry, or crush the seeds before use. In this case, the oils come out and the flavor is quite lush and extravagant. In the region, poppy seeds appear in pastas and their sauces, in salad dressings, on breads, tossed with fruit, and in many baked goods.

Radicchio

This is not the red-and-white streaked ball that is from Chioggia in Veneto or the red and white lettuce shaped like romaine that is from Trevisio. In Friuli-Venezia Giulia (and certain other Italian regions), radicchio is any one of several delicate greens that give character to a salad or buttery softness to an herb mix. To approximate it, you should use baby spinach, lamb's quarters, small pieces of bibb or limestone lettuce, or mâche. Sometimes *radicchio* is translated as chicory or wild chicory, but the version you may have available may be sharper in taste than is radicchio, so use it sparingly.

Rosemary *(Rosmarinus officinalis)*

A sweet-scented, highly aromatic perennial with characteristic needles. It is often sold dried, but you really should use it fresh. It is a classic Mediterranean herb that grows near the sea. Its name derives from *ros maris,* or dew of the sea.

Rue *(Ruta graveolens)*

Very bitter, and therefore used sparingly, in frittatas, for example. But it has an appealing taste.

Saffron *(Crocus sativus)*

The most expensive of all spices, highly prized for its subtle taste and the vibrant red or golden color that it can infuse a dish. It derives from an autumn crocus, and it takes 75,000 hand-picked blossoms to make 1 pound / 454 g of saffron powder. One can use either the powder or the copper-colored strands that are the spice in its truest form. Saffron is planted in Spain, Italy (particularly in Abruzzo), Greece, Iran, India, Kashmir, and China. One of the finest of all is found in Austria, and it is very possible that this is a spice that came down the Friulian spice road first rather than arriving at the port of Trieste. In the region it flavors risotto and is added to flour when bread doughs are made.

Sage (*Salvia officinalis*)

A popular herb in Friuli and throughout Italy. In Carnia they often fry sage leaves which become a tasty appetizer called *salviade*. When dipped in sugar, they make an even tastier dessert. The tendency in many places outside of Italy is to use dried sage, especially with poultry; but in Italy, fresh sage is preferred. It is a classic taste when heated in melted butter and then used on top of filled pasta.

Savory (*Satureja hortensis, Satureja montana*)

Summer savory (*S. hortensis*) matches beautifully with string beans, sauerkraut, beef, veal, rabbit, venison, and in herb mixes. Winter savory (*S. montana*) is particularly suited for herb mixes.

Sesame Seed (*Sesamum indicum*)

Primarily used in the region as a flavoring for breads and bread sticks.

Shallot (*Allium ascalonicum*)

A hardy bulb in the onion family, but more subtle in flavor. It is great with fish, game, stews, liver, and chopped over vegetables. In herb mixes, it gives a special perfume.

Silene (*Silene*)

This herb is little known or appreciated in much of the world, but it is a touchstone taste in Friuli. The local name is *sclopit* or *sclupit*. This peppery, slightly musty, and very grassy herb appears in the spring and, in addition to appearing in herb mixes, very often appears on its own as a flavoring in risotto. You will not likely see *sclopit* elsewhere, but Friulians dote on it, and you will find it everywhere if you are there in April.

Sorrel (*Rumex acetosa*)

It has a slightly sharp, acidic flavor that is perfect with eggs, salmon, spinach, lettuce, and is a great component in herb mixes.

Tarragon (*Artemisia dracunculus*)

With rare exceptions, not popular in Friuli-Venezia Giulia, although it does turn up in a couple of dishes in Slovenia.

Thyme (*Thymus vulgaris*)

In the mint family, thyme finds broad use in the region and is almost always consumed fresh rather than dried. A tisane made with thyme is considered ideal for two things: fighting colds and reducing pressure in the stomach from gas.

Turmeric *(Curcuma domestica)*

This spice is in the same family as ginger and is an essential ingredient in curry, to which it imparts its golden-orange color. It grows in China (where it is more green than orange), Africa, Australia, India, and Haiti. It is made from an aromatic root that is washed, dried, and ground. Its flavor is warm and sweet, and it is often the undercurrent in prepared mustard.

Verbena or Lemon Verbena *(Lippia citriodora)*

Immensely popular in the region, especially in Carnia, where it appears in every herb mix, and often on its own with fruit.

Watercress *(Nasturtium aquaticum)*

Peppery leaves that form a nice minor note in herb mixes.

Zucchini Flowers *(Cucurbita pepo)*

Also called zucchini blossoms or courgette blossoms. These flowers grow attached to baby zucchini (courgettes) and should not be discarded. Gently remove the pistil and stamen within and use the flowers in many ways. They can be stuffed with soft cheese and sautéed as an appetizer, or chopped and used in an herb mix, or sautéed and used in risotto.

The Vineyard of the World: The Fascinating Wines of Friuli-Venezia Giulia

Chi ga inventado il vin, se no 'l xe in paradiso, el xe vizin
La terra, la zappa e il contadino sono gli amici che ci danno il vino.
La vit dis dammi, che ti darai

He who invented wine, if he was not in paradise he was near
The earth, the hoe and the farmer are the friends who give us wine.
The vine says "give to me so that I may give to you"

—FOLK SAYING

We do not know who invented wine but, as this saying from Isonzo would suggest, from the very start, wine making was a spiritual pleasure as much as a sensory one. Wine making is very close to the soul of Friuli-Venezia Giulia and the region has innumerable proverbs about wine and its pleasures.

There is evidence of the vine being in the land we now call Friuli-Venezia Giulia at least thirteen centuries before Christ. Wine from here was exported to outposts on both shores of the Adriatic and all the way to Rome. Pliny the Elder wrote about the wines quite enthusiastically. Roman Empress Livia Drusilla (second wife of Augustus) attributed her health and longevity to a red wine from the Carso called Pucinum. This wine is thought to be the forerunner either of Terrano or Prosecco, which have been shown to be unusually high in health-giving mineral content because of the soil they grow in.

The Romans certainly produced and enjoyed wine during their hegemony in the area, which was centered in Aquileia (founded 181 B.C.). The city was a vital port for trade and a link to northern Europe. It was also a chief center of production of glass objects. When the Aquileians were driven from their city by the invasion of Attila the Hun (A.D. 452), they took their glass-making skills with them to the islands in the Adriatic where they founded the city that would become Venice.

In ancient times, wine was made in open vats of terra-cotta, clay, wood, or even marble. It was stored and transported in terra-cotta amphorae, although some drinking glasses were already used. When more elaborate glasses and good bottles became central to wine, northeastern Italy was one of the first places where this happened, thanks to the Aquileian/Venetian tradition.

Through the Middle Ages, wine making continued on estates in which indentured servants produced for landowners. An innovation of medieval wine making, in Friuli and elsewhere, was fermentation of wine in wood barrels. During this era, the church played a key role in keeping vines healthy and in use. Perhaps no place was more vital than the Abbazia di Rosazzo, an abbey that maintained high standards and cultivated native varieties, most notably Pignolo and Picolit. When they almost disappeared elsewhere, they still flourished here. Picolit had a revival in the eighteenth century, while Pignolo was saved from extinction in 1979 when vintner Walter Filiputti took the only two known vines and bred them back to life.

When most of what we now call Friuli and a few areas of the current Venezia Giulia came under the Republic of Venice in 1420, this region supplied some of the most important wines consumed at the tables of doges and merchants. Many of the hams of San Daniele also went to Venice, along with polenta, fruit, vegetables, and anything else of value. What was left for the Friulians were grape skins with which they made grappa and a few ingredients with which they would find a way to feed themselves.

By the early eighteenth century, Trieste was the chief port for Austria and its empire and this area benefited from Empress Maria Theresa's affection and benevolence. But it was in other parts of Venezia Giulia, also under Austria, that wine history was being made. The quality of all fruit that grew in this area made it a prized source for the markets of Vienna and elsewhere. It was also recognized that some of the best wine in the empire came from these zones, now referred to as Collio and Isonzo. The Austrians, in their efficient bureaucratic way, documented the foremost wine-producing communities (in terms of quality) and at or near the top were Cormons, Farra, Oslavia, Russiz, San Floriano, and Spessa. These are still among the best wine towns in the whole region. They furnished Vienna with wine until 1914 and had a comfortable existence until the vineyards were destroyed by war.

An important figure in the region's history of wine making was Count Fabio Asquini (1726–1818), who lived in Fagagna, northwest of Udine in Friuli. He produced wine from several grape varieties, but understood that Picolit was something special. In 1762 he decided that if a whole bottle of Picolit was impressive, a half bottle would be even more so. A liquid dispensed in such small quantities *just had* to be extraordinary. There was no market for this luxury product locally, so Asquini thought in terms of exporting. But first he had to deal with bottling. He had special, unmistakable blown-glass bottles produced in Murano and then sought to sell the wine in Venice.

Venetians loved complex sweet wines, which were referred to as "meditation wines," to be sipped in beautiful chalices in a slow and deliberate way. Doge Manin and the wealthy class of the city tasted Asquini's wine and it became all the rage. He hired a sales agent in Venice and announced that the only authorized sellers (and therefore guarantors of quality) were Asquini and his agent.

Rather than sell all of his Picolit to Venice, as he could have, Asquini held some back to make it more desirable. When the court in Vienna learned of Picolit, they had to have some too. It would rival Tokaj, the wonderful Hungarian dessert wine that came into fashion around 1750, and, by creating a second market, Asquini was not putting all of his fate in Venice's hands. As it happened, the Venetian Republic was in decline and would collapse in 1797, with its holdings divided by Austria and France.

Asquini strategically saw to it a few bottles also found their way to Paris in the pouch of a diplomat from Udine. Soon, three of Europe's most important capitals vied for whatever few bottles of Picolit they could have, and Asquini became a famous early example of the benefits of the laws of supply and demand. Interestingly, once he had a faithful client, he did not raise the price for the wine.

He was a brilliant marketer, but he was not as vigilant as he could have been with the quality of the wine. One reason was that, curiously, he did not drink alcoholic beverages. He had to rely on a group of expert wine makers and tasters, but they were not with him through all of his long life. The vineyards were not always well tended, and the situation was complicated by the fact that Picolit is one of the most fragile and difficult to work with of all wine grapes. With Asquini's passing, Picolit was too expensive a product for most wine producers to think about, and the grape almost disappeared until it was rescued in the post–World War II revival of the region's wines. The story of Asquini is fascinating because it presages so much that would happen to wine in Friuli-Venezia Giulia more than two hundred years later.

In the nineteenth century, the best wines (mostly from Venezia Giulia) went to Vienna, while regular ones were sold locally or in the Veneto. The phylloxera epidemic that raged through European vineyards in late century affected this area in 1879, and planting new vines became necessary. But unlike the rest of the continent, where growers replanted grapes they knew, growers in Friuli and Venezia Giulia would make a radical innovation: They planted both native and foreign varieties.

*T*hroughout the centuries, this small region has been amazingly hospitable to almost any grape variety that has been planted there. This is due to the soil and the many microclimates that offer sun, shade, breeze, or warmth that different grapes need to flourish. Above all, these grapes were (and are) tended by a population that has acquired and passed on centuries of intimacy and knowledge of these grapes and their different needs.

Because there has been a tradition of many more grapes in Friuli-Venezia Giulia than elsewhere in Italy and most of the world, when disaster (phylloxera and wars) made it necessary to replant most of the region's vineyards, it was decided to use not only the many native varieties but foreign ones as well. In the town of Rauscedo (UD) is the largest grape nursery in Italy, where varieties are studied, cloned, and improved through breeding. This activity has been an incredible benefit for wine producers in Friuli-Venezia Giulia and elsewhere.

There are more important native grape varieties in this region than any other in Italy. Note that I say *important*. Regions such as Puglia have many grapes, but the wines they produce can in no way rival those of Friuli-Venezia Giulia. Among the native grapes are Picolit, Verduzzo, Pignolo, Tazzelenghe, Schioppettino, Ribolla Gialla, Prosecco, and probably Malvasia Istriana. All of these ancient grapes are still used to make outstanding wines of extraordinary and singular character. Tocai Friulano is in a category unto itself. Technically, it probably is not native to the region, but it has been there for such a long time that it is the only grape to have the region as part of its name.

Friuli and Venezia Giulia, which had always been open and friendly to foreigners, and often under outside domination, had a natural inclination to internationalism. In the late nineteenth century, growers received and planted grapes from elsewhere decades before international varieties were used in most of the world's wine zones. It was the first Italian region to have Merlot, and certainly among the very first to have Cabernet Sauvignon, Cabernet Franc, Chardonnay, Sauvignon Blanc, Pinot Blanc (or Bianco), Pinot Gris (Grigio), Pinot Noir (Nero), Traminer, and Müller Thurgau. All of these grapes were present and accounted for prior to 1900. Compare this with the internationalization of grapes in the 1970s, when Chardonnay, Cabernet, Merlot, and Pinot grapes spread all over the world.

INDIVIDUAL GRAPE VARIETIES USED IN FRIULI-VENEZIA GIULIA

Here is a list of all of the major grapes used in the region, although there are numerous other ones that are tended by growers with an historical bent. Those grapes are made into lovely wines for local consumption, but are not easy to find beyond their hometowns. Remember, as you read this section, that grapes are used in one of two ways. The first is to make 100 percent varietal wines. That is, a wine will come from one grape and be named for the grape. The other way, always popular in Friuli-Venezia Giulia, is to make an *uvaggio,* or blend. In the Collio zone, this is very popular with white wines, and each blend is an expression of the ideas and taste of its producer.

When you ask most wine experts to talk about the wines of Friuli-Venezia Giulia nowadays, they immediately mention the extraordinarily fragrant, luscious, and complex white wines that are considered Italy's best. Few of these experts know that historically this was a region that excelled in red wines and also made good whites. Even today, 52 percent of the wine made in the region is red. While you should definitely get to know the region's whites, which are now among the world's best, don't forget that world-class reds from Italy are not the exclusive province of Piedmont and Tuscany.

White Grapes

Chardonnay

The product of a long-ago cross between a little-known French white grape called Gouais with a grape from the Pinot family, Chardonnay is probably the most popular grape in the world. It is hearty and produces a structured wine that can conform to different tastes and styles. In Europe it is often prized for its fruit flavor and adaptability. Typically, it is vinified in steel and might have some contact with wood during aging to give it an accent. It might be served with delicate vegetables, risotto, or white meats.

In the United States and elsewhere in the "New World," Chardonnay is typically aged in oak for quite a while, so that it acquires the fragrance and flavor of oak, vanilla, and butterscotch. In California, the abundant heat boosts the sugars and therefore the alcohol levels, so that the strong flavors must come with an increased amount of alcohol. Many Americans dote on this style and seem disappointed when they encounter Chardonnay from Italy or France that speaks of grape rather than tree. In Friuli-Venezia Giulia, some producers age their Chardonnays in oak, but not to the extreme found in California. As often as not, they blend their barrel-aged Chardonnay with other wines aged in steel, so the result is more interesting and sophisticated than the straightforward assault that wood creates.

The typical alcoholic gradation ranges from 11° up to 13.5°. By contrast, California Chardonnays can reach 14.5° and, unofficially, even higher. (Note that in the Aquileia DOC there is also a Chardonnay Spumante, and it is at the lower end of alcoholic gradation.)

Malvasia Istriana

In the province of Trieste, this grape is simply called Malvasia (mahl-vah-ZEE-uh), but it is important to make geographic distinctions. There are many grapes in Italy called Malvasia, both red and white, some vinified dry and others as sweet dessert wines. Perhaps the most famous Italian Malvasia is a honey-colored dessert wine produced in Sicily. In Friuli-Venezia Giulia, all Malvasia wines are white. There is the little-seen Malvasia del Friuli that is an all-purpose white produced in Buttrio in the Colli Orientali. Malvasia del Collio Goriziano (or Malvasia Collio DOC) is grown in Venezia Giulia's premier wine zone. Its color ranges from straw to light gold, and it is a round, lively white wine that is not overly alcoholic. Malvasia di Trieste is virtually interchangeable with the region's most famous Malvasia, the Istriana. The original grape dates to antiquity and was grown in the Peloponnese in Greece. The variety is thought to have reached Istria by 1300, perhaps on the ships of Venetian sailors. It is planted in various zones throughout Friuli-Venezia Giulia, including Carso, Collio, Isonzo, and Colli Orientali. There was a brief period in the early 1990s when certain producers turned their backs on this grape, but now it is making a welcome return. When served in Istria, it is usually more rustic and pungent, with great charm. In Friuli-Venezia Giulia, Malvasia Istriana is more delicate. Straw-colored, with an aromatic nose (sometimes of exotic fruit or white pepper) and dry flavor, it is the ideal match for seafood, especially mussels.

The typical alcoholic gradation ranges from 10.5° to 12.5°.

Müller Thurgau

This grape was bred in 1891 by a Swiss man named Hermann Müller Thurgau. It is also known as Riesling Sylvaner, because it is cross between those two grapes. It arrived in

Friuli-Venezia Giulia in the 1930s. As a wine, it has a delicate aroma, light and fresh taste, and sometimes a hint of spiciness. It does not appeal to everyone, but it is very well suited to delicate foods or for drinking on its own. I have found that this wine matches beautifully with vegetables such as endive, red radicchio, various green lettuces, and herbs. More classically it goes with seafood.

The typical alcoholic gradation ranges from 11° to 13°.

Picolit

Thought to originate in or near Premariacco in the Colli Orientali del Friuli (COF), this is a very difficult grape to care for, and many growers disdain it because it is high maintenance and risky. Many of the buds die before they mature to grapes. This is known in oenology as "floreal abortion," which is a rather severe term for an event that occurs in nature in which less hardy buds do not grow into grapes. It is also, in effect, a form of natural selection, and the grapes that do mature result in one of the most magnificent dessert wines you will ever taste.

Typically Picolit is served at important occasions, in small amounts from half bottles. The tendency is to serve it in small glasses with small rims that concentrate the fragrance. However, one leading producer showed me that the wine is just as exciting if served in small amounts in huge glasses normally reserved for big reds. By swirling it in this giant globe, the fragrances are released in a way that cannot happen in the little glass. Try it both ways and make your own decision.

Picolit can range from rich to almost syrupy, with honeyed scents, plus many other characteristics that range from one producer to another: flowers, spice, apples, pears, and other mysterious notes. One can smell this wine for a long time before moving on to tasting it. It will be sweet, but not overly so. It is usually consumed at the end of a meal, sometimes with cake but often on its own—it is better than any dessert. It should be served cool, but not ice cold, which would dull its fragrance and flavor. Obviously, prized wine like Picolit is quite expensive, but it is also a rare treat.

The typical alcoholic gradation is around 15°, but the wine is so rich and complex that alcohol is not a dominant note. A few producers have added small amounts of Picolit to their white blends, which is a luxurious gesture that produces special results.

Pinot Bianco

This is an ancient grape that is thought to have its origins in Burgundy, where it is known as Pinot Blanc. In Germany it is Weissburgunder (echoing its provenance), and in Italy it is sometimes referred to as Borgogna bianco. It existed in small amounts in

Friuli-Venezia Giulia in the early nineteenth century and was planted extensively in the late 1880s after the region's vineyards were devastated by phylloxera. This is an elegant, fragrant grape of medium weight, and it produces a wine that is pleasing when young but also has some aging possibilities. Its fine and persistent fragrance can be that of fresh baked bread or of almonds. It is a wine I find very pleasing, but some wine makers I have great respect for are dismissive of this grape. Try it for yourself and decide. It often goes with vegetables, risotto, pasta, and some meats. It is usually a wine that does not have contact with wood during aging, but several producers in Collio (especially Castello di Spessa) have done a good job of using wood as an accent that is very flattering to the wine.

The alcoholic gradation of Pinot Bianco ranges from 10.5° to 12.5°.

Pinot Grigio

There is documentation of Pinot Grigio in Friuli as far back as 1863, when the grape was called Auvergnat Grigio. This wine found great favor for a few years as the white of choice for many Americans making their way into Italian wine. Most of it came from the Veneto, and some from the Grave del Friuli. At first it was very respectable, but as demand outstripped supply, the quality declined, and the Pinot Grigio found in America was rather insipid. Do not confuse this stuff with the fragrant and tasty wine made by the fine producers of Friuli-Venezia Giulia. Here the wine has a golden color, delicate fragrance, and notable body, and wine makers are adept at expressing great things with it. Pinot Grigio is eclectic in its food pairings in the region. It is served with fish (raw, marinated, or cooked), white meats, and poultry. It matches well with some flavorful cheeses, including aged Montasio. The typical alcoholic gradation ranges from 10.5° to 12.5°.

Prosecco

This grape, grown in very small quantities in the province of Trieste, is thought to be the source of the white grape used with great success in the province of Treviso (in Veneto) to make a dry sparkling wine. In Venezia Giulia it is known as la Glera di Prosecco, because the grape is called la Glera and it grows in the little Carso town called Prosecco, which is known as Prosek in Slovenian. Some scholars think this was the grape used to make a wine loved in ancient Rome, but there is not definitive proof of this. Prosecco as made in Venezia Giulia is a lean still wine, clear in color, mildly fragrant, and more sweet than dry. The typical alcoholic gradation ranges from 10.5° to 12°.

Ramandolo

Often called Verduzzo di Ramandolo, this was the first Friulian wine to gain its own geographic designation. It is a sweet wine, often quite rich and tannic, and it is made mostly in the town of Nimis (Udine). It is wonderful with veined cheeses, such as Gorgonzola, and with dry desserts flavored with nuts or fruit. The typical alcoholic gradation ranges from 12° to 13.5°.

Ribolla Gialla

One of the region's great secrets, this prized, wonderful white grape, almost unknown outside its native Friuli-Venezia Giulia, makes world-class wine. The grape is thought to have originated near Rosazzo in the COF in ancient times. Ribolla Gialla was once grown throughout the region, although now it is largely confined to the Colli Orientali, Collio, and Isonzo zones. Centuries ago it was a popular local white in Trieste. We know that in 1202, Venetians drank what was called *optimi vini puri ribolei,* which were really excellent Ribolla wines sent from Trieste. Before World War II the term "Ribolla" often suggested a white blend from Collio that included Sauvignon Blanc, Pinot Grigio, and other grapes. Since the war, the regional tradition is to call varietal wines by their grape names and give other names to blends.

Pure Ribolla Gialla has an elegance of fragrance and flavor, with creamy undertones. It is a wine that is intense, lively, and harmonious, and goes beautifully with a wide range of dishes from seafood to preparations that include fruit. If you have never sampled it, an exciting wine awaits you. The typical alcoholic gradation ranges from 12° to 13°.

Riesling Italico

Although the name suggests the grape is Italian, it is either of German or of French origin, depending on whom you ask. It arrived in the Veneto from Germany in 1869 but did not come into Friuli. Rather, around 1900, the grape came to Venezia Giulia from Styria, in Austria, where it is very popular. This golden-yellow grape produces wine with a dry and inviting fragrance and flavor and good body. It grows primarily in the Collio zone, although it appears elsewhere in the region, notably in Lison-Pramaggiore. It is occasionally vinified and bottled by itself, but in Friuli-Venezia Giulia it is more typically used for blending with other grapes, especially Ribolla Gialla and Sauvignon Blanc. The typical alcoholic gradation ranges around 11°.

Riesling Renano

Renano is the Italian for Rhenish, suggesting that the provenance of this grape is around the Rhine River. It is very popular in Alsace-Lorraine and in Germany, and also in parts of Italy. It has been in Friuli-Venezia Giulia since at least the 1880s, and perhaps earlier.

The wine is straw-colored, the fragrance is unmistakable—ranging from ethereal to intense, depending on where it is grown. Riesling Renano appears in most of the region, including the zones of Aquileia, COF, Grave, and Isonzo. Occasionally 100 percent Riesling Renano is bottled on its own, but more customarily in Friuli-Venezia Giulia it is used for blending. The typical alcoholic gradation ranges from $10.5°$ to $12°$.

Sauvignon Blanc

Not a native of Friuli-Venezia Giulia, the grape has been there so long that it has acquired permanent residency. Although it is found a little bit near Piacenza (in Emilia-Romagna) and in the Alto Adige and Veneto, Sauvignon Blanc in those places has none of the status that it does in this region. Wine made with this grape is dry, generous, full-bodied, with a distinct fragrance that pleases most sophisticated wine drinkers. No one has come up with the perfect description of it. Some say it smells of sage, others anise, still others talk of certain fruit or spices or egg yolk. The point is that the fragrance of Sauvignon Blanc is singular and pleasing, and most people describe it using terms that have positive connotations for them. The taste is equally hard to describe, but beguiling. The wine is round, has a significant presence of fruit from the grapes, and often has a very long finish. Most producers will make a Sauvignon Blanc to bottle on its own, but will also reserve some to use for blending. Sauvignon is delicious when made in steel, and it is equally interesting when it has contact with wood before being bottled. The wine goes well with seafood, is perfect with eggs, omelets, asparagus, and many herbs. The typical alcoholic gradation ranges from $11°$ to $13°$.

Sciaglin

A little-seen native of the region, this makes a charming white wine for an aperitif. There is evidence of this grape as far back as the fifteenth century in Spilimbergo, in the Grave zone. It used to be quite bitter and only became interesting with years of aging. With modern wine-making methods, it has found a small niche among cognoscenti, but it is almost never seen outside of its zone. It happens to match particularly well with trout and other river fish. It is also very suitable for dishes based on fresh herbs. The alcoholic gradation is around $10.5°$ to $11.5°$.

Tocai Friulano (usually called Tocai)

More than any other wine, Tocai Friulano is the emblem of this region's wine making and character. A fair percentage of the bloodstream of most Friuli-Venezia Giulians is made of Tocai. This is a white wine that has been produced here for centuries, but whose origin remains a subject of hot controversy and debate. One theory is that it originated near Gradisca more than 1,200 years ago. Another is that it is from somewhere between Pordenone and Treviso, was planted in Hungary, and then planted near Gradisca. Yet another refers to it as Sauvignonaz (Green Sauvignon) and that it has French origins. People in the region are deeply sensitive on this topic, as they feel that Tocai Friulano is an essential part of who they are.

Tampering with Tocai in any way to a citizen of this region would have the same effect as telling a New Yorker that the Statue of Liberty would have to be removed from New York Harbor. So you can imagine the devastating effect that a decision by the European Union in the early 1990s had on lovers of Tocai. The bureaucrats in Brussels said that there were three wines that have historic claims on the name, but that only one could continue to use it. There is Tocai Friulano. Then there is Tokai, which is essentially Pinot Gris (confusingly, this is Pinot Grigio in Italy), and which is popular in Alsace in France. And then there is the famous Hungarian dessert wine, Tokay, named for the principal town in the zone where it is produced. This wine is made from a blend of grapes: Furmint (thought to be related to the Formentino seen occasionally in Collio), Harsevilii, golden Muscat grapes, and sometimes one or two other varieties. All of these grapes are dried and their intense juices make the famous Hungarian wine.

When the European Union decided that, as of 2006, the only wine that could be called by the homophonic name was the Hungarian one, there was deep shock in Friuli-Venezia Giulia. The French decided to rename their wine Tokai-Pinot Gris, and the Tokai part will vanish in 2006. By contrast, in Friuli-Venezia Giulia wine makers wrung their hands and lamented at how their history and identity were being stolen from them yet again. (Remember, this is a region that has often been invaded and has maintained its identity despite terrible adversity.) Various names were proposed by producers and government officials, but none gained consensus. For a long time it was thought that Bianco Friulano would become the name, but it was ultimately rejected as pallid and generic. The new name had to be recognizable, meaningful, memorable, and easy to say.

The debate heated up in 1999 as it became clear that if a name were not selected soon, the wine would be forgotten outside the region when the name Tocai could no longer be used. Out of these discussions came Furlan, which is the name of the Friulian language and also the word to indicate a person from Friuli. For years before, people would use the expression *"O soi Furlan"* (I am Friulano) in marketing campaigns describing things made in Friuli. The saying also indicates a sense of quiet pride about identity, of which Tocai

Friulano is an essential component. When it was realized that the name Furlan is easily pronounced all over the world, it seemed likely that this would be the new name of Tocai Friulano. Therefore, when you see the name Tocai in this book, bear in mind that it will soon have a new name that will likely be Furlan or, perhaps, Friulano. But you can be certain that in the region it will always be known as Tocai.

When you enter an *osteria* anywhere in Friuli-Venezia Giulia, it is traditional to order a *tajut,* which means "a cut" in Friulano. Some wine writers who describe the *tajut* mistakenly assert that this implies that the local white wine is "cut" with (that is, has the addition of) more substantial wine from Southern Italy. This is completely wrong—they are confusing this with the practice in the past in Piedmont, where red wines were fortified with strong reds from Puglia. "Cut" in the Friulian sense suggests a measurement, usually one-tenth of a liter, that is poured for the customer. Nowadays, one is given whatever amount the proprietor pours, but the term *tajut* persists as an affectionate evocation of older, more rustic times.

The fragrance of Tocai can be a little peachy or nutty or have herbal notes. It varies according to the place it is grown, the amount of sugars that it develops, and how it is vinified. It has a clean, delicate flavor and some persistence. Although it is very popular to drink 100 percent Tocai, the wine is also very prized for blending, especially in Collio and COF.

Tocai can go well with many foods, but its most traditional pairings are with two classic foods of the region, frico and prosciutto di San Daniele. It also goes well with other pork products from the region. These foods might be accompanied by bread sticks or grilled wedges of polenta. With the *tajut* in one hand and a little food in the other, many happy hours are spent in the *osteria* nibbling, sipping, talking, laughing, and singing.

The typical alcoholic gradation of Tocai ranges from $10.5°$ to $12.5°$.

Traminer Aromatico

The Traminer family of grapes are Italian, although they are typically associated with Germany. They originated in the town of Tramin in the neighboring Alto Adige, and some clones of this have found fame as spicy Gewürztraminer. In the mid-nineteenth century, it arrived in the zones of Friuli and Venezia Giulia that were under Austria.

In the region, the Aromatico is prized for its fragrance that distinctly resembles roses. Nonetheless, the scent is not overbearing, and the flavor is balanced and generous. It is often consumed with substantial fish (such as monkfish) or shellfish. It is also lovely to drink on its own. It is produced in Grave and Aquileia in particular, but is also found in Collio and Isonzo. The typical alcoholic gradation is around $12°$.

Ucelut

A white wine grape that may or may not be native to the region. There are several grapes with similar names in Veneto and Trentino-Alto Adige. What all of these grapes have in common is that their wild varieties sprouted at the edges of forests or stands of trees. The grapes were delicious to birds (*uccelli,* in Italian) who lived in the trees. Ucelut was documented in the region as far back as 1863 and makes a pleasant light wine. It is consumed primarily by people who want to connect with their regional identity, but almost none is sold outside the region.

Verduzzo

This versatile Friulian native can be vinified as an appealing white wine or as a very special dessert wine. In the latter form it is not as rich and imposing as Picolit, but it is more easily grown and can be consumed in more contexts. Verduzzo gives pleasure and comfort; Picolit stops traffic. Dessert Verduzzo (and to a lesser extent also dry Verduzzo) have color that ranges from straw to gold to amber and a fragrance that ranges from fruity (especially apricots and plums) to winey. Verduzzo has had a significant revival since 1973, when several producers around Nimis sought to give the wine a great deal of care and thought. In 1977, an excellent version by Ronchi di Cialla triggered interest in the grape among other COF growers. The grape has also become an interesting supporting player when blended with other white grapes, both as a dry wine and as a dessert wine. The typical alcoholic gradation ranges from 11° (for the dry) to 15° (for the dessert wine).

Vitovska

While in the rest of the region, Tocai is the grape that most tells people who they are, in Trieste and the Carso, people see themselves in the red Terrano and the white Vitovska. It can have flavor notes of cream and caramel and certainly reflects the minerals of the soils where it grows. Probably the leading producer is Edi Kante, who has endeavored to make this grape more respected and known. There is not a lot produced, but it is worth trying if you encounter it. The typical alcoholic gradation is around 11°.

Red Grapes

Cabernet Franc

This old grape, with provenance in Gironde, France, found its way to northeastern Italy in the nineteenth century, if not earlier. There is a frequent misapprehension about this grape. The Cabernet Franc used in Friuli-Venezia Giulia is not the one used in Bordeaux wines of today. Rather, it is the Carmenère grape, which is a bit different. The grape arrived in Friuli around 1870, although it had been planted in Marengo, near Alessandria (in Piedmont) as far back as 1820. However, nowhere else in Italy has it found the acceptance that it enjoys in Friuli-Venezia Giulia. While in France Carmenère and Cabernet Franc are usually blended with Cabernet Sauvignon, here it is often vinified on its own.

In the nose it has an unmistakable grassy, herby quality. There are hints of blackberry in the mouth, along with plums. This wine matches incredibly well with game and with spices. In an *osteria* in Udine, I once tasted goat flavored with nutmeg. It was served with a Cabernet Franc, and the results were unforgettable. It also goes well with cold roasted meats. The typical alcoholic gradation ranges from 11.5° to 13.5°.

Cabernet Sauvignon

This is now the most popular red wine grape in the world, at least if you measure popularity by the number of countries in which it is planted. Just about every wine-producing nation has Cabernet Sauvignon, and if you say "Cabernet" it is assumed to be Sauvignon and not Franc. (Incidentally, Cabernet Sauvignon is the product of a cross between Cabernet Franc and Sauvignon Blanc.) It has been in Friuli-Venezia Giulia since at least 1863.

In many countries that have recently adopted it, the wine is vinified on its own and usually spends time in contact with wood before bottling. In its native France, it is usually a blending wine as one of the principal components of Bordeaux. In Tuscany, it has invaded Chianti, whose traditional formula did not include it. Since about 1985 more and more Cabernet has crept into Chianti and other Tuscan wines. It appears in other Italian regions on its own.

Friuli-Venezia Giulia, ever different, has the best of both worlds. The wine is vinified and bottled on its own, especially in Grave. But it also is a marvelous blender, and finds increasing acceptance in the great *uvaggi* (blends) of COF and Collio. Its fragrance recalls violets, and the flavor is balanced and robust. It ages very well and takes to wood nicely, whether in large barrels or in *barriques* (small oak barrels). Cabernet Sauvignon matches well with meats, poultry, game, and mature cheeses. The typical alcoholic gradation ranges from 11.5° to 14°.

Forgiarin

A sturdy native red grape that is little known in the region and unknown elsewhere, Forgiarin is thought to have originated in western Friuli, perhaps near San Daniele. It comes from the peasant tradition and matches well with foods of that type. It is wonderful with bean soup, grilled or roasted chicken and game birds, and dishes flavored with ham or pork. The typical alcoholic gradation is around 12°.

Franconia

This grape produces a ruby-red wine used for blending in Isonzo and in Aquileia, where it occasionally appears as a wine all on its own. Some people think it originated in Croatia, while others insist it is German. It is known to have been in the region since 1920, and perhaps earlier. The wine is dry, the flavor slightly fruity and herbal. The typical alcoholic gradation is about 11°.

Merlot

This grape has been gaining on Cabernet Sauvignon in recent years for the title of the world's most popular red grape. It is often lighter than Cabernet and benefits from a two-syllable name that is easy to pronounce anywhere. (This was not lost on producers of Tocai [see pages 66 to 68) who, in having to rename their wine, found that people who could say "Merlot" for their red wine could say "Furlan" for their white.)

But Merlot was not suddenly planted in Friuli-Venezia Giulia because of its recent popularity. Originally from Gironde in Bordeaux, Merlot was brought to Friuli in 1880 and later was planted in Veneto as well. By 1903 it had spread to other parts of Italy, but in Friuli it found its first and most congenial soil. The earliest documentation of recognition of Merlot was when it took first prize among red wines at a fair in Cividale in 1896. It is grown throughout the region and is the dominant red grape in the Grave zone. Many people consider it the region's traditional red grape, even though it was not born there.

Merlot can range from a modest and pleasing wine to something with immense power and subtlety (such as the Sossò made by Livio Felluga). It is also a wonderful blending wine that has found favor in many of the region's *uvaggi* (blends). It is relatively easy to cultivate and vinify, is likable young, and ages well. It suits all kinds of foods and manages to be casual or elegant as the occasion calls for. It happens to match beautifully with porcini and responds to the slight nutty flavor of golden polenta. It goes with pork products, poultry, lentils, and rice. Younger Merlot goes nicely with certain fish, such as grilled sardines and braised cuttlefish. With a typical alcoholic gradation range from 10.5° to 12.5°, it also is less imposing than its Cabernet cousins.

Molinara

One sees this red grape (also called Rossara or Rossanella) occasionally. Native to Veneto, it is a blending grape for Bardolino and Valpolicella. It sometimes winds up in Friulian red blends, especially in Grave and Latisana. The typical alcoholic gradation ranges from 10.5° to 11°.

Moscato Rosa

The Moscato family of grapes is one of the largest, and perhaps the largest, of native Italian grapes. They vary greatly from region to region, from the pale one that makes a delicate sparkling wine in Piedmont to the rich, dark golden ones that produce a splendid still dessert wine in Sicily. Moscato Rosa is typical of Collio and the Alto Adige. The name means pink Moscato, but the wine is notable for its unmistakable rose fragrance. Depending on the producer, this wine can be still or have a slight sparkle. It makes a beautiful dessert wine that matches well with dry cake. It is also lovely to drink on its own. The typical alcoholic gradation ranges from 10.5° to 12.5°, depending on how it is produced.

Piculit-neri (a.k.a. Picolit-neri, Picolit Nero, and Picolit Neri)

Don't confuse this red table wine with Picolit, the marvelous dessert wine. I have been privileged to try this rare wine on a few occasions. By itself it works as an intriguing alternate red to drink in an *osteria*. It occasionally gives extra character to certain blends.

It has some flavor and fragrance characteristics in common with Refosco. While not strictly a food wine, it goes well with prosciutto, soft creamy cheeses, cheese frittatas, and creamy soups. The typical alcoholic gradation is around 12.5°.

Pignolo

There is documentation of this native Friulian grape since at least 1380, when it was described as growing at the Abbazia di Rosazzo. By the postwar era in the middle twentieth century, the variety had almost disappeared. When Walter Filiputti arrived at the Abbazia in the 1970s, he found two surviving vines and nursed them back to health. He is now one of the few wine makers who vinify this grape, along with Le Vigne di Zamò, Girolamo Dorigo, and only a few others. There are only small amounts available because it requires great care and attention to tend this grape. It is, to me, one of the finest red wines produced anywhere. Occasionally it is used in COF blends. The typical alcoholic gradation ranges from 12° to 13°.

Pinot Nero

The Pinot family of grapes is the oldest attested variety in Burgundy, referred to in the first century A.D. by Columella, a Roman agricultural writer. The red grape in this family is known in French and English as Pinot Noir, and in Italian as Pinot Nero. It finds certain terrains particularly congenial, such as Oregon in the United States. It is difficult to work with because of the fragility of the grape skins. Yet it is prized for its relative delicacy of flavor and fragrance among red wines. In Collio it is occasionally vinified and bottled on its own with success. In several parts of the region it lends character to blends. The typical alcoholic gradation is around 12.5°.

Refosco dal Peduncolo Nero

This is a little-seen wine that once had greater currency. The grapes grow from a black stalk, hence the name, and make a gratifying wine much like Refosco dal Peduncolo Rosso (see below). Most Refosco nowadays grows from a red stalk.

Refosco dal Peduncolo Rosso

Another native of the region, this grape was described as far back as 1390. Its name means that it is the Refosco grape from the red peduncle (stalk). It has a violet color and fragrant notes of blackberries. It makes a dry wine, full in the mouth with some bitter notes in the finish. The wine matches well with pork products and is especially nice with gnocchi. This is a wine that merits wider discovery outside the region. Many people believe that Refosco is the future star red wine of Friulian wine making. The typical alcoholic gradation ranges from 10.5° to 12.5°.

Refosco di San Dorligo

A robust red suited to aging, this grape is found in the province of Trieste. It is also called Refosco Nostrano. It is a cousin of the Refosco found in Friuli, but it is distinct because of the soil it grows in from San Dorligo to Muggia. This same zone is also where olive trees historically grow, and many local dishes might be cooked in oil and flavored with Refosco. It is ruby red in color, and has a winey nose and a dry finish. The typical alcoholic gradation ranges from 10.5° to 12.5°.

Schioppettino

This historic grape faced extinction until it was revived from a few vines by Paolo Rapuzzi at his Ronchi di Cialla winery in COF around 1970. This is a gracious red often referred to as feminine. It goes well with many foods, but particularly with barley, liver from different animals, and certain firm fishes. It also goes well with small game. The typical alcoholic gradation is around 11°.

In 1977, at the suggestion of Walter Filiputti, Rapuzzi vinified his Schioppettino in small *barriques,* creating a wine of astonishing power and durability that was wonderful when I tasted it in 1993. It had an alcoholic gradation of more than 13°, and was very special. Other producers now vinify this grape in two ways: either for drinking young and pleasurably or, in its best years, creating a wine with great aging possibilities.

Tazzelenghe

This gutsy wine, whose name means "tongue-cutter," has always held a place in the hearts of *osteria* denizens who responded to its straightforward character. A native of Friuli, it is not the sort of wine that will win awards, but it goes very well with many foods, especially those with a high fat content, which are tempered by the acidic edge in this wine. It goes perfectly with all pork dishes, plus polenta, beans, frico, and wild mushrooms. If you are in the region, be sure to try Tazzelenghe. It is as close as you can come to tasting wine that still maintains a proud rusticity. The typical alcoholic gradation is around 12.5°.

Terrano

This is the beloved red wine of the people of Trieste and the Carso. Just as the basic glass of wine in Udine is Tocai, in Trieste it is Terrano. It is one of the oldest red wines in Italy, having been produced continuously for at least two thousand years. It was shipped to Rome, where it was prized not only for flavor but for its medicinal properties. It is often prescribed by doctors to patients with digestive problems, because it has acids that are thought to be beneficial, and to anemic patients who need iron.

Terrano is made with a grape from the Refosco family, but takes its particular characteristics from the strong sun and the high mineral content of the Carso's red soil. In Istria and other areas where Slovenian is spoken, the wine is known as Refosk, suggesting that the grape is part of the Refosco family. Terrano is ruby red in color, with a taste that is slightly acidic, dry, and a bit salty, with a fragrance that has a hint of raspberry in it. At 10° or 11°, it is lower in alcohol than most reds. The growing zone hugs a road known as the Strada del Vino Terrano and includes Carso towns such as Duino-Aurisina, Sgonico, Monrupino, Sistiana, and Opicina. It is a versatile wine that pairs with many foods from the Triestine and Carso kitchens, including *cevapcici* (ground meat patties), pork products, cheeses, potatoes, cabbage, and fruit. The most famous pairing is one of the simplest: the Terrano and *ovi duri* (hard-boiled eggs) that one can consume in any buffet in Trieste.

A *rosato* wine is what is known in English and French as rosé. This is usually made with red wine grapes by allowing the skins (which give color and tannins) to have only minimal contact with the juice during vinification. When red wine is made, the skins have contact with the juice during all of the fermentation. As you might expect, a *rosato* is lighter and has less alcohol than a red, is not intended for aging, and does not quite achieve the character of important reds or whites. It is, nonetheless, very pleasant with light food or for drinking on its own. In Italy, the most notable *rosati* come mostly from Puglia. Friuli-Venezia Giulia has three DOC *rosati* (Aquileia, Grave, and Latisana).

Rosato di Aquileia

This rosé combines Merlot (about 70 percent) with Cabernet Franc, Cabernet Sauvignon, and Refosco. I like it with grilled meat patties, such as *cevapcici*. The typical alcoholic gradation ranges around 10.5°.

Rosato di Grave del Friuli

This rosé combines Merlot, Pinot Nero, Cabernet Franc, Cabernet Sauvignon, and Refosco. It is good for quaffing and matches well with dishes made with ricotta. The typical alcoholic gradation ranges around 10.5°.

Rosato di Latisana

A wine similar in composition to Rosato di Grave del Friuli, the typical alcoholic gradation ranges around 10.5°.

Typical Uvaggi (Blends) of Friuli-Venezia Giulia

Collio Bianco

The most traditional white blend in Collio will usually contain at least two of the following wines: Malvasia Istriana, Ribolla Gialla, and Tocai. But more and more wine makers now consider Sauvignon Blanc an essential grape in their blends, and then it is likely that either Pinot Bianco or Pinot Grigio will appear with it. This formula is also followed in Isonzo and in the COF, where producers occasionally sneak in a little Verduzzo or even Picolit.

Collio Rosso

Almost invariably this blend will contain Merlot and one or both of the Cabernets. It might also contain local grapes such as Refosco or Schioppettino. It suits grilled or roasted meats and game.

Collio Cabernet

Typically this is a blend of Cabernet Franc and Cabernet Sauvignon. It is intensely fragrant and has solid structure, making it ideal for aging. When younger, it goes well with grilled meats and, when older, with roasted meats and game. Its alcoholic gradation is usually between 13° and 13.5°.

Prato delle Rose

This is a little-seen and unusual dessert wine from Grave that combines Moscato Rosa and Verduzzo. Its alcoholic gradation is around 11.5°.

Rosso del Carso

A DOC designation was granted to this blend of red grapes that grow in the hard red soil of the Carso. It always has Terrano, which gives it its particular color and fruitiness and may contain any or all of the following: Refosco, Merlot, Cabernet Franc, and Cabernet Sauvignon. One does not find much of this wine exported, but it is an eminently pleasing and drinkable wine that pairs well with dishes from the Carso. The typical alcoholic gradation is around 12.5°.

*I*n so much of the history of Friuli-Venezia Giulia, its peoples' actions and decisions were based on strategies for survival. Many vineyards were destroyed or abandoned during World War I, and the region was economically devastated for much of the next two decades. This is the period that many refer to as *la miseria,* and there were mass migrations, especially to Argentina and Canada. Many of those who moved to Argentina went to Mendoza and became the heart and soul of the Argentine wine business.

Most of what had been salvaged or rebuilt after the first war was wiped out during World War II. As the people of Friuli-Venezia Giulia tried to pull themselves up yet again, several key figures in wine making, including Mario Schiopetto, Livio Felluga, and Vittorio Puiatti, tried to figure out how to create a niche in the wine market that the region could capture. They looked abroad to see how wine was made, what people drank, and how they ate. France, which made excellent red wines, had whites that did not enjoy the same status. The vineyards of Austria and Germany, both specializing in white wine, were ruined by war. Nations such as Spain, Portugal, the United States, Argentina, Chile, and Australia did not figure in the international market for table wines.

Most wines that came from Italy were reds from Piedmont, Tuscany, Veneto, Sicily, and Puglia. The few whites that Italy exported (Frascati, Soave, Orvieto, Verdicchio, Lacryma Christi) were light and drinkable but not special. So while Friuli-Venezia Giulia continued to produce excellent reds mostly for home consumption, it concentrated on making white wines that would be Italy's best and a valuable export item.

There was room in the international wine market for excellent white wines that would cost less than those of France. The wine pioneers of Friuli-Venezia Giulia planted new vines of white varieties and began exporting tasty, affordable wines. The biggest markets then were neighboring Austria and Germany, and they still are.

Among the first whites to catch on was Pinot Grigio, which also was the first Friulian wine to have any impact in the United States. It was very good when it reached American shores, but a few Friulian producers and many from the neighboring Veneto began to shortchange quality to increase profits. But as the rest of the world (especially California) showed improvement in their white wines, Germany and Austria became producing nations again, and countries such as Chile undercut Italian prices, Pinot Grigio's stock fell. This proved to be an important lesson for the wine makers of Friuli-Venezia Giulia. They had to redouble their efforts and create white wines that were unique. A tacit consensus emerged that quality had to be high across the board, because if anyone put "Friuli-Venezia Giulia" on his label and sold a less than excellent wine at a lower price, the whole region would suffer.

*T*heir approach was to make a new kind of white wine with concentrated fragrance and flavor, much like the world's important red wines. Such wines were made in small amounts in parts of France and Germany, but had not yet appeared in California. It is notable that because of a warmer climate and reliable sun in California, whites there tended to be higher in sugar (and therefore ultimately higher in alcohol) than in Europe. To cut the alcoholic edge, Californian wine makers let the white wines age in barrels so that they would acquire a rounder taste and aroma that often included notes of vanilla and butterscotch. This became emblematic of California style. When well done, there was a fascinating balance of fragrance and flavor. But too often the Californians overdid it, so that the characteristics of the white grape (usually Chardonnay) were hardly noticeable underneath all that wood.

The Friulians learned from this example that wood could be an *accent* in some white wines, but it has to be subordinate to the fragrance and flavors of grapes. How does concentration of flavor and fragrance occur? The guiding principle was to favor quality over quantity. The number of grapes per hectare (1 hectare = 2.47 acres) was reduced so that each bunch of grapes had more exposure to sun. Similarly, vines were trained along wires and posts to permit even more sun exposure. Soils were carefully analyzed for their mineral content, with the knowledge that this would influence the final flavor of the grapes.

Then came the famous intangible: the intuition on the part of the grower to know when grapes are ready to be harvested. Usually the lighter white grapes (such as Pinot Grigio) were harvested earlier than more substantial whites (Chardonnay); and then lighter reds (Pinot Nero) were harvested before bigger reds (such as Pignolo and Cabernet Sauvignon). If a grape is harvested too soon, it will not have achieved its maximum potential to make a concentrated wine. If it is harvested too late, it may have dried a bit and passed its peak.

In the past, growers relied on tradition, their senses, and phases of the moon. There are countless proverbs that represent peasant knowledge of weather and land. But this would not do for modern wine making.

Advances in the science of grape growing also helped the Friulians change their style of wine making. By the 1960s, some producers began to use chemical analysis to assess the quality of a grape. Nowadays, most use laboratory evaluation to decide when to pick grapes, but there is always a sense of gambling. In the past, it was difficult to determine if rain was in the offing. Even now, with more sophisticated meteorological forecasting, surprise rainstorms can come just around harvest, flooding vineyards and waterlogging grapes.

I observed this firsthand during the 1998 harvest. There had not been much sun that September and many growers hoped to hold on a bit longer to get sun that would boost sugars in the grapes. Some growers decided not to take the risk and harvested a little early. Others waited and saw many white and red grapes ruined. While the skillful wine makers of the region managed to create excellent wine (such as Rosa Bosco's Sauvignon Blanc), it was a year in which talent in the winery *(cantina)* made up for unforgiving nature in the fields. Many of the growers sold their grapes to less demanding wineries that transformed them into drinkable but unremarkable wines. The more serious growers were willing to take a financial loss rather than produce indifferent wine with their names on the labels. This sense of pride has made the average quality level of wine bottled each year in Friuli-Venezia Giulia the highest in Italy, along with Alto Adige, followed by Piedmont and Tuscany.

Successful grape growing and picking is only the beginning. Once the grapes are brought to the *cantina,* more decisions are made. It is these choices that result in the marked differences in wines from one producer to another, even if each is using superb examples of the same grape. Continuous technological progress since World War II has changed the face of wine making in Italy, and the people of Friuli-Venezia Giulia were among the very first to embrace this technology.

To make white wine, machines called stemmers are first used to separate the grapes from the stems without damaging the grapes. (Red grapes are sometimes stemmed, sometimes not.) Another machine crushes the grapes and separates the sweet juice from the skins, which often contain bitter flavors. The skins are saved to make grappa. Some producers believe that by leaving the juice of certain white grapes in contact with skins for a longer period of time, a wine with more aroma will be produced. When the wine maker decides the moment is right, the juice is placed in stainless steel tanks or oak barrels.

Juice from red grapes is kept in contact with the skins. Reds are fermented with their skins, which provide color and tannin. The skins are later removed from the tanks and are often used for making grappa.

Fermentation occurs thanks to yeasts. Ideally, one wants to use the natural wild yeasts that exist on grape skins. But to assure consistency, many growers add commercial yeasts to launch the fermentation process.

Most wine is now fermented in stainless steel tanks. Steel offers a neutral, sterile environment that does not add any odors or tastes to the wine. Because steel tanks are made of metal, the heat of fermentation could ruin the wine, so the tanks are cooled during fermentation. In the years before computers, these tanks were cooled by running cold water through their seams. With the advent of computers, it became possible to maintain constant temperatures in steel tanks. Each wine maker has a formula for each grape as to how long, and at what temperature, fermentation should take place. During fermentation, much of the sugar in the juice is transformed into alcohol while malic acid is naturally released. The alcohol, acid, and the flavors and aromas of the grapes (which derive from natural substances called polyphenols) are the components that make up a wine.

In many countries where weather may result in grapes that are not high in sugars, it is permissible to add sugar to the vats where wine is fermenting. Some sugar converts to alcohol, while the rest adds to flavor. In Italy it is strictly against the law to add sugar during the wine-making process. In some extreme cases, wine makers add concentrated grape musts (cooked skins and juice that yields sugars) to a vat for fermentation. But this is not a common practice, and it is only done when the state of the grapes is poor.

Not all producers ferment their wines in steel, especially when it comes to red wines. The older way of fermenting wine, in oak barrels, is still the preferred method for some. New oak barrels are usually slightly toasted within before the juice is added for fermentation. This lets the juice interact with the inner surface of the barrel so that some of its characteristics are imparted at the same time that the barrel absorbs some of the tannins of a red wine. There are some producers (most famously Josko Gravner) who believe that the juice and skins of grapes should have no contact with any material except wood for the entire wine making and aging process, up to the moment that the wine is bottled. So substances such as steel and plastic are not to be found in these wineries. (Recently, Gravner has gone further and is reported to be making wine in terra-cotta, as was done by the ancient Romans in this area.)

A few producers use *barriques* (small oak barrels) for fermentation, though this is an expensive proposition and a risky one too. Because the barrels are small, a greater percentage of the wine has contact with the sides of the barrel. Therefore, its flavor and aroma characteristics become more pronounced. Many producers now use *barriques* later in the wine-making process, for aging wine, to give it distinct woody traits.

*O*nce the fermentation occurs, there are two choices for how to proceed. Either the wine can be left as is to age in steel or wood where it fermented, or it can undergo a second fermentation. The wine will slowly mature during the aging process. It is usually drinkable by mid-November (this is *nouveau* or *novello* wine), though inevitably it will improve if it is left to age further. Because producers of Friuli-Venezia Giulia use such high-quality grapes for which they have spent large sums to acquire and nurture, it is considered a waste to sell off new young wine before it has achieved any special characteristics. If a wine is intended to be drunk young (emphasizing its fruit and liveliness), it will probably be bottled and released in the spring following the harvest of the autumn before.

Producers who do not choose to simply age their wine after fermentation often take another approach, called malolactic fermentation. This is a natural second fermentation that may take place immediately after the first (if the wine maker permits temperatures in a barrel or tank to go high enough), or the following spring. Malolactic fermentation transforms the harsh malic acid in many wines into softer lactic acid, which shifts the sensory expression of the wine from bluntly acidic to something more complex.

Whether wine has one or two fermentations, and whether it ages in steel or wood, will contribute to its various distinctive characteristics. The producer may wait until spring before putting a wine in wood, and then let it age for months or even years. (A wine aged for at least two years will be referred to as *riserva* on the label.) Or the wine maker may choose to bottle the wine and let it age that way. Or the wine may be sold right away. All of these decisions are based on taste, intuition, finances, and a desire for personal expression.

When most of the rest of Italy made local wines by traditional formulas, wine makers in Friuli-Venezia Giulia sought to improve quality, break down formulas, and create new styles. They would influence the rest of Italy, especially Tuscany, whose producers slowly evolved the formulas for making Chianti and, when they became restless to do something original, created the so-called Supertuscans, red wine blends that combine Sangiovese, Cabernet Sauvignon, and sometimes Merlot. Although Friulians made outstanding blends of reds and whites much earlier, the Tuscans were better marketers and benefited from tourists who tasted Supertuscans and wanted more. In the year 2000, the term "Super-whites" was coined to promote the marvelous white blends of Friuli-Venezia Giulia.

What makes the wine of this region extraordinary cannot be found just in examining the amount of alcohol, the purity of the grapes, and the chemical makeup that provokes those glorious fragrances and flavors. A chemical analysis of a wine is like a blood test. You can learn what the wine is made of, but you don't learn what makes it special. You must experience it, as you would a person, to feel that you know it.

*W*hen, in the early 1960s, the wine pioneers of the region sought to make a qualitative leap in their products, they were both helped and hindered by Italian national law. Friuli-Venezia Giulia is one of five autonomous regions in Italy and therefore has more self-determination than the fifteen regions that are completely under the Italian Republic. In 1963, in Trieste, regional law number 29 was passed to give significant economic advantages to growers who planted native grapes. With the added income, wine producers were able to invest in technology that enabled them to make strides before producers in most other regions.

It was at this same time that national legislation created the DOC *(Denominazione di Origine Controllata)* laws that codified the formulas for hundreds of Italian wines and specified the maximum yield per hectare that could be used for a DOC wine. The intention of this was to set minimum standards of quality. This was beneficial for most of Italy and helped improve both quality and sales. However, the producers of Friuli-Venezia Giulia aimed for international quality, and some bridled under the constraints of DOC laws. Also, because they had spent more for the best grapes, the cost of producing their wines was higher, and they faced competition from the decent wines of other regions that inevitably cost less. At the time (and even today), most international consumers had never heard of Friuli-Venezia Giulia and to them one Italian wine was indistinguishable from another. Placing the name "Friuli-Venezia Giulia" on labels is an important step that many, though not all, regional producers have taken to identify their wines.

*A*s wine producers in Friuli-Venezia Giulia sought to expand their market abroad, an interesting and rather unexpected development would really help their cause. In the 1960s and 1970s, as the economic status of most of Italy blossomed, consumers in other parts of the nation (especially in Milan) decided that the best white wines were from Friuli-Venezia Giulia and they were willing to pay for them. At long last the strategy of the pioneers had worked, though not as they had planned. Instead of sending their top whites to Munich or Vienna, they went to Milan, Turin, Bologna, and Rome. Germans, Austrians, and Americans who visited those cities tasted these marvelous whites there and then wanted them in their home countries. The only major importing nation that was indifferent to Friulian wines was Great Britain.

This raises an interesting point. Most people who consider wines, certainly those of us with English as a native tongue, derive much of our opinion and vocabulary from the British, who probably formed the first group of wine journalists in the late nineteenth century. They set standards and determined taste. For them Bordeaux (Claret) was the gold standard, although Burgundies were also significant. White wines from France also became the ones against which others were compared. A few German whites were approved of, but that was it.

For the British, the top Mediterranean wines were all fortified (having about 15° alcohol) and were meant for drinking away from meals: Marsala from Sicily, Sherry from Spain, and Port from Portugal. A few more daring writers later found merit in Chianti and Barolo from Italy, but not much else. Nowadays, some top Italian wines are known to cognoscenti in Britain, but most are from Tuscany, Piedmont, and Veneto. For the average British consumer, the most typical Italian wine is cheap and cheerful, while for an important expenditure for a special occasion only French will do.

As a group, those original wine experts never paid much attention to how wine and food interact. At most it was red wines with meat and whites with fish. In Italy, wine has always gone with food and Friuli-Venezia Giulia is the most advanced region in terms of understanding the marriage of food and wine flavors and fragrances. Until that tradition becomes a key part of wine-drinking in Britain, the wines of Friuli-Venezia Giulia will probably be a novelty there, which is a shame. One excellent producer who has a following in smart London restaurants is Alvaro Pecorari of Lis Neris.

Beside the big markets, there are other interesting niches for Friulian wines. Pighin, a producer with a good quality/price ratio, is considered the leading seller of white wine in Sweden. Here is a case of a market that was identified early and pursued intelligently. Two other key markets are Australia and Canada. The former has a major wine industry of its own; the latter does not make a lot of wine but much of it is impressive in quality. Yet both have very large and united immigrant communities from Friuli who proudly form a fanatically devoted clientele.

*I*n Friuli-Venezia Giulia all of the top wine makers have their own philosophy about the land, grapes, wine making, and marketing. Although they all work with the same range of grapes, they come up with astonishingly individual choices. What I find so interesting is the extent to which producers assert their individuality, politics, gender, and economic outlook. You can meet more than 110 of these producers in a chapter on discovering the region's wines (page 355), but I want to describe some of them here. It is notable that most of the categories I am about to discuss are agreed upon by most people in the region, even if they disagree with the philosophies of the producers in some of these groups.

Pioneers and grand old men: In this group are Mario Schiopetto, Livio Felluga, his independent brother Marco Felluga, and Vittorio Puiatti. Puiatti was one of the first proponents of stainless steel vats and resolutely refuses to make wine that touches wood. Also in this group are Paolo and Dina Rapuzzi of Ronchi di Cialla, who were among the leading advocates for the recovery of disappearing native grapes, making them valid for wine again. Pietro Pittaro is probably the most famously political producer, and he became prominent in agricultural circles in Rome and was an officer in international wine organizations. In so doing, he brought attention to the region and was influential when necessary in the Italian government.

Scholars: The most important is Walter Filiputti, who has written extensively about grapes and wine in his region. He has also put his knowledge into practice as a consultant and as a producer. Walter and his wife, Patrizia, live in the Abbazia di Rosazzo and lease the vineyards to produce Pignolo and other excellent wines. Filiputti understands the balance between knowledge, scholarship, and seriousness of purpose on the one hand, and pleasure, sensuousness, and excitement on the other. He is controversial but you cannot ignore him. He and his wife are in the DNA of this book. Also in the scholar category is Girolamo Dorigo, who built one of the region's top wineries with his ex-wife Rosetta. His home is full of books, and he reads widely to create the philosophy of the Dorigo winery. It is well known that Rosetta is every bit as knowledgeable as Girolamo, and she has gone on to exciting new wine adventures of her own.

Heretics: Josko Gravner is in a class by himself. "Heretic" is not my term, but one used all over the region. It is a label usually said with reverence and awe. Gravner has always pursued his own vision of wine, and he is almost entirely removed from the marketing, politics, and culture of wine making in his region. He works by himself in his vineyard and *cantina* in Oslavia and produces wines that sell for very high prices. He has several disciples who make excellent wine and go their own way, including Nicola Monferrari and Edi Kante.

In Gravner's mold, but entirely his own man, is young Enzo Pontoni of the Miani winery. His approach to grape growing and wine making is all his own, and there are more than a few people who think that the best wine now made in the region comes from Miani.

Sons with a Single Vision: These include Alvaro Pecorari, Edi Keber, and Sandro Princic. All grew up in their fathers' wineries and have a sense of connection to these hard-working men who through their hands, their instinct, and sheer will created small but important wineries that had local respect. The sons are mindful of honoring their fathers, but also pursue their own visions and are making statements of independent identity.

Marketers: Most producers in the region have figured out in one way or another how to sell their wines. Years ago, Vittorio Puiatti created different price categories and segmented his market with great success. More recently, the champion has probably been Silvio Jermann, whose wines are familiar to wine buffs. What is interesting is that most Jermann fans I meet know his name and wines but don't associate him with his region. Instead, he is known for wines with intriguing names and labels.

Women of Wine: In Italy there is an important organization called Le Donne del Vino, and Friuli-Venezia Giulia has one of the most vital chapters. Everybody knows that these women have been an essential part of the scene for a long time, but only recently have they received the acclaim they deserve. Rosa Bosco (formerly Rosetta Dorigo) is one of the most respected and beloved wine producers in Italy. Her wines are outstanding, and she miraculously infuses much of her character in them. Barbara Maniacco guides Le Vigne di Zamò, which combined several smaller wineries of distinction into a larger institution that ranks with the region's best. Marina Danieli leads by example, operating a large winery in Buttrio with gorgeous vineyards, plus a hotel, an agritourism (a winery with a restaurant and guest rooms), two restaurants, and an organic farm. Her beliefs translate into action, and she has been very supportive of other women trying to find their way. Patrizia Stekar (Castello di Spessa and La Boatina) pursues a singular vision of the perfect winery and agritourism, and in a short period of time has garnered international respect. Elda Felluga and Patrizia Felluga have each become protagonists in their fathers' wineries (Livio and Marco, respectively). They are responsible for many of the operations and the directions these historic companies are taking. Roberta Borghese (Ronchi di Manzano), Wanda Gradnik, and Ivana Adami all run quality wineries that are growing in stature. And in grappa, which is intimately linked to wine, there is the irrepressible trailblazer, Giannola Nonino (and her three daughters), who is probably the most important heir to the legacy and innovation of Count Asquini.

Young Couples: Flavio and Silvana Basilicata of Le Due Terre and Gabriele and Serena Palazzolo of Ronco del Gnemiz are all custodians of the soil, devoted to the legacy and tradition of Friulian viticulture and deeply involved in environmental preservation, which is the highest calling of people who love their land. Their wines are magnificent, and I respect these four people because they have resisted the blandishments of marketing to dedicate themselves entirely to making wine they believe in, confident that it will sell.

WINE ZONES IN FRIULI-VENEZIA GIULIA

Friuli-Venezia Giulia is a very small place, and it produces only about 2.5 percent of all the wine made in Italy. Much of it conforms to DOC regulations, though at a very high level. The region has eight wine-producing zones completely within the region, and one that is shared with the Veneto. There are many subzones in these larger entities.

It is important to note that many wines produced in Friuli-Venezia Giulia may or may not have the region's name on the label, but will very likely have the name of the DOC zone. This is a key fact because there are remarkable historical and geographical differences among the zones, and if producers have one giant unresolved problem, it is that they insist on identifying these zones, which is confusing to most consumers who cannot remember the many names. A wine from Collio, Colli Orientali del Friuli (COF), or Isonzo may cost much more than those from Grave, Aquileia, Latisana, or Annia, and producers from the more expensive zones (where much of the best wine in the region is made) want to make sure a wine buyer knows what she or he is getting. Then there is Carso, in the province of Trieste, which very defiantly asserts its own identity and wants its name on the label. For these reasons, a label that simply says "Friuli-Venezia Giulia" gives you some good information, but not enough.

And there are indeed differences. Grave del Friuli is by far the largest zone and makes the most wine. Colli Orientali del Friuli (usually referred to as COF) and Collio (in Venezia Giulia) compete to make the best wines in the region. They are separated by the narrow Judrio River and have many similarities. People always ask me whether wineries in COF or Collio make the best wines, and I find it impossible to answer that question. Taste hundreds of wines and then decide for yourself!

Just behind the wineries in COF and Collio in quality are those in Isonzo, which get better every day. Carso is the producing zone in the province of Trieste and has a tradition all its own. The other zones are Aquileia, Annia, and Latisana. Each is rather small and can be found along the rim of the Adriatic in the Bassa Friulana. Given their location, it is not surprising that they have sandy soils. The wines produced there are mostly for local and regional consumption, but are pleasurable.

In terms of geography, the Grave, COF, Latisana, Annia, and most of the Aquileia zones are in Friuli, while most of Collio and Isonzo, plus Carso and the rest of the Aquileia zone are in Venezia Giulia. Finally, one should note a zone called Lison-Pramaggiore, some of which is in the western part of Friuli, and much of which is in Veneto. The wines produced there are similar to those of Grave and Latisana.

In parts of the region, air currents play a role in how the vines are positioned. In Isonzo, Grave, and Aquileia, there are fewer hills, so the wine producer must be even more creative and vigilant than elsewhere. Soils differ in all of these zones. Some of the soil in COF is described as poor, which means that the vine has to work harder to yield great fruit. But the final product of that struggle is outstanding.

In many zones of the region, but especially COF, small or big hills are thought to provide better exposure to sun and therefore make better grapes. The vineyards are terraced on these hills to assure maximum exposure for the most grapes possible. A hill in these parts is called a *ronco* (*ronc,* in Friulano) and wine labels will indicate the name of the hill as a source of pride and geographical interest. This is not the only

Italian region that does this. In Piedmont a hill is called a *bricco,* while in Tuscany it is a *poggio.*

Annia

The newest DOC zone, Annia received its designation in 1995. Many of the region's grapes are found here and grow in a relatively mild climate.

Aquileia

Received DOC recognition in 1975. This zone has an ancient wine-making tradition and a particularly sweet climate that benefits viticulture. This is the zone that makes the most notable rosé wines and also very fine grappas. Riesling, Tocai, Pinot Bianco, Refosco, Merlot, and Cabernet Franc are the most popular grapes.

Carso

This zone received DOC recognition in 1986. Its name (karst in English and German) is thought to be of Celtic origin and means "land of rock." It is largely limestone and red rocks, but beneath it run rivers that have created huge caverns and the largest grotto in the world. The largest river, the Timavo, begins in Slovenia and runs 95 kilometers (about 60 miles) to the Adriatic, of which 38 kilometers (23 miles) run in a continuous underground flow beneath the Carso, which is in the area of the province of Trieste north of the city. There are also a few Carso towns in the province of Gorizia. The climate shares the warming breezes of the Adriatic with the cold driving gales from the north known as the Bora. The Carso is where vegetation changes from the rest of the region. Here you find olive trees and maritime pines. Terrano, Malvasia Istriana, and Vitovska are the most popular grapes grown here, all of ancient origin. Refosco di San Dorligo is another smaller variety.

Colli Orientali del Friuli (COF)

This zone received DOC recognition in 1970. The soil here and in Collio (a.k.a. Collio Goriziano) is known either as *ponca* (the local word) or *flysch di Cormons* and consists of alternating strata of marl and sandstone. Among the leading towns are Buttrio, Rosazzo, Manzano, and Cividale.

COF differs from Collio in that it has delineated subzones where certain grapes flourish. So Ramandolo, farther north in COF is the coolest and has the most rainfall. Here is where delicious Verduzzo (sometimes called Ramandolo) is made. Cialla, in the eastern part of COF, is where many Friulian native grapes grow: Refosco, Ribolla Gialla,

Picolit, Schioppettino, and Verduzzo. The southernmost subzone, Rosazzo, has Picolit, Pignolo, and Ribolla Gialla, and is more likely to produce blends (as in the tradition of neighboring Collio).

The COF zone runs mostly north/south and borders on Slovenia. Historically, this is where Friuli bordered with the lands of the Austrian empire. A good part of the frontier is defined by the Judrio River, which is often so small that I thought it was a brook. But to this day, people define themselves as being on one side or the other, and Friulano or Giuliano as a result. Here is the heartland of Pignolo and Picolit, and many of the region's best wines. It is notable that the leading business in the area is Friuli's world-famous furniture industry, and people who became rich on chairs then invested in wineries. You can meet many wine producers who are relatively new to wine but devote themselves to it with great passion as a means of supporting the region's land and heritage.

Collio

This zone received DOC recognition in 1968. Occasionally the combined zone of COF and Collio is thought of as Collio Goriziano (with the dividing line being the Judrio River, separating the provinces of Gorizia to the east and Udine to the west), but you should think of them as distinct. Various ancient Greek writers described the wine from around Gorizia, which they called Adriano. Collio runs east/west and has some of the most idyllic scenery you will ever see. It is sheltered by the Giulian Alps to the north (in Slovenia), enjoys breezes from the Adriatic, and has lots of sunshine. While COF makes important reds and whites, Collio has become so famous for its extraordinary whites that people forget to try the reds, which is a shame. Among the leading towns are Cormons, Capriva, Spessa, Oslavia, and San Floriano. Cormons is the seat of the consortium and one of Italy's great wine towns.

War and devastation are part of the collective memory of citizens of Collio, and they have had to rebuild twice in less than fifty years. Oslavia was one of the towns in Europe that suffered most in World War I and has one of the largest ossuaries in the world to serve as a constant reminder of the horrors of war. The producers in Collio make a wine each year called the Vino della Pace (the Wine of Peace), which is used to promote amity among world peoples. The idea was born in 1983 in Cormons, and a vineyard was set aside that includes 540 grape varieties from Europe, Asia, Africa, Oceania, and North and South America. There is even one from Yemen. Eighty percent of the grapes are white. They are used to produce a wine each year that is bottled and sent to leaders of every nation and religion. Famous artists are commissioned to design labels and, each year during the Sagra dell'Uva harvest festival in Cormons, large reproductions of the art are displayed. With the gift of another harvest, the people of Collio give thanks for peace and prosperity and wish them for everyone.

Grave del Friuli

Far and away the biggest producer of wine in Friuli-Venezia Giulia, Grave del Friuli received DOC recognition in 1970. The wearing down of alpine ridges over the centuries filled the lowlands with alluvial debris rich in gravel and sand, the combination of which is known locally as *grave*. (The term is like *Graves* in Bordeaux, referring to the gravelly soil). The center of this zone is traversed by the Tagliamento River, which flows from the Alps to the sea. The river was the ancient conduit for much of the materials that give this terrain its character. The land with Grave soil extends from the border of the Veneto to the west across Friuli and into the zone known as the Isonzo, in Venezia Giulia. Two former small subzones in the Friulian part (Latisana and Annia) are now independent because their character is distinct. Both are closer to the Adriatic and have moister air and warmer temperatures than farther north.

The Grave zone has fifty-nine towns in the province of Udine and thirty-five in the province of Pordenone. Many of these towns form subzones, and one of the most intriguing is Casarsa della Delizia, in which all wine is produced and sold collectively, with growers receiving money for their grapes. This is known as a *cantina sociale* and has roots in the collective farming in Italy of decades ago. These exist in many other Italian regions, but there are only a few in Friuli-Venezia Giulia, where individual expression is the rule. Casarsa has more vines than any subzone in the region (891 hectares / 2,202 acres). Its wines are moderate in price, of good quality, and widely available.

Merlot is the most popular grape in Grave, followed by Tocai, Pinot Bianco, Pinot Grigio, and Refosco.

Isonzo

This zone received DOC recognition in 1974. It is, topographically, the eastern part of the Grave del Friuli in soil that is drained by the Isonzo River, which flows from the Julian Alps in Slovenia through Gorizia and down to the Adriatic. Wine making has gone on here since antiquity, and in recent times some Isonzo producers, despite soil less desirable than COF and Collio, have begun to make wines that fully rival those other two zones. Isonzo extends to the Slovenian border, with the Collio zone to the north and Carso and Aquileia to the south. Leading towns include Farra, Villanova, San Lorenzo, and Gradisca. Farra and Villanova are sometimes called part of Collio, even though they are in Isonzo, because their soils are more typical of those in Collio. All the major grapes of the region grow in Isonzo.

Latisana

A thin strip of land extending from the Veneto border east toward the left bank of the Tagliamento River, this zone received DOC recognition in 1975. The soil is sandy and the climate is mild. Its wines are similar to those of Annia and, like that zone and Grave, it produces more reds than whites.

Lison-Pramaggiore

This zone received DOC recognition in 1986. It ranges from the westernmost part of the province of Pordenone into the Veneto (the provinces of Treviso and Venice). The Friulian part ends at the Piave River. It is a fertile zone, and the most popular grapes are Tocai, Merlot, and Cabernet Franc.

STORING AND SERVING WINE

Storing wine is both more difficult and easier than you might imagine. You do not have to be fancy, but you must assure that the storage conditions are as close to ideal as possible. If you have a temperature-controlled wine cellar, this is the best of all possible worlds for keeping your valuable collection. But most of us do not. So it is necessary to find an environment in your home that is dark and maintains a cool temperature. I have a closet that has a constant temperature of about 64°F (18°C). This is at the high end of acceptable, but because the temperature changes little throughout the year, my bottles don't suffer.

My wines rest on a simple metal rack, and I always make sure to keep the door shut so the outside light and air do not penetrate. People with more space than I have in my New York City apartment often purchase whole cases to put in their cellars. This is wise if you develop a particular affection for a few wines that you intend to make your "house" reds and whites. If you buy a case and don't intend to put the bottles on a rack, place the box on its side so that the wine bottles will be horizontal. The wine keeps the cork moist, preventing it from drying and cracking, which would admit air that would spoil the wine.

Wine changes in character as it ages, sometimes for the better and sometimes for the worse. Tannic red wines become rounder and smoother with age. Acid in both reds and whites softens, and sometimes the intensity of fruit diminishes. As a general rule, white wines cannot age for too many years (usually three is the maximum). However, many Friulian whites (Sauvignon Blanc, Chardonnay, blends, and even some Pinot Grigio and Ribolla Gialla) have a great deal of structure and age beautifully for up to ten years. It often is written on the label whether the producer believes a white wine has aging possibilities. But Tocai, Malvasia Istriana, Pinot Bianco, and some Pinot Grigio and Ribolla Gialla should be consumed within two years to get their maximum effect. Most sparkling and dessert wines do not age particularly well, although Picolit and some Verduzzo can be astonishingly rich and intense when they have aged.

Serving Temperatures

Temperature is important for storage and even more so when it comes to serving wine. As a general rule, Americans and some other peoples serve red wines too warm and white wines too cold. What follows is a good general list of proper temperatures for all wines, and is absolutely correct for those from Friuli-Venezia Giulia.

Reds: Serve between 57° and 64°F (14° and 18°C). Wines that are aged in steel or bottles should be served cooler than those aged in wood. Look at the back label of the wine for this information or ask your wine seller.

Dry White Wines: Serve between 43° and 50°F (6° and 10°C). Typically, barrel-aged Chardonnay and other whites are served just a little warmer, up to 57°F (14°C), so that their complex flavors can be better appreciated.

White Dessert Wines: Serve between 43° and 50°F (6° and 10°C). If a dessert wine is sweet, it can be served a bit cooler. A wood-aged Ramandolo should be served a little warmer.

Because my wine closet is at the high end of the permissible temperature range (it is ideal for some reds), it is necessary for me to cool most of the wines before drinking them. Many people err by putting a white wine in the refrigerator for one or more days so that it has a temperature of 34° to 36°F (1° to 2°C). They then serve it this cold, which is a waste of good wine. You cannot get the full aroma or taste. A better idea is to put a white wine in the refrigerator a few hours ahead of drinking it. Typically it will be just right when you take it out. The same applies for rosé wines. Most red wines that are stored in overheated homes are also too warm to serve. I usually put a light or medium-bodied red in the refrigerator for 30 or 45 minutes before serving it so that it is just slightly cool. Most dessert wines should be cooled for a few hours at most. Only sparkling wines should be good and cold, about 37°F (3°C).

Except for sparkling wines, I never put my bottles in an ice bucket. This chills the wine too much and dulls its fragrance and flavor. Usually a white wine will be consumed quickly enough that no further cooling is necessary. But there are nice containers made of marble, terra-cotta, or good plastic in which you can place a bottle at the table. These tend to maintain the temperature of a wine.

Opening Bottles and Decanting Wines

How far in advance should a bottle of wine be opened? For most whites and dessert wines, it can be opened just before serving. The same applies to red wines intended to be consumed young. Some young reds are tannic and acidic, so they might benefit from opening about 15 minutes before service.

If you are opening a wine that is at least five years old, uncork it 30 to 45 minutes before pouring. Sometimes older wines require decanting so that the sediment that comes with age does not flow out of the bottle with the wine. If the bottle has been in your cellar for a long time, stand it up (in your cellar) for 2 hours so that all the sediment will gather at the bottom. Handle this bottle carefully before opening so that the sediment is not shaken. Uncork it and then carefully decant.

Decanting wine is not as daunting as you might expect. It requires patience, a steady hand, and a watchful eye. Your decanter or carafe should be clear glass or crystal and have a broad bottom and a tapered neck. After uncorking the bottle, hold it in one hand and the base of the decanter in the other. Tip the decanter about 60° to 75° (or about 2 o'clock if you are thinking of the face of a clock). Tip the wine bottle toward the decanter and rest it gently on the lip. Let the wine slowly pour from the bottle, taking care that the sediment at the bottom is not stirred up. If you see any sediment in the neck of the decanter, put down the wine bottle (do not change the angle of the decanter) and wipe the inside of the neck with a clean cloth. Then put down the decanter and wait a while for the wine to settle. If, when you resume decanting, you find that more sediment is coming out of the bottle, then you probably have poured all of the wine that you will be able to drink. Let the wine in the decanter rest in a cool, poorly lit place for about 30 minutes.

Wine Glasses

Many wine buffs have an endless series of glasses, each seemingly suitable for a different wine. For the great majority of us (myself included), this is not necessary. I have three types of glasses, and they are suitable for almost every wine I serve. Each glass has a sturdy, medium-length stem that I hold when drinking so that the temperature of my hand does not affect the wine. The white wine glass is tulip-shaped and taller than it is wide. It closes ever so slightly at the top, so that it concentrates the fragrance. The red wine glass has a larger capacity, is somewhat more square and also closes slightly at the rim. Some people like their red glass to be exaggeratedly large so they can really swirl the liquid to release its fragrance. That is fine with me, but these glasses break a little more easily. My third glass is a traditional champagne flute, tall and thin with a slight closure. Another good reason to limit the number of types of glassware you own is that when they break (as they inevitably do), you can replace them with more of the same type.

This collection is suitable for most purposes. If I serve a meal with two wines, I have several options. If there are two whites, the lighter one will go in the tulip glass and the bigger one will go in the red wine glass. If I serve one white and red, each will go in its typical glass, although I might choose to serve a big white in a red wine glass. If I serve two reds, they might both go in red glasses, or a lighter one could even go in the white glass. If I serve a meal with more than two wines, I alternate the type of glass, or remove a used one and replace it with another of the same type if it is the most suitable for the wine being served.

I tend to pour most dessert wines in my flutes, although a structured Picolit or aromatic Verduzzo often winds up in the white or even the red glass. They have an intense fragrance that only comes forth fully when the wine is swirled. People usually serve fine grappa and distillates in snifters. If you have these, that is fine. But I will often put a little bit of this precious liquid in the white wine glass or the flute, and the effect is the same.

Needless to say, only buy glasses that are clear so that you can regard the wine. I have been served wine or water in blue, green, or red glasses and had no idea what I was drinking!

Pouring Wine

One area in which most wine drinkers sorely lack knowledge concerns how much wine to pour in a glass. They tend to take their cues from waiters and wine stewards in restaurants, many of whom do things wrong. In most restaurants, wine is filled to almost the brim of the glass for two reasons. The first is the perceived notion that anything less would not be giving the customer his money's worth. This is particularly the case when wine is ordered by the glass.

The other case happens when a customer orders a bottle of wine. The waiter will bring the wine to the table with a basket of bread. Glasses will be filled to near capacity, and diners will drink and eat bread while their meal is being prepared. Restaurant owners hope that much of the wine will be consumed early on so that another bottle of wine might be ordered. This is a cynical way to try to make more money.

This does not happen in Friuli-Venezia Giulia and other parts of the world where wine is truly understood and appreciated. If you inebriate a client he will not fully enjoy his meal. People who order wine by the glass know that they will receive one that is partially filled, and they will be charged a fair price for it. In New York, London, and other major cities in the world, a glass of average wine in a fancy restaurant can easily cost $12, while in Italy an excellent glass of wine might cost $3 to $4. In most restaurants in Italy (except those that are blatantly geared to tourists), there is still a sense of care and respect for the customer. In big international capitals, dining out has become a competitive event in which diners are expected to feel grateful for getting a good table and then pay vast sums to occupy it for a couple of hours before being handed the check (whether or not it was requested) and then encouraged to leave. Accelerated wine pouring is part of this phenomenon, and you should make sure that the waiter or steward pours the right amount or insist that you do it yourself.

As a general rule when drinking still (non-sparkling) wines, never fill a glass more than one-third full. With big structured wines or those that have aged for a long time, fill the glass one-quarter full. The reason for this is that wine tastes better when you can swirl it to release its fragrance. Smell is the second major sense you use with wine. The first is sight and the third is taste (touch is used in handling the bottle and the glass and the ear is gratified with the clink of glasses).

With less liquid in the bowl of the glass, wine will not rush into your mouth as you drink it. You can let the wine trickle down the side of your glass and into your mouth, savoring it more fully as you feel it on your lips, tongue, palate, and cheeks. A small sip brings the fragrance to your nose again from within your mouth.

The key revelation as you approach the marriage of food and wine in Friuli-Venezia Giulia (and anywhere else, for that matter) is that you will discover new things when you combine a sip of wine with a small bite of food. Think about it: Most people eat, chew, and swallow their food, then drink wine, then eat, and so on. They are not truly combining the flavors and discovering the mysteries of the interaction between wine and food. By having a more manageable amount of wine in the glass, this can become possible.

Opera, which I love as much as food and wine, is the marriage of words and music. Each on its own is important, but when combined they create something incomparable that resembles neither of the individual components. Once you come to love the fusion of food and wine (you decide which is words and which is music) you will understand why the separate elements are wonderful but the combination is outstanding.

ON PAIRING FOOD AND WINE

People in Friuli-Venezia Giulia have a greater knowledge of how to pair food and wine than in any place I have ever been. This wisdom is not merely the province of sommeliers and food experts, but resides in most everyone I have ever met in the region. I think this owes to a rather strong attachment to the region's terrain and flavors—a legacy both of hunger and a sense of attachment to a land that was so frequently invaded.

Rather than dictate hard-and-fast rules to you, I encourage you to look at the wine recommendations that accompany most recipes in this book. And the more you taste different varietal wines (that is, made from one grape), the more you will learn their characteristics and develop your own preferences. Sauvignon Blanc in much of the world is thought of as something of an acquired taste, but in Friuli-Venezia Giulia it is abundantly fragrant and full of complex flavor. It often goes with foods that have a pronounced flavor rather than those that are delicate. Ribolla Gialla often has a creaminess about it that makes it a lovely companion to traditional "white wine foods" that are opulent in the mouth— scallops, for example, rather than clams. The undercurrent of cherry in many Merlots makes this wine a nice match with creamy cheeses, foods with almond flavoring, and dishes cooked with fruit. And so on and so on. This is a wonderful path to go down for many years of discovery.

When you look at what food you are about to eat and think of what wine to pour with it, there are a couple of things to keep in mind. A good general rule, at least for the dishes in this book, is that if you prepare a recipe using a particular wine, then that is a safe wine to serve with it. The concept that red goes with meat and white with fish is not really true, especially in Friuli-Venezia Giulia, where whites go with many meats and either Refosco or Merlot is served with fish stews. Moreover, when you look at a dish, do not simply think meat or fish. Think about the flavoring of the food and not simply the principal ingredient. Among these flavorings may be fruit, vegetables, cheese, vinegar, oil, spices, or herbs. So gnocchi filled with plums and topped with cinnamon and melted butter will taste different if you serve a white Pinot Bianco, a red Schioppettino, or a sweet Verduzzo. All, I believe, are appropriate, but distinct. Each wine responds to different ingredients: cinnamon and butter with Pinot Bianco, plum and the gnocchi dough with the Schioppettino, plum and cinnamon with the Verduzzo. Therefore, I would not dictate to you which is the best, but encourage you to follow your instincts and preference.

The red wine / red meat pairing does have some validity, of course. The tannin in the wine blends with the protein in the meat, facilitating digestion. A light red wine can go with a substantial oily fish, such as swordfish or tuna, but would overwhelm a delicate white fish, such as trout or sole.

Vinegar, an important component in this region's cuisine, often presents a problem in wine pairing. This is not so much the case here for two reasons. One is that the vinegar used in Friuli-Venezia Giulia is usually less acidic. The second is that many wine makers produce vinegars from individual grapes. So a vinegar made with Tocai that is cooked with ham will have fat from the meat neutralize some of the acid in the vinegar. You can safely serve a glass of Tocai wine with it. If you are making a salad, either cut the vinegar with a little bit of water, or consider lemon juice instead of vinegar for the dressing. Light white wines that are not very acidic, such as Pinot Bianco, are a good match for salads dressed with oil and lemon juice.

You can play around with cheese and wine to your heart's delight. A crisp frico is an ideal match with Tocai. A runny melting frico goes well with medium-weight reds. Aged or ripe cheeses go well with big reds or, sometimes, with dessert wines, such as Verduzzo or Ramandolo. A granular cheese such as Parmigiano-Reggiano or very aged Montasio are nice with sparkling wines. Smoked ricotta, for me, is wonderful with Ribolla Gialla, but it also matches with numerous wines from this part of the world.

It is hard to generalize about spices because there are so many different types: Sharp, hot, aromatic, herbal, mild, floral are all adjectives one can apply to spices. Spicy wines such as Traminer, Müller Thurgau, and some Cabernet Franc and Syrah often go well with spices. Wines with pronounced fruit (Pinot Grigio, Pinot Bianco, Ribolla Gialla, Picolit, Verduzzo, Refosco, Pignolo, and some Merlot) also go well with some spices. Finally, more vegetal varieties (especially Cabernet Franc and Sauvignon Blanc) match with very aromatic spices such as nutmeg, clove, and ginger. Remember, when you attempt to match wines with spices, to observe what other ingredients are in a recipe. This will give you further insight into which wine to select.

$\mathcal{F}$inally, wine is first and foremost a source of pleasure, and it should be viewed that way. It can sometimes be defeated by the pomposity and unrelieved seriousness of those who describe it or sell it. People who competitively toss around statistics about sugars, yields, and good vintage years are about as interesting as sports fans who can tell you everything about a game but no longer take pleasure in watching one. So gather some friends and family, select yourself a nice bottle, and pour the wine into normal glasses. Admire it, swirl it, breathe it in, taste it, and let it slide down your throat as your mouth breaks into a smile. This is the secret to knowing and loving the wines of Friuli-Venezia Giulia.

A Few Words About Measurements in the Recipes

Because this book is intended for an international readership, measurements are indicated both in the sober metric system used in most of the world and in the archaic but charming ounces, cups, and pounds preferred in the United States of America and a few other places. Sharp-eyed readers will note that in some cases there are not exact translations of weight or volume from one system to the other. The reason is that I have presented what I call parallel recipes. In other words, if you stick to the U.S. system, the recipe will work; and if you use metric, it will also succeed. The total weight or size of the finished dish will be very nearly the same whichever measurement system you adopt. And, above all, the final product will *taste* as close as possible to the original preparation in Friuli-Venezia Giulia.

Stuzighet

There is not a long list of traditional appetizers (starters) in Friuli-Venezia Giulia. In a place that knew significant poverty as recently as the early 1960s, meals were one or two courses that provided necessary nourishment and staved off hunger. Appetizers connote an entirely different economic condition and approach to a meal. They require a longer time at table, and therefore those present can afford the time. They are served as a part of a meal in which flavors of food and wine are orchestrated by a knowing chef or host, and therefore where attention is paid by those who prepare and those who consume. This does not imply that the food will be fancy or necessarily expensive, but the presence of an appetizer signals a certain seriousness of purpose.

Nowadays, a meal in the region may have one, two, or even three appetizers, but they will only be small tastes. Most of the antipasti in this book were once whole courses, or whole meals. You will find numerous recipes in which I describe portion size as *up to* 4 or 6 servings. This is because as a main course a frittata or frico may serve 1 or 2 persons. But as an appetizer in a series of courses, a small tantalizing piece can be presented as one tasty step in a procession.

Large seafood preparations, such as those using scallops, shrimp, or mussels, may be given in small portions to please the palate and tease the diner. An example is one large, perfect sea scallop broiled in its shell with a drop of olive oil, and perhaps a hint of thyme or tarragon. It is often customary to make a portion of three of these as an appetizer and six as a main course. But at a meal in which you might be sampling many different dishes, three scallops are almost too much of a good thing. The one perfect scallop is like a passionate kiss from a lover who then goes to the other room to change into something more comfortable.

The most famous antipasto in the region, and one of the most prized anywhere, is

Friuli's own prosciutto di San Daniele. It is now possible to find it in most places, and you will never go wrong serving it at the start of your meal with a glass of Tocai.

Leftover polenta is useful for many appetizers, including Polenta Wedge with Prosciutto and Ricotta-Chive Sauce (page 218), Fried Polenta Squares with Anchovy (page 219), or Fried Polenta Cubes (page 220).

It is certainly possible to fashion a meal as a parade of appetizer-sized portions that are designed to show off the best qualities in one or more wines. In that case, you can use just about any recipe in this book and reduce the serving size.

The Secret of San Daniele

To most people the word *prosciutto* means the delectable air-cured ham that is produced in Langhirano, a town in the province of Parma in Emilia-Romagna. This ham typically goes by the simpler name of prosciutto di Parma. Langhirano sits on a high hill in such a way that it receives breezes from both the Tyrrhenian and Adriatic seas. This location, combined with clean local air, meticulous care of pigs from the moment they are born to when they are slaughtered, and careful curing and aging is what makes prosciutto di Parma an almost incomparable product.

I say *almost* because there are other air-cured hams in the world that are delectable. The Serrano ham from Spain deserves its growing respect. In Italy there are a couple of other prosciutti that are niche products: One is from Carpegna in the Marche and the other is an exquisite ham scented with fourteen herbs and spices and produced in small quantities in Valle d'Aosta.

And then there is prosciutto di San Daniele, a historically famous and prized ham from the town of San Daniele in the province of Udine. This ham, according to most experts, is in every way a rival to that of Parma. Each has its ardent defenders. In 1997, a typical year, San Daniele made 1,800,000 hams. This may sound like a lot until you consider that Parma produced 9 million hams.

In the simplest terms, there are only five elements required to make superb prosciutto: a pig, salt, air, time, and human intervention. The first three must be of the highest quality, the fourth is a constant, and the last is a combination of eye, nose, touch, and taste, plus education, sensitivity, and the gift of tradition.

A pig in Italian is called *un maiale* or, sometimes more crudely, *un porco*. This latter word is often combined with other terms to use scatologically. The word for the meat of a pig in Italian is also *maiale.* The word *prosciutto* comes from the verb *prosciugare,* which basically implies "to dry slowly," perhaps "to air-dry." Confusingly, there is *prosciutto cotto* and *prosciutto crudo. Cotto* is boiled ham, often made from pork butt or shoulder (called *spalla cotta*). Italian boiled ham, made in many regions but most notably in Emilia-Romagna and Friuli-Venezia Giulia, is one of the world's best, along with those of France, Poland, Denmark, Prague, and a few other places. Do not confuse it with baked ham, made well in many countries.

Prosciutto crudo sounds unappealing if translated literally into English, because *crudo* means "raw." It is made from the hind legs of pigs that are slaughtered at a minimum of nine months old to a maximum of eighteen months old. The average weight of the pig is about 170 kilos (374 pounds) and the leg weighs about 13 kilos (28.6 pounds). All these pigs must be virgins at their sacrifice to provide the most delicate meat. In fact, they are neutered when they are quite young so that their hormones, which would change flavor and texture, are not produced.

There are twenty-seven producers of prosciutto di San Daniele, all of whom have their plants just outside of town in a place where the air currents were once considered most favorable for the curing of the hams. The unique position and wonderful sweet air is one of the secrets to this product's uniqueness. Sweet air, it seems, leads to sweet ham. Remember, sea air flows to Parma from both directions, while it only comes to San Daniele from one—the Adriatic.

For most of its history, San Daniele thrived thanks to its hams. This was a free town under the Patriarchs of Aquileia, and it paid its taxes with prosciutto. When it fell under Venice in the sixteenth century, the Venetians used Friuli as an area of conquest and exploitation of resources. Yet San Daniele was able to preserve its independence by furnishing twenty hams to the doge each year. It also supplied ham to the Hungarian royal family and later to the Court in Vienna. In 1797, when Napoleon came to the region to sign an agreement ceding most of the territory to Austria, his general, Massena, was sent to occupy San Daniele and take the approximately two thousand hams that were there. In 1997 the people of the town considered sending a letter to French President Chirac seeking the return of two thousand hams.

People who raised their own pigs did not necessarily slaughter them. In the past a professional butcher would journey from town to town in the late autumn to do the job, called *purcitade* in Friulano. He would produce numerous cuts of pork and bacon, make salami, and leave one hind leg. The other would be taken as payment for his work. The legs would then be salted and cured and, if the weather conditions were favorable, the result would be prosciutto. Now that agriculture and climate-control technology permit production of prosciutto throughout the year, more hams are made than when it was a seasonal occurrence every fall.

It bears noting that every ham made in Parma and San Daniele is made from the leg of a pig born in Italy. As a nation with stringent food standards, Italy will not allow foreign pigs to be used for this purpose. In Italy it is strictly against the law to inject hormones or antibiotics into animals used for meat. Laws are not necessarily as strong in every other European nation and in North America, and Italians fear that as regulations in the European Union are standardized by bureaucrats in Brussels, there will be a decline in quality because inferior products from elsewhere will compete with the scrupulously cared-for Italian ones. It should be noted that many hams from elsewhere in Europe (especially the Netherlands and Germany) are sent to Italy for boiling, curing, or baking and then sent elsewhere in Europe. But an Italian-born pig used to make ham or other pork products in Italy is always labeled as such.

The actual process of making a prosciutto has changed little over the century. A newly butchered hind leg is weighed and then rubbed with sea salt. The standard rule is that the ham remains salted for 1 to 1½ days for each kilo of the total weight. Typically, the salt content in the finished product is about 5.5 percent, usually lower than in Parma ham. While the latter is not salty, per se, the higher percentage of salt in Parma makes the San Daniele ham seem sweeter in contrast.

After the ham is hand-salted, it is carefully cleaned to prepare it for its next phase. It is pressed into its form, resembling a mandolin. They refer to the shape as a *goccia* or *lacrima* (teardrop). This process enhances taste and delicacy as the fat merges better with the lean meat, making it more suitable for aging. After resting for 3 months (including a daily inspection), the hams are carefully washed and cleaned so they will be ready for at least 8 months of aging (also called seasoning). During the seasoning, the "ham masters" feel by hand the tenderness of the meat and the resilience of the surface. Then, they cover the surface with a natural lard and flour mixture to prevent the meat from drying up too quickly.

The hams hang in temperature- and humidity-controlled rooms that are cross-ventilated so that the historic tradition of curing the hams with San Daniele air is maintained. In Parma, hams can age for as little as 10 months and then be sold, while in San Daniele the minimum is 12 months and the average is 14. When the ham is thought to be ready, the ham master will puncture it in five places with a needle made of horse bone, which is thin and porous. If there is any suspect odor, the ham is examined for flaws and inevitably destroyed. If the smell is clean, fresh, and a bit spicy, then the ham is ready.

A major distinction between prosciutto di San Daniele and Parma ham is that the Friulian hams are made with the trotter left intact, while in Parma it is removed. In San

Daniele the belief is that by leaving the trotter on the leg, there is no cut or injury that can allow bacteria to enter the leg. The leg bone acts as a drain pump, removing extra water and permitting the ham to dry well. Many cooks in Friuli-Venezia Giulia use the bone to flavor soups. The point of view in Parma seems to be the opposite, believing that the hoof is unsanitary or perhaps unsightly. In Parma, they seal the site after the trotter is cut off.

Importation of Italian prosciutto to the United States was banned in the mid-1960s because, apparently, one Parma ham arrived infected. It took about thirty years for Italian prosciutto to gain readmittance, with Parma coming first and San Daniele following. The U.S. Department of Agriculture insists that prosciutto arrive without the hoof, on the theory that it has touched the ground and could be dirty. For this reason, San Daniele hams destined for the United States (and Japan, too) are preselected and receive different treatment for the four hundred days it usually takes for it to complete its curing and drying. The hoof is removed at slaughter and the hams are pressed in such a way that they maintain their shape; as they age, they hang in separate areas with little American or Japanese flags attached to them. The ham bone is removed before packaging, which is done with firm plastic bands so the distinctive shape is maintained. In 1998, thirty thousand hams were made for the American market. It is now found in most major American cities, especially on the coasts.

After all the effort to make this splendid product, it is important that you buy it sliced properly. In Italy, most stores that sell it know to slice it thin and only at the moment of purchase. In Germany, there is a tradition of slicing cold cuts before a store opens so that the customer does not have to wait. This makes the ham dry out, which ruins it. In France and America, the ham is usually sliced much too thick. As of 1998, San Daniele producers began to export vacuum-packed sliced prosciutto. This will never compare to freshly sliced prosciutto, but the thin, even slices in these packages are often more reliable than poorly handled prosciutto in your local market. The goal should be to have slices that are thin enough to almost see through, but still firm enough to twirl on a fork.

Store prosciutto slices in the refrigerator, tightly wrapped in waxed paper or foil covered with a plastic bag. The slices dry out when exposed to air, so keep them wrapped until the last possible moment. At its best, the ham, when sliced, seems a miraculous hybrid of flesh and silk. It can be used in many ways, but perhaps the most wonderful is to simply eat a slice of it while sipping a glass of Tocai. A marriage made in heaven, and in Friuli-Venezia Giulia. 🍇

Persut cui Fics

PROSCIUTTO DI SAN DANIELE WITH FRESH FIGS

SERVES 1

This is the antipasto of choice in Friuli in September, when figs are at their peak. After a summer of sunshine, the figs heat up as they hang on the trees. When freshly picked, a hot fig provides a degree of pleasure that makes one forget all other pleasures (and I mean all). You may serve this recipe as a nice appetizer. Double the portion for a decadent lunch. For more portions, simply multiply by the number of diners. Thin plain bread sticks go well here.

2 ounces / 60 g prosciutto di San Daniele, sliced paper thin
2 very ripe figs, green or black

Spread the slices of prosciutto on a pretty plate (preferably with a white or clear center), making sure not to place one slice atop another. Wash and dry the figs, cut lengthwise (top to bottom), and place them invitingly on the plate.

Eat by sticking a piece of prosciutto in your mouth with one hand, and then lift a fig half to your mouth with the other hand and suck out the pulp. Let the flavors mingle in your mouth at length before swallowing. Continue until you have eaten everything. Better still, have someone feed you.

WINE: Tocai

Mosaico di Sapori Nostrani

MOSAIC OF "OUR FLAVORS"

SERVES I
(MULTIPLY
QUANTITIES BY
NUMBER OF
PORTIONS)

Nostrano *is a particular Italian word. Very simply, it means "ours." Yet it implies much more: home, family, terrain, tradition. So* sapori nostrani, *in which the word is used in its plural form, would immediately suggest the comfort and intimacy derived from familiar flavors. I tasted this dish in Spilimbergo, one of Italy's foremost centers of the art of making mosaics. Many dishes there have that name even if they are more a combination of distinct ingredients that retain their characteristics rather than joining in a mosaic. This recipe uses most of the classic foods found in central Friuli .*

1 tablespoon / 15 g unsalted butter

5 slivers fresh garlic

4 ounces / 115 g funghi porcini, carefully cleaned and sliced thin

¼ teaspoon / 2 g minced fresh parsley

1 cup / 225 ml hot, soft, freshly made yellow polenta

2 thin slices prosciutto di San Daniele

2 ounces / 60 g fresh young Montasio cheese, sliced quite thin

Preheat oven to 350°F / 180°C.

Once all of the ingredients are at hand, melt the butter in a small frying pan. Add the garlic and swirl until the butter takes on the garlic fragrance. Add the mushrooms and saute actively just until they are soft and have yielded their liquid. Then toss in the parsley and remove the pan from the heat.

Pour the polenta into the middle of an ovenproof plate, forming a well in the middle. Line the well with the slices of prosciutto and then add the mushroom mixture. Cover this thoroughly with the slices of cheese and then place the dish in the oven. Bake for about 5 minutes, or just until the cheese has melted without burning.

WINE: Merlot, preferably from Grave

Buste di Radicchio Rosso con Petto di Oca Affumicato

SERVES 4

Here is an antipasto that inevitably pleases. I have had different versions of it throughout the region, but the common denominators are the red radicchio, a smoked or air-cured meat, and an outstanding vinegar as a finishing flavor. You have a fair degree of latitude in making variations on this dish, based on what meat you have available and which vinegar you select. If you are using smoked breast of either goose or duck, a superb vinegar made from a single red wine grape (Cabernet or Merlot, for example) works very well. Genuine balsamic vinegar is also perfect. If you are using bresaola or prosciutto di San Daniele, then a white wine vinegar (Pinot Bianco or Grigio, for example) or balsamic vinegar are best. Remember, what English-speakers call radicchio is red radicchio to Friulians, who also dote upon delicate green radicchio.

8 ounces / 225 g red radicchio, washed, separated into leaves

8 slices smoked goose or duck breast (or bresaola or prosciutto di San Daniele), sliced ¼ inch / .6 cm thick

Extra virgin olive oil

1 tablespoon / 15 g unsalted butter (optional)

5 or 6 juniper berries (optional)

2 tablespoons / 30 ml high-quality wine vinegar (or 1 teaspoon / 5 ml genuine balsamic vinegar)

Steam the radicchio leaves for 5 minutes. Divide them into 8 equal bundles. Fold the leaves in each bundle in half lengthwise and then stack them one on top of another, holding them with one hand so that the stack does not come undone. Take a piece of goose or duck breast (or bresaola or prosciutto) and wrap it entirely around the radicchio to form a packet. Stab a toothpick through so that the packet holds tight. Prepare 8 "envelopes."

Lightly grease a skillet with olive oil and place the pan over medium heat. If you are using prosciutto or a meat that does not have a high fat content, you may add some butter in addition to (or instead of) the olive oil. Add the 8 "envelopes" and give the pan a quick shake so that they do not stick. Return the pan to the heat and shake continuously for a minute or so. If you plan to use wine vinegar later on, add the juniper berries. If you are going to use balsamic vinegar, do not use the juniper berries. With a spatula, carefully flip over the "envelopes," and give the pan another shake.

Add the vinegar, turn up the heat to medium-high, and continue shaking the pan so the flavors are distributed and the "envelopes" do not stick. The dish is ready when the meat is somewhat transparent. Serve immediately, with a few drops of the vinegar sauce, but do not serve the juniper berries.

WINE: Tocai or Ribolla Gialla

Foie Gras al Picolit

FOIE GRAS FLAVORED WITH PICOLIT

SERVES 4

You might think that foie gras (fegato grasso, in Italian) might be too extravagant for a cuisine born largely of a peasant tradition. As it happens, the people of Friuli and, especially, Venezia Giulia, have always eaten a lot of roasted duck and goose, the livers of which go on to greater glory. This is, after all, a region that produces some of the most luscious plums in Europe, and these are fed to the ducks and geese. I have tasted this dish several times as an appetizer, but I believe that it works best as the final course (before dessert) of a sumptuous meal. There is not much I would want to eat after this dish with a glass of Picolit.

4 cups / about 1 l Polenta (page 209)

4 tablespoons / 60 g unsalted butter

8 ounces / 225 g terrine of pâté de foie gras, cut into 8 slices

⅓ cup / 80 ml Picolit

Prepare the polenta, using yellow cornmeal. Stir in 2 tablespoons / 30 g unsalted butter.

Melt the remaining butter over low heat in a broad, nonstick pan. Carefully add the pieces of foie gras and heat them by shaking the pan. After 15 seconds, carefully turn the pieces over using a spatula. Add the Picolit and cook about 1 minute at most.

Remove the pan from the heat. Quickly spoon the portions of polenta onto warm plates. Carefully place 2 pieces of foie gras on each bed of polenta, forcing the pieces of liver down slightly in the process. Evenly distribute the pan liquid over the 4 portions and serve immediately.

Eat this dish with deliberate slowness so that you can savor the flavors and the pairing with the wine.

WINE: Picolit

Capesante al Forno

BROILED SEA SCALLOPS

SERVES 1

Here is an easy and exquisite preparation that one finds all along the coastal areas of Friuli-Venezia Giulia and, to a lesser extent, in the Veneto. It is a classic appetizer. To successfully make it you must become friends with your fishmonger and ask him to find you sea scallops that are still in their shell. When you buy them whole in the shell, the flavor will be incredibly fresh. You will see the orange-colored roe (also called coral) in addition to the white scallop. Many Europeans eat both scallop and roe, while North Americans customarily consume only the scallop. If you manage to purchase scallops intact, eat everything. If it is not possible to find these, then buy the freshest scallops you can find and also buy scallop shells. Always keep the scallops as cold as possible (without freezing) until you are ready to use them. I have adapted this recipe from the delicious preparation served at Ristorante ai Campi di Marcello in Monfalcone. Typically, an appetizer portion has three scallops in their shells. Simply multiply this recipe by the number of portions, and remember the key is delicacy.

3 sea scallops, still in their shells (or 3 scallops placed in 3 shells)

Coarse sea salt

Freshly ground pepper (preferably white)

3 teaspoons / 15 ml white wine (Sauvignon Blanc, Pinot Grigio, or Pinot Bianco are preferred choices)

1½ teaspoons / 9 ml delicate extra virgin olive oil

Preheat your oven to broil or your broiler.

Carefully open each scallop. Sprinkle a *tiny* pinch of sea salt and a slightly larger amount of white pepper (use less pepper if it is black) over each.

Add 1 teaspoon / 5 ml white wine to each shell, pouring it down the side rather than over the scallop. Drizzle ½ teaspoon / 3 ml olive oil over the scallop and roe.

Place the shells in an ovenproof pan and place it under the broiler for 1½ minutes or for 2 minutes, if the scallops are quite large or if you have the roe as well. Remove from the broiler, place the shells on a plate, and serve immediately.

VARIATION: Sometimes I have seen the addition of the tiniest amount of torn fresh thyme leaves to the oil. This gives the scallop a nice flavor, but tends to mask the fresh briny flavor of the scallop.

WINE: Serve the same wine that you have used in cooking.

Capesante alle Mandorle

SCALLOPS WITH ALMONDS

SERVES 2 *This preparation from Trieste calls for scallops removed from their shells.*

2 tablespoons/30 g unsalted butter

1 teaspoon/5 g flour

2 teaspoons/10 g finely minced white onion

8 ounces/225 g sea scallops, washed, dried, and sliced in thin slivers

Small pinch fine sea salt

1 tablespoon/15 ml brandy or 1½ teaspoons/8 ml fine grappa

½ cup/120 ml light cream

3 tablespoons/45 g almond slivers

1 teaspoon/5 g finely minced fresh flat-leaf parsley

Melt 1 tablespoon/15 g butter in a heavy-bottomed skillet over very low heat. Roll the rest of the butter in the flour and set aside. Once the butter in the pan has melted, add the onion and gently sauté until it is soft. Add the slivers of scallop and salt. Add the brandy and, once it has evaporated, add the cream, almonds, and parsley.

Cook gently for 4 minutes over medium-low heat, and then add the floured butter. Cook for another 2 minutes, just until the sauce has thickened. Serve immediately in small hot bowls or ramekins.

WINE: Ribolla Gialla

File e Daspe

POTATOES IN A CHEESE SAUCE

SERVES 4, 2 AS

A MAIN COURSE

I learned this dish in Zuglio, in Carnia. It has all the hallmarks of food from that area: a mixture of egg and cheese, potatoes as a foundation, a dash of fresh herbs, and apple cider vinegar rather than one made from grapes. It is often served as an appetizer (this recipe would be for 4), but it can also be a more substantial course in a meal that has fruit and vegetables to balance it.

8 small potatoes, perhaps red bliss or waxy yellow

4 yolks from large eggs

10 ounces/300 g soft latteria or young Montasio cheese, cut into tiny cubes

Pinch freshly ground black pepper

Tiny pinch salt

4 tablespoons/60 ml apple cider vinegar

6 tablespoons/90 ml whole or partially skimmed milk

1 tablespoon/6 g minced fresh chives

Place the potatoes in a pot with cold water to cover. Bring to a boil and cook until the potatoes are tender.

While the potatoes are cooking, warm the serving plates and make the sauce. Combine the yolks, cheese, pepper, and salt in a bowl with a whisk. Add the vinegar and then the milk; beat until the ingredients are combined. Pour this mixture into a nonstick pan and place it over low heat. Cook, stirring continuously with the whisk, until the sauce is creamy. Do not let it boil.

Drain the potatoes and place 2 potatoes each on warmed serving plates. Split each potato in half. Spoon some sauce over them and sprinkle one-quarter of the chives on top to finish it. If this is a main course, divide the chives between 2 portions.

WINE: Sauvignon Blanc or Merlot

Salviade

SAGE FRITTERS

MAKES 25 TO 30

FRITTERS

Yolks from 3 large eggs (reserve the whites for another use)

4 tablespoons / 60 g sugar

6 ounces / 150 ml whole milk

3 tablespoons / 45 ml grappa

Freshly grated zest of ½ lemon

Approximately 10 tablespoons / 150 g unbleached all-purpose flour

Canola, corn, peanut, or delicate olive oil, for deep-frying

25 to 30 unblemished sage leaves

Sugar (optional)

Make a batter by combining the yolks and 4 tablespoons / 60 g sugar. Then add the milk, then the grappa, then the lemon zest. Stir with a wooden spoon and gradually add the flour until you achieve a consistency that is creamy and uniform. The amount of flour indicated is approximate, but your result should be a light- to medium-weight batter. Let it sit, covered, for at least 2, or up to 3, hours.

Using a wide deep pot, heat at least 3 inches / 7.5 cm of oil until hot but not smoky. Dip a few sage leaves in the batter, and then toss them in the oil. Each leaf should be fried until golden brown but not darker. Fish them out with a slotted spoon and drain briefly on paper towels.

Serve hot or warm. These can make a nice appetizer with Tocai, Sauvignon Blanc, or Traminer wine. To serve at the end of a meal, roll them in sugar (granulated—not confectioners'—sugar) and serve warm or at room temperature.

Točh e Cuince

It was the ancient Romans who probably first introduced sauces to Friuli-Venezia Giulia. For them, sauces were sometimes a means of imparting special flavors to a food (usually cooked meat), but otherwise were intended for preservation of foods. At the base of many of the sauces used to preserve food was salt, which the Romans prize highly to this day. The word *sale* is the root for many others in which salt is used: *salami, salsiccia* (sausage), and *salsa* (sauce). It also is linked to *insalata* (salad, or greens that are salted) and *salary* (salt being equivalent to currency). *Salsa,* the Italian word for sauce, clearly derives from salt, even if every sauce does not necessarily contain salt. Foods that are savory are thought to taste good, but what often gives them that savor is salt.

In the northern Adriatic, there is a tradition of preserving fish and other foods in a sauce called *savòr* in Trieste. It predates the similar *saòr* found in Venice. *Savòr* dates back to Roman sauces, such as *garum* and *agreste,* which had sour elements (such as vinegar or citrus juice) essential for preserving food.

Of course, these preserving sauces also taste good and are a part of the richness and diversity of a region's cuisine. But Friuli-Venezia Giulia, like much of the world, has also fashioned sauces that are meant strictly to impart certain flavors and to lend a creaminess to the various taste sensations one finds in a meal.

Sauces in this region are vehicles of the flavors of the land. Fresh herbs are often blended with dairy products such as ricotta, feta cheese, or yogurt. Horseradish is a ubiquitous flavor here and appears in many sauces, as well as appearing as a garnish when freshly grated. Spices also contribute to sauces, as do vegetables, fruit, wine, and vinegar. Coffee, another archetypal flavor in this region, gets a sauce of its own.

One distinction between sauces from Friuli and Venezia Giulia is that the former often used lard, while the latter used olive oil. It should be said, of course, that lard was also used in Venezia Giulia, but more for cooking. Nowadays, butter is often substituted for lard, and that is what I have done for the lard-based sauces presented in this chapter. In Carnia it has long been traditional to use *ont,* which is clarified butter that has been allowed to harden and then is stored in a cool place, but now regular butter is used more. If you wish to substitute *ont* in recipes from Carnia, feel free to do so.

In almost all cases you should make sauces just before you use them so that they will retain their lively flavor. The only exception is prepared horseradish, which is really a condiment more than a sauce.

Horseradish Sauces

Horseradish is a cardinal flavor throughout Friuli-Venezia Giulia. It is another example of a food that is dismissively said (by some Italians and friends of Italy) to be of Germanic importation. In fact, horseradish has always been in this ground no matter what nationality of person was above it. It was very popular in the cooking of ancient Rome, where it was often used with pork. While it was forgotten in most of Italy, it never left Trieste, where it was paired with ham baked in bread and with the boiled pork that is the forerunner of the Triestine buffet. By the way, both of the aforementioned pork dishes are of Roman, not Germanic, origin.

Part of the confusion about horseradish is its name in this multilingual region. *Cren* is the word most used in Friuli-Venezia Giulia, although the Italian word, *rafano,* is sometimes used. In German it is *Meerrettich,* although in parts of southern Austria it is called *Kren.* The Italian word is close to the French one, *raifort,* and in parts of the region where France ruled I have heard the strange word *raiforte.* In France it is popular to combine horseradish with oysters and other seafood and fish. Whether the combination of scallops and horseradish found by the Adriatic is in any way related is hard to tell.

The nostril-opening fragrance of horseradish is hot and spicy, and its flavor becomes addictive by the third time you taste it. When available fresh, it is grated like large flakes of snow next to boiled meats, especially ham. It is an inevitable condiment in Triestine buffets, and is often stirred into ricotta or other soft cheeses to give zip. A teaspoon in boiled carrots is a pleasant combination, and it is a perfect match when tossed with sliced cooked beets. Fresh horseradish is also turned into what is called a sauce, but might also be referred to as pickled or prepared horseradish. This is available for purchase in many stores around the world, but it is typically made with horseradish that is too finely minced or chopped, so that the ratio of vinegar to horseradish is too high. In Friuli-Venezia Giulia, the horseradish is grated more coarsely, as a carrot might be, so that it and not the vinegar dominates. When stored in a sterilized mason or other jar, it can last unopened for about 4 months in a cold part of the refrigerator.

A word about handling horseradish: Once you have touched it, be sure to wash your hands thoroughly before touching your eyes, or you will be in for a very unpleasant reaction. ❦

Salsa di Cren

PREPARED HORSERADISH SAUCE

If you want to make your own prepared horseradish rather than relying on a store-bought variety, this is how to do it.

Select a jar or jars with tight-fitting lids. I recommend that you use several small jars, because once opened the horseradish is quite perishable. Sterilize the jars by boiling in water to cover for 10 minutes. Grate the horseradish into a bowl and then pack it rather tightly into the jars, leaving a little space at the top. Pour in white wine vinegar and, as it seeps into the horseradish, add more. Continue until the vinegar reaches the same level as the grated horseradish. Close tightly and refrigerate. If unopened, this prepared horse-radish will last about 4 months. Once opened, it should be consumed within 30 days.

VARIATION: Some people like to add sugar to this sauce. Use it sparingly if you choose to, stirring it into the first batch of vinegar you add.

Salsa Calda di Cren

WARM HORSERADISH SAUCE

This is milder than the previous recipe, but still imparts the special taste.

2 tablespoons / 30 g unsalted butter

1 tablespoon / 15 g unflavored dry bread crumbs

½ cup / 120 g freshly grated horseradish (see Note)

2 teaspoons / 10 g sugar

¼ cup / 60 ml vegetable or chicken broth, or diluted apple juice

½ cup / 120 ml heavy cream, or ¼ cup / 60 ml sour cream

Melt the butter in a small pan over medium heat and add the bread crumbs. Cook gently for 3 to 4 minutes, stirring often, until the crumbs are golden brown. Add the horseradish and stir well. Add the sugar and stir again until the ingredients are combined. Add the broth (or juice) and bring to a boil. Stir in the cream or sour cream, lower the heat, and bring to a simmer. Stir continuously for 2 minutes. Serve hot or warm.

NOTE: If fresh horseradish is unavailable, use 2 tablespoons / 30 g prepared horseradish, thoroughly drained.

Salsa di Cren e Meluz

HORSERADISH-APPLE SAUCE

This sauce is a bit different from others in that the horseradish should be finely grated, with the result that the sauce is creamy rather than coarse. Use it as you would other horseradish sauces. The proportions as indicated make a small amount. If you wish to make more, then you should use the proportion of 1 horseradish root (about 4 ounces / 115 g) to 1 medium apple and about 3 tablespoons / 45 ml white vinegar.

3 tablespoons / 45 g finely grated fresh horseradish

3 tablespoons / 45 g finely grated peeled green apple

1 tablespoon / 15 ml white wine vinegar or apple cider vinegar

Combine the horseradish and apple in a bowl and pour in the vinegar. Use a spoon to vigorously stir the sauce until it becomes creamy and uniform. Then taste. If it is too vinegary, add a little more apple. If it is too mild, add a little more horseradish.

Salsa di Cren all' Arancio

HORSERADISH-ORANGE SAUCE

MAKES ABOUT

I CUP / 250 ML

This somewhat exotic sauce is wonderful with roasted goose or duck, or with the grilled breasts or sautéed livers of these birds.

2 medium juicy oranges
¾ cup / 175 ml white wine, such as Tocai or Pinot Bianco
½ teaspoon / 2.5 g ground cinnamon
1 tablespoon / 15 g sugar
3 tablespoons / 45 g freshly grated horseradish (see Note)
Pinch salt

Squeeze the juice from the oranges and reserve. Grate about 2 tablespoons / 30 g orange zest and combine it in a saucepan with the wine. Heat gently over low heat for about 1 minute. Add the orange juice, cinnamon, and sugar, and heat for 1 minute. Add the horseradish and salt and cook, stirring, for about 5 minutes, until the sauce is somewhat concentrated. Serve hot, warm, tepid, or cold.

NOTE: If fresh horseradish is unavailable, use 2 tablespoons / 30 g prepared horseradish that has been completely drained.

Salsa di Ûe Ribis

RED CURRANT SAUCE

This is a popular sauce throughout the region because it lends sweetness as a garnish to certain meats. It is often served in tandem with horseradish sauce. Together, they are wonderful with hot baked or boiled ham, or with slices of prosciutto made from game.

1 pound / 450 g red currants

¾ cup / 175 ml red wine

2 tablespoons / 30 ml red wine vinegar

2 tablespoons / 30 g sugar

Freshly grated zest of ½ lemon

Pinch salt

Combine the currants, wine, vinegar, sugar, lemon zest, and salt in a saucepan. Simmer, stirring constantly, until the sauce thickens and reduces by half. The cooking time will depend on the thickness of the currants you use. Serve hot, tepid, or cool.

Salsa di Mela Verde e Basilico

GREEN APPLE–BASIL SAUCE

MAKES ABOUT

1 CUP / 225 ML

This versatile sauce from Carnia pairs well with ricotta cheese, with grilled or roasted pork, or with pastries such as Friulian Apple Cake (page 334). It is more a relish than a sauce. Traditionally it is made in a food mill, but you may use a blender or food processor so long as you pulse rather than puree it. If you liquefy the ingredients, the sauce will lack the texture it needs.

2 green apples, such as Granny Smith, peeled and cored

6 large or 10 small basil leaves

Juice of 1 large lemon

5 tablespoons / 75 g confectioners' sugar

If you are using a food mill, pass the apples and basil together through it and into a bowl containing the lemon juice. The texture should be slushy. Stir in the sugar and refrigerate until you are ready to serve it.

If you are using a processor or blender, combine the apples, basil, lemon juice, and sugar. Pulse until the mixture is slushy. Refrigerate until needed.

If you are thinking of using this as a dessert sauce, it is a nice idea to freeze the sauce for about 10 minutes to make it a cold slush.

Salsa Haivar

HAIVAR SAUCE

This sauce, presumably of Slavic origin but very possibly Turkish, is found up and down the length of the Carso and is the ideal accompaniment for cevapcici, pljescavica, and other patties made of ground meat. In the past it was made by dicing the vegetables and passing them through a food mill, which you may do, but it is also fine when made in a blender or food processor. This recipe is made with either red or green sweet peppers—I prefer red.

Olive oil

1 small eggplant, cut into small chunks

2 large bell peppers, cored, seeded, and cut into thick strips

2 garlic cloves, split

1 to 2 teaspoons / 5 to 10 ml freshly squeezed lemon juice

After dicing the eggplant, sauté the chunks in a skillet containing a thin layer of hot olive oil. Then drain the eggplant and let cool.

If you are using a blender or food processor, combine the peppers, garlic, eggplant, and lemon juice. Pulse until the sauce is pulpy and thick. You should be able to spread it with a spoon or butter knife. If you are using a food mill, pass the peppers, garlic, and eggplant through together and then combine them in a bowl, stirring in the lemon juice.

VARIATION: If you roast the vegetables and then cool them before making the sauce, it will have a slightly smoky flavor.

Squazeto

RICH MEAT GRAVY

MAKES ABOUT

1 CUP / 225 ML

Do not confuse this sauce with the veal stew on page 258. Sguazeto is an all-purpose term used in the region (but especially in Venezia Giulia) for any meat sauce that is enhanced with pine nuts, spices, and prunes. You may use pan juices or stewing liquid from beef, veal, pork, lamb, goose, duck, rabbit, kid, or venison to make this sauce. The quantities in this recipe are for 1 cup of pan juices. Multiply the quantities by the number of cups you are using.

2 prunes, pitted (or substitute 1 tablespoon / 15 ml prune lekvar or apricot butter)

1 heaping tablespoon / 18 g pine nuts

1 scant teaspoon / 4 g sugar

½ teaspoon / 1 g ground cumin

1 cup / 225 ml pan juices

Soak the prunes in warm water until softened, about 30 minutes. Drain.

Combine the pine nuts, sugar, and cumin in a mortar and pound with a pestle until you have a fine powder. Transfer this powder to a small saucepan. Pound the prunes in the mortar until they form a nice pulp. Transfer the pulp to the saucepan, add the juices, and cook gently over low heat, stirring often until the sauce just reaches a boil.

Salsa Triestina

TRIESTINE SAUCE

MAKES ABOUT

2 CUPS / 500 ML

This is a particular preparation I found in Trieste that goes well on salads as a dressing, but also works beautifully with boiled beef or roasted pork. Also try it on boiled potatoes, broccoli, cauliflower, or carrots, or any vegetable that you think it will flatter. This sauce is light enough for even the most delicate of greens.

The use of feta cheese is due to the long presence of Greeks in Trieste. Many of them are Jews, and feta figures prominently in the cooking of Triestine Jews for that reason.

This is a recipe that relies heavily on your own preferences and the qualities of the ingredients you have at hand. If the feta cheese is dense, you will need more liquid to soften it. If it is soft, you will need less. If the cheese is tangy, then use less lemon juice. If it is bland, use more lemon juice. The addition of oil is up to you. I aim to have this sauce sing with lemons and feta, and oil is only a minor note. So you must taste the feta and lemon juice before proceeding.

8 ounces / 225 g fresh feta cheese

Juice of 1 to 2 large lemons, preferably a sweet perfumed lemon such as Meyer

1 teaspoon / 2 g poppy seeds, crushed in a mortar

Delicate extra virgin olive oil or other pure vegetable oil

In a glass jar, combine the cheese, lemon juice, and poppy seeds and shake vigorously to combine. Then add a little bit of oil, just enough to give the sauce a silky texture. The sauce should be creamy and runny rather than thick. To make it thinner, add a little more lemon juice. Shake again and serve.

NOTE: I like this sauce without lumps of cheese. To accomplish this, I pour the shaken sauce into a bowl and then use a whisk to beat the sauce until smooth.

Toc' di Vòres

RICOTTA SAUCE

MAKES ABOUT

I CUP / 225 ML

This is a sauce of very humble origins and every Friulian is familiar with it. It is the food that women in Carnia who worked in the fields would have for their daily lunch as they took a break from their labors. The sauce would be served atop a bowl of soft polenta. This recipe would be enough for 2 servings of polenta.

1 tablespoon / 15 g unsalted butter

4 tablespoons / 60 g grated smoked ricotta

1 tablespoon / 15 g coarsely ground polenta or cornmeal

¾ cup / 150 ml whole milk

Small pinch salt

Melt the butter in the top of a double boiler over simmering water. Add the ricotta and let it heat without stirring. It should toast somewhat. Sprinkle the polenta over the cheese and leave for 1 minute. Add the milk and salt and stir gently and continuously until everything melts and the sauce thickens slightly. Spoon over hot soft polenta and serve immediately.

Salsa di Yogurt e Aneto

YOGURT-DILL SAUCE

MAKES ABOUT

1½ CUPS / 350 ML

The sauce will be more interesting if you use a very tangy yogurt instead of a bland commercial one. If you live near a Greek grocery that sells imported yogurt, buy it there. Serve with meat patties, as a salad dressing, or tossed with cold chicken or turkey chunks.

4 to 5 ounces / 125 g yogurt

1 to 2 teaspoons / 5 to 10 g paprika

Pinch salt

1 teaspoon / 5 g freshly grated lemon zest

2 tablespoons / 30 g fresh dill leaves

2 to 3 tablespoons / 30 to 45 ml extra virgin olive oil

Pour the yogurt into a mixing bowl. Add the paprika and salt and beat with a whisk. Add the lemon zest and beat. Then add the dill and beat to make the sauce creamier. Add 1 tablespoon / 15 ml oil and beat. Repeat with a second tablespoon / 15 ml. Then taste. If the sauce is to your liking, beat a little more and then serve. If you want it more velvety, beat in the third tablespoon / 15 ml of oil. Serve immediately.

Toc cun Scueta (ed Erba Cipollina)

RICOTTA-CHIVE SAUCE

MAKES ABOUT
2 CUPS / 500 ML
(ENOUGH FOR
1½ POUNDS / 675 G
GNOCCHI)

This delicious and delicate sauce is lovely with plain gnocchi or stirred into soft polenta. A nice antipasto is lightly grilled bricks of leftover polenta draped with prosciutto di San Daniele and topped with this sauce (see page 218).

8 ounces / 225 g fresh ricotta

1 cup / 225 ml whole milk

3 heaping tablespoons / 50 g minced fresh chives

1 teaspoon / 5 g freshly ground black pepper

Combine the ricotta and milk in the top of a simmering double boiler for 20 minutes, always cooking gently. Never let the sauce approach a boil. Stir in the chives and pepper. Heat for 2 minutes. Serve the sauce immediately with gnocchi or pasta.

Toc cui Capârs

CAPER SAUCE

MAKES ABOUT

2 CUPS / 500 ML

Use this sauce to accompany roasted or boiled meats or for boiled, poached, or grilled freshwater fish. Capers can be found a little bit in Istria and the Carso, but most of them came to Trieste by importation and then headed to Vienna. People in Friuli tasted them along the way and added them to the local repertoire of sauces. Notice the presence of herbs and spices that you would never see in caper sauces from other places.

1 tablespoon / 15 g unsalted butter

1 tablespoon / 15 ml delicate olive oil or seed oil

2 tablespoons / 30 g minced onion

1 tablespoon / 15 g unbleached all-purpose flour

2 tablespoons / 30 ml delicate red wine vinegar (dilute, if necessary; see page 00)

2 tablespoons / 30 g salt-packed capers, rinsed

½ teaspoon / 2.5 g ground cinnamon

¼ teaspoon / 1.25 g freshly ground nutmeg

½ teaspoon / 2.5 g minced fresh thyme

½ teaspoon / 2.5 g freshly grated lemon zest

⅓ cup / 100 ml broth (beef or vegetable)

Gently heat the butter and oil together in a small saucepan. Add the onion and cook until it softens and gives off a fragrance. Stir in the flour and heat for about 15 seconds. Remove from the heat and stir in the vinegar.

Add the capers, cinnamon, nutmeg, thyme, and lemon zest and stir. Then pour in the broth and return to the low heat. Cook until the sauce begins to concentrate and thicken.

Serve hot, tepid, or cold.

Pestât Furlan

FRIULIAN SEASONED BUTTER

MAKES

I CUP / 250 G

I have taken liberties with this condiment in anticipation that you would do the same. Traditionally this is made in early winter at the time that hogs are slaughtered. The lard is reserved and seasonings are blended in. It is then kept in a cold place (pre-refrigeration it was kept outside) and used as needed. The primary use was as a cooking medium for making risotto or to flavor soups or polenta. I also use this butter to make omelets and scrambled eggs. It is also used to rub on meats to give them tenderness and flavor before roasting. If you have excellent fresh pork fat available to you, then use it. Otherwise, opt for butter and store the finished product in an airtight container in a cold part of the refrigerator, far away from anything else fragrant.

1 small carrot, finely grated

2 fresh sage leaves, torn into tiny bits

1 teaspoon / 4 g fresh rosemary needles, crushed

1 teaspoon / 4 g minced fresh chives

1 teaspoon / 4 g minced fresh parsley

1 teaspoon / 4 g fine sea salt

1 teaspoon / 4 g freshly ground black pepper

½ teaspoon / 2 g rose or sweet paprika

½ cup / 1 stick / 115 g whipped unsalted butter (or fresh pork fat)

Combine the carrot, sage, rosemary, chives, parsley, salt, pepper, and paprika in a glass bowl and mix well. In a larger glass bowl, soften the butter with a wooden spoon or plastic spatula. Then add the seasonings and fold in until the butter and flavorings are well amalgamated. Taste for intensity. If you find that it is too strong, fold in more butter.

Store in an airtight container in the coldest part of your refrigerator for up to 30 days.

Salsa di Senape e Vino Cabernet

MUSTARD-WINE SAUCE

I tasted this sauce in the Isonzo area of Venezia Giulia. It is very nice with boiled meats or roasted game, especially venison. The preferred wine is Cabernet Franc, though you may use Cabernet Sauvignon as well.

3 heaping tablespoons / 50 g dry mustard powder

3½ ounces / 100 g sugar

½ cup / 100 ml Cabernet Franc or Cabernet Sauvignon

½ cup / 100 ml red wine vinegar

5 tablespoons / 90 g high-quality tomato paste

Stir all of the ingredients together in a bowl until the combination is creamy and even. Use a whisk if you wish.

WINE: Serve the wine that you used to make the sauce.

Salsa de Pomidoro co' la Sivola

ISTRIAN TOMATO-ONION SAUCE

MAKES ABOUT

3 CUPS / 750 ML

You may use this sauce to dress pasta, but in Istria it is cooked until thick and becomes a sauce for boiled meats. It is so tasty and basic that you will probably find your own uses for it.

3 garlic cloves, with green heart removed, cut into slivers

1 tablespoon / 7 g minced fresh parsley

Pinch sea salt

Extra virgin olive oil

4 large white or yellow onions, cut into paper-thin slices

2¼ pounds / 1 kg plum tomatoes, peeled and coarsely chopped

An easy way to peel tomatoes is to drop them into boiling water for 30 seconds and then lift them out with a slotted spoon. The skins should slip off easily. Once you have prepared all of the ingredients, combine the garlic and parsley in a dish with the salt.

Pour a few drops of olive oil into a large casserole or saucepan with a broad bottom, and swirl them around. Then arrange a layer of onions in the pan. Top with a thin layer of chopped tomatoes. Then toss on a bit of the garlic-parsley-salt mixture. Add a few drops of oil, then onions, and continue the layering process until all the ingredients are used up.

Cover and cook over medium heat for 20 minutes. The result should be thick and rather sweet. Remove from the heat and stir just so that the ingredients combine but do not break.

Serve hot as a pasta sauce, or serve hot, tepid, or cool as a sauce with meat.

Salsa di Montasio e Menta

MONTASIO-MINT SAUCE

MAKES ABOUT

2 CUPS / 450 ML

An elemental sauce with the flavors of Carnia. If you wish to use this as a pasta sauce, rigatoni or penne are your best bets. This sauce is enough for 1–1½ pounds / 450–675 g of uncooked pasta. To serve with polenta, use soft polenta and add the sauce. Another possibility is to grill a brick of leftover polenta and then pour the hot sauce on top.

1 tablespoon / 15 g unsalted butter

1 pound / 450 g young Montasio cheese, cut into small cubes

2 tablespoons / 20 g fresh mint leaves, wiped clean with paper towels and torn into tiny pieces

1 teaspoon / 5 ml apple cider or white wine vinegar

In the top of a double boiler over simmering water, melt the butter. Add the cubes of Montasio and, on top, the mint. Cover the pot and cook gently for 5 minutes. Remove the lid and stir as the cheese melts thoroughly. Once it forms long strings when tugged with a wooden spoon, add the vinegar and stir vigorously until the sauce is creamy. If you think the sauce is still too thick, add a little more vinegar and stir vigorously.

To serve with pasta, add the cooked pasta to the sauce, toss, and serve. To serve with polenta, spoon the polenta into individual bowls, form a well in the middle of each, and pour in the sauce.

WINE: A medium to robust red is perfect.

Salsa di Caffè

COFFEE SAUCE

With coffee a touchstone flavor of Friuli-Venezia Giulia, one finds versions of this sauce throughout the region. It goes beautifully with ice cream, but I also like to pour some onto a plate before setting a piece of sponge cake, chocolate cake, gubana, or pinza on top of it. Once, in Lignano, I had an unusual dish that did work well, but it raises culinary eyebrows because it is really far afield from classical combinations and would taste dreadful unless made by the most accomplished chef: roasted cod with a small amount of coffee sauce beneath it. The vanilla flavor in the sauce came forth and worked well with the snowy white flesh of the cod.

1 cup / 250 ml whole milk

⅔ teaspoon / 3 ml vanilla extract or ½ vanilla pod

8 large egg yolks (reserve the whites for other uses)

3½ ounces / 100 g sugar

4 ounces / 1¼ cups / 115 g fresh, fragrant Italian espresso beans

Combine 1 cup / 250 ml cold water (preferably spring or distilled), the milk, and vanilla in a saucepan and heat just to a low simmer. If you are using a vanilla pod, break it up in the liquid. Once this is done, let cool.

Using a whisk, beat the eggs and sugar in a glass or metal bowl until you have a smooth creamy texture. Add about ¼ cup / 60 ml of the vanilla mixture to the egg mixture and beat just until everything is combined. Pour this into the saucepan with the vanilla mixture and return to low heat. Stir with a wooden spoon until it is thick enough to adhere to the spoon. Add the espresso beans.

Remove from heat and let cool, stirring every so often to prevent the sauce from sticking to the pan. Strain the sauce to eliminate the coffee beans. You may use this sauce immediately at room temperature. Otherwise, refrigerate it in a tightly sealed jar or container until it is needed. Do not keep for more than 24 hours.

WINE: A small glass of Verduzzo dessert wine usually goes well.

Ûs e Formadi

EGGS AND CHEESE

Cheese and eggs are fundamental building blocks of Friuli-Venezia Giulia's cookery. The reason should be obvious. Poor families with one cow and a few hens could not afford to slaughter these beasts. So milk and cheese and eggs became the chief sources of protein.

Because of the seemingly boundless resourcefulness of the local women, these humble ingredients were used in many ways to create dishes that pleased the nose and mouth before filling the stomach. The recipes in this chapter (along with most of the soup, pasta, grain, vegetable, and fruit chapters) will be ideal for a reader who is an ovo-lacto vegetarian.

Eggs present an almost infinite range of possibilities for the resourceful cook. As Balzac said, "If one truffle falls onto my plate, that will suffice. It is the egg which immediately hatches ten characters for my 'Comédie Humaine.'" The most famous egg preparation in Friuli-Venezia Giulia is *fritàe* or *fertae* (frittata), a filled omelet that can be served hot, tepid, or cold. In Trieste, eggs are called *ovi,* and dishes that use them go by that name. Frico, melted Montasio cheese brought to greater glory, is Friuli's most famous cheese dish. The fascination of frico and frittata comes in how they are prepared and, often, in what ingredients they are filled with. The choices are almost endless, but include ham, potatoes, onions, shrimp, asparagus, mountain herbs, apples, pears, mussels, berries, zucchini, mushrooms, and even hops.

Typically, hens in Friuli-Venezia Giulia are free range and dine on a wider variety of fare than mere chicken feed. Their egg yolks are an orange-red and incredibly fresh and flavorful. North American eggs are larger than those in Italy, and are indicated by size (medium, large, extra large, jumbo). Italian eggs are more or less equivalent to large eggs in the New World.

*M*ontasio cheese, the foundation of frico, is now the name of a delicious, if generic, cow's milk cheese that is produced at various large cooperative dairies around the region, but especially at Campoformido, near Udine. The way you distinguish Montasio is by its age. At cheese stores in Udine, little signs indicate whether it is *fresco* (young: about 30 days old), *semi-stagionato* (semi-aged: about 90 days), or *stagionato* (aged: up to 18 months). In its youth, Montasio is buttery and creamy and melts very easily. This is the ideal cheese to make a runny *frico fondente*. Semi-aged Montasio also melts well, but when cooked can form a crisp crust. This is the preferred cheese for a frico that will be filled. Finally, the very well-aged cheese is granular (it makes for great snacking) and must be grated to use for the crunchy *frico croccante*.

It is not necessarily easy to determine how old a soft Montasio might be. If it smells milky, then it is quite young. If there is a bit of a tang in the fragrance and taste, it is probably semi-aged, the cheese you are most likely to see in North American, British, and Australian markets. If you have a relationship with a caring cheesemonger, he or she can probably order cheese of a specific age for you. This can be encouraged if you give your cheesemonger a frico recipe from this book so that he or she will know what Montasio is used for.

Montasio is a good standard product that I can heartily endorse, but it is only the tip of the Friulian cheese wedge. Things get confusing after this because, unlike most cheese-producing areas, Friuli has very few names for its product. The generic word wherever you go is *latteria*. In pure Italian this means dairy and the word for cheese is *formaggio*. In Friuli latteria practically means cheese, although the Friulian word for cheese is *formadi*. The latteria, always made of cow's milk, is different from one producer to the next. This is part of the fascination. The cheese from Buttrio might be granular and forward in taste, while that of nearby Cividale might be smoother and less assertive. As I have wandered from town to town, I have found that each has a very different cheese with the identical name of latteria. The distinction, therefore, is made by where it is from.

I am sad to report that the Consortium of Montasio producers in Campoformido has tried to curb the production of these local latteria cheeses. Its standard Montasio cheese is being marketed as Friuli's cheese. It is delicious and perfect for most frico preparations, but I would never want to be forced to live on only one cheese. So I encourage you, when you visit a *baita* (cheese shop) in Friuli and Venezia Giulia to ask for different types of latteria cheese so that you will support the work of small, independent producers. And if you find one you really adore, get the name and address of the cheesemaker and bring it to your cheesemonger at home.

The Carnia Alps of upper Friuli is the ideal summer grazing area for cattle, and some of the region's most tasty, complex cheese is produced here. In springtime, the cows feast on the first mountain herbs that push through melting snow. Then they spend a couple of months eating fresh grass. The fragrant, tangy result invariably is more intriguing than cheese produced from cows who dine on hay.

In the highest reaches of Carnia the cattle spend the cold months in sheds, and adjacent to them is the *malga*. Here is another tradition that a few Friuliani are bravely attempting to preserve. The *malga* is where cheese is handmade each day by the cowherd. This is hard, lonely work, and the winters are long. Few young people have embraced this tradition, so it will only continue if city people of a certain age decide to go back to the land.

There are two principal cheeses in Carnia: latteria (and the range that that implies) and ricotta. We tend to think of ricotta as a cheese of Rome and Southern Italy, but this fresh soft cheese has been standard in Carnia and central Europe since ancient times. In German it is called *topfen* and, when lightly sugared, is the cheese filling in strudel and other pastries.

Ri-cotta, in Italian, means twice-cooked. This cheese is the milky liquid (a by-product of cheese making that is left after production of latteria) that is heated again, with the addition of an acidulated whey (locally called *siz*). This was done by placing the whey in a jug near a fire and dipping in a wine-soaked piece of bread. The heat causes fermentation of the whey so that it can then be used to make ricotta. *Siz* was also used as a dressing for cooked greens.

The cheese (which also contains water and salt) is then hung in canvas sacks so that extra liquid seeps out. The result is a soft, creamy cheese that is sensational when warm and is also delicious served cool or cold if it is very fresh. The Friulian word for ricotta is *scuete* (SHOO-et-eh) and this is how it will be indicated in smaller towns in the region. Ricotta is used for eating plain, as part of a pasta filling, as a sauce for polenta or pasta, and in many desserts. To make ricotta a little more fluffy, Friulians often whip in just a little bit of sweet cream or egg white before using it in a recipe. You may do this in many of the preparations in this book that call for ricotta.

One of the great delicacies of the region is *ricotta affumicata,* or smoked ricotta. This was probably created because the cowherd in the *malga* had more ricotta each day than he knew what to do with. In a corner of most *malgas* is a hearth where food is cooked and warmth is found. Some enterprising cheesemaker must have once placed his rounds of ricotta above the flames, and the smoke preserved the cheese.

When ricotta is smoked it takes on an ocher or burnt-orange exterior with a gray-beige interior. *Ricotta affumicata* is an exquisite grating cheese that pairs perfectly with many foods, but especially pumpkin and squash. Until trade and more cash on hand fostered the arrival of Parmigiano-Reggiano and Pecorino Romano, the grating cheeses of Friuli-Venezia Giulia were *ricotta affumicata* and aged Montasio. Both are gradually finding their way outside the region to good cheese shops elsewhere, and this demand has created work for men in the *malgas* and is helping to hold together the somewhat threadbare social fabric of Carnia. Smoked ricotta, when vacuum-packed, can keep for quite a while, and travels well. If a recipe calls for smoked ricotta and you absolutely cannot locate it, then use half the amount of Pecorino Romano.

In the Val Canale, the strikingly beautiful Alpine area that surrounds Tarvisio, there is a cheese called *sasaka*. It is a sort of acidulated ricotta that is an example of this region's taste for sweet and acidic together (you find this taste in pasta fillings, in the combination of pork and vinegar, and many other examples). If you have a recipe in which you want a bit of tanginess in your sweet ricotta, you can approximate *sasaka* by stirring a little bit of apple cider vinegar into your cheese before using it.

The only significant non–cow's milk cheese in the region is the feta cheese found in Trieste. This is typically made with sheep's or goat's milk, or a combination of both. Feta cheese is known throughout the world and is easily found. The tradition of eating feta in Trieste probably came with the arrival of Jews from Corfu, who are a prominent part of the Jewish community in the city. It is eaten on its own, can be folded into crêpes (Palacinche, see page 332) as a savory dish, or used in a sauce (Salsa Triestina, page 124).

A Visit to a Malga in Carnia

In the Friulian language, the word for cheesemaker is *fedâr*. I have tried to do some etymological research on this word, which does not seem to have any roots in words relating to milk or cheese. It does, however, link to the family of words that suggest faith, and that is the best way to consider the difficult work of the few people who continue the tradition of producing cheeses by hand in faraway places, high up in mountain pastures, where dairy cattle graze on fresh grass and herbs in the late spring and summer.

The *fedâr* who works in a *malga* is a dying breed in Friuli. The *malga* is the small building situated in the remote areas where cattle roam. The cheeses he or she makes are distinct for at least three reasons. First, the cheesemaking commences the moment the cow is milked. There is no fresher milk than this. The milk itself reflects the land on which the cow has grazed. It will taste of that place, with its particular soil, grass, herbs, and air, making it more distinct than the milk drawn from a cow who dines on hay. Finally, the eye, nose, and hand of the cheesemaker combine to make this cheese unique. This is hard, lonely work, and as the public comes to accept generic, mass-produced cheeses, these individualistic cheeses, which necessarily command higher prices, are less sought.

The tradition of the *malga* continues in the remotest parts of alpine northern Italy, from Friuli in the east, through the Veneto, Alto Adige, Trentino (the region with the greatest number of *malga* cheeses), to Lombardy, Piedmont, and Valle d'Aosta. In most of these areas, however, cheesemaking is dominated by more industrialized processes that replicate en masse the work once done by hand. Milk is transported from dairy barns to central plants, where cheese, butter, yogurt, and cream are produced and milk is put into containers. In the north, most of these cheeses are of cow's milk.

In Tuscany, Marche, Umbria, Lazio, Campania, and Sicily, many cheeses are made from sheep's milk to produce a type known as pecorino. This generic name only begins to describe the vast range of cheeses that are produced, all with their distinct and blissful characteristics. Some are made in *malghe,* but they are few and far between. Only in Sardinia does a strong *malga* tradition continue, and the sheep's milk cheeses of that island region are among the most exquisite you will ever taste.

One late September afternoon, when the sun had already set behind the western side of the peaks, leaving mountain passes in complete darkness, I traveled high into the alps of Carnia to visit one of the few remaining *fedârs*. The name of this area of Carnia is Valdajer (4,950 feet / 1,500 meters), past Ligosullo and close to Monte Paularo (6,742 feet / 2,043 meters). Most buildings are abandoned and, like much of Carnia, there is a sense that few people can be found.

Historically, men in Carnia went away from autumn through early summer to work as manual laborers while women stayed behind to tend the land and maintain the home. In the 1980s and 1990s, young people left Carnia for study and took office jobs in Udine, Trieste, or Milan. Only a few older people remain in rural Carnia. It is notable that as man has left this zone, bears, deer, lynxes, and elk have returned after hundreds of years, and their populations are growing. Carnia's sylvan aspect, in which man seems like an intruder, is quite startling.

In the middle of the forest there is a small clearing, which leads to a high mountain pasture full of grass and herbs. This is where Sergio Craighero lives with his wife, Guglielmina, in their *malga,* a sort of one-room shed with two small additional chambers, one for making cheese, the other for storing it.

There is a refrigerator, a wooden table, a few assorted chairs, a sink, a bed, a telephone, and a television set. In one corner of the main room is a very large hearth where Guglielmina cooks and Sergio builds fires to smoke his ricotta cheese. This is also the source of heat on the many cold nights. Most cheesemakers who work in a *malga* stay from mid-June to mid-September. Their cattle are then walked down to stalls in the valley, or travel by truck with their owners.

Sergio said to me, "I stay up here all year. I have done it for seven years now, since 1991. Winter is cleaner. There is always sun up here, even too much. Down below it is gray much of the time." For many years, Sergio toiled as a construction worker in France, returning in summers to make cheese. Most of his clients are local, although tourists come by in the summer to purchase whole cheeses to take home.

Before the snows come, Sergio makes hay while the sun shines, and this is what his cattle are fed in the winter months. Cheese from hay-fed cattle is straw-colored and uniform, and is based on the flavor of the hay. Cheese made from grass-fed cattle is sweeter, more golden in color, more aromatic and nutty. The butter will be intensely yellow.

Sergio's latteria cheeses, as they are called in Friuli, range from young and soft to semi-aged and firm to quite aged and granular. He specifically says that the only wines to serve with his aged cheese are Cabernet Sauvignon or Cabernet Franc. He pours me enough of both to amply prove his point.

During my visit, he had just received a large purchase of Merlot grape skins left over from wine making that occurred the day before near Udine. He will take cheeses that range in age from 21 to 120 days and soak them in the skins for 8 days. The result, sometimes called *ubriaco* (drunken cheese), has a reddish-black exterior and a wonderful cheese-wine flavor.

After the latteria cheese is made, he produces ricotta. He hangs large canvas sacks of the cheese so that it may drain. He then forms small bricks of ricotta (1¾ to 2¼ pounds / 800 to 1,000 g each) and places them on a metal grate in the upper part of his hearth. He sets and tends a small fire using chestnut wood ("You need a small fire to make a lot of smoke," he cautions). For the next 4 days the ricotta is enveloped in smoke.

According to Sergio, the smoked ricotta must be stored in a very dry place, where it can last for up to a month. After that it must be refrigerated, where it can stay for 2 to 3 months, wrapped in plastic. It is important to know that the cheese must be taken directly from the refrigerator when used for grating, and then immediately returned.

Guglielmina and I made frico together. Hers is more old-fashioned than restaurant frico, and very tasty. She sautés a chopped onion in an 8-inch / 20-cm cast-iron pan that she has rubbed with lard. Then she adds pieces of raw potato she has chopped to the size of dice. Then she adds assorted pieces of latteria cheese of various ages and puts it over a very low flame. She will cook this frico for 2 *hours,* at first stirring the cheese with a wooden spoon as it melts, then turning the frico often (otherwise it will become hard) and shaking the pan. It requires great patience and vigilance. Because of the potatoes, this frico is softer than one made only of cheese.

To make a lacy, crunchy frico (*frico croccante*), she only uses older cheese, and grates all of it. She adds a tiny drop of vegetable oil to her pan and then distributes the grated cheese in a layer across the bottom. She cautions that it must only be slightly golden—if it cooks to a deep gold, the frico will be bitter. Once it is golden on one side, she flips it over and cooks it briefly on the second side. She then folds the frico onto the bottom of a clean glass or bottle to form a basket shape that it will keep as it cools. In the past, when there were a lot of lumberjacks in Carnia, this crunchy frico was the one they took with them into the woods.

Above the central part of the hearth, where the largest fire can be built, is a large, heavy metal hook. When they make polenta, stews, or soups, Sergio and Guglielmina will hang large copper pots from this hook and raise or lower it over the flame to adjust the temperature.

They eat stone-ground dark polenta, often blended with buckwheat. The taste is earthy and delicious, especially when combined with one of their cheeses. "Now they make polenta a side dish," she said. "It is not special that way. Once our polenta was the center of a meal, it was our bread. We ate polenta every day for lunch and minestrone for supper." They eat no canned food except tuna. "After World War Two, we had care packages from America: condensed milk, powdered milk, chocolate. It kept us alive and we were grateful, but we were happy when we had fresh milk again."

Before I left with the local friend who had driven me up, Sergio took out a notebook that was carefully wrapped and stored. In it, written in a perfect hand, was the knowledge of a *fedâr* from the mid-1920s on how the cheeses on this piece of land should be made. I wanted to hold the book, but did not ask to. Sergio held it like a premature baby, so delicate, so precious.

As we were at the door, at nearly 11 P.M. (the middle of the night for people in these parts), Guglielmina came forth with a farewell drink. It was *mosto di pere,* newly crushed pear juice that had just the slightest alcoholic prickle. Soon it would mature to cider, which she called *vino dei vecchi,* wine for old people. With the leftover pear pressings, they will make a sort of grappa. With my pear juice she popped a piece of fresh young cheese in my mouth bringing me back full-circle, after an unforgettable evening, to the elemental taste of their piece of *terra fortunata.*

Fritàe/Fertàe/Ovi

FRITTATA

There are at least three ways of making a frittata in Friuli-Venezia Giulia. The most typical way is in a skillet using either butter or olive oil (and on some occasions lard). In Trieste, they make a fluffy frittata by beating the whites first before adding other ingredients. Another type of frittata involves cooking the eggs in the oven. Any way you prepare it, the resulting frittata has a chestnut-brown, slightly firm skin on both sides. Most frittatas have fillings and can be served hot, tepid, or cold.

Frittata Method 1

Have an 8- or 9-inch/20- or 23-cm skillet on hand. In Friuli they often use heavy cast-iron, but a heavy-bottomed pan clad with copper, stainless steel, or aluminum is acceptable. Warm the pan slightly over medium heat. If you are using olive oil, you might grease the pan before putting it on the heat. If you are using butter, add it after the pan is warm. Either way, it is very important that you grease not only the bottom but the sides, all the way up to the rim.

In some cases, you will cook ingredients in the pan before adding eggs. In other cases, the eggs will go into the pan with all of the ingredients. Either way, use a fork to move the ingredients about, taking care to never scrape the fork along the bottom, because you do not want to tear the skin that is forming on the bottom of the frittata. While working with the fork in one hand, shake the pan continuously with the other. This will prevent the frittata from sticking. Every 30 seconds or so, lift the pan from the heat as you shake it, just to slightly lower the temperature and slow the cooking. You may also use a spatula (plastic or metal, according to the needs of your pan) to lift the frittata and move it about once it has a somewhat firm skin on the bottom.

Once the frittata has a rather firm skin on one side (typically after 4 to 5 minutes), slide it out of the pan and onto a plate. Now lift the plate with one hand and, with the other hand, grab the handle of the pan and cover the frittata with the pan. In one motion, flip both hands in an arc so that the plate is now on top of the pan and the less-cooked side of the frittata is now face-down in the pan. Return to the heat and cook for 3 to 4 minutes, shaking the pan continuously to prevent sticking. The frittata is done when the bottom is firm and light chestnut-brown.

Slide the frittata into a dish for serving. If you plan to cool the frittata, cover it with a clean cloth or paper towels. In Friuli-Venezia Giulia it is customary to cut the frittata into 4 or 6 wedges before serving.

Frittata Method 2 (Ovi alla Triestina)

This particular recipe serves 4 persons, although you may adapt it to your needs. You can make this frittata without added ingredients (beat the eggs as indicated, and add heated oil from another pan). If you use additional ingredients, as is typical, they must be prepared apart and then added to the eggs. The most common version is ovi con zivola, eggs with onions, but other ingredients can be used, including thinly grated carrots, chives, bits of celery, and so forth. I have made a Triestine-type frittata with onion, carrot, celery, chive, and feta cheese (a combination I never saw in that city) and it was delicious. Because Trieste is in an olive oil–producing area, that is the cooking medium of choice for these eggs. You must use delicate oil or the taste of the eggs will be overwhelmed. Triestine, Ligurian, or Lake Garda oils are acceptable; Tuscan and Umbrian oils are not.

2 to 3 tablespoons / 30 to 45 ml delicate olive oil (from Trieste, Liguria, or Lake Garda; if the oil is too fragrant, use half olive oil and half neutral oil, such as sunflower or canola)
3 small onions, cut into very thin slices
6 large eggs

Have 2 pans at the ready: one for cooking the onions and the other (8- or 9-inch / 20- or 23-cm) to make the frittata. In the pan for onions, heat 2 tablespoons / 30 ml oil over medium heat. If this oil is not sufficient for your pan, add a little more. Once it is hot but not yet smoky, add the onions and cook them until they are translucent. Use a slotted spoon to remove them from the pan to a dish, carefully squeezing out any oil from the onions before lifting them out of the pan.

Separate the egg whites from the yolks and beat the whites in a chilled mixing bowl until they are frothy but not firm. Carefully fold in the yolks, one at a time, and beat the eggs just enough so that they keep their frothiness. Spoon the cooked onions atop the egg mixture and fold them in gently.

Pour half the oil from the onion pan into an 8- or 9-inch / 20- or 23-cm omelet pan. Place it over medium heat. When the oil is hot, add the egg mixture using a wooden spoon that you will use to gently stir the eggs into the pan. Then stop stirring and let the frittata form a skin on the bottom. Shake the pan continuously so the eggs do not stick.

Once a skin has formed (after about 3 to 4 minutes, typically), slide the frittata out of the pan and onto a plate. Flip the frittata onto another plate so that the cooked side is facing upward.

Add the rest of the onion-scented oil to the pan, let it heat up, and slide the frittata back into the pan so that the less-cooked side will brown. Shake the pan as you cook to assure that the frittata does not stick. When it is ready (typically about 2 to 3 minutes), slide it back onto one of the plates.

If you plan to cool the frittata, cover it with a clean cloth or paper towels. Cut into wedges before serving.

Frittata Method 3 (alla Rustica)

It is only partially correct to refer to this preparation as rustic. But this is how it is called in much of Italy, and I have noticed that this dish is found more in rural areas such as Carnia and the flat plains of southern Friuli. Nonetheless, I have seen it in Udine and Trieste and other cities around Italy. A frittata rustica almost always has cheese as an ingredient, and comes out firm on the outside and custardy within.

To make this frittata, preheat the oven to 300°F/150°C. Beat the eggs with milk in a bowl. Add cheese and other ingredients. Pour the mixture into a buttered casserole or baking dish (glass or enamel work best) that is 8 inches/20 cm in diameter. Bake for about 15 minutes.

Let cool, then unmold it onto a plate, cut, and serve. An example of this frittata is Frittata with Montasio (page 147).

Fertàe cu lis Jàrbis

SERVES 4 TO 8

This is one of the real classics of this region's cuisine. You will find it wherever you travel, especially in springtime when wild herbs sprout in fragrant profusion all over la terra fortunata. *The key here is to use as large a variety of herbs, grasses, and greens as you can locate. It is traditional that there be at least five different types. Among the most famous are silene, hops, melissa, mint, verbena, basil, marjoram, sage, parsley, spinach (just a little), fennel leaves, Swiss chard, zucchini (courgette) flowers, wild fennel, beet greens, chervil, sorrel, and celery leaves. This frittata is served piping hot, tepid, or cold. As always, it should be covered if allowed to cool, and cut into wedges before serving.*

2 tablespoons/30 g unsalted butter, or more if needed

2 tablespoons/30 g minced chives or onions

1½ cups/400 g fresh herbs and greens, all carefully cleaned and dried, then torn into small pieces

12 large eggs

6 tablespoons/100 ml whole or low-fat milk

1 tablespoon/15 g unbleached all-purpose flour

2 tablespoons/30 grams grated aged or semi-aged Montasio cheese

Freshly ground black pepper

Thoroughly butter the bottom and sides of an 8-inch/20-cm nonstick skillet. If 2 tablespoons/30 g are not sufficient, use more butter. Place the pan over low heat; when the butter becomes warm, add the chives or onions. Heat gently, just until they give off a little fragrance. Add the herbs and greens and, if necessary, a little more butter. Stir so that all the flavors mingle.

While the greens are heating, beat the eggs, milk, flour, cheese, and a little pepper into a large bowl. Add the egg mixture to the greens and stir with a fork, taking care to avoid scraping the fork along the bottom of the pan. While working with the fork in one hand, shake the pan continuously to prevent the frittata from sticking.

Once the frittata has a rather firm skin on the bottom, slide it out of the pan and onto a plate. Invert the frittata back into the pan so that the less-cooked side of the frittata is now face-down in the pan. Return to the heat and cook for 2 to 3 minutes, shaking the pan continuously to prevent sticking. The frittata is done when the bottom is firm and light chestnut-brown.

Slide the frittata onto a dish for serving. If you plan to cool the frittata, cover it with a clean cloth or paper towels. Cut into wedges before serving.

VARIATIONS: To make a baked omelet, preheat the oven to 300°F/150°C. Prepare the greens as above and transfer to a buttered 8-inch/20-cm baking dish. Beat the eggs, milk, flour, cheese, and pepper in a large bowl and pour over the greens. Bake for 15 minutes, unmold onto a plate, cut into wedges, and serve.

Although usually served plain, you can drape a paper-thin slice of prosciutto di San Daniele over the frittata before serving.

WINE: Many wines seem to go well with this preparation, including Collio Bianco, Tocai, Sauvignon Blanc, dry Verduzzo, and dry Prosecco.

Ovi Triestine alla Fred

Here is my improvisation using ingredients popular in Trieste in a frittata as they make it in that city.

2 tablespoons / 30 g feta cheese

2 to 3 tablespoons / 30 to 45 ml delicate olive oil
(from Trieste, Liguria, or Lake Garda; if the oil is
too fragrant, use half olive oil and half neutral oil,
such as sunflower or canola)

1 small onion, sliced very thin

1 carrot, grated as for carrot salad

1 celery stalk, thinly sliced

1 tablespoon / 6 g minced fresh chives

6 large eggs

Soften the feta cheese with 1 to 2 teaspoons / 5 to 10 ml warm water, stirring until you have a thick cream. Set aside.

Heat the oil in an 8- or 9-inch / 20- or 23-cm omelet pan over medium heat. When the oil is hot, add the onion and carrot, and sauté for 1 minute. Add the celery and cook until the onion is translucent. Add the chives. Quickly stir all the ingredients together vigorously and remove from the heat. Use a slotted spoon to remove the vegetables from the pan, squeezing out all of the oil.

Separate the egg whites from the yolks. Beat the whites in a chilled mixing bowl. Fold in the feta cheese. Carefully fold in the yolks, one at a time, and beat the eggs just enough to combine but keep their frothiness. Spoon the vegetables atop the egg mixture and fold them in gently.

Pour half the oil from the vegetable pan into an 8- or 9-inch / 20- or 23-cm omelet pan. Place it over medium heat and, when the oil is hot, add the egg mixture. With a wooden spoon, gently stir the eggs into the pan. Stop stirring and allow the frittata to form a skin on the bottom. Shake the pan continuously so the eggs do not stick. Once a skin has formed (about 3 to 4 minutes), slide the fritatta out of the pan and onto a plate. Add the rest of the oil from the vegetable pan to the omelet pan and let it heat up. Invert the frittata back into the pan so that the less-cooked side of the frittata is now face-down in the pan. Shake the pan as you cook to assure that the frittata does not stick. The frittata is done when the bottom is firm and a light chestnut-brown.

Slide the frittata onto a dish for serving. If you plan to cool the frittata, cover it with a clean cloth or paper towels. Cut into wedges before serving.

WINE: A white wine from the Carso, or Pinot Bianco

Fritàe cul Montasio

SERVES 2 TO 4

I first tasted this dish when it was made for me by Gianni Cosetti, who used to rule in the kitchen of the Ristorante Roma in Tolmezzo. He was one of the first chefs whose fame extended beyond the region's borders, and his influence on younger cooks is palpable. His great achievement was to combine the flavors of Carnia with a master's approach to cooking. I am grateful to him for sharing this recipe.

Unsalted butter

8 large eggs

6 tablespoons / 75 ml whole milk

Salt and freshly ground black pepper

7 ounces / 200 g young Montasio cheese, cut into small cubes

2 tablespoons / 30 g finely minced fresh chives or scallions

1 tablespoon / 15 g finely minced flat-leaf parsley

Preheat the oven to 300°F / 150°C. Generously butter a 7-inch / 17.5-cm nonstick pan or casserole.

Beat the eggs in a large bowl using a whisk to aerate them. Beat in the milk and salt and pepper to taste. Add the cheese, chives, and parsley. Pour the mixture into the buttered pan or casserole. Bake for 15 minutes, until the frittata is cooked and somewhat puffed up, like a soufflé. Serve hot or tepid. Cut into wedges before serving.

WINE: Sauvignon Blanc or Collio Bianco

Frittata con Gamberetti e Asparagi Bianchi

FRITTATA WITH BABY SHRIMP AND WHITE ASPARAGUS

SERVES 2 TO 4

This dish is ubiquitous in springtime in the plains that extend from the Isonzo Valley in Venezia Giulia across southern Friuli and to the border of the Veneto. Typically the shrimp used are tiny crayfish from local rivers, but you can use boiled baby shrimp. The white asparagus is an exquisite delicacy, but if you cannot find it, use the most tender green asparagus you can locate. You may use frittata methods 1, 2, or 3. All will succeed.

8 ounces / 225 g white asparagus, bottoms scraped

8 large eggs

6 tablespoons / 75 ml whole milk

8 ounces / 225 g boiled baby shrimp

Butter or olive oil

In a large pot of boiling salted water, boil the asparagus until tender (when they can be stabbed by a fork). Let cool slightly, and then cut off the tips and reserve. Cut the rest of the stalks into ½-inch / 1.25-cm pieces.

Beat the eggs and milk in a medium-size bowl. Add the asparagus pieces and shrimp. If you are using olive oil, grease the sides and bottom of an 8- or 9-inch / 20- or 23-cm omelet pan and place over medium heat. If you are using butter, warm the pan over medium heat, then add the butter and swirl to coat the bottom and sides of the pan. Add the egg mixture to the pan and briefly stir with a fork, taking care to avoid scraping the fork along the bottom of the pan. Shake the pan continuously to prevent the frittata from sticking.

Once the frittata has a rather firm skin on the bottom, slide it out of the pan and onto a plate. Invert the frittata back into the pan so that the less-cooked side of the frittata is now face-down in the pan. Return to the heat and cook for 2 to 3 minutes, shaking the pan continuously to prevent sticking. The frittata is done when the bottom is firm and light chestnut-brown.

Slide the frittata onto a dish for serving, cut into wedges, and serve immediately.

VARIATIONS: To make a baked omelet, preheat the oven to 300°F/150°C. Transfer the egg mixture to an 8-inch/20-cm baking dish. Bake for 15 minutes, unmold onto a plate, cut into wedges, and serve.

You may make a frittata only of shrimp or only of asparagus. It is also possible to substitute thin disks of tiny baby zucchini (courgettes) for the asparagus. Use only tiny zucchini, which have a low percentage of water. Thinly slice the zucchini and then sauté the slices in olive oil. Use the same pan to make the frittata. It will retain the flavors of oil and zucchini, which will be delicious. Of course, it is also possible to make a zucchini frittata by itself, or with some added cheese.

WINE: Sauvignon Blanc goes beautifully with eggs, shrimp, and asparagus, so it is the perfect wine here. For a zucchini frittata, choose Tocai or Merlot.

Ovi con Pedoci

MUSSEL FRITTATA

SERVES 2 TO 6 *This is a popular preparation along the coast of Venezia Giulia from Muggia to Grado.*

2¼ pounds / 1 kg mussels in their shells
Water or white wine
4 garlic cloves, split
10 large eggs
3 tablespoons / 45 g minced flat-leaf parsley
Salt and freshly ground black pepper
Olive oil

Scrub the mussels very well, removing their beards and any dirt that clings to the shell. Put a little water or white wine just to cover the bottom of a broad pan or pot. Add the garlic and then the mussels. Cover and steam over medium-high heat for a few minutes until the mussels have opened. Remove the mussels from their shells and place in a bowl. Discard any mussels that have not opened.

Separate the egg whites from the yolks and beat the whites in a chilled mixing bowl until they are frothy but not firm. Carefully fold in the yolks, one at a time, and beat the eggs just enough to combine but keep their frothiness. Spoon the mussels and sprinkle the parsley and salt and pepper atop the egg mixture and fold in gently.

Pour half the oil into an 8- or 9-inch / 20- or 23-cm omelet pan. Place it over medium heat and, when the oil is hot, add the egg mixture. With a wooden spoon, gently stir the eggs into the pan. Stop stirring and allow the frittata to form a skin on the bottom. Shake the pan continuously so the eggs do not stick. Once a skin has formed (after 3 to 4 minutes), slide the frittata out of the pan and onto a plate. Add the rest of the oil and let it heat up. Invert the frittata back into the pan so that the less-cooked side of the frittata is now face-down in the pan. Shake the pan as you cook to assure that the frittata does not stick. The frittata is done when the bottom is firm and a light chestnut-brown.

Slide the frittata onto a dish for serving. Serve hot or tepid. Cut into wedges before serving.

WINE: Pinot Grigio or Malvasia Istriana

S'cipi

This ancient farmworker's preparation will not appear on any heart-healthy lists, but it is an example of how poor people in Carnia once ate when they had more imagination than food. It is also delicious and might make a good dish for Sunday brunch.

8 ounces / 225 g young Montasio cheese cut into ½-inch / 1.5-cm cubes

2 to 3 tablespoons / 30 to 45 g finely ground polenta or cornmeal

3 tablespoons / 45 g unsalted butter

2 to 4 large eggs

Pinch salt

Roll the cheese cubes in the polenta.

Set 2 nonstick pans side by side over medium heat. Melt half of the butter in each pan. In one pan, when the butter is hot but has not turned brown, add the little cubes of cheese. Shake the pan so the cubes move about. Cook until they are crunchy, then remove from the heat. In the other pan, make 1 or 2 sunny-side-up eggs per person. Once the whites become firm, sprinkle a little salt on them.

Place each portion of eggs on an individual plate and surround them with the cubes of cheese. Serve immediately.

WINE: Sauvignon Blanc

Ovi Duri

HARD-BOILED EGGS

You may find it strange that I would include a seemingly standard recipe to which Friuli-Venezia Giulia can exert no special claim. However, hard-boiled eggs are made with great care there, and they are a classic accompaniment to a glass of wine (ideally Sauvignon Blanc) in the region's casual eateries: the buffet *of Trieste, the* osmizza *in the Carso, the* gostilna *around Gorizia, the* osteria *in the province of Udine, and the* frasca *wherever wine is produced. The term* ovi duri *is Triestine because you will see them more in that city than any place else. Hard-boiled (sometimes called hard-cooked) eggs are also important in dishes such as Asparagus with Egg Sauce (page 279) and are tasty when combined with sardines, anchovies, or sauces such as Salsa Triestina (page 124).*

Select the freshest eggs possible. In many so-called developed countries eggs are sold refrigerated. In other advanced nations, including Italy, they are often sold at about 20°C/68°F and at home will sometimes be refrigerated and sometimes not. If you purchase refrigerated eggs in a carton, be sure to keep them refrigerated until you need them.

To hard-boil, take a medium-size saucepan made of glass, enamel, or stainless steel and gently place the eggs in. There should be enough room for the eggs to move about easily. Add enough cold water to the pan so that the eggs are entirely covered but the water will not bubble out when boiling.

Bring the water to a boil over medium heat. Then lower the heat to a simmer, cover, and cook the eggs for another 10 minutes. If you are using eggs that were cold from the refrigerator, cook the eggs for 12 minutes rather than 10. Once the eggs are cooked, immediately place them in cold water (I use ice in the water). This will prevent further cooking and discoloration of the yolks. If you intend to eat the egg hot, then remove it from the water. Otherwise, let it cool in the water.

To shell a hard-boiled egg, gently tap one end of it against a hard surface. Then roll the egg in the palms of your hands for a couple of moments. This will loosen the shell, which should then be relatively easy to pull off if you start at the point at which you made a crack.

WINE: Sauvignon Blanc, Terrano, or a wine suited to the dish you are using the eggs in

Amlet di Frutta

You will not be melancholy after tasting this amlet. *It is delicious for brunch, at lunch, or to end a meal. The fruit omelet is particularly popular in Trieste and the rest of Venezia Giulia. There is a great selection of fruit to choose from, but my general recommendation is to use the ripest fruit at its peak and combine it with a congenial alcoholic beverage to flavor it. Three secrets to the success of this dish: 1) Have the fruit prepared before starting your omelet; 2) Use eggs that are as close to room temperature as possible; 3) Use a pan that is solely dedicated to making omelets. The standard one is 7 inches / 17.5 cm in diameter and is often nonstick.*

FOR THE GARNISH ON THE PLATE:
Confectioners' sugar
Ground cinnamon

FOR THE FILLING:
1 tablespoon / 15 g unsalted butter
½ cup / 125 g cut fruit (see below)
1 tablespoon / 15 ml distillate, eau-de-vie, or liqueur
    (see below)

FOR THE OMELET:
2 to 3 large eggs
1 tablespoon / 15 g confectioners' sugar (optional)
1 tablespoon / 15 g unsalted butter, preferably clarified

First, set up your serving plate. Sprinkle small pinches of confectioners' sugar and ground cinnamon on the plate. Swirl it around by grasping the sides of the plate and twisting the plate. The sugar and cinnamon should blend all over the plate.

Now make the fruit filling. Melt the butter in a pan over medium heat. Add the pieces of cut fruit. Stir vigorously for a minute or so to let the fruit soften. Add the recommended alcoholic beverage, increase the heat, and stir well until the alcohol has evaporated and you have a slightly chunky fruit filling.

Now make the omelet. Beat the eggs ever so slightly in a bowl, just until the yolks and whites have blended. You might wish to beat in a little confectioners' sugar at the same time (this is often done in Trieste, but I omit it).

Heat the omelet pan over high heat. Add the butter and swirl it so the whole surface is covered. Add the eggs. As you make the omelet, you should often lift the pan with one hand and swirl the eggs around by jerking your hand. Use the tines of a fork to move the omelet around the pan, but be careful never to scrape the fork along the pan's bottom.

When the omelet is soft but uniform and slides back and forth in the pan, it is ready. This whole process takes between 30 and 50 seconds. Remove it from the heat.

Now you must work fast to fill the omelet. You have two options: filling the omelet in the pan, which is the method I prefer, though some find it more difficult, or filling it on a plate.

To fill the omelet while it is still in the pan, spoon the fruit filling (leaving a tablespoon/15 g of fruit in its pan) in a straight line (parallel to you) across the middle of the omelet. Then quickly take your fork and lift the part of the omelet nearest you and fold it away from you to cover the fruit filling. Immediately move to the serving plate. Using the fork, roll the omelet out of the far end of the pan and onto the plate in such a way that you have entirely enfolded the fruit filling. Place the omelet slightly off center on the plate and then spoon the remaining fruit onto the other side of the plate for an appealing presentation.

Or, to fill the omelet outside the pan, slide it out of the pan and onto a clean plate. Spoon all of the fruit (except 1 tablespoon/15 g) in a straight line across the middle of the omelet. Working fast, use your fingertips to roll the omelet over itself and then quickly transfer it to the sugared serving plate. Spoon the remaining fruit onto that plate and serve immediately.

NOTE: To clarify butter, melt butter over low heat. Pour into a glass, jar, or dish. Let stand for a few minutes. The milk solids will sink to the bottom and the butterfat will rise to the top. Skim off the fat and, when you need the clarified butter, pour the clear golden liquid out leaving the milk solids behind.

Pairing the Fruit and a Suitable Beverage for the Filling

The Nonino distillery in Friuli makes exquisite fruit distillates and grappas that are perfect to use. You should also serve a tiny glass of the same beverage along with the omelet. Try:

Pears with pear eau-de-vie (distillate)
Apples with a single grape distillate, such as Moscato, Ribolla Gialla, or Müller Thurgau

Raspberries with framboise or raspberry eau-de-vie

Plums with plum eau-de-vie or Slivovitz

Apricots or peaches or nectarines with apricot eau-de-vie

Plums and apricots with plum eau-de-vie or Slivovitz

Raisins and walnuts with a single grape distillate, such as Moscato, Ribolla Gialla, or Müller Thurgau

Pitted orange, mandarin, or tangerine with vodka

Cherries (pitted and cut in half) with cherry eau-de-vie [I am a cherry lover, and become grumpy when they are not in season. To satisfy this problem, I purchase cherry preserves and pull out the fruit and only some of the preserve. Some of the brands I use are the Morello cherry preserves by Tiptree in England, D'Arbo fruit conserve from Austria (which makes both sour and black cherry conserve), and FiordiFrutta organic fruit spreads that are made in the Veneto. These are all acceptable substitutes. There are some other good Italian cherry preserves too, especially from Modena and Verona. You want to use a preserve that has whole pitted fruit. I have also revived dried cherries with hot water and then added a bit of eau-de-vie.]

For Replacing Other Fruits

The D'Arbo and Fiordifrutta companies offer fruit preserves that can replace fresh fruit. The plum and apricot conserves from D'Arbo taste very much like those from Venezia Giulia. The Fiordifrutta spreads have a bright Italian taste to them and have the great advantage of being sweetened only with fruit juice. Of course, these cannot replace fresh fruit, but the advantage of these 2 brands (both increasingly available in stores) is that the fruit grows in land that borders Friuli-Venezia Giulia, and has a taste closer to the real thing.

Pirus e Formadi

PEAR AND CHEESE SALAD

SERVES 1 TO 4

This simple dish can be an appetizer served on small plates or a nice lunch for one person. As always, its success rises and falls on the quality of the ingredients you use, so select them with care. Try to find pears that are fragrant, flavorful, sweet, and just slightly soft to the touch. Abate and Forelle pears are good choices. Otherwise, use the best pears available.

6 to 7 ounces / 200 g arugula, trimmed

6 to 7 ounces / 200 g young Montasio cheese

2 perfect medium pears, peeled and cored

Freshly ground black pepper (optional)

2 drops (literally) extra virgin olive oil (optional)

Place the arugula on one large plate for a single portion, or on individual plates. Using a grater with large holes, grate the cheese in a little mound in the center of the plate(s). Then, with the same grater, grate the pears on top of the cheese. If the arugula you are using is not too peppery in taste, you might choose to grind a little fresh pepper on top (be sparing—this is a delicate dish). You might also add one or two drops of olive oil, although the dish is traditionally served without it.

WINE: Pinot Bianco or a young Pinot Nero

Formadi cu lis Jàrbis

CHEESE WITH FRESH HERBS

This is a classic springtime dish in Carnia, where a seemingly endless variety of herbs grow. If you live in a place where unusual herbs and greens grow, or have access to them, consider making this dish. Among the herbs to select are silene (called sclopit *locally), hops, valerian, marjoram, fennel leaves, parsley, mint, sage, melissa, a little spinach, Swiss chard, verbena, celery leaves, or lemongrass. You will need chives or scallions separately, so do not include them in this mixture. The key is to have a great variety, and no single flavor should dominate.*

3 tablespoons / 45 g unsalted butter

1 tablespoon / 15 g minced fresh chives or scallions

1 pound / 1¾ cups / 450 g mixed herbs and greens, trimmed, washed, and dried

1 pound / 450 g semi-aged Montasio cheese, cut into 6 to 8 pieces

1 teaspoon white wine or apple cider vinegar (optional)

In a large skillet, combine 2 tablespoons / 30 g butter together with the chives or scallions over medium-low heat. When the butter is soft and fragrant, add the herbs and greens. Sauté so that all the flavors mingle and the ingredients lose whatever crunch they may have.

While sautéing the greens, warm an 8-inch / 20-cm nonstick skillet over medium-high heat. When it is quite warm, add 1 tablespoon / 15 g butter and let it melt. Raise the heat a little and add the cheese. Sear them quickly on one side, then flip them over. Sear on the other side and then start moving the pieces around the pan. Once they get a little soft, add the herb mixture. Cover, reduce the heat to low, and let melt for about 2 minutes. Uncover and stir so that you combine the ingredients. If you wish, add a little vinegar to give the dish some lightness and zing.

When the cheese is soft but in no way crisp, transfer the contents of the pan onto a warm plate. Cut into portions and serve immediately, before the cheese becomes firm.

WINE: Collio Bianco or Tocai

Frico Croccante

SERVES UP TO 4

I am a frico freak. This is the most delicious and addictive snack to have while drinking a pre-meal glass of wine. And once you get the knack, it is very easy to make. All you need is Montasio cheese, which is now available in most major markets in North America. The version presented here is the traditional kind that becomes slightly crunchy. You will occasionally find a version that has a crunchy crust and a creamy interior, such as at Ai Cacciatori in Cerneglons, that is just as wonderful (see Frico Fondente on page 159). For tips on making Frico Croccante from the wife of a cheesemaker, see page 139.

1 pound / 450 g aged Montasio cheese, 16 to 18 months old, coarsely grated

Heat a large well-seasoned or nonstick frying pan with slightly curving edges over medium heat until it gets hot. Sprinkle one-quarter of the cheese all over the pan, and then push any scattered bits toward the whole so that it looks like what you have is a cheese crêpe. Push down with a fork all over the frico so that the fat is rendered. Once the frico is relatively firm and the bottom is light gold in color, turn it over and heat the other side, again pressing down to let some of the fat run out. The whole process takes about 10 minutes. Have a clean empty wine bottle or drinking glass nearby.

When the frico is firm and has a bit of pull, slide it onto a plate. Press the bottom of the bottle or glass into the middle of the frico and fold the edges upward around the bottle. Lift the bottle out and leave the frico, which is now shaped like a flower, to cool.

Repeat the process 3 more times, or until you have used all of the cheese.

When the frico has cooled, it will be crunchy. You break off a piece and eat it (I'll bet you can't eat just one). You can serve certain foods, including soft polenta or some risotto, gnocchi, and pasta dishes, inside the frico flower. This makes for a very attractive presentation.

NOTE: If you feel your pan needs a little greasing, use a *very sparing* amount of extra virgin olive oil before making a frico.

WINE: The ideal match is Tocai, but any Friulian wine will go well.

Frico Fondente

SERVES UP TO 4

Frico, as made in most of Friuli, is a crunchy golden yellow cheese crisp, which can be referred to as frico croccante *(see page 158). One can also fill a crunchy frico with ingredients such as potatoes or onions. There is, however, another kind of frico, but one seldom encounters it anymore. I first tasted it at the Trattoria ai Cacciatori (The Hunters' Trattoria) in the tiny town of Cerneglons in the province of Udine. This is the town's principal social institution—the trattoria bestrides the two main roads of Cerneglons and sooner or later every citizen will come in for coffee, wine, and a game of cards, to look for friends or family, or simply to read the news and announcements posted on the long wall to the right of the entryway. Smart people also stay for delicious food, starting with the frico. On my first visit I was told that the chef, Marcello, would never reveal his secret recipe, and it took several more visits before I could even have access to the kitchen. Finally, I was allowed to watch the* frico fondente *being made, and then prepared a dozen or so of them that were sent out to the dining room. No one noticed the difference, and Marcello said I may pass his recipe on to you. The secret, he said, is that the Montasio cheese you use must be 30 to 40 days old. This is something you can easily determine in Friuli, but it may be harder if you live somewhere else. I have dealt with the problem by asking for the youngest, freshest Montasio my cheese seller has. A somewhat older cheese may warrant a few more minutes of cooking, but if it is pale yellow and soft, you will achieve good results. On average, you need about 7 to 10 ounces / 200 to 250 g of cheese per person.*

About 2 pounds / 1 kg young Montasio cheese, 30 to 40 days old

Cut the cheese into 2-inch / 5-cm cubes, discarding any rind. Place a good nonstick pan, about 7 inches / 17.5 cm in diameter over medium heat. When the pan gets somewhat hot, place the cubes of cheese in so that all touch the bottom of the pan and none are atop one another. Turn the heat up somewhat and let the cheese melt. Give the pan a good shake every so often so that the increasingly runny cheese is distributed all over the bottom.

When the frico has formed an even disk of melted cheese and the top is still yellow-white (this usually takes 5 to 7 minutes), turn the frico over. If you are an assured or daring cook, you may simply flip the frico over with a quick jerk of the pan. A safer way is to slide the frico into a dish and then invert the frico back into the pan so that the browned side faces up. Lower the heat slightly (it should still be a bit more than medium) and cook for 3 to 4 minutes, shaking the pan periodically. At this point you will want a spatula or rubber scraper (if you can't use metal utensils with your pan) at hand. Use the tool to slide the frico onto your plate if you do not want to flip it. Otherwise, flip it. Be careful as you turn the frico over that you do not puncture it. If you do, the dish is not ruined, but the result will be more delicate if you can avoid breaking it. When you have turned the frico over, you will notice that it begins to rise, like a soufflé.

When the frico has formed a thin crust and seems on the verge of bursting, it is time to flip it again. Either slide it onto the plate (to then return to the pan) with the help of your spatula or scraper, or flip the frico in the pan. When the frico rises on this side and forms an air pocket, it is ready.

Slide it onto the plate and serve with a fork and a sharp knife. The bubble will subside as the frico cools, but inside the cheese will be runny and delicious. Cut it into 4 quarters and serve immediately. This can be eaten on its own, but is often paired with firm white polenta.

WINE: Most Friulian whites or a light and lively red

Frico del Fattore

FARMER'S FRICO

A filled frico such as this one and those that follow uses less cheese because it has other ingredients as well. Farmer's Frico is typical of the remotest towns in Carnia, such as Sauris and Ampezzo. Speck is bacon that is cured and smoked before being aged for 6 months.

5 ounces / 150 g speck or pancetta, diced

1 yellow onion, cut into thin slices

Salt and freshly ground black pepper

4 large mealy potatoes (such as Idaho), peeled and cut into large cubes

12 ounces / 375 g semi-aged Montasio cheese, about 90 days old, cut into pieces about
   1 inch / 2.5 cm long and ½ inch / 1.25 cm wide

Heat the speck or pancetta in a medium-size pot or casserole for a few seconds over medium heat until it begins to render some fat. Then add the onion slices. Once they begin to give off a fragrance, add some salt and pepper to taste, and then the potatoes. Stir with a wooden spoon to combine the ingredients. Add ⅓ cup / 75 ml cold water, spread the ingredients evenly over the bottom of the pot, and cover. Cook over low heat for about 30 minutes. If the water completely evaporates, add a little more—just enough so the ingredients do not stick or burn.

Add the cheese to the pot, a piece at a time. Stir continuously until the cheese has largely melted but does not brown.

While melting the cheese, warm a 7- or 8-inch (about 20-cm) nonstick pan over medium heat. Once the cheese mixture has melted, pour it into the nonstick pan. Brown the frico first on one side and then the other (using a plate to flip it, if necessary). As the frico renders fat while cooking, drain it out of the pan. The result should be golden brown and crunchy.

Transfer the frico to a plate, cut into 4 quarters, and serve immediately.

WINE: Pinot Grigio, Refosco, Pinot Nero, or a young Merlot

Frico con i Melus / Frico con i Pirus

FRICO WITH APPLES OR PEARS

SERVES UP TO 4

Cheese and fruit are a natural combination, but here they come in a slightly different form. This is a traditional preparation in the fall and winter. Try to find fruit that is not particularly juicy, such as Golden Delicious apples or Bosc pears.

1 tablespoon / 15 g unsalted butter

1 pound / 450 g apples or pears, peeled, cored, and cut into paper-thin slices

1 pound / 450 g young or semi-aged Montasio cheese, cut into thin strips

Warm a 7- or 8-inch (about 20-cm) nonstick pan over medium heat. Melt the butter in the pan and add the apple or pear slices. Heat for just a couple of moments until they give off a slight perfume. Add the cheese and fold the ingredients together so that the fruit slivers are distributed throughout the frico. Gradually the frico will condense and form a crust. Brown the frico first on one side, then the other (using a plate to flip it, if necessary). As fat is rendered, pour it off.

Transfer the frico to a plate, cut it into 4 pieces, and serve immediately.

WINE: Ribolla Gialla

Frico con le Cipolle

SERVES UP TO 4   *This is a particular favorite in Tolmezzo, the principal town of Carnia. Its preparation is very similar to that of frico made with apples or pears (page 162).*

1 tablespoon / 15 g unsalted butter

⅔ pound / 300 g yellow or Vidalia onions, cut into paper-thin slices

1 pound / 450 g young or semi-aged Montasio cheese, cut into thin strips

Warm a 7- or 8-inch (about 20-cm) nonstick pan over medium heat. Melt the butter in the pan and add the onion slices. Cook until they are a light golden color. Add the cheese and fold the ingredients together so that the onion slices are distributed throughout the frico. Gradually the frico will condense and form a crust. Brown the frico first on one side, then the other (using a plate to flip it, if necessary). As fat is rendered, pour it off.

Transfer the frico to a plate, cut it into 4 pieces, and serve immediately.

WINE: Pinot Grigio

Frico cun Cartufùles (a.k.a. Frico cu lis Patatis)

FRICO WITH POTATOES

SERVES 2 TO 4

This preparation is similar to Farmer's Frico (page 29). While that preparation is very place-specific to upper Carnia, Frico cun Cartufùles is found in much of the region.

2 tablespoons / 30 g unsalted butter

1 yellow onion, cut into thin slices

Salt and freshly ground black pepper

3 large mealy potatoes (such as Idaho), peeled and cut into matchsticks

12 ounces / 375 g semi-aged Montasio cheese, about 90 days old, cut into pieces about 1 inch / 2.5 cm long and ½ inch / 1.25 cm wide

Melt the butter in a medium-size pot or casserole for a few seconds. Add the onion slices. Once they begin to give off a fragrance, add some salt and pepper to taste, and then the potatoes. Stir with a wooden spoon to combine the ingredients. Then add ⅓ cup / 75 ml cold water, spread the ingredients evenly over the bottom of the pot, and cover. Cook over low heat for about 30 minutes. If the water completely evaporates, add a little more—just enough so the ingredients do not stick or burn.

Add the cheese to the pot, a piece at a time. Stir continuously until the cheese has largely melted but does not brown.

While melting the cheese, warm a 7- or 8-inch (about 20-cm) nonstick pan over medium heat. Once the cheese mixture has melted, pour it into the nonstick pan. Brown the frico first on one side and then the other (using a plate to flip it, if necessary). As the frico renders fat while cooking, drain it out of the pan. The result should be golden brown and crunchy.

Transfer the frico to a plate, cut into 4 quarters, and serve immediately.

WINE: Merlot, Refosco, or Tazzelenghe

Liptauer

MAKES

2 CUPS / 900 G

This is a creamy cheese spread (also called Liptovsky syr) *that is popular in Trieste and Gorizia. It is also widely consumed in Hungary and eastern Austria. Surely it is a legacy of the years when Venezia Giulia was under the rule of Vienna. I first tasted it as a child at Zabar's, the well-known Manhattan emporium. To this day they produce huge amounts that New Yorkers love. It is customary in Venezia Giulia to eat liptauer spread on rye bread as an appetizer or a snack. You see this combination in most every buffet in Trieste. I usually accompany it with a beer rather than wine.*

I have also used liptauer to stuff in celery stalks as a canapé. Another delicacy that I enjoy (though I have not seen it in the region) is to smear it over hot white or green asparagus. Put a little dollop of liptauer next to a frittata with shrimp and asparagus (see page 148) and dab a little on each forkful. I also like it as a flavor element on a plate of hot prosciutto such as Ham Baked in Bread (page 268).

10 ounces / 275 g fresh ricotta

3½ ounces / 7 tablespoons / 100 g unsalted butter (use whipped, if available)

1 tablespoon / 15 g minced capers (use brine-packed)

1 tablespoon / 15 g ground sweet or rose paprika

1 tablespoon / 15 g dry mustard powder

1 tablespoon / 15 g finely minced flat-leaf parsley

1 teaspoon / 5 g finely minced scallion or spring onion

The secret to making a winning liptauer is that it be creamy. I start by stirring the ricotta (you may also use pot cheese or farmer cheese as long as it has firm curds and not too much liquid). Stir until the cheese itself is creamy. Then stir in the butter. Stir in the capers. Continue by stirring the paprika, then the mustard, then the parsley, and then the scallions. Once the scallion has been stirred in well, you should have a yellow-orange mixture with green specks. It is ready to serve, or will keep, if well covered and refrigerated, for up to 72 hours. Some people in Trieste insist that the paprika should be the last ingredient to be added. Try it both ways and decide for yourself.

Sope e Mignestre

Of soup and love, the first is best

—SPANISH PROVERB

No Italian region has more soups than Friuli-Venezia Giulia. An old saying in the region has it that there are 365 days, so you can make 365 different soups. This was an admonition to be creative, and it flourished in this region's approach to food. The basic idea was that when all that was available was water and whatever ingredients could be gathered, those would be combined to make the *soup du jour*. Until the region became more affluent, for many residents soup was the *meal* du jour. So there is a legacy of intriguing and substantial soups in Friuli-Venezia Giulia with a wide range of ingredients, some of which you will find presented below.

Most thick vegetable-based soups are better the day after the soup is made, although asparagus soup should be eaten fresh. Also remember that any soup containing barley can only be reheated once. A second reheating will cause the barley to turn bitter and ruin the soup.

Jota

SERVES 8 TO 10

There are several spellings of this word, though jota *is the most used.* Jote *is the term in Friulano, and* iota *is often used in Trieste and Gorizia. There is a fair amount of debate about the origin of this name. Many people think it derives from the Spanish* jota, *which is a stew of meat and vegetables. The Spanish word probably had Arabic roots. I am not convinced about this etymology because, even though Trieste had trade with Spain, the traditional* jota *preparation seems strictly local and without Spanish influence. It is more plausible that the word derives from the Latin* jutta, *which loosely means a concoction of assorted foods in one dish.*

Jota is on the short list of essential dishes of the region, especially in Venezia Giulia. This recipe is a combination of recipes I learned in Trieste plus input from Majda Cicigoj of the Trattoria da Majda in Gorizia, home of a luscious jota. *Many women told me that they make this soup early in the day because they want to pay attention to it before the phone starts ringing. Also, it is tastier when it has sat for a few hours or, better still, for a day or two.*

1 pound / 450 g dried beans, such as cranberry, borlotti, red kidney, or pinto

8 ounces / 225 g boiled ham or smoked pork butt (1 chunk cut into pieces)

1 bay leaf

Freshly ground black pepper

3 large mealy potatoes (such as Idaho), peeled

1 pound / 450 g sauerkraut

⅓ pound / 150 g pancetta or speck (1 chunk cut into small dice)

1 garlic clove, mashed

Extra virgin olive oil or 1 tablespoon / 15 g lard

1 teaspoon / 5 g unbleached all-purpose flour

Salt

Soak the beans for at least 8 hours, up to overnight, in cold water, adding at least 4 inches / 10 cm water above the top of the beans. Drain thoroughly and transfer the beans to a large pot along with the pieces of boiled ham or pork butt, the bay leaf, and a little pepper. Add water just to cover the ingredients, bring to a rapid boil, then reduce the heat to a simmer for 45 minutes. Do not add salt.

Meanwhile, boil the potatoes in salted water to cover for 45 to 50 minutes.

Taste a little bit of the sauerkraut. It should be tangy and slightly crunchy. If you feel it is too acidic, rinse under running water. But the acid is part of its character, so don't overdo it.

Place the pancetta or speck in a tall heavy-bottomed pot with the garlic and a few drops of olive oil or a tablespoon/15 g of lard. Let cook over medium-low heat until the pancetta becomes slightly fragrant. Keep moving the ingredients about so that nothing sticks. Add the sauerkraut and sauté to flavor it, about 5 minutes. Add the flour and continue sautéing until it has been incorporated into the mixture. Turn off the heat.

When the beans are tender but still intact, remove half of them with a slotted spoon and mash them in a food mill or a blender so that you have a thick paste. Add this paste to the pot with the sauerkraut and stir well.

Drain the potatoes and reserve the cooking water. Cut half into chunks and mash the other half. Add the mashed potatoes to the pot with the sauerkraut. Cut the rest of the potatoes into cubes. Return the pot to low heat and let the flavors blend, about 5 minutes. Then add the rest of the beans and the pork, along with their cooking water. Discard the bay leaf. Add the potato cubes. Stir well so that all the ingredients combine.

There should be some liquid in the pot, but not an excessive amount. Cover partially and cook over low heat for another 45 minutes. The potatoes and many of the beans will fall apart, making a thick, delicious soup. Stir periodically so that the soup does not stick to the bottom of the pot. If the soup is just too thick, stir in some of the potato water, scraping the bottom of the pot. Be careful not to let the ingredients burn, or you will ruin the delicate flavor of the soup. Once done, taste for salt and add a little, if you think necessary. Salt should be a present component, but not a dominant flavor.

Let the soup stand for at least 15 minutes before serving. If you serve it a day later, reheat to a simmer and serve warm, not hot. No matter when you serve *jota,* you might wish to add a few drops of extra virgin olive oil to each individual serving of soup.

VARIATIONS: In Trieste one often finds sauerkraut in this soup, while in parts of Slovenia they might use fresh cabbage, which actually has a more bitter taste as opposed to the acidic tang of the kraut. In Gorizia, cornmeal is sometimes added instead of potatoes. In the Carso they use fewer beans but add some barley, and prefer sausage to ham. In Friuli a *jote* would have fresh beans instead of dried ones and would use *brovada* (fermented turnips) in place of sauerkraut.

WINE: Terrano, Refosco, or Merlot

Minestra di Orzo e Fasio

BARLEY-BEAN SOUP

SERVES 6 TO 8

Here is Friuli's favorite soup; they like it in Venezia Giulia, too, although jota *dominates there. Remember that a soup with barley can only be reheated once. After that the barley becomes bitter and ruins the soup.*

1½ cups / 300 g dried beans such as borlotti, cranberry, or pinto

1 tablespoon / 15 ml extra virgin olive oil (or 1 heaping teaspoon / 8 g of lard)

1 garlic clove, crushed

5 ounces / 150 g pancetta, in one piece

3 generous grindings black pepper

1 bay leaf

1 cup / 200 g pearl barley

Pinch salt

High-quality extra virgin olive oil (optional)

Soak the beans for at least 8 hours, up to overnight, in cold water, adding at least 4 inches / 10 cm water above the top of the beans. Drain well.

In a large soup pot, heat the olive oil at medium temperature. Add the garlic and sauté just to flavor the fat. Then remove the garlic. Add 8½ cups / 2 l cold water, the beans, pancetta, black pepper, and bay leaf. Cook over medium heat and let boil gently for 1 hour.

Add the barley and salt, stir well, reduce the heat, and simmer partially covered for another 45 minutes. Stir every so often to assure that the ingredients combine well and that nothing sticks to the bottom of the pot. Remove the bay leaf when the soup is done.

The soup should be thick and velvety. The beans will be tender and the barley slightly chewy. Much of the pancetta should have cooked down, but you may remove what is left, dice it, and return it to the soup. Serve hot or warm, perhaps with a few drops of extra virgin olive oil added to each bowl.

WINE: A young Merlot is perfect.

Pasta e Fagioli

PASTA AND BEAN SOUP

This recipe is adapted from the soup at the Trattoria ai Cacciatori in Cerneglons. Make a lot and save some for the next day, when it is always better.

1⅓ pounds / 600 g dried cranberry beans

8 ounces / 225 g yellow onions, coarsely chopped

8 ounces / 225 g medium waxy potatoes, peeled and coarsely chopped

1 large carrot, coarsely chopped

1 celery stalk, trimmed and coarsely chopped

½ pound / 225 g firm ripe fresh tomatoes (or 1 cup / 225 g canned peeled tomatoes), coarsely chopped
   with seeds discarded

1 long stem fresh rosemary

¼ pound / 115 g pancetta, cut into small bits

3 tablespoons / 45 g fine sea salt

1 tablespoon / 15 g freshly ground black pepper

⅓ pound / 175 g ditalini rigati (or, if not available, pennette)

High-quality extra virgin olive oil

Combine the beans and 5 quarts / 4.75 l fresh cold water in a large (8-quart / 7.5-l) soup pot. Cover and let soak for 12 hours.

Place the pot over medium heat and add the onions, potatoes, carrot, celery, and tomatoes. Remove enough rosemary needles from the stem to fill 1 tablespoon, mince them well, and add to the pot. Cover and cook over very low heat for 2 hours, until the beans are very tender.

Using a slotted spoon, remove slightly more than 1 cup/225 g beans and set aside. Using a slotted spoon, remove the rest of the solid ingredients and pass through a food mill into a very large bowl. It is preferable to use a manual food mill to get a nice thick consistency. If you use a blender or food processor, pulse them very gently to break down the ingredients. The key to this soup is that it be thick. Reserve any liquid that might be left in the pot in another bowl.

Return the soup pot to the top of the stove. Place the pieces of pancetta in the pot and sauté over medium heat just until they begin to render some of their fat. If you wish, add more whole rosemary needles, to taste, and sauté for 15 seconds with the pancetta. Then add the bean and vegetable mixture. (You may, if you wish, omit the pancetta from this preparation. In this case, simply add the bean-vegetable mixture to the pot.) Add the whole beans, salt, and pepper.

After giving the ingredients a good stir, bring to a slow boil. Add the ditalini and cook, with the pot partially covered, for 10 minutes. The soup should be quite thick. If you wish to make it a little thinner, add judicious amounts of the reserved cooking liquid.

Serve in warm bowls, and add a few drops of extra virgin olive oil at the table. Stir well, and eat.

WINE: Merlot, Refosco, Cabernet Franc, Terrano, or Pinot Nero

Minestra di Bobici

SERVES 6 TO 8 *This soup is most popular in Trieste and the Carso, but all evidence indicates it was created in Friuli, combining as it does the beans and corn so popular in the Bassa Friulana. You want to use very fresh corn. Check this by puncturing a kernel. If the liquid that comes out is milky, then all is well.*

1 cup/225 g dried beans, such as cranberry, borlotti, red kidney, or pinto

2 tablespoons/30 ml extra virgin olive oil

¼ pound/115 g pancetta or prosciutto di San Daniele with fat still attached, diced

Salt and freshly ground black pepper

2 large mealy potatoes, washed, peeled, and cut into bite-size chunks

Kernels scraped from 2 ears fresh corn

Soak the beans for at least 8 hours, up to overnight, in cold water, adding at least 4 inches/10 cm water above the top of the beans. Drain thoroughly.

In a large, heavy-bottomed soup pot, heat the olive oil over medium-low heat. Add the pancetta and sauté for a few minutes, until the meat gives off a fragrance. Add the beans and stir for a minute. Add 8½ cups/2 l cold water. Bring to a boil, cover the pot, reduce the heat, and cook just below boiling for 45 minutes.

Add salt and pepper to taste and cook partially covered for another 45 minutes. Many of the beans will break down, some water will evaporate, and the soup will thicken. Add the potatoes and corn. Cook, partially covered, for 20 minutes, until the potatoes are tender when pierced with a fork. Stir frequently and make sure nothing sticks to the pot.

Let sit for 15 minutes before serving.

WINE: Terrano, Tazzelenghe, Refosco, Merlot, or Pinot Grigio

Paparot

SPINACH-CORNMEAL SOUP

SERVES 6 TO 8   *This is one of my favorite soups anywhere, not just in Friuli-Venezia Giulia.*

2¼ pounds / 1 kg fresh spinach (use baby spinach, when available)
1 garlic clove, peeled
3 tablespoons / 45 g unsalted butter
4 ounces / 115 g fine polenta or slow-cooking fine cornmeal
3 tablespoons / 45 grams unbleached all-purpose flour
3 cups / 750 ml high-quality hot chicken or vegetable broth
Salt and freshly ground black pepper

Wash the spinach and remove any tough stems. Cook it over medium heat in a covered pan using only the water clinging to the leaves. When the leaves are tender, remove from heat and thoroughly squeeze all the liquid from the spinach. Save this liquid. Finely mince the spinach.

Place the garlic in a casserole or broad soup pot over low heat. Add the butter and gently melt it. Briefly sauté the garlic until it flavors the butter. Once the garlic begins to turn color, remove the clove and reserve for another use. Add the spinach and gently sauté until it is coated with the garlic butter. Do not allow the ingredients to burn.

While the spinach is cooking, combine the polenta and flour in a bowl and add a ladleful of broth. Stir well so that no lumps remain. When the spinach is fragrant, add the remaining broth to the pot plus the cooking liquid from the spinach. Stir well, and then add the flour mixture a little at a time. Stir continuously while adding the flour mixture. Cook partially covered over medium-low heat for 30 minutes, stirring often.

Add a dash of salt and pepper and let sit for 1 hour. Reheat and serve hot.

VARIATION: Boil 6 ounces / 175 g garlic-scented soft pork sausage in a casing in water for 15 minutes to remove some of the fat. Then peel the sausage, crumble it, and add it to the soup pot as you add the spinach.

WINE: Pinot Bianco or Merlot

Crema di Asparagi

CREAM OF ASPARAGUS SOUP

SERVES 6 TO 8   *This soup is excellent using either white or green asparagus. Select fat stalks, if available.*

2¼ pounds / 1 kg fresh white or green asparagus

2 medium waxy potatoes, peeled

1 small leek, trimmed and chopped

1 tablespoon / 15 g unsalted butter

½ cup / 120 ml light cream

Pinch ground white or black pepper

4 tablespoons / 60 g prosciutto di San Daniele, diced (optional)

Chop off the tips of the asparagus and reserve. If the stalks are woody, peel the lower third and chop off the base. Then cut the stalks into large pieces.

Add the potatoes and leek to a large pot of salted boiling water. When you can, with a bit of effort, penetrate a potato with a fork, add the asparagus stalks. Place the tips in a colander or strainer and set over the boiling water. Steam for 3 minutes, then set aside. Drain the vegetables.

Pass the potatoes, leek, and asparagus stalks through a manual food mill to make a creamy puree. If you prefer, use a food processor or blender, but make sure not to make the puree too thin.

Melt the butter in a medium-size pot over medium heat and add the puree. Use a whisk to stir and gradually add the cream. Add the pepper and keep stirring until the soup is very hot but not yet boiling. Serve immediately.

VARIATION: If you wish, sauté some diced prosciutto di San Daniele in a bit of butter in a separate pan. Top each portion of soup with some of the ham, taking care not to get much pan liquid into the soup.

WINE: Sauvignon Blanc or Traminer

Briža

POTATO-SQUASH-BEAN SOUP

SERVES 8 TO 10

This soup is of Slovenian origin and is found in the Natisone Valleys in the province of Udine. This recipe is from Teresa Covaceuszach who, with her husband Franco Simoncig, owns the Trattoria Sale e Pepe in Stregna, just a stone's throw from the Slovenian border. This is a popular soup in the summer.

5 medium acorn squash, halved and seeds and fibers discarded

Salt

2¼ pounds / 1 kg waxy medium potatoes, peeled

10 ounces / 300 g fresh cranberry beans (the weight is measured after they are removed from their pods so buy at least double this weight)

1 small carrot, coarsely chopped

1 bay leaf

½ onion, peeled and cut into 4 pieces

1 celery stalk, coarsely chopped

5 cups / 1200 ml whole milk

3 cups / 700 ml sour cream

Grate the squash pulp into a large bowl, using the coarse holes of a box grater. Sprinkle generously with salt, cover, and set aside for 2 hours.

Meanwhile, cook the potatoes in a large pot of boiling salted water until you can penetrate one easily with a fork. Drain and chop the potatoes into bite-size pieces. Cover and keep warm.

Combine the beans in a pot with the carrot, bay leaf, onion, and celery and add enough water to cover the ingredients. Cook over medium heat just until you can penetrate a bean with a fork. Turn off the heat; discard the carrot, bay leaf, onion, and celery.

Squeeze all of the liquid from the squash and set about making the soup. Gently heat the milk and sour cream in a large pot, stirring frequently. Add the squash, then the potatoes, then the beans and their liquid, stirring all the while. Now turn the heat up to medium and stir constantly. When the liquid just starts to boil, turn the heat down as low as possible and simmer for 20 minutes, stirring periodically. Add a pinch of salt, if you wish, and serve tepid.

WINE: Tocai or Traminer Aromatico

Mignestre di Melus e Vin

COLD APPLE AND WINE SOUP

I tasted this soup in Ampezzo in western Carnia, practically at the border with Veneto and Alto Adige. In the latter region they make a wine soup (without apples) with Terlano wine, which is a blend of Pinot Bianco, Chardonnay, Riesling Italico, Sauvignon Blanc, Sylvaner, and Müller Thurgau. To make the Friulian soup, with apples, I would recommend a similar blend, if you can find it. Certainly you may use a Collio Bianco, which usually contains Tocai, Ribolla Gialla, and Sauvignon Blanc, although Chardonnay sometimes finds its way into the mix. As for the apples, try to find very fragrant, spicy apples, such as Northern Spy. If you use a generic apple, such as Golden Delicious, the soup will be less interesting. Avoid tart apples, such as Granny Smith.

4 medium to large apples, peeled, cored, and diced

½ / 125 g cup sugar or more to taste

Fresh juice and finely minced zest of 1 lemon

2 tablespoons / 30 g unbleached all-purpose flour

1 cup / 250 ml white wine (preferably a blend such as Collio Bianco)

½ cup / 125 ml heavy cream

Combine 3 cups / 750 ml hot water, the apples, ½ cup / 125 g sugar, the lemon zest, and lemon juice. Cook over medium-low heat until the apples are tender. Blend 2 tablespoons / 30 ml cold water and flour together and add to the soup. Simmer for 5 minutes. Stir in the wine and sweeten the soup to taste. Chill well covered. Add the cream before serving.

Zuppa di Comino

CARAWAY SEED SOUP

SERVES 2 TO 6

For people in Friuli-Venezia Giulia, caraway seeds are not only about flavor. They are medicinal, too. I tasted this soup in a family home in Gorizia, and the daughter confided to me that when grandfather has had a little too much to drink, this is what they serve him. It is supposed to be the best thing for an upset stomach. Interesting, of course, but I would not have included this recipe if it were not delicious.

5 tablespoons / 75 g unsalted butter

⅓ cup / 75 g unbleached all-purpose flour

1 tablespoon / 15 g caraway seeds

1 tablespoon / 15 g sea salt

Over medium-low heat, gently melt the butter in a large pot. Add the flour a little at a time, stirring constantly with a wooden spoon until the mixture becomes frothy. Add the caraway seeds, and stir continuously until the mixture is golden brown, about 2 to 3 minutes. Remove from the heat.

Gradually add 6 cups / 1.5 l cold water, stirring constantly. Then toss in the salt and stir. Return to the heat and bring to a boil, continuing to stir. Cover tightly, turn down the heat, and simmer for 15 minutes. Pour through a sieve and serve.

VARIATIONS: Beat 2 large eggs and add them to the soup just before you plan to serve it. Stir the soup with a whisk, turning the eggs into shreds. Or, just before serving, stir in 2 tablespoons / 30 g sour cream.

WINE: It is probably not typical to drink wine with this soup, but if you do, a Pinot Bianco might be suitable.

Minestra Dalmata

DALMATIAN SOUP

SERVES 4
GENEROUSLY

This is not a soup created by the malevolent Cruella deVil from 101 spotted dogs. It refers instead to the plainest of plain soups that originated in Dalmatia, over the eastern border from Venezia Giulia. I am including it in this book because it is a tangible legacy of la miseria, *the time period between the two world wars, when thousands of people in the region starved and lived primarily on polenta, grappa, and this type of soup. It is important to include these recipes because of their historical interest, but also because it contrasts with the opulence and sophistication of contemporary food in the region. Minestra Dalmata happens to be tasty in its plainness, as some foods of privation are; but for Friulians of a certain age, this soup inevitably brings back memories of the struggles for survival that are so much a part of Friulian history. It was meant to provide warmth and a use for bread that had become stale. I have adapted this recipe for the modern cook by omitting the lard that was once used and replacing it with prosciutto di San Daniele or speck.*

4 ounces / 115 g prosciutto di San Daniele or speck (bacon), cut into cubes

1 garlic clove, minced

4 slices stale bread, cut or broken into large cubes or pieces

Salt

1 tablespoon / 15 ml extra virgin olive oil

Grated aged Montasio or Parmigiano-Reggiano cheese (optional)

Place the prosciutto or speck in a skillet or saucepan over medium heat. After a few seconds, add the garlic. Sauté for about 2 minutes, making sure nothing burns but that some of the fat is rendered. The garlic should give off some of its perfume, but should not turn color.

While the ham and garlic are cooking, place the pieces of bread in the bottom of a large tureen or serving bowl. Add 6 cups / 1½ l boiling water, the salt, and olive oil. Stir carefully to combine, but do not break up the bread. Add the ham and garlic combination, stir to combine, and serve. Grated cheese would have been a luxury when this soup was often consumed, but adds meaningfully to the flavor and texture when consumed nowadays, so go for it.

Zuppa di Ostriche

OYSTER SOUP

This recipe is the creation of Patrizia Filiputti, a marvelous home cook who benefits from having her husband Walter's wines to serve with her food. Making this soup is very labor-intensive, but the results are worth it. Patrizia insists on two things to make the broth successful. The first is that the bass be from the sea because this is the source of its flavor. The second is that the bass must be "sacrificed" for the sake of the broth, which is to say that it be cooked for all of its flavor and then discarded. (I must confess that I discarded the bones, mashed the fish, and used it for stuffing in lettuce leaves that I braised in a very light tomato sauce, and it was delicious.)

FOR THE BROTH:

2¼ pounds / 1 kg whole sea bass, cleaned and scaled

1 onion, coarsely chopped

1 celery stalk, coarsely chopped

1 carrot, coarsely chopped

FOR THE SOUP:

2 tablespoons / 30 ml delicate extra virgin olive oil

1 leek, finely chopped

8 cherry tomatoes, finely chopped, liquid saved

1 radish, finely chopped

3 sprigs flat-leaf parsley, finely chopped

1 medium carrot, finely chopped

1 medium zucchini (courgette), finely chopped

2 ounces / 60 g minced beet greens

½ cup / 120 ml Pinot Grigio or Ribolla Gialla

Pinch fine sea salt

80 oysters, shucked, with liquid reserved separately

First make the broth. Place the sea bass in a large pot with the onion, celery, carrot, and 8½ cups / 2 l cold water (preferably spring). Simmer, partially covered, for 50 minutes, until the fish is entirely cooked. Strain the broth, discarding the fish and vegetables.

Using the same pot, heat the olive oil and add the leek, tomatoes and their liquid, radish, parsley, carrot, zucchini, and beet greens. Sauté briefly, until the vegetables give off a fragrance. Add 2 ladlefuls of broth and a bit of wine. Keep simmering this liquid, adding a little more broth and wine until they are all used up. Add a pinch of salt and the liquid from the oysters. Bring to a boil. Toss in all 80 oysters and immediately turn off the heat. If you are cooking on an electric stovetop, remove the pot so the ingredients do not heat further.

Serve immediately.

WINE: Pinot Grigio or Ribolla Gialla

Paste

Friuli-Venezia Giulia's location as a crossroads region drawing influence and flavors from other places is perhaps most striking when we deal with dishes that fall under the general category known as pasta. This is one of the foremost gnocchi-making regions of Italy. Ancestors of these delicate little dumplings were surely Roman in origin, so the tradition of forming a dough with a starch (once wheat, now usually potatoes) and liquid has been around for more than two thousand years.

Nowhere else in Italy can one find such a wide range of gnocchi that adapt to basic sauces such as tomato or meat, but also to herb sauces, cheeses, spices, and even chocolate. Other gnocchi are made with ingredients such as pumpkin or ricotta cheese instead of potatoes. Then there are the larger gnocchi (more delicate than the dumplings of Mitteleuropa) that are made with bread and served with butter, cheese, or a spicy cucumber sauce. The greatest gnocchi of all are probably those filled with fruit such as plums, apricots, or cherries.

The region also uses typical Italian pasta, such as penne or tagliolini, combined with native flavors such as prosciutto di San Daniele, shellfish, or cheese, and blended with spices.

There are many specialty pastas in Friuli that reflect the region's diversity of flavors and pair beautifully with its great wines. Ones seen nowhere else include *cjarsòns* (40-ingredient—including spices, lemon zest, cheese, mint, nuts, and chocolate—filled pasta from Carnia) and *lasagne da fornel* (Christmas lasagne with raisins, almonds, and poppy seeds). These exotic flavor combinations tend to include everything that was available to poor people, but have evolved into dishes of great sophistication.

Although some of the recipes in this chapter seem more geared toward the end of a meal, they are intended to be eaten when pasta courses are normally served. Consider serving smaller portions than you normally would and savor every mouthful.

Pay close attention to wine pairings with food and spices in your pastas from Friuli-Venezia Giulia. This is a real area for developing your palate as you see how flavor notes interact with sips of wine.

Gnocchi

SERVES 4 TO 8

(ABOUT 2 POUNDS /

900 G GNOCCHI)

This recipe is for potato gnocchi, the standard type found in most of Italy. At their best, gnocchi are delicate, airy little pillows that should melt in your mouth. People often think that gnocchi are heavy, but this is usually the result of poor execution and oversaucing. To avoid this, coat gnocchi very lightly with sauce.

1¼ pounds / 570 g mealy potatoes, such as Idaho

2½ cups / 285 g unbleached all-purpose flour plus more for dusting

Pinch sea salt

1 extra-large egg

Boil the potatoes in water to cover until you can easily poke a fork through them. Drain, peel, and mash them.

Form a mound of potatoes on a work surface (smooth wood, formica, or marble). Let cool for 5 minutes. Then combine the potatoes with the 2½ cups / 285 g flour and the salt and gently work the mixture together with your hands. Do not work the mixture more than necessary. Form a well in the center of this mixture and break the egg into it. Work this mixture together until you have formed a dough.

Once the dough is made, divide it into several pieces. Take a piece and roll it out with your hands until you form a ropelike cylinder the thickness of your index finger. With a sharp knife, cut pieces of the "rope" ½ to ¾ inch (1.25 to 2 cm) long. Press each gnocco with your thumb against the back side of a cheese grater or the tines of a fork. These indentations will become receptacles for sauce when you dress your gnocchi. Repeat this process until you have used all the dough.

Dust with a little more flour and do not pile them one on top of another. Let the gnocchi rest in a draft-free, cool place. Cook them the same day they are made.

To cook the gnocchi, bring a large pot of cold water to a boil. Add a pinch of sea salt. As soon as the water returns to a rapid boil, add the gnocchi. Unlike most foods, the gnocchi will tell you when they are ready. Properly cooked gnocchi rise to the surface of the boiling water. You must fish them out using a slotted ladle or spoon. Do not drain them in a colander like pasta. I usually cut the first one in half to see if it is done to my liking, and then I taste it. If the doneness is right, I proceed as described. If it is a bit grainy, I let them cook a bit longer. If it is mushy (this seldom happens), I try to retrieve them a bit sooner.

Once you have removed the gnocchi from the cooking water, transfer them to a warmed bowl to which you have added a drop of whatever sauce you are using. Once the gnocchi are all cooked, add the rest of the sauce, but make sure that the gnocchi are only lightly coated and not swimming, or the final result will be too heavy. Serve at once.

VARIATION: Gnocchetti are simply small gnocchi. Proceed with the recipe above but once you have formed the dough into a rope, cut it into pieces ¼ inch / 65 mm long. Do not make indentations with a fork or cheese grater, gnocchetti are too small. Cook as above, removing them once they rise to the surface of the water.

Macarons cu'i Savors di Mont

GNOCCHI WITH MOUNTAIN HERBS

SERVES 4 TO 6

This is a specialty of Carnia, and the sauce is made only with newly gathered fresh herbs. Use the most fragrant and flavorful herbs you can find.

1 pound / 450 g Gnocchi (half the recipe on page 181)

2 cups / 250 g fresh herbs (of which 25 percent should be parsley, plus about 12 leaves of basil, and a mixture including sage, lemongrass, marjoram, and mint, plus small quantities of others)

½ tablespoon / 8 g softened (with a few drops of warm water) ricotta or light cream

Tiny pinch salt

Tiny pinch freshly ground black pepper

1 tablespoon / 15 ml delicate extra virgin olive oil (such as Ligurian)

Minced parsley and basil, for garnish

Make the gnocchi and set aside. Set a large pot of cold water to boil.

Tear the herbs into pieces, discarding the stems. Place them in a large colander and set the colander atop the boiling water so the herbs steam (but are not boiled) for about 5 minutes. Remove from the colander and place in a blender or food processor and pulse quickly, only until the leaves are broken into small bits. Place in a bowl and add the softened ricotta, salt, and pepper, and whisk until the ingredients are combined. Add a little of the oil and whisk again so that the sauce acquires a silkiness. You will need more oil if you use ricotta instead of cream, but under no circumstance should you use more than 1 tablespoon / 15 ml oil. The sauce should be thinner than most pasta sauces. If it is still dense, add a little bit of hot water from the pot and whisk again. Spoon thin pools of sauce on small plates and decorate the sauce and rims of the plate with bits of minced parsley and basil.

When the water for the gnocchi comes to a boil, add a pinch of salt. Let the water return to a boil, add the gnocchi, and boil until done. Remove with a slotted spoon and place portions in the middle of each plate. Serve immediately. Diners should move the gnocchi about in the sauce as they eat.

WINE: Sauvignon Blanc or Pinot Blanc

Gnocchi con Crema di Montasio e Semi di Papavero

GNOCCHI IN A MONTASIO SAUCE WITH POPPY SEEDS

SERVES 4 TO 6 *This is a very simple sauce that I have had with gnocchi, but you may also use dried pasta, such as penne. The sauce is mostly made of fresh or semi-aged Montasio, but becomes more interesting when you also grate in some aged Montasio. If you do not have it, a little Parmigiano-Reggiano is an acceptable substitution. A serving suggestion: As a lovely small pasta course for 6, make 6 frico flowers (see page 158). Let them cool, and then spoon the gnocchi and sauce into each and serve.*

1 pound / 450 g Gnocchi (half the recipe on page 181)

½ pound / 225 g young or semi-aged Montasio cheese

2 tablespoons / 30 g grated aged Montasio or Parmigiano-Reggiano cheese

⅓ cup / 100 ml light cream or whole milk

Pinch salt

2 tablespoons / 30 g poppy seeds, pounded or crushed just before use

Make the gnocchi and set aside. Set a large pot of cold water to boil.

While the water heats, prepare the sauce. Cut the young cheese into small pieces, and grate the aged cheese. Heat the cream or milk in the top of a double boiler to just a simmer. Add the pieces of young cheese and stir gently so that everything melts. Add the grated cheese and keep stirring.

When the water has reached a rolling boil, toss in a pinch of salt and let it return to a boil. Add the gnocchi to the boiling water. As soon as they rise to the top, fish them out with a slotted spoon, shaking off excess water. Transfer the gnocchi to the sauce. Once all the gnocchi are in the sauce, toss in the poppy seeds. Give one thorough stir to combine all of the ingredients, and serve immediately.

WINE: Refosco, Merlot, Schioppettino, or Tazzelenghe

Gnocchetti al Cioccolato

CHOCOLATE GNOCCHETTI

This is a holiday preparation in Carnia. It is tasty as a dessert, but really works better as a small plate in the early part of a festive meal. For instructions on making gnocchetti, see page 182.

1 pound / 450 g Gnocchetti (half the recipe on page 181)
4 tablespoons / 60 g freshly grated smoked ricotta
3 tablespoons / 45 g freshly grated curls of bitter chocolate
1 tablespoon / 15 g sultana raisins
1 teaspoon / 5 g ground cinnamon
½ cup / 1 stick / 120 g unsalted butter
Pinch salt

Make the gnocchetti and set aside. Set a large pot of cold water to boil.

Combine the ricotta, chocolate curls, sultana raisins, and cinnamon in a bowl and set aside in a cool place.

In a small saucepan, melt the butter over low heat. Do not let it burn.

When the water is at a full boil, add a pinch of salt. When it returns to a boil, add the gnocchetti. They will rise to the surface quickly, which means they are done. Remove them with a slotted spoon and place on individual warm plates. Distribute the ricotta-chocolate mixture evenly on all the gnocchetti, and then pour the hot butter in equal amounts over the mixture. Serve immediately.

WINE: A small glass of Verduzzo, Ramandolo, or Picolit is ideal.

Gnocchi di Susine (o di Altra Frutta)

MAKES 12
GNOCCHI

Gnocchi di Susine is a classic regional dish that one can never eat enough of. It is seasonal, made only when small plums (usually called Italian, Hungarian, or prune plums) are available. You may substitute fresh apricots for plums when they are in season, and there are other fruit fillings that appear at other times of the year (see page 187). The traditional way to sauce these gnocchi is by dusting them with cinnamon and sugar and then topping them with melted butter. There is also a nice variation in which the gnocchi are sautéed in butter.

2¼ pounds / 1 kg medium mealy potatoes

Salt

1 large egg

About 2 cups / 450 g unbleached all-purpose flour

6 small ripe plums, halved and pitted

12 pinches granulated sugar

½ cup / 1 stick / 120 g unsalted butter

3 tablespoons / 50 g unflavored dry bread crumbs

Ground cinnamon

2 tablespoons / 30 g granulated sugar

In a medium-size saucepan, cover the potatoes with water. Cook, partially covered, for 30 minutes over medium-high heat. Peel the potatoes while they are still hot and mash them with a fork or pass through a potato ricer. Sprinkle on a little salt and let cool.

When the potatoes are cool, add the egg and half of the flour. Work into a dough, adding enough flour to make a dough that is firm but not hard. Separate the dough into several pieces and roll it out gently with your hands to form cigar-shaped lengths.

Cut a piece about 1½ inches / 4.5 cm long, flatten it slightly in the palm of your hand, place a plum half and a pinch of sugar within the dough, and fold it around the plum until it is completely covered. Moisten your thumb slightly and then seal the gnocco gently with your thumb. Set it aside. (Note: Do not put flour at the seam, for it will only come apart.) Make 12 gnocchi, each about the size of a tangerine. Cover the gnocchi with a cloth and let them rest for about 30 minutes.

Set a large pot of cold water to boil. There should be enough space in the pot so that when the gnocchi are added, they do not touch. If you do not have one pot that is sufficiently big, then use two.

When the water reaches a boil, toss in a pinch of salt. When the water returns to a boil, add the gnocchi carefully and cook. While the gnocchi boil, prepare the sauce. Melt the butter in a pan, add the bread crumbs, and let them toast slightly. Set aside.

There are two schools of thought about when the gnocchi are done. One says to cook them for 8 to 10 minutes. These tend to be gnocchi that do not rise to the top, especially at higher elevations. If you are closer to sea level, the gnocchi may rise during cooking. When the gnocchi rise to the top, let cook another 2 minutes. In either case, fish the gnocchi out with a slotted spoon, shake off excess water, and, if you plan to sauce them in the traditional way, place them on warm individual plates dusted with cinnamon around the edges, giving 2 or 3 per portion. Sprinkle some sugar and cinnamon over them, then pour on the butter and bread crumb mixture. Serve immediately on plates with cinnamon powder at the rim.

WINE: A Friulian white of your choice, such as Sauvignon Blanc, Pinot Bianco, Ribolla Gialla, Tocai, Traminer Aromatico, or Riesling Italico; or, a small glass of Verduzzo, Ramandolo, or Picolit

VARIATION: After trying Gnocchi di Susine the traditional way, consider finishing them as I have sometimes tasted them in Tarvisio. Combine the bread crumbs, sugar, and cinnamon on a broad plate. You will likely need more of these ingredients than indicated above, but keep them in the same proportion. When the gnocchi are cooked, roll them in the crumb mixture so they are lightly covered. Once they are all prepared, melt the butter in a large heavy pan and sauté quickly so that the crumb mixture is light golden in color and crunchy. When served this way, Verduzzo, Ramandolo, or Picolit is the ideal wine to pair with the gnocchi.

Other Fruit-Filled Gnocchi

There are other magnificent fruit-filled gnocchi from Friuli-Venezia Giulia. The most traditional filling is apricot, but many home cooks throughout the region use local fruit (and sometimes spices) to make exquisite fruit-filled gnocchi for much of the year. All of these preparations can be sauced in the traditional or alternative way, with one caveat: If there is a spice other than cinnamon enclosed in the gnocchi, then that is the spice to pair with sugar and bread crumbs outside. For stronger spices, such as ginger, be more sparing than you would be with cinnamon.

Apricots.   In early summer, apricot gnocchi are delicious if you have beautiful fresh apricots. Prepare these exactly as you would plum gnocchi, substituting apricots. If you do not have fresh apricots, find excellent unsulphured dried ones (check mail-order sources). Steam each dried apricot just until it puffs up but is not mushy. Discard any excess liquid before enclosing them in the gnocchi. Serve as you would plum gnocchi.

Cherries.   When cherries are in season, get the most flavorful ones you can find. Discard the stems and use an olive pitter to remove the cherry pits. If you do not have this tool, cut the cherries in half and discard the pits. Combine the cherries with a bit of cinnamon or nutmeg (or both) and sugar, then enclose them in the gnocchi. Have cinnamon and nutmeg in the dressing.

Red Currants.   Red currants should be combined with a little fresh lemon juice and sugar before stuffing. Cinnamon should be part of the dressing.

Pears.   Fresh pears with ginger is a sublime combination. Find fresh juicy pears, peel and core them, and chop into small pieces. Grate about 1 teaspoon/5 g fresh ginger for each pear you use. Combine the two ingredients, cover, and let sit for 15 minutes before making the gnocchi. If you do not have fresh ginger, use ⅓ to ½ teaspoon/2 to 3 g of ground ginger per pear. Either way, add a small amount of ground ginger to the dressing.

Apples.   Apple-walnut gnocchi are a wonderful combination. Peel and core flavorful apples and cut them into small bits. Crush a few walnuts and combine them with the apples and a few bread crumbs and sugar before filling. Use cinnamon in the dressing. If you are using the alternative method of dressing, add pounded walnuts to the bread crumbs.

WINES: Verduzzo is a classic match with all fruit-filled gnocchi, but I also like a big round Ribolla Gialla. Verduzzo reinforces the idea of sweetness, whereas the Ribolla lends a lush roundness and matches nicely with the gnocchi dough. Other excellent selections are a structured Pinot Bianco or, if you want a red, a Schioppettino.

Manici

RICOTTA GNOCCHI

SERVES 4 TO 8

This is a divine preparation of humble origin that can grace the tables of kings and delight the most jaded gourmand. It is an ancient dish that I learned from the delicate hands of Dina Rapuzzi, wife of Paolo, the owners of the historic Ronchi di Cialla winery. The name means "knife handles" and comes from the particular shape of these gnocchi, which are more like clouds.

3⅓ pounds / 1½ kg fresh ricotta cheese, drained in a colander or strainer

3 medium or large eggs (or 2 extra-large or jumbo eggs)

3½ ounces / 100 g freshly grated Parmigiano-Reggiano cheese

Pinch salt

Pinch freshly ground white pepper

Slightly larger pinch ground nutmeg

¼ cup / 60 g unbleached all-purpose flour plus additional flour for dusting

4 zucchini flowers (squash blossoms), torn in half, with pistils and stamens removed (optional)

3 tablespoons / 45 g unsalted butter

2 fresh sage leaves, wiped clean, stems discarded, torn into little bits

4 baby zucchini (courgettes), cut into matchsticks

In a large mixing bowl, pulverize the ricotta curds very finely with a wooden spoon. Beat the eggs and add them to the cheese. Add the Parmigiano-Reggiano, salt, pepper, and nutmeg. Combine the ingredients thoroughly, then add the flour. Stir very gently, just until the flour is incorporated.

Very lightly dust a clean surface, such as marble or wood, with flour. Place the ricotta mixture on the work surface. Divide the mixture into 8 batches. Take a batch and enclose it in your hands as if you are praying. Form a flat oval shape that is 2 inches / 5 cm long and about ¾ inch / just under 2 cm wide. The height will be determined by the shape of your hand, but it should be no more than 1¼ inches / about 3 cm. After you have briefly given it a form, open your hands and keep the gnocco in one. If you have the half zucchini flower, press it into the middle of the gnocco, which you should then take back in your hands and give its final form (the shape described above). Place the gnocco in a large glass dish and make the other 7. Cover the dish and place in the refrigerator for 10 minutes.

Fill a large wide pot that will hold all the gnocchi without touching with cold water and bring to a boil. When the water has come to a boil, add a pinch of salt. When it returns to a rapid boil, add the gnocchi. Set a timer for *exactly* 12 minutes from the moment the gnocchi were placed in the water.

While the gnocchi are boiling, melt the butter and sage in a saucepan. Add the zucchini sticks. Sauté just until they are soft. Divide them evenly among 4 plates so that they form little beds on which the gnocchi will rest. Spoon some of the pan liquid onto each bed.

When the timer sounds, remove the gnocchi quickly with a slotted spoon, shaking off all of the water. Place 2 on each bed of zucchini and serve immediately. If you are doing a meal of several small plates, you can make 8 portions of 1 *manico* each.

WINE: Dina Rapuzzi served this with their light and lovely Ciallabianco. You should think of a white blend from COF or Collio, preferably one made primarily of classic Friulian grapes, such as Tocai, Ribolla Gialla, and Malvasia Istriana.

Macaróns di Cóce (Gnocchi di Zucca)

BUTTERNUT SQUASH GNOCCHI

SERVES 4 TO 6 *These are often mistakenly referred to as pumpkin gnocchi. They can be made with pumpkin instead of squash, but the traditional vegetable in Friuli is closer to what people elsewhere might call butternut squash. Either way, you need about 1½ pounds / 675 g of the vegetable you select. The classic preparation includes a topping of smoked ricotta, melted butter, and a little sage, and it is scrumptious.*

FOR THE GNOCCHI:

1½ pounds / 675 g butternut squash (or pumpkin)

2 large eggs, beaten

1 teaspoon / 5 g salt

1½ cups / 350 g unbleached all-purpose flour

FOR THE TOPPING:

4 tablespoons / 60 g freshly grated smoked ricotta
   (or substitute half the amount pecorino from Lazio or Sardinia)

4 tablespoons / 60 g unsalted butter

A few fresh sage leaves

Preheat the oven to 350°F / 180°C.

Cut the squash in half or thirds and place on a sheet of aluminum foil in the oven. Bake until tender when stabbed with a fork, usually 30 to 35 minutes. Remove from the oven and, when it is cool enough to handle, scoop out and discard the seeds and membrane. Scoop the flesh of the squash into a fine strainer placed over a large bowl. Place in the refrigerator so that the squash cools and liquid drains away. Leave for at least 6 hours, or overnight.

If the squash is still chunky, puree it in a manual food mill or in a processor with a brief whirl. You don't want to make this too liquidy. Transfer the squash to a large bowl, then add the eggs and salt. Stir well, then add the flour a little at a time, stirring to amalgamate all the ingredients. The result should be soft but not runny.

Bring a large pot of cold water to a boil. Add a pinch of salt, and allow the water to return to a boil. With a teaspoon, scoop up some of the dough. Use your fingers (or perhaps another spoon) to form the gnocco before it goes into the boiling water. It can either have the shape of the spoons or, if you prefer, be smaller and more traditional. When the gnocchi rise and stay up in the water, fish them out with a slotted spoon. Make about 12 to 16 at a time, which should be enough to serve 4 people. Arrange the gnocchi prettily on a plate (3 or 4 spoon-shaped gnocchi per person), with their points facing one another so the result looks like a flower. Smaller portions can serve up to 6 persons.

While cooking the gnocchi, melt the butter in a small saucepan. Add the sage leaves and coat well with butter.

Add 1 tablespoon/15 g smoked ricotta (or ½ tablespoon/8 g good grating pecorino from Lazio or Sardinia, only if the ricotta is unavailable) to the top of the flower, pour some melted butter over each dish, and serve.

WINE: Pinot Bianco, Traminer Aromatico, or a dry Verduzzo

Gnocchi di Pane (Knödel) con Salsa di Cetrioli

BREAD GNOCCHI WITH CUCUMBER SAUCE

MAKES 10
GNOCCHI

There is a Friulian saying, Vida in sasso, cugúmeri in téren grasso, *which means "vines in stony soil, cucumbers in rich earth." It expresses well the origins of this recipe. Boris Aita of Cormons makes fine Tocai and white blends, and his wife Rosi cooks dishes with foods from her garden that make the wines even more delicious. The cucumber sauce is not the fresh-tasting kind that goes with salmon but rather is a spicy, concentrated sauce that I use with gnocchi of all kinds, as well as roasted or boiled meats. Note that these bread gnocchi also pair well with goulash and roasted meats where there is a sauce nearby.*

To make bread gnocchi successfully you need a careful eye and a sense of what works. Quantities are approximate because this was initially a recipe made of leftovers, and you used what you had.

About 1 pound / 450 g stale bread (all white or a mixture of white, rye, pumpernickel, and others)

1 cup / 250 ml hot milk or more as needed

1 tablespoon / 15 g unsalted butter

4 tablespoons / 60 g finely diced speck or pancetta

2 tablespoons / 30 g minced onion

3 to 4 large eggs

Pinch salt

Pinch freshly ground black pepper

1 tablespoon / 15 g minced fresh chives

½ cup / 120 g unbleached all-purpose flour, plus more for your hands

Place the bread in a flat dish and pour the hot milk over it. Turn the pieces so that the milk covers both sides. If all the pieces of bread have not been bathed in milk, add more milk. Let soak for 1 hour.

While the bread is soaking, melt the butter over medium heat and sauté the speck and onion until they are soft and fragrant. Remove the pan from heat.

Beat 3 eggs in a very large bowl. Add the salt and pepper. When the bread is soaked, squeeze out all excess liquid and put cube-size chunks in the egg mixture. Add the speck / onion mixture, including the pan liquid. Add the chives. Combine the mixture well with a wooden spoon. Add the flour and mix until the ingredients are well blended. Do not over-work the ingredients. The dough should be moist and shiny, not liquidy and not dry. If you think it is too dry, add another beaten egg. If, at that point it is too moist, add a little more flour.

Bring a large pot of cold water to a boil. When the water boils, add a pinch of salt.

The secret to the success of these gnocchi is that when you form one the ingredients stick together. Flour one hand generously and place a large spoonful of the mixture from the wooden spoon in your palm. Generously flour the other hand. Form a ball the size of a tennis ball or small orange. Press your hands together and compact the ingredients so that the ball is firm. If the ball is too loose, add a little more flour to your hands and keep rolling and shaping.

Lower the ball into the boiling water with a slotted spoon. The cooking time varies with the type of bread in the gnocco, how much flour was used, and the size of the ball. Estimate about 10 minutes, but watch it cook carefully. If it shows signs of falling apart, scoop it out and cut it in half. If it is cooked through, then that is just beyond the proper cooking time. If it is still uncooked within, then the ball was too moist and you need to add more flour to the mixture. I can tell you that with these proportions, things should work well as long as you have diligently squeezed all of the milk out of the bread. Once 1 gnocco has served as a trial, make the others and boil them right away. Remove from the water with a slotted spoon.

Serve topped with cucumber sauce or in consommé as a first course. For a main course, serve beside meats with gravy or sauce, with goulash or game. The traditional way to eat these is with a fork only, cutting them in half and swirling the pieces in sauce.

Salsa di Cetrioli

CUCUMBER SAUCE

MAKES ABOUT

1½ CUPS / 400 ML

Pinch fine sea salt

2 huge cucumbers (about ¾ pound / 375 g, if possible), peeled, seeded,
    and cut into small chunks

1 tablespoon / 15 g unsalted butter

1 garlic clove, minced

1 small onion, minced

1 tablespoon / 15 g caraway seeds

1 tablespoon / 15 g rose or sweet paprika

3 tablespoons / 45 g fresh dill leaves

2 tablespoons / 30 ml sour cream

Sprinkle the salt over the cucumber chunks and set aside for 1 hour. Drain well.

Melt the butter over medium heat in a heavy-bottomed pot, add the garlic and onion, and sauté until they are soft and fragrant. Add the cucumber pieces, caraway seeds, paprika, and dill. Cook over low heat for 1 hour, stirring occasionally as the cucumber pieces break up. Remove from heat, thoroughly stir in the sour cream, and serve.

WINE: The ideal wine with bread gnocchi and cucumber sauce is Tocai.

Tagliolini al Prosciutto di San Daniele

TAGLIOLINI WITH PROSCIUTTO DI SAN DANIELE

SERVES 2 TO 6   *Here is an exquisite, crowd-pleasing recipe that looks as good as it tastes. I discovered it in the town of San Daniele, where people dote on their local ham, and serve it all the time.*

Pinch salt

1 pound / 450 g fresh or dried tagliolini (aka tagliarini)

1 tablespoon / 15 g unsalted butter

¼ pound / 115 g (cut in 2 thick slices) prosciutto di San Daniele, minced

½ cup / 120 ml light cream

1 teaspoon / 5 g poppy seeds (optional)

2 teaspoons / 10 g freshly grated Parmigiano-Reggiano cheese

¼ pound / 115 g prosciutto di San Daniele, cut in paper-thin slices

1 teaspoon / 15 g poppy seeds, pounded just before use

Set a large pot (at least 6 quarts / 6 l) of cold water to boil. When it comes to a rolling boil, add the salt and let the pot return to a boil. Add the tagliolini and cook until al dente, according to the package instructions if you are using dried pasta; check periodically for doneness.

While the pasta is cooking, begin warming plates in the oven and prepare the sauce. Melt the butter over medium heat in a saucepan or skillet that will be big enough to hold the pasta. When the butter has melted, add the minced prosciutto. Sauté briefly, just until the ham gives off some fragrance. Add the cream and the optional poppy seeds and stir well. Add the cheese and stir well. Remove from the heat.

When the pasta is cooked, drain thoroughly in a colander (do not rinse) and then add the noodles to the saucepan. Return the pan to the heat and use a fork to quickly toss the noodles and sauce until well combined.

Using tongs or a pasta fork, fill a 6-ounce / 175-ml teacup or bowl with pasta and then carefully turn it onto the middle of each serving plate so that a nest of pasta is formed. Cover each nest entirely with a layer of paper-thin slices of prosciutto and toss a few poppy seeds around the outside. Serve immediately.

VARIATION: You may use "prosciutto" made of other animals, such as fallow deer or elk. See the listing about Wild on page 381 for more details.

WINE: Tocai or Merlot

Pasta allo Zafferano con gli Asparagi

PASTA WITH SAFFRON AND ASPARAGUS

SERVES 2 TO 6

I discovered this recipe purely by chance. I was in Tavagnacco, where asparagus is king, and I was walking down a street when a sudden April downpour drenched the town. I ducked under a bus shelter, and next to me was a woman also seeking refuge. Her bag was brimming with white asparagus, and I asked her how she was going to use them. "Al modo mio," she replied, with no ring of defensiveness in her voice. "How?" I asked again. Here is "her way"—a wonderful combination of outstanding local products with a generous use of spices.

¾ pound / 350 g white asparagus (or pale green)

3 ounces / 80 g grated young Montasio cheese or Gruyère

3 ounces / 80 g grated aged Montasio or Parmigiano-Reggiano cheese

2 tablespoons / 30 g unsalted butter

1 teaspoon / 5 g minced onion

2 cups / 500 ml Ribolla Gialla

Salt and freshly ground pepper (preferably white)

⅓ cup / 100 ml light cream

½ teaspoon / 2.5 g saffron, preferably threads

1 pound / 450 g dried pasta (penne or farfalle)

To prepare the asparagus, cut off and discard the hard ends. Cut off the tips and set aside. Cut the stalks into pieces ½ inch / 1.25 cm long.

Set a large pot of water to boil for cooking the pasta. Combine the cheeses in a dish and set aside.

While the water heats, prepare the sauce. Melt the butter over medium-low heat in a medium-size saucepan. Add the asparagus pieces (though not the tips) and onion. Sauté for 30 seconds. Pour in a little bit of wine, and add a pinch of salt and pepper. Then add a little more wine, and then some more, until all has been added and the alcohol has evaporated.

Add the asparagus tips, the cream, and half of the cheese mixture and stir until the cheese has melted into the sauce. Add the saffron and continue to cook.

When the pasta cooking water comes to a boil, toss in a pinch of salt and let it return to a boil. Then cook the pasta until al dente, according to the package instructions; check periodically for doneness. Drain well. Add the pasta to the sauce along with the rest of the cheese. Stir for about 1 minute, until the pasta is thoroughly coated. Serve immediately.

WINE: Ribolla Gialla (if unavailable, substitute Sauvignon Blanc or Pinot Bianco)

Penne con Ricotta e Cannella

PENNE WITH CINNAMON RICOTTA

SERVES 6 TO 8

This dish is popular in Carnia, where ricotta is so loved, and down through Pordenone and into the Veneto. It introduces an imported spice to a local flavor. In the past, this sauce might have flavored polenta, and it still can, but nowadays you are likely to find it blended with pasta. In Friuli, the ricotta is naturally sweet, so added sugar is unnecessary. If you are using a bland cheese, consider adding at most just a pinch of sugar. The cinnamon should be a subtle note rather than a dominant flavor. This is a rich dish, and a small portion can go a long way.

Pinch salt

1 pound / 450 g penne

12 ounces / 335 g fresh ricotta

2 teaspoons / 10 g freshly ground cinnamon (adjust to taste)

½ teaspoon / 2.5 g sugar (optional)

Set a large pot of cold water to boil. When it reaches a full boil, add a pinch of salt. When the water returns to a boil, add the penne and cook until al dente, according to the package instructions. One minute before the penne are supposed to be done, taste one and decide for yourself how much more cooking you need.

While the pasta is cooking, prepare the sauce. Put the cheese into a large bowl (big enough to contain the hot pasta). Stir the cheese with a wooden or plastic spoon for a minute to make it more creamy. Add the cinnamon and stir in well. Taste for sweetness and, if you wish, stingily add a little sugar and cinnamon. Add 1 tablespoon / 15 ml hot water from the pasta pot and stir it into the cheese to make it creamier. You might wish the sauce to be even creamier, in which case you should then stir in another tablespoon / 15 ml hot water.

Once the pasta is cooked, drain in a colander but leave a little hot water clinging to the penne. Transfer to the ricotta sauce, toss well, and serve immediately.

WINE: Ribolla Gialla, Pinot Bianco, or Tocai

Spaghetti con Scampi all' Aglio

SPAGHETTI WITH SHRIMP IN A GARLIC SAUCE

SERVES 4 TO 6

I first sampled this in Trieste in 1983, and it has become a standard in my repertoire of dishes. Many people back away in horror at the prospect of any dish made with 15 cloves of garlic, but they are pleasantly surprised if they agree to taste it. The sauce becomes smooth and creamy, and the garlic flavor is more mild than sharp. The key is to remove the green core of each garlic clove, which is where the bitterness resides. Split the clove in half and use the tip of your knife to remove the green portion from both halves of the clove.

¼ cup / 30 ml extra virgin olive oil

15 garlic cloves, finely minced

1 teaspoon / 5 g tomato paste

1 cup / 75 g unflavored dry bread crumbs

1¼ cups / 30 ml dry white wine (Malvasia Istriana, Tocai, Pinot Bianco, or Pinot Grigio)

¼ cup / 30 ml cognac

Zest from 1 unsprayed, uncolored lemon, grated

Salt and freshly ground black pepper

2¼ pounds / 1 kg (approximately 16 to 20 large fresh shrimp), peeled and deveined

¼ cup / 15 g finely minced flat-leaf parsley

Water or fish broth (optional)

1 pound / 450 g spaghetti

Combine the olive oil, garlic, and tomato paste in a deep pot over low heat and cook gently, stirring with a wooden spoon. When bits of garlic start to stick to the bottom of the pot, add the bread crumbs. Then add, in the following order, the wine, cognac, lemon zest, salt and pepper to taste, shrimp, and parsley. Raise the heat to medium-high or high (near boiling) for about 15 minutes. If the sauce becomes too thick, add a bit of water or, if you have it, fish broth. The result should be creamy. Remove from the heat, and let sit for 2 hours to concentrate the flavors.

When the sauce is ready, set a large pot of cold water to boil and begin to warm the pasta bowl. When the water reaches a boil, add a pinch of salt and let it return to boiling. Begin to gently reheat the sauce. Cook the spaghetti until al dente, according to the package instructions. Drain well in a colander (do not rinse!).

Add the spaghetti to the sauce pot. Toss well and serve immediately in warm bowls.

WINE: The same wine you used in the sauce

Blècs di Cjanâl di Guart

BUCKWHEAT AND CORN FLOUR NOODLES

SERVES 4 TO 6 *Blècs di Cjanâl di Guart, I can assure you, taste a lot better than their name sounds. These are maltagliati (irregularly cut pasta) as eaten in a valley near Tarvisio. This is another example of the Friulian love of grains. The result is simple, yet delicious.*

1¼ cups / 150 g buckwheat flour

1¼ cups / 150 g unbleached all-purpose flour

3 medium eggs

Pinch salt

10 tablespoons / 150 g unsalted butter

1¼ cups / 150 g corn flour (finely ground cornmeal)

3 tablespoons / 45 g freshly grated aged Montasio or
    Parmigiano-Reggiano cheese

2 teaspoons / 10 g minced chives (optional)

On a clean, lightly floured work surface, combine the buckwheat and unbleached wheat flours with your hands. Form a mound and make a hollow in the center. Add the eggs and a pinch of salt. Move the sides of the mound into the egg and gradually make a ball of dough. If it is too dry, judiciously add tepid water, just enough for the dough to become more elastic. Use a cylindrical wooden rolling pin to roll it out as flat as possible. When the dough is about ⅛ inch / .3 cm thick, use a knife or a fluted pastry wheel to cut triangles of dough about 2 inches / 5 cm per side. Let these triangles rest for about 30 minutes, covered by a clean cloth.

Set a large pot of cold water to boil. While the water is heating, melt the butter in a saucepan over medium heat. Do not let it turn brown. When the butter is melted, add the corn flour and cook slowly so that the flour browns and begins to look nutty and crunchy.

When the pasta water comes to a rolling boil, add a pinch of salt and let it return to a boil. Add the pasta triangles to the boiling water. Cook for only 3 minutes and then drain carefully into a colander or fish them out and place them in a colander.

Immediately add the pasta to the saucepan, and cook them quickly over high heat for 2 minutes, coating the noodles with the crunchy corn flour.

Serve immediately on individual plates, topped with a little freshly grated cheese and a bit of minced chives.

WINE: Sauvignon Blanc

Lasagne da Fornel

CHRISTMAS LASAGNE

SERVES 6 TO 8

This recipe is popular in Carnia. It is a festive dish that finds great approbation whenever I serve it. Lasagne da Fornel is customarily served at Christmas, but you can enjoy it throughout the year.

4 large or 6 medium apples, preferably a fragrant or spicy variety, such as
    Northern Spy, Macoun, McIntosh, Braeburn, or Gala
2 teaspoons / 10 ml freshly squeezed lemon juice
4 ounces / 115 g dried figs, cut into bits
4 ounces / 115 g sultana raisins
4 ounces / 115 g walnuts, crushed
Pinch of salt
1 pound / 450 g dried egg lasagne
¾ cup / 1½ sticks / 150 g unsalted butter
4 tablespoons / 60 g poppy seeds
3 tablespoons / 45 g sugar (preferably cane sugar)

Preheat the oven to 375°F / 190°C. Set a very large pot of cold water to boil.

While the water is heating, peel, core, and grate the apples into a mixing bowl. Add the lemon juice to prevent oxidation. Add the figs, sultana raisins, and walnuts. Stir gently until the ingredients are combined.

When the water is actively boiling, toss in a pinch of salt and bring to a boil again. Cook the lasagne a few at a time until they are three-quarters done (see suggestions on your box of lasagne). Drain them on a clean cloth or towel, taking care not to stack one atop another.

Melt the butter in the top of a double boiler and add the poppy seeds. Remove from the heat.

When all of the elements are prepared, lightly butter a 9-inch by 13-inch / 23-cm by 32-cm lasagne pan. Place a layer of noodles on the bottom. Add some of the apple mixture, then some melted butter. Repeat in the same order. Finish with a top layer of lasagne, then butter and poppy seeds. On top of this sprinkle the sugar.

Bake for 15 minutes. Let sit for 5 minutes before cutting.

WINE: If you want sparkling wine for a festive occasion, Prosecco is a good choice. Tocai or Chardonnay are suitable whites, and Refosco or Merlot are top picks among reds.

Cjarsòns

SAVORY FILLED PASTA FROM CARNIA

SERVES 8 TO 12

The story of this astonishing dish—unlike anything else in the repertoire of Italian pasta preparations—is inextricably linked to the history of the cramars. *This is another of the interesting and unique professions that seem to be a part of the heritage of Friuli—especially Carnia. The Friulian word* cramar *is a corruption of the German* Kramer, *which means seller of goods. In the years from 1400 to 1780, a* cramar *was a familiar sight throughout much of central Europe. Essentially a* cramar *was a spice seller, but he was very much more. He had regular routes and customers and would leave Carnia every September and travel to Salzburg and then on to other points. They were a common sight in Bavaria, where they were known as* Südfruchten, *selling wine, spices, and luxurious and humble fabrics.*

You could always spot a cramar *when he walked through town because he carried on his back a wood cabinet with many drawers called a* crassigne. *The little drawers were filled with spices that he would weigh on a scale that hung from the cabinet. His spices (which came to him from the ports of Trieste and Venice) were not so much for cooking as for medicinal needs. The more expert* cramars *would make concoctions of spices and herbs that may actually have provided relief for certain ailments. Others were more palliative only in psychological terms. Think of the character of Dr. Dulcamara, who sells the Elixir of Love (in the opera of that name) to rustic mountain people. Nonetheless, this is how they made their living. In many of the German lands,* cramars *were regarded with suspicion because they were somewhat exotic.*

The life of the cramars *declined around 1780 for two reasons. The first is that advances in medicine made more folkloric preparations obsolete. Second, a wave of protectionism and nationalism swept Austria, Switzerland, Bohemia, and German states, so that outside products were considered inferior. When they no longer traveled, the* cramars *learned other professions, including building trades, forestry, and woodworking. Their descendants used these skills to travel the world as talented and tireless manual laborers.*

The cramars *had great social and economic impact on Carnia. In 1679, for example, 2,000 emigrants (mostly male—in fact 30 percent of all males over 15) from a population of 21,000 left Carnia for most of the year. Each year, in September, Carnia became a female domain. Women worked the land, ran families and businesses, and dealt with all emergencies. When they came back in June, the men had to be integrated into the families again. They brought a lot with them: foods, customs, sometimes wives. They also spoke other languages, giving Carnia a degree of sophistication other Alpine regions did not know.*

Life was lived fully in the summer in Carnia. Fields were tended, families reunited, couples coupled. In the parish of San Daniele di Paluzza, 48.8 percent of the births in the years 1612 to 1800 occurred in March, April, May, and June. The reason is that women had been impregnated during the cramars' visit the previous summer and early fall.

And what, you ask, does all of this have to do with cjarsòns? These are filled pastas that often have up to 40 different ingredients in them. When the cramar came home in June, he emptied all of the drawers of his crassigne on the kitchen tables. The wives would gather them up, mix them with mashed potatoes, fresh or smoked ricotta cheese, fruit, herbs (especially lemon balm), chocolate, coffee, and other flavors. Each woman had her own version, and from town to town there were different preferences. The following recipe for cjarsòns (pronounced Key-Ar-SHONS, and spelled variously as cialciòns, cialsòns, cialzòns, ciarzòns, cjalsòns, cjalzòns, cjarciòns, cjarzòns, gjalsòns) is representative of the kind served in much of Carnia and is inspired by the preparation made by Signora Fides of the wonderful Ristorante Salon in Arta Terme.

In the mouth, cjarsòns speak in many flavor languages: sweet, sour, astringent, herbal, soft, buttery, toasted, smoky, and more. This is not something you would make every day, but is a marvelous festive dish. Here is a modern adaptation.

FOR THE FILLING:

2¼ pounds / 1 kg medium potatoes

7 tablespoons / 100 g minced fresh parsley

3 tablespoons / 45 g basil leaves,
  wiped and torn into small bits

3 tablespoons / 45 g lemon balm (melissa),
  wiped and torn into small bits (or substitute
  3 tablespoons / 45 g grated lemon zest) preferably
  from organic lemons

1 tablespoon / 15 g fresh marjoram leaves,
  wiped and torn into small bits

1 tablespoon / 15 g mint leaves,
  wiped and torn into small bits

1 pear, peeled, cored, grated,
  and sprinkled with lemon juice

1 apple, peeled, cored, grated,
  and sprinkled with lemon juice

3 tablespoons / 45 g sultana raisins or
  raisins, softened in a little grappa or rum

3 heaping tablespoons / 50 g grated smoked ricotta
  (or substitute good aged pecorino)

1 tablespoon / 15 g fresh ricotta

1 tablespoon / 15 g ground cinnamon

1 teaspoon / 5 g ground nutmeg

1 tablespoon / 15 g cocoa powder

1 teaspoon / 5 g freshly ground coffee beans

3 tablespoons / 45 g sugar

1 teaspoon / 5 g salt

2 tablespoons / 30 g walnut meats,
  pounded to a powdery meal

3 ladyfingers (or substitute 6 amaretti cookies
  or 10 vanilla wafers), crumbled

1 tablespoon / 15 g apricot jam

2¼ pounds / 1 kg unbleached all-purpose flour

Generous pinch salt

⅔ cup to 1 cup / 160 to 240 ml warm milk

Grated smoked ricotta or aged Pecorino Romano

Sugar

Cinnamon

About 1 cup / 2 sticks / 225 g unsalted butter, melted

Make the filling first. Boil the potatoes in water to cover until fork-tender. When cool enough to handle, peel and mash the potatoes. Place the potatoes on a large clean work surface or in a very large mixing bowl. Mix in the other filling ingredients, a few at a time. First mix in the parsley, basil, lemon balm, marjoram, and mint. Then mix in the pear, apple, and raisins, followed by the smoked and fresh ricotta. Mix in the cinnamon, nutmeg, cocoa, coffee, sugar, salt, walnuts, ladyfingers, and finally the jam. If you taste the filling uncooked, you will find that one flavor comes through after the next. Cover with plastic and set aside.

Next, make the dough. Place the flour and salt on a work surface and form a well in the middle. Add some of the warm milk and work it into the flour to form a dough. Add more milk as needed. The result should be smooth, firm, and just a little moist. If it is too moist, add a little more flour. Knead as little as possible.

Once the dough is ready, divide it into 2 or 3 pieces and let them rest for a few minutes. Then roll one piece of dough out using a rolling pin, placing the dough in front of you and rolling directly away from you. Do not change the direction of the pin. Rather, turn the dough clockwise and keep rolling directly away. Once the dough is very thin (about ⅛ inch / .3 cm), it is ready to be filled.

Take a wine glass that has a bowl about 3 inches / 7.5 cm in diameter. Wet the rim slightly, then press down into the dough to form individual circles that will become the *cjarsòns*. Save the scraps of pasta to cook in soup.

Place 1 teaspoon/5 g filling in the center of a circle of dough. Imagine the circle to be the face of a watch. Fold the dough in half so that 6 o'clock meets 12 o'clock. Seal the edges with moist fingers. Pinch and slightly raise the dough at 11 o'clock and 1 o'clock. Then squeeze the ends (3 o'clock and 9 o'clock) so that you have the tips sticking out slightly. The resulting pasta should look like a little hat. Before making the next one, make sure that the edges of the pasta are entirely sealed.

Make all the *cjarsòns* from the first batch of dough. Continue the procedure using the remaining dough and filling. Set aside for about 30 minutes to rest before cooking (by now, you will probably need a rest, too!).

To cook *cjarsòns*, set a very large pot of cold water to boil.

While the pasta water heats, grate a little smoked ricotta (or even less aged pecorino) onto each individual serving plate. Sprinkle on a pinch of sugar and a pinch of cinnamon. Pour on a bit of hot melted butter to soften the cheese.

Add a pinch of salt to the pasta water when it comes to a boil. When the water returns to a full boil, carefully add the *cjarsòns*. They will be fully cooked when they rise to the surface of the pot (often, the seam of the pasta points upward). Usually this takes about 5 minutes, more or less depending upon the density of the filling. Lift out with a slotted spoon and place the *cjarsòns* (about 6 to 8 per serving) on the softened cheese. On top of these place a very little more cheese (too much will make this dish heavy and blot all the flavors in the pasta), plus sugar and cinnamon. Spoon over 2 tablespoons/30 ml melted butter so the topping melts. Serve immediately.

WINE: A rich Sauvignon Blanc, a Verduzzo, or, if you want a red, a Schioppettino

Polente, Rîs, e Vuardi

POLENTA, RICE, AND BARLEY

And he gave it for his opinion that whoever could make two ears of corn grow upon a spot of ground where only one grew before, would deserve better of mankind, and do more essential service to his country than a whole race of politicians put together.

—JONATHAN SWIFT

It has been frequently observed to me that although Friuli-Venezia Giulia has made enormous contributions to Italy for such a small region, it has not given the nation too many politicians. You may say this is a good thing (though I believe that we need to develop and support talented leaders rather than disdain all politicians), but the people of Friuli-Venezia Giulia have their own outlook. It is a society that is fundamentally egalitarian, while Italy is a nation where politicians have incredible privileges.

In Friuli-Venezia Giulia, there is a strong sense of doing good for one's own region. The politicians I have met have all had other jobs and seem to be involved in politics as a form of public service. While researching this book, I met the region's president, Roberto Antonione, who is a practicing dentist. The mayor of Trieste, Riccardo Illy, is of the famous coffee family. Mayors I have met elsewhere are farmers, jewelers, mothers, wine makers, and teachers. And all of them eat polenta, the most egalitarian of foods in this region.

Polenta is a staple in much of northeastern Italy, but it is eaten in more ways in Friuli-Venezia Giulia. It can be creamy soft or quite firm. It serves as a cereal, a side dish, or a dessert with sugar or fruit. While other Italians exclusively consume golden yellow polenta, Friulians also have white polenta and black polenta, the latter taking a charcoal gray color when cooked. This is the most essential grain in this region, and its significance extends far beyond the table. For example, there is the tradition of the *balote*. This is a loaf of golden yellow polenta filled with a soft cheese. When the *balote* is prepared by the mother of a young woman and given to a young man, this means that his proposal of marriage has been accepted. I have noticed that when people in Friuli-Venezia Giulia list their region's leading food products, they mention prosciutto, cheese, trout, wine, grappa, fruit, and baked goods, but seldom include polenta (or, for that matter, roasted coffee). Polenta is something so fundamental, so innate, that it is second nature. And it is also omnipresent.

Corn first appeared in Friuli-Venezia Giulia at the start of the seventeenth century. The earliest documentation of it in Udine was in 1627. The traditional assertion is that corn was an ingredient brought back to the Old World from the New, but it probably did not arrive here directly. It may have gone to Spain, then across the Mediterranean to Turkey, from which it traveled to Romania (where soft cooked cornmeal is called *mamaliga*) and then moved west with the Turks to Serbia, Hungary, Slovenia, and then Venezia Giulia and Friuli.

The land of the Bassa Friulana, the plains north of the Adriatic in the provinces of Gorizia, Udine, and Pordenone, turned out to be ideal for growing corn. If you go to towns such as Mortegliano and Varmo in August, there may be a few wine grapes around, but the dominant and very beautiful view is of fields of tall stalks of corn as far as you can see. Corn grows throughout the region as far north as Carnia. Each fall, throughout the region, ears of corn are hung to dry outside homes plain and fancy to be ground into cornmeal.

In Friuli-Venezia Giulia, both yellow and white polenta are popular. A basic rule of thumb is that yellow goes with meat dishes and white with fish. Vegetables and cheeses can be used for either, although the more flavorful ones go with yellow and the more delicate ones go with white.

Before corn arrived, people in the region ate other kinds of cereals, especially millet. With the arrival of cornmeal, though, the other cereals fell into disuse. Versatile polenta was a lifesaver in a region afflicted by hunger. Rice and barley, however, were never replaced by polenta. They were served as side dishes to meat or fish; but most of the time, these grains were cooked with other ingredients or flavorings and served as the first or only course of a meal. Hence risotto, that creamy and delectable dish, and orzotto, barley cooked more or less as risotto, except that the final product is a little firmer and chewier.

Friulians are formidable risotto makers. Among the flavoring ingredients they use are radicchio, asparagus, fresh herbs, funghi porcini, sausage, chicken livers, seafood, and acacia flowers. Friulians are also Italy's foremost consumers of barley, an ingredient not really seen in the rest of the country. Note that in Italy there is also a pasta called orzo that looks like almonds. Do not confuse this with the same word, *orzo,* which means barley. Another important thing to remember about barley is that any dish you have that includes it (including soups) may be reheated only once. If you heat it a second time, the barley becomes quite bitter and ruins the dish.

As with so many food preparations in Friuli-Venezia Giulia, remember that you may make portions of polenta, risotto, and orzotto as large or small as you wish, depending upon how you intend to use them in the meal.

Polenta

As with most traditional foods, polenta is not difficult to prepare but it does take time and energy. There are instant polentas and ones that are sold prepackaged in small bricks, but none can outdo the genuine article. You should have a heavy pot that holds at least 6 quarts / 5½ l and a sturdy wooden spoon with a long handle. The pot should be stainless steel and, preferably, have a copper-clad bottom. Friulian women who are serious about their polenta have a large copper pot called a paiolo that is shaped so that the polenta can be easily turned out. In older times they would cook polenta in large cauldrons and make enough to last several days. At first it would be eaten hot, and the rest would be allowed to cool. This would be sliced as needed into wedges for toasting or grilling.

I have a traditional Friulian polenta spoon, shaped more like an oar than a spoon, which permits stirring with less resistance as the polenta thickens. If manual stirring is difficult for you, only then may instant polenta be substituted. It will not be as rich and delicious as that made by the slow method, but it is still acceptable.

You should also have on hand a board or bowl onto which the cooked polenta can be turned. In Friuli they customarily use a clean round wooden board about 15 inches / 38 cm in diameter, but you might also use a broad, flat pasta, salad, or fruit bowl.

A note about the quantities in this recipe: What we have here is the typical proportion of water and polenta as used in Friuli-Venezia Giulia. You should do all you can to purchase Italian polenta, which is now available in specialty shops and by mail order (see Sources for Ingredients). In every case you should read the recommended proportions on the package and use that as a point of departure. If you are using grits or other American cornmeal, try to purchase a product that is stone-ground and certified organic. It will be more healthful and delicious, and it is more likely that you are not buying meal made from genetically modified corn.

1⅜ tablespoons / 20 g salt

3 cups / 450 g coarsely ground polenta or cornmeal

Unsalted butter (optional)

Grated aged Montasio, Parmigiano-Reggiano, or smoked ricotta cheese (optional)

In a large pot, bring 8 cups / 1800 ml cold water to a rolling boil. Add the salt and then allow the water to return to a boil. With one hand, add the polenta to the water in a continuous stream (the Italians say, *a pioggia,* like rain) while stirring continuously with a wire whisk to prevent lumps. Set the whisk aside and use a wooden spoon to stir the polenta in one continuous motion (either clockwise or counterclockwise) to assure the final product will be silken and creamy. It will also prevent the polenta from sticking to the sides of the pot. This stirring should continue for about 40 minutes. You may pause every so often to let the polenta simmer, but then return to stirring. You will notice that sometimes the polenta will make a plopping sound as steam bubbles form and rise to the top. Some Friulian mothers let some polenta stick to the sides when the polenta is almost done. The crispy result, when cooled, is a particular favorite of children. The polenta is ready when it begins to separate from the sides of the pot.

If the polenta is to be consumed hot and creamy, you may add some butter or grated cheese. This will probably be served as a first course. Turn out the polenta, as described below, while it is still soft.

If the polenta is to be consumed firmer or left to cool, cook for a few extra minutes until the polenta is more solid. Then turn it out, preferably onto the customary wooden board, and let cool. If you know that all of the polenta will be served cool or used for grilling, cook it until it has achieved a very firm consistency.

Turning Out Polenta: First wet another wooden spoon (not the one you used in cooking) in cool water. Use it to nudge the polenta away from the sides of the pot. Gradually turn the pot so that the polenta slides out and onto the wooden board or into the broad, flat dish. Take care as the full pot will be rather heavy and cumbersome.

Slicing Polenta: After the polenta has cooled for 30 minutes or more, use a clean, sharp knife to cut square, rectangular, or triangular wedges about 1 inch / 2.5 cm thick. This may be served to accompany a meat as a second course or chilled to be served with jam, fruit butters, or cinnamon and sugar. These wedges may also be grilled or pan-fried in unsalted butter for use as an accompaniment.

There is another lovely and traditional way to cut polenta that makes very even wedges. Once the polenta has cooled for 10 to 15 minutes, take a long strand of white thread (I used strong unwaxed dental floss) in your two hands, pull apart so the thread is taut, and cut the polenta as you would a pie. Face the polenta and first lower your hands to horizontally bisect the polenta. Then walk 90 degrees to the right or left and bisect again so that you have created quarters. Then make eighths and, if you wish, sixteenths. If you prefer to have rectangular wedges, use the thread to make a series of horizontal and then vertical cuts and you will have perfect pieces of polenta to serve immediately or to use later on.

Storing Polenta: To keep any leftover polenta, cover it tightly in plastic wrap and refrigerate. In the past, leftover polenta was covered with a clean towel and stored in a place high enough to escape the reach of hungry children and animals.

Saucing Soft Polenta: While it is wonderful as is, polenta also benefits from certain dressings and sauces. Whichever one you use, the procedure is the same. After pouring soft polenta into an individual plate or bowl for serving, make a hollow in the middle using the bottom of a spoon or ladle. Then add the sauce or dressing. You may either stir it into the polenta (a good idea if it has cheese in it), or just let the sauce sit and then use your spoon to move polenta into it. Melted butter by itself, or with a spice such as cinnamon, ginger, paprika, or anise, can work. Butter and sugar is a lovely treat at the end of a meal, especially for children. You might also look at the sauce chapter (pages 113 to 133) for some ideas.

Leftover Polenta: You can always grill it to serve with fish, meat, vegetables, or cheese. A divine preparation from Lombardy is to bake a wedge of polenta in the oven with Taleggio or Gorgonzola on top until the cheese melts.

Polenta con lo Zenzero

GINGER POLENTA

SERVES 6 TO 8
AS A MAIN DISH,
10 TO 12 AS A
SIDE DISH

This is not, as far as I know, a traditional dish in Friuli-Venezia Giulia. However, the method and flavors are very much in the tradition, and I devised it for a couple of reasons. One was to see how creative cooks in the past may have taken what was available to them and fashioned something new. The second reason was to develop a polenta that would go well with fish. I like the results, and I have served it to enough people from the region who think it must be traditional because they understand the logic behind it. Typically, I use white polenta, although it is also delicious with the yellow variety. In the latter form, I have served it as a side dish with braised beef and game and roasted duck and goose. The most natural seafood matches seem to be scallops, mussels, and shrimp, although cod and monkfish also work very well. Oily fish (salmon, tuna) do not work, nor do delicate fish, such as sole and flounder.

You can make the polenta with fresh ginger, candied ginger, or ground ginger and butter. In each case, use my recommended amount of ginger as a point of departure to find the intensity of ginger flavor that pleases you. Fresh ginger is the most vivid in the mouth and you should use as much as you think would let you have the suggestion of ginger but still taste the complex flavor of the polenta. Candied ginger has a special taste because there is sugar in it. This is a really wonderful combination, especially with meat dishes. Powdered ginger will give more of a burn in the mouth. If you find that pleasing, go for this option. I think it is the least interesting choice of the three, but I know that not everyone likes to work with fresh ginger.

1 recipe Polenta (page 209)

2-inch/5-cm piece fresh ginger, or 2 tablespoons/30 g candied ginger,

  or 1 heaping teaspoon/6 g ground ginger and 2 tablespoons/30 g unsalted butter

Make the polenta according to the recipe instructions. About 10 minutes before it is done, prepare the ginger.

If you are using fresh gingerroot, peel the ginger using a vegetable peeler. Grate it into a little dish using a grater with a very fine mesh. I usually take a piece of plastic wrap and hold the root with it so the smell does not get on my hands. If you are using candied ginger, mince with a knife as finely as possible. If you are using ground ginger and butter, melt the butter carefully in a little saucepan. Remove the pot from the heat and stir in the ginger.

Stir the prepared ginger thoroughly into the polenta and keep stirring until the polenta has separated from the sides of its pot.

Serve the polenta hot or cooled.

WINE: When served with fish, Pinot Grigio is a magical combination. When served with meat and game, Pignolo is best and Merlot is very good, too.

Polenta Pasticciata

BAKED AND GARNISHED SOFT POLENTA

SERVES I

An easy and popular preparation to use either as a small plate or as a hearty first or main course. Cheese is essential, but the mushrooms or sausage are optional. Do not use both options. This is a delicious dish.

1 bowl hot, soft yellow Polenta (either an appetizer or large portion) (page 209)

1 ounce / 30 g sliced porcini, cremini, or cultivated mushrooms, cut into thin slices, about ⅓ cup (optional)

1 tablespoon / 15 g unsalted butter (optional)

2 ounces / 60 g young Montasio or latteria cheese, cut into thin strips

2 ounces / 60 g soft, crumbly pork sausage (optional)

Preheat the oven to 350°F / 180°C.

Prepare the polenta according to the recipe directions. Pour the polenta into a heat-proof dish or ramekin that is taller than it is wide (or, at the very least, not a flat dish).

Place the cheese strips over the polenta. If you are using either mushrooms or sausage, make a hollow in the polenta with the bottom of a spoon or ladle.

If you are using mushrooms, melt the butter in a small skillet over medium heat. Add the mushrooms and sauté briefly just until they are soft. Pour the mushrooms and butter into the hollow of the polenta. Place the strips of cheese across the mushrooms and polenta. If you are using sausage, peel away any casing and sauté the meat in a small skillet over medium heat until browned. Pour the sausage and pan liquid into the hollow of the polenta. Place the strips of cheese across the sausage and polenta.

Once the dish is assembled, bake for 5 minutes in the oven to give the cheese a light crust outside while leaving the polenta creamy within. Serve piping hot.

WINE: Merlot or Refosco

Toc' in Braide

SERVES 4

This is one of the real classics of the cuisine of Carnia. The ingredients are the simplest, the preparation is easy if you are attentive, and the results are gratifying. To say that this is polenta and sauce only begins to hint at how good it is. Typically Toc' in Braide is served as a first course.

FOR THE POLENTA:

¾ cup / 175 ml whole milk

Pinch salt

Heaping ¾ cup / 200 g finely ground polenta or cornmeal

FOR THE SAUCE:

¾ cup / 200 g fresh ricotta

Scant 4 ounces / 100 g young Montasio or latteria cheese, cut into small pieces

6 tablespoons / 90 ml whole milk

FOR THE GARNISH:

7 tablespoons / 100 g unsalted butter

3 heaping tablespoons / 50 g finely ground polenta or cornmeal

First, make the polenta. In a large heavy saucepan, bring ¾ cup / 175 ml cold water and the milk to a simmer. Add the salt. With one hand, add the polenta in a continuous stream while stirring continuously with a whisk to break up any lumps. Cook for 30 minutes over medium-low heat. During the cooking, stir continuously with a *whisk* (this is different from the standard polenta recipe). The goal is to have a thinner polenta than usual. This should be like a thick cereal that you can eat with a soupspoon.

While the polenta is cooking, make the sauce. Melt the cheeses in milk in the top of a double boiler set over simmering water. Do not allow the sauce to boil. Stir frequently with another whisk to make it creamy and almost frothy.

Once the sauce is made, begin warming flat soup bowls and make the garnish. Melt the butter in a small pan and toss in the polenta meal. Swirl the pan so that the polenta meal absorbs the butter and becomes toasted in color and taste. Do not let it burn.

When all the ingredients are ready, pour some polenta into the heated bowls. With a ladle, pour some cheese sauce into the middle of each bowl. With a spoon, lightly add some of the garnish over the cheese sauce. Serve immediately, with soupspoons.

WINE: A change in the fate of this most humble of farm dishes is that while it used to be served with rustic wine, it is now usually paired with big whites that have been aged in wood. Chardonnay or a Collio blend are good choices, but any wood-aged white (such as the Castello di Spessa Pinot Bianco) would fill the bill. The toasty and creamy sensations in both the food and the wine make a wonderful match.

Polenta con Montasio e Menta

POLENTA WITH MONTASIO-MINT SAUCE

Here is a delicious and typical preparation that is very easy. You may use it as a small plate in a multicourse meal, a traditional primo *before a meat and vegetable course, or as a filling one-course lunch.*

1 recipe Polenta (page 209), using yellow polenta or cornmeal
1 recipe Montasio-Mint Sauce (page 132)

Make the polenta according to the recipe instructions. This may be more than you need, so save the rest for another use. About 10 minutes before it is done, prepare the sauce.

Fill small, medium, or large bowls full of piping hot polenta. Burrow a hole in the middle of it using the bottom end of a tablespoon or ladle. Then pour in some Montasio-Mint Sauce and stir immediately. Do not overwhelm the polenta with sauce—simply fill the hole you have made. Serve immediately.

WINE: Tocai or Cabernet Franc

Polenta e Prosciutto con Salsa di Ricotta ed Erba Cipollina

POLENTA WEDGE WITH PROSCIUTTO AND RICOTTA-CHIVE SAUCE

SERVES 1

I tasted this dish in a farmhouse not far from San Daniele and will never forget how exquisite the first bite was. So were the second and third. You may serve it as an appetizer or, in a larger portion, as a lunch with a glass of wine and a salad. This recipe is for one serving because it uses leftover polenta. Simply multiply the quantities by the number of diners you will serve.

1 wedge or rectangle leftover polenta about 3 inches by 4 inches / 7.5 cm by 10 cm, at room temperature
Butter (optional)
1 very thin slice prosciutto di San Daniele
2 tablespoons / 30 ml hot Ricotta-Chive Sauce (page 127)

Begin by warming the serving plate(s) in the oven. If you have a grill or pan with a raised grid that permits grilling, heat it well and then place your wedge of polenta on it. Cook until it is browned or even a little black, if that is your preference, on both sides, turning once. If you don't have this sort of pan, melt a little butter in a skillet over medium-high heat and warm the polenta wedge on both sides.

Place the wedge on a warm plate and immediately drape the prosciutto on top of it. The heat of the polenta will soften the ham and bring out a lovely fragrance. Spoon on the sauce and serve immediately.

WINE: Tocai or a light-bodied Merlot

Rebecchine

FRIED POLENTA SQUARES WITH ANCHOVY

SERVES 6

A rebechin (with one c) is any kind of snack in Trieste. This recipe is for a specific preparation of a different origin. Rebecchine *are usually thought to be named for Rebecca and are considered part of Jewish Triestine cooking. They are popular snacks in the city and no longer confined to the Jewish kitchen.*

Extra virgin olive oil or corn oil for frying
6 to 8 salted anchovy fillets, mashed
1 tablespoon / 15 ml extra virgin olive oil
12 pieces cold white or yellow polenta, cut into squares that are ½ inch / 1.25 cm in height
    and 1 inch / 2.5 cm in length
2 large eggs, beaten
Unbleached all-purpose flour

In a pot or deep-fryer, add 5 inches / 12.5 cm olive or corn oil. Slowly warm over medium heat.

Combine the mashed anchovies with olive oil to make a paste. Spread the paste on 6 squares of polenta. Top these squares with others of equal size so that you have, in effect, made a polenta-anchovy sandwich.

Dip the sandwiches carefully in egg so that they are coated. Do not let them absorb the egg. Then roll the sandwiches in flour. Using tongs or a slotted spoon, immerse them in hot oil (olive or corn), frying them until golden—approximately 3 minutes. Drain on paper towels. Serve hot or warm with a glass of wine.

WINE: Terrano, Refosco, or Pinot Grigio

Polenta Fritta

FRIED POLENTA CUBES

Here is yet another traditional method for using leftover polenta. Cubes of polenta were fried in oil or butter and topped with sugar and cinnamon and served hot to children. I have made a modern adaptation of this to serve with cocktails or sparkling wine.

Traditional Method

Cut leftover polenta into cubes with 1-inch/2.5-cm sides. Heat enough corn oil (or a neutral vegetable oil) or unsalted butter in a skillet to cover the bottom of the pan. Once the oil or butter is hot, gently add the cubes in a single layer. Be careful not to burn your fingertips. Fry until the cubes are browned but not burnt, turning them with a slotted spoon. Lift the cubes out with the spoon and serve hot with some sugar and a light dusting of cinnamon on top.

New Method

Set aside polenta while still soft and stir in a generous amount of grated or cut cheese so that it melts into the polenta. Smoked ricotta, Montasio, Gorgonzola, Taleggio, and Parmigiano-Reggiano are all good choices. When the polenta/cheese combination is cool, cut it into cubes and fry as above. Serve piping hot with glasses of sparkling wine.

VARIATION: Use ginger polenta and omit the cheese.

WINE: Sparkling wine

Making Risotto

Here are some tips for making a basic risotto. Consult these when you work on individual recipes in this chapter.

About the Rice: Use only short-grain rice grown in Italy. The preferable varieties include Arborio, Carnaroli, and Vialone Nano. Examine the rice and use only pristine pearly kernels. Discard any that have blemishes.

Broth (Stock) or Other Cooking Liquid: While making your risotto, keep an adjacent pot of hot, though not boiling, stock to ladle into the rice as needed. For most *risotti,* you will use either chicken, vegetable, or fish stocks. In the best of all possible worlds, you will want to make your own stocks. Nothing can match a stock made to order, but it is quite time-consuming. If you make a chicken stock, use a healthy bird that has not been injected with hormones or antibiotics. Many Italians use bouillion cubes, but I discourage this. They can be tasty, but they are laced with chemicals and lots of salt. If you use broth packed in containers or cans, try to use an organic brand, and one that is low in sodium. Organic vegetable broths can be purchased, packed in containers, from health food stores in North America and elsewhere. Of course, the best option is to make your own vegetable broth from carrots, onions, celery, leafy greens, parsley, parsnips, chives, and shallots. When it comes to fish broth, you have no alternative but to poach a fish and reserve the liquid.

Most risottos as prepared in Friuli-Venezia Giulia call for the addition of some wine. In most cases, this should be a light white wine (which has had no contact with wood) such as Pinot Bianco, Pinot Grigio, or Malvasia Istriana. Also interesting, especially for vegetable risottos, is Tocai.

Oil or Butter: This choice varies from place to place throughout Italy. I often like to combine the two (heating oil gently and melting butter in it before adding other ingredients). One often-applied rule is that extra virgin olive oil should be used with fish preparations, while butter works with cheese, vegetables, or meats. In Friuli-Venezia Giulia many people tell you that oil is used around Trieste, while butter or rendered pork fat is used elsewhere.

Adding Other Ingredients: Some vegetables may be added with the onions, while others should be added a few minutes before the risotto is done. Meat, fish, and seafood should be cooked separately and added just before the risotto is ready. Fresh herbs should be chopped or torn and added to the risotto no more than 5 minutes before the risotto is done. Cheese is usually not used with fish or seafood risotto.

Consistency: This is a matter of taste. Many people like risotto *all'onda* (wavy) so that it is quite creamy. Others prefer it firmer. This preference will determine whether you add some additional stock toward the end of the cooking process.

Equipment: You will need a 4-quart / 4-l pot that is wide and heavy plus a separate pot to keep stock warm. You will also need a ladle and a wooden spoon, perhaps with a hole in the middle, so that the rice passes through during stirring.

Eating Risotto: Many Italians, when they are served a plate of risotto, flatten it with the tines of their forks so that it will cool evenly. They then scoop some up with the fork and eat it. It is important not to tarry. Risotto must be eaten hot. 🍇

Risotto

SERVES 6 TO 8

3 tablespoons / 45 ml extra virgin olive oil or 3 tablespoons / 45 g unsalted butter
   (or a combination totaling 3 tablespoons / 45 g)
½ cup / 120 g minced onion
2½ cups / 575 g Italian short-grain rice
½ cup / 100 ml white wine
6½ cups / 1500 ml hot stock or broth
½ cup / 120 g freshly grated Parmigiano-Reggiano, aged Montasio, or other suitable cheese (optional)
Freshly ground black pepper (optional)

Heat the oil and / or butter in a wide 4-quart / 4-l pot over medium-low heat. When almost hot (do not allow the butter to burn), add the onion and sauté until it is translucent. Stir frequently. Add the rice and continue stirring so that the rice toasts. It should become opalescent after a couple of minutes.

Pour in the wine and cook, stirring, until the wine has evaporated.

Add ½ cup / 100 ml stock and keep stirring until it has been absorbed. Lower the heat so the ingredients are simmering. Continue adding stock, one ladle at a time, until the rice is very creamy but firm. The total cooking time from the time you toasted the rice is about 20 minutes. The creaminess is a result of starch being released from the rice.

Stir in most of the cheese, until it has melted. Add a little pepper, if you wish. Serve immediately in flat bowls or on a broad plate. Sprinkle the rest of the cheese around the risotto.

Risotto con Asparagi

ASPARAGUS RISOTTO

SERVES 6 TO 8

This is a masterpiece of Bassa Friulana cooking each springtime. If at all possible, use white asparagus, which is wonderfully delicate. If you use green asparagus, opt for thick stalks.

1 pound / 500 g white or green asparagus, trimmed

3 tablespoons / 45 g unsalted butter

½ cup / 120 g minced onion

2½ cups / 575 g Italian short-grain rice

½ cup / 100 ml white wine

5½ cups / 1300 ml hot stock or broth

½ cup / 120 g freshly grated Parmigiano-Reggiano, aged Montasio, or other suitable cheese

Steam or boil the asparagus until you can stab the thick end of one with a fork. Remove from the water and drain, reserving the cooking liquid. Cut off the tips and reserve. Then cut the stalks into small pieces.

Heat the butter in a wide 4-quart / 4-l pot over medium-low heat. Add the onion and asparagus stalks and sauté until the onion is translucent. Add the rice and continue stirring so that the rice toasts. It should become opalescent in a few minutes.

Pour in the wine and cook, stirring, until the wine has evaporated.

Add ½ cup / 100 ml stock and keep stirring until it has been absorbed. Turn down the heat to low, so the ingredients are simmering. Continue adding stock and 1 cup / 225 ml asparagus cooking liquid, one ladle at a time, until the rice is creamy but firm.

Just 2 minutes before the risotto is done, thoroughly stir in the asparagus tips. Stir in most of the cheese, until it has melted. Serve immediately in flat bowls or on a broad plate. Pass the remaining grated cheese, which should be added sparingly by each diner.

VARIATION: Risotto con Asparagi e Gamberetti (Risotto with Asparagus and Baby Shrimp). Make the asparagus risotto. Two minutes before it is ready, melt 2 tablespoons / 30 g unsalted butter over medium heat in a small pan. Add 1 teaspoon / 5 g minced onion. Immediately add 8 ounces / 225 g boiled baby shrimp and 1 tablespoon / 15 g chopped fresh flat-leaf parsley. Cook quickly so that the shrimp are coated with onion butter. Stir the contents of the pan into the risotto and serve immediately, without the additional cheese passed at the table.

WINE: Sauvignon Blanc

Risotto con Erbe Spontanee

RISOTTO WITH FRESHLY GATHERED HERBS

SERVES 6 TO 8

This is a very popular risotto throughout the region. No two taste alike because the herbs you will find will always be different. If you do not live in a place where you can gather herbs, then purchase a combination of as many different types as you can, including flat-leaf parsley, basil, marjoram, and lemon verbena.

3 tablespoons / 45 ml extra virgin olive oil or 3 tablespoons / 45 g unsalted butter
    (or a combination of both totaling 3 tablespoons / 45 g)
1 teaspoon / 5 g minced pancetta (optional)
½ cup / 120 g minced onion
1 pound / 450 g mixed fresh herbs, chopped
2½ cups / 575 g Italian short-grain rice
½ cup / 100 ml white wine
6½ cups / 1500 ml hot stock or broth
½ cup / 120 g freshly grated aged Montasio or Parmigiano-Reggiano cheese (optional)

Heat the oil and / or butter and optional pancetta in a wide 4-quart / 4-l pot over medium-low heat. Add the onion and herbs and sauté for 1 minute, until the herbs are wilted. Move the herbs to the side of the pot and add the rice. Continue stirring so that the rice toasts. It should become opalescent after a couple of minutes.

Stir in the wine and cook, stirring, until the wine has evaporated. Add ½ cup / 100 ml stock and keep stirring until it has been absorbed. Lower the heat so the ingredients are simmering. Continue adding broth, one ladle at a time, until the rice is creamy but firm; this will take about 20 minutes from the time you toasted the rice.

Stir in some or all of the cheese, until it has melted. Serve immediately in flat bowls or on a broad plate. Do not pass additional cheese.

WINE: Tocai

Risotto con lo Sclopit o con i Bruscandoli

SERVES 6 TO 8

Sclopit *(silene) is hard to find outside of Friuli-Venezia Giulia, but this book would not be complete without this recipe. Every springtime people throughout the region dote on this herb, which has a sweet-sour taste, a very grassy fragrance, and is really very good. The other cardinal dish is risotto made with* bruscandoli, *which are fresh hops. These you might find if you live in the midwestern United States, in Germany, the UK, or anywhere beer is brewed.*

3 tablespoons / 45 ml extra virgin olive oil plus 2 tablespoons / 30 g unsalted butter
 or 5 tablespoons / 75 g unsalted butter
½ cup / 120 g minced onion
2¼ pounds / 1 kg silene or hops, coarsely chopped
2½ cups / 575 g Italian short-grain rice
½ cup / 100 ml white wine
5¾ cups / 1350 ml hot stock or broth
¾ cup / 75 ml light cream
½ cup / 120 g freshly grated aged Montasio or Parmigiano-Reggiano cheese (optional)
Chopped fresh parsley

Heat the oil and butter in a wide 4-quart / 4-l pot over medium-low heat. Add the onion and silene or hops. Sauté until the onion is translucent. Move the herbs to the side of the pot and add the rice. Continue stirring so that the rice toasts. It should become opalescent after a couple of minutes.

Stir in the wine and cook, stirring, until the wine has evaporated. Add ½ cup / 100 ml broth and keep stirring until it has been absorbed. Lower the heat so the ingredients are simmering. Continue adding broth, one ladle at a time. When the broth has all been added, add the cream and stir vigorously so that all the ingredients are combined and the rice is creamy but firm. Total cooking time will take about 20 minutes from the time you toasted the rice.

Stir in some or all of the cheese, until it has melted. Serve immediately in flat bowls or on a broad plate. The bowls or plate should be garnished with lots of chopped parsley before the risotto is added. Do not pass additional cheese.

WINE: Tocai

Risotto con le Carote

CARROT RISOTTO

SERVES 6 TO 8 *This dish is a specialty of Raveo, in Carnia, that I have slightly adapted for this book. This difference is that in Raveo they only use cut carrot pieces, while I have added thin strips of carrot, which add flavor and body.*

4 medium to large carrots

3 tablespoons / 45 ml extra virgin olive oil or 3 tablespoons / 45 g unsalted butter
  (or a combination totaling 3 tablespoons / 45 g)

½ cup / 120 g minced onion

2½ cups / 575 g Italian short-grain rice

½ cup / 100 ml white wine

6½ cups / 1500 ml hot stock or broth

½ cup / 120 g freshly grated aged Montasio cheese

2 tablespoons / 20 g chopped fresh chervil

Peel all of the carrots. Cut 1 carrot into thin disks. Chop up 2 carrots into bits. Save the largest carrots and, using a vegetable peeler, cut long flat strips of carrot by sliding the peeler lengthwise down the carrot. When you have gotten as many strips as possible, chop the rest of the carrots.

Heat the oil and/or butter in a wide 4-quart / 4-l pot over medium-low heat. Add the onion and carrots. Sauté until the carrots cook down a bit (become slightly soft). Move them to the side of the pan and add the rice. Continue stirring so that the rice toasts. It should become opalescent after a couple of minutes.

Stir in the wine and cook, stirring, until the wine has evaporated. Add ½ cup / 100 ml broth and keep stirring until it has been absorbed. Lower the heat so the ingredients are simmering. Continue adding broth, one ladle at a time, until the rice is creamy and firm, stirring vigorously. Total cooking time will take about 20 minutes from the time you toasted the rice.

Thoroughly stir in the cheese until it is melted. Then stir in the chervil. Serve immediately in flat bowls or on a broad plate.

WINE: Tocai

Risotto del Pescatore

SEAFOOD RISOTTO

SERVES 6 TO 8

There are endless variations to this preparation, based on what you might have available at the time. This particular recipe reflects some of the flavors that you would typically find in coastal towns such as Grado, Lignano, or Muggia. Absolutely do not add cheese to the finished risotto and be a little more generous than usual with black pepper, which should be ground into the pot 5 minutes before the risotto is ready.

FOR THE SEAFOOD:

8 ounces / 225 g sole or other delicate white fish (flounder, snapper, or even grouper)

1 tablespoon / 15 g minced fresh garlic

Extra virgin olive oil

½ cup / 100 ml white wine

1 teaspoon / 5 ml tomato paste

Pinch cayenne pepper or hot paprika (optional; this is used in Trieste)

8 ounces / 225 g mussels in their shells, scrubbed and debearded

1 tablespoon / 15 g unsalted butter

1 tablespoon / 15 g minced scallion or shallot

8 ounces / 225 g sea scallops, cut in half (preferably lengthwise to form disks)

8 ounces / 225 g boiled shrimp, perhaps baby shrimp

1 teaspoon / 5 ml grappa

FOR THE RISOTTO:

3 tablespoons / 45 ml extra virgin olive oil or 3 tablespoons / 45 g unsalted butter
   (or a combination totaling 3 tablespoons / 45 g)

½ cup / 120 g minced onion

2½ cups / 575 g Italian short-grain rice

½ cup / 100 ml white wine

5½ cups / 1300 ml hot fish broth

Freshly ground black pepper

¼ cup / 60 g freshly grated Parmigiano-Reggiano, aged Montasio, or other suitable cheese (optional)

First, poach or steam your sole or other white fish. Let cool before flaking.

Combine the garlic and a little olive oil in a large pot and heat slightly, just until you smell the garlic. Add the wine, ¼ cup / 50 ml water, the tomato paste, and cayenne or paprika. Stir well and bring to a gentle boil. Add the mussels, cover, and cook until the mussel shells have steamed open, about 5 minutes. Turn off the heat. Discard any mussels that do not open. Remove the mussels from their open shells and place in a dish. Discard the shells. Strain and reserve the liquid from the pot.

To make the risotto, heat the oil and / or butter in a wide 4-quart / 4-l pot over medium-low heat. Add the onion, and sauté until translucent, stirring frequently. Add the rice and continue stirring so that the rice toasts. It should become opalescent after a couple of minutes.

Stir in the wine and cook, stirring, until the wine has evaporated. Stir in the mussel liquid and cook until it has been absorbed. Add ½ cup / 100 ml broth and keep stirring until it has been absorbed. Lower the heat so the ingredients are simmering. Continue adding broth, one ladle at a time.

When half the broth has been added to the risotto, cook the remaining seafood. In a small skillet, melt 1 tablespoon / 15 g butter with the green onion or shallot. Add the scallops and shrimp and sauté for 15 seconds. Add the grappa, being careful that flames from your stovetop don't lick into the pan, and cook the scallops and shrimp for another 30 seconds. Pour the contents of the pan into the risotto. Then add the flaked sole (or other fish). Keep stirring the pot, add the cheese and black pepper to taste, and gradually add the remaining broth until the risotto is creamy and the rice is tender but firm. Seafood risotto should be a little thin and creamier than other risottos, so do not overcook.

Serve immediately.

WINE: Sauvignon Blanc, Pinot Grigio, Malvasia Istriana, Pinot Bianco, Tocai, or an unwooded white blend

Risotto con Capesante, Fiori di Zucca, ed un Arcobaleno di Spezie

RISOTTO WITH SCALLOPS, ZUCCHINI BLOSSOMS, AND A RAINBOW OF SPICES

SERVES 4 TO 6

I tasted this dish at the dinner table of a small wine-making family near Pordenone. They were using it to show off their Tocai. At first, the idea of this dish seemed too forced, too nouvelle, but I discovered that it was an old recipe, dating back to the nineteenth century. It seems that a relative was a spice seller from Carnia, and like the cramars of old he would come home with an assortment of spices at the end of his journey. These flavors have been in Friuli-Venezia Giulia for centuries. Scallops are the most popular shellfish in the region, and zucchini (courgette) blossoms have always been a traditional ingredient among local cooks who wasted almost nothing. The combination is therefore traditional, and the flavor beguiling. Ideally, you want to use whole spices and crush them just before tossing them into the risotto, but this is also an occasion for you to use up spices you have had too long in little jars, so gather as many of the spices called for that you can find.

FOR THE SPICE MIX:

Use as many of the following spices as you can
    gather, totaling about 2 tablespoons / 20 g:

Ground ginger

Cinnamon

Star anise (whole)

Red peppercorns

Green peppercorns

Cardamom

Cumin seeds

Juniper berries

Cloves (whole)

Dash sugar (just enough to cover the
    tip of a teaspoon)

FOR THE RISOTTO:

5 tablespoons / 75 g unsalted butter

1¾ cups / 14 ounces / 400 g Italian short-grain rice

18 to 20 zucchini blossoms, pistils and bases removed,
    cut into lengthwise strips

4 cups / 1 l boiling vegetable broth, or more, as needed

Extra virgin olive oil or unsalted butter

8 ounces / 225 g sea scallops, rinsed and left to dry on
    paper towels, then sliced into
    coin-shaped disks

Combine the spices in a pepper mill or mortar. Grind or pound them until they form a very fine powder. If you are using spices that have already been ground, combine in a bowl. Stir in the sugar. Set the spices aside, covered.

Melt 1 tablespoon/15 g butter over medium-low heat in a wide 4-quart/4-l pot. Add the rice and toast it, stirring constantly. It should become opalescent in a couple of minutes. Then add the zucchini flowers. Stir so that the ingredients combine and nothing sticks. Add one ladleful of vegetable broth. Keep stirring until it has been absorbed. Then add another, until it has been absorbed. Continue the process until you have used all of the broth.

Add the remaining 4 tablespoons/60 g butter, stir thoroughly, and let the risotto cook for another 5 minutes, stirring occasionally. Then add the spices. When I first tasted this dish it was very spicy. You need to determine how much is sufficient for you. I find that 2 tablespoons/20 g is quite enough to give the dish character without being overbearing. You may want more or less. Stir thoroughly, and cook for about 5 more minutes.

Lightly grease a nonstick pan with olive oil or butter and heat at medium-high. Add the scallops and cook rapidly, stirring for 30 to 45 seconds, just until they are done. Spoon the scallops and any pan liquid into the risotto. Stir thoroughly. The risotto should be creamy. Serve immediately.

WINE: Tocai, Pinot Grigio, or Sauvignon Blanc

Risotto con Grancevola e Piselli

RISOTTO WITH CRABMEAT AND PEAS

SERVES 6 TO 8   *This lovely dish is popular in small trattorias and restaurants in Trieste.*

3 tablespoons / 45 ml extra virgin olive oil or 3 tablespoons / 45 g unsalted butter
   (or a combination totaling 3 tablespoons / 45 g)
½ cup / 120 g minced onion
2½ cups / 575 g Italian short-grain rice
½ cup / 100 ml white wine
6½ cups / 1500 ml hot fish or vegetable stock or broth
¾ cup / 180 g fresh baby peas
1 pound / 450 g cooked crabmeat, cut or torn into shreds or strips

Heat the oil and/or butter in a wide 4-quart / 4-l pot over medium-low heat. Add the onion, and sauté until it is translucent. Add the rice and continue stirring so that the rice toasts. It should become opalescent after a couple of minutes.

Stir in the wine and cook, stirring, until the wine has evaporated. Add ½ cup / 100 ml broth and keep stirring until it has been absorbed. Lower the heat so the ingredients are simmering. Continue adding broth, one ladle at a time. Five minutes before the risotto is done, toss in the peas and stir thoroughly. One minute before the risotto is done, thoroughly stir in the crabmeat. Total cooking time will take about 20 minutes from the time you toasted the rice.

Serve immediately in flat bowls or on a broad plate. Do not serve cheese.

WINE: Pinot Bianco or Ribolla Gialla

Risotto alla Cannella e Miele

RISOTTO WITH CINNAMON AND HONEY

I tasted this lovely dish at the Trattoria La Primula in San Quirino near Pordenone and adapted it for this book. Note that you should try to use a very light chicken broth. If you have one that is fragrant, dilute it with spring or distilled water.

5 tablespoons / 75 g unsalted butter
2½ cups / 575 g Italian short-grain rice
½ cup / 100 ml white wine
6½ cups / 1500 ml hot light chicken broth or stock
Freshly ground black pepper
¼ cup / 60 g freshly grated aged Montasio or other suitable cheese
1 tablespoon / 15 g ground cinnamon
¼ cup / 60 ml honey (preferably orange flower, clover, or chestnut)

To make the risotto, heat 3 tablespoons / 45 g butter in a wide 4-quart / 4-l pot over medium heat. Add the rice and continue stirring so that the rice toasts. It should become opalescent after a couple of minutes.

Stir in the wine and cook, stirring, until the wine has evaporated. Add ½ cup / 100 ml broth and a little black pepper, and keep stirring until it has been absorbed. Lower the heat so the ingredients are simmering. Continue adding broth, one ladle at a time. Total cooking time will take about 20 minutes from the time you toasted the rice.

Stir in the cheese until thoroughly melted. Remove the risotto from the heat and stir in the cinnamon. Add the honey and remaining 2 tablespoons / 30 g butter. Serve immediately in flat bowls or on a broad plate.

WINE: Tocai or Traminer

Risotto di Mele o di Pere

APPLE OR PEAR RISOTTO

SERVES 6 TO 8

Here again is the Carnia fruit tradition, and the result is subtle and delicious. Use the most fragrant and flavorful apples or pears you can locate. Peel them, core them, chop them in little pieces, and toss them with a little lemon juice to prevent oxidation. Do not combine apple or pear flavors in this dish; use one or the other.

Note that spices, such as cinnamon or nutmeg, do not work well in this dish. However, a stinting addition of chopped fresh mint (with apple) or verbena (with pear) is very nice. But the first time you make this recipe try it without the added herbs.

2 cups / 450 ml apple juice or pear nectar

3 cups / 675 g diced apple or pear

Freshly squeezed lemon juice

3 tablespoons / 45 g unsalted butter

2½ cups / 575 g Italian short-grain rice

1 teaspoon / 5 ml Calvados or pear distillate (preferably Friulian) (optional)

½ cup / 100 ml white wine

Chopped fresh mint (with apple) or lemon verbena (with pears), torn into small bits (optional)

½ cup / 120 g freshly grated aged Montasio or Parmigiano-Reggiano cheese

In a medium saucepan, combine the apple juice or pear nectar with 4½ cups / 1050 ml water and bring to a boil.

Toss the fruit with the lemon juice to prevent oxidation.

Heat the butter in a wide 4-quart / 4-l pot over medium-low heat. Add 1 cup / 225 g fruit and sauté for about 2 minutes, until the fruit is slightly soft. Push some of the fruit to the side and add the rice. Continue stirring so that the rice toasts. It should become opalescent after a couple of minutes.

Stir the Calvados or distillate into the wine and pour into the saucepan. Cook, stirring, until the wine has evaporated. Add ½ cup / 100 ml fruit juice and keep stirring until it has been absorbed. Lower the heat so the ingredients are simmering. Continue adding fruit juice, one ladle at a time, until the rice is creamy but firm; this will take about 20 minutes from the time you toasted the rice. About 5 minutes before the dish is finished, toss in the remaining 2 cups / 450 g fruit. If desired, add the mint or lemon verbena and continue stirring until the rice is done.

Stir in the cheese, until it has melted. Serve immediately in flat bowls or on a broad plate.

WINE: The best choices would be an unwooded Pinot Bianco, Ribolla Gialla, or Tocai. Another interesting option is a big wood-aged Chardonnay or Collio white blend; however, do not add wood-aged wine to the risotto because it would overwhelm the delicate flavors and ruin the dish. Instead, use a delicate white of the types listed above.

Risotto al Vino

RISOTTO WITH WINE

With the great wines Friuli-Venezia Giulia offers, you might be tempted to try each one in risotto. I would recommend that you skip all the white wines and every dessert wine except for sparkling ones. The best bets are good, well-crafted grapey reds such as Refosco, Schioppettino, or Merlot.

3 tablespoons / 45 g unsalted butter

½ cup / 120 g minced onion

2½ cups / 575 g Italian short-grain rice

1½ to 2 cups / 175 to 225 ml red wine, such as Refosco, Schioppettino, or Merlot

5 cups / 1200 ml hot broth or stock

Freshly ground black pepper

¼ cup / 60 g freshly grated Parmigiano-Reggiano, aged Montasio, or other suitable cheese

To make the risotto, heat the butter in a wide 4-quart / 4-l pot over medium-low heat. Add the onion and sauté until it is translucent, stirring frequently. Add the rice and continue stirring so that the rice toasts. It should become opalescent after a couple of minutes.

Stir in ½ cup / 100 ml wine and cook, stirring, until the wine has evaporated. Stir in the remaining wine, ½ cup / 100 ml at a time, until it has been absorbed. Add ½ cup / 100 ml broth and keep stirring until it has been absorbed. Lower the heat so the ingredients are simmering. Continue adding broth, one ladle at a time. Total cooking time will take about 20 minutes from the time you toasted the rice.

Season with pepper. Stir in the cheese until thoroughly melted. Serve immediately in flat bowls or on a broad plate.

WINE: Either no wine at all or a small glass of the wine used in the risotto

A flower of frico croccante filled with gnocchi in a Montasio cheese sauce
with poppy seeds and prosciutto di San Daniele

Duck breast with pink peppercorns and sautéed figs

Risotto with shrimp, asparagus, and saffron

Polenta with ricotta-chive sauce draped with prosciutto di San Daniele

Palacinche filled with cherries (left) and lemon-scented ricotta (right)

Orzotto (barley risotto) with mushrooms, carrots, and grapes

Lasagne da fornel *(Christmas Eve lasagne)*

Insalata triestina

Orzotto

SERVES 4

Barley has been in Friuli-Venezia Giulia for a very long time and is part of the food tradition. It can be used in two ways: as a vegetable side dish (you will find recipes on pages 299 to 301 for this preparation) or cooked in a manner similar to risotto. You will find below the standard method for making orzotto, and you should add ingredients in the manner called for in individual risotto recipes. I don't believe that everything that goes with rice goes with barley, which has a more insistent flavor and texture. Most fish and seafood do not work well, although I like sautéed rings of squid or strips of cuttlefish. Vegetables work very well and herbs are perfect. All sorts of mushrooms go well with barley, as do currants, grapes, dried cherry, and slivers of fresh cherry. Ground pork, sliced or diced prosciutto, small bits of lamb, rabbit, or venison are also congenial. While most wine for risotto is white, you can drink some light to medium-weight red wines with some orzotto preparations.

3 tablespoons / 45 ml extra virgin olive oil

3 tablespoons / 45 g unsalted butter

2 tablespoons / 30 g minced onion

2 tablespoons / 30 g minced scallion or chive

10 ounces / 300 g pearl barley

4 cups / 1 l cold water (preferably spring or distilled), brought to a boil

2 heaping tablespoons / 35 g freshly grated aged Montasio or Parmigiano-Reggiano cheese

Combine the olive oil and butter in a wide 4-quart / 4-l pot and heat over low heat, taking care not to burn the butter. Add the onion and scallion and sauté gently until the onion is translucent.

Add the barley and increase the heat slightly. Toast the barley for about 5 minutes. Add the boiling water, ½ cup / 100 ml at a time. When ½ cup / 100 ml has been absorbed by the barley, add more. Continue until all the water has been absorbed. At a certain point the barley will yield some of its starch, making the dish more creamy. If it is dry, add some softened butter, perhaps a drop of milk or cream, and the grated cheese. At this point, add the optional flavor ingredients. The total time for making the orzotto should be about 25 minutes.

Possible Additional Flavor Ingredients for Orzotto

- ⅓ pound / 150 g porcini or cremini mushrooms, sliced and sautéed in 2 tablespoons / 30 g unsalted butter

- ⅓ pound / 150 g diced prosciutto di San Daniele sautéed in 1 tablespoon / 15 g unsalted butter with 1 tablespoon / 15 g dried currants or cherries

- ½ pound / 225 g small chunks of lamb sautéed in 2 tablespoons / 30 g unsalted butter and a pinch of salt; toss in 1 teaspoon / 5 g finely torn mint leaves

- ½ pound / 225 g small squid rings or strips of cuttlefish, cleaned, sautéed in 3 tablespoons / 45 ml extra virgin olive oil to which ½ cup / 100 ml light white wine is added; the seafood is ready when tender

Orzotto alle Erbe Spontanee

BARLEY WITH WILD MOUNTAIN HERBS

SERVES 4

This is a recipe from Chef Gianni Cosetti of the Ristorante Roma in Tolmezzo, just at the foothills of the Carnia Alps. Gianni works hard to preserve the traditional flavors of Friuli and is also one of the leading innovators in the creation of modern classics in the Friulian style. Because the Alps are nearby, he has access to a great variety of herbs that grow wild. To create this recipe effectively outside of Friuli, it is important to have flat-leaf parsley, basil, marjoram, lemon verbena, and other green herbs. Above all, mint is absolutely indispensable; if there is none at hand, you should not make this dish. The idea is to make a broth of these herbs, and the overall effect should be of springtime freshness. Vegetarians may eliminate the speck or prosciutto and will find this to be a wonderful first course.

1¾ pounds / 800 g assorted mixed fresh herbs

Salt

1½ onions, minced

1 celery stalk, minced

1 carrot, finely grated

1 small zucchini, ends removed, chopped into small pieces

3 tablespoons / 45 ml extra virgin olive oil

3 tablespoons / 45 g unsalted butter

2 ounces / 50 g speck or prosciutto di San Daniele, cut into small cubes (optional)

10 ounces / 300 g pearl barley

3 tablespoons / 45 g freshly grated Parmigiano-Reggiano or aged Montasio cheese

Wash all of the herbs carefully, ridding them of any dirt or discolored leaves. Bring 33 ounces / 1 l fresh cold water (preferably spring water) to a boil in a large pot, adding a pinch of salt. Add the herbs and cook for 3 to 4 minutes. Strain the liquid and return it to the pot. Put the herbs on ice so they will retain their color.

Add two-thirds of the minced onions, the celery, carrot, zucchini, and another pinch of salt to the pot and boil for 30 minutes to make a vegetable broth for the barley. Strain the broth once it is done.

In a wide 4-quart / 4-l pot, heat the olive oil and butter over medium heat. Add the remaining minced onion and the diced speck or prosciutto. Sauté for a few minutes, until the onion becomes translucent and the speck slightly pink. Add the barley and toast it slightly, moving it around with a wooden spoon. Lower the heat and add ½ cup/100 ml cooking broth; stir until it is absorbed. Then add another ½ cup/100 ml, and continue this process for 35 minutes, until most of the liquid has been added, stirring very frequently.

Remove the herbs from the ice and finely chop them. Add the chopped herbs and stir well. Add the remaining broth. Stir in the freshly grated cheese (grate it just before using it), and keep stirring for 2 minutes. Serve immediately.

WINE: Pinot Bianco

Peš e Frutam di Mâr

You need only look at the undulating floor in the ancient basilica in Aquileia to know that the people of Friuli-Venezia Giulia have enjoyed a huge selection of fish and seafood for thousands of years. The mosaics depict many types of sea creatures in all of their beauty and mystery, and you can still see most of these in the fish markets of the region.

Nature was generous and creative in the bounty it offered. Along the eastern shore of the Adriatic, in the province of Trieste and farther south in Istria are coves where all kinds of shellfish grow and fish feed and breed. There are beds of mussels all around Trieste.

The northernmost part of the sea is a beautiful network of canals, lagoons, bird sanctuaries, and a sandy sea floor that provides the right nourishment for the fish in residence. Fine white fish such as sole, turbot, sea bass, bream, and monkfish are taken from these waters. There is also an abundance of fresh anchovies and sardines that are especially popular in Trieste. Eel that swim in bays and river mouths wind up in many fish stews. This area is also full of scallops, shrimp, and soft-shell crabs, all of which star on tables from Trieste to Venice.

While Grado, set in the lagoon just like Venice, is the chief fishing port of the region, there is significant activity in Lignano, Monfalcone, Trieste, and Muggia. With towns such as Pordenone, Udine, Cormons, and Gorizia no more than 40 minutes from a port, fresh fish can be found on tables in most of the region.

When a railway was created to run from Trieste to Vienna in the late nineteenth century, there was a daily train with carriages full of blocks of ice that left at 3 in the morning carrying fresh fish to Vienna. It stopped to make deliveries at a couple of towns en route before arriving at 10 A.M. The fish was in the markets of Vienna at 11:30 A.M. and on lunch tables by 1 P.M. I learned of this from Manny Peck (born 1896), who was the last surviving fisherman of the Austrian Empire in this area. He had the daily routine of a 2:30 P.M. card game (with wine) at an *osteria* in Brazzano.

Northern Friuli produces and consumes more trout than any part of Italy. The fish swims free in the rivers and is also farmed in real and man-made lakes near San Daniele and Venzone. A recent delicacy is smoked trout, produced in San Daniele and now exported.

An interesting side note is that people in this region are the only Italians who eat a significant amount of herring. It is not a local fish, but has arrived from the Baltic and North Seas for many centuries. In Carnia, smoked herring provided cheap yet highly nutritious sustenance to poor people in midwinter. In Trieste, smoked herring is a favored specialty. It is soaked in milk until it softens, and then it is split and boned, topped with a bit of olive oil, and served with hot squares of polenta.

As fish becomes more popular throughout the world, many of them come from waters that are polluted or overfished. It seems that Friuli-Venezia Giulia has not been affected by this in a major way, in part because of the regional devotion to civic-minded environmentalism. Late each spring, the Italian government and Italia Nostra, the nation's leading environmental organization, release statistics documenting the cleanliness of beaches and waters in Italy's twenty regions. For many years now, Friuli-Venezia Giulia has been the national champion. Its beaches have received perfect ratings, and the rivers, lagoons, and sea are among the most pristine in southern Europe. One of the reasons for this is the innate awareness among people in the region that protecting the land and sea is not only a question of food and tourism. To pollute this land would be a stain on one of the foremost senses of identity that people here have.

For more recipes using fish and seafood, see the appetizer, soup, pasta, and rice chapters.

Sogliola al Vapore

SOLE FILLETS COOKED OVER BOILING WATER

SERVES 2 TO 3

People in Friuli-Venezia Giulia brag that their sole is the world's best because of the particular microclimate of the northern Adriatic. It is indeed delicious, but I have had outstanding sole in England, France, and elsewhere. This particular preparation is interesting because it really brings out the flavor of the fish. I first had it on a small fishing craft near Muggia made with a fish caught minutes before. The key to making this recipe at home is to use a shallow covered heatproof dish, preferably of glass. Or substitute two glass pie plates of equal size, and use great care in handling them so you do not burn yourself or break the dishes.

1 pound / 450 g sole fillets
1 tablespoon / 15 g freshly minced garlic
1 tablespoon / 15 g minced fresh marjoram or fresh Italian parsley
Pinch fine sea salt
3 tablespoons / 45 ml delicate extra virgin olive oil

Fill a large, wide-mouthed pot with water and set a metal rack across it. Bring the water to a boil.

While the water heats, wash and carefully dry the fillets. Lay them flat in a shallow heatproof dish, taking care that they overlap as little as possible. Sprinkle the garlic, marjoram, and salt over the fillets. Drizzle the oil on top of this.

Cover the dish and place it on the rack over the rapidly boiling water. Leave covered for 5 minutes so that the steam that develops will cook the fish. Using the tines of a fork, test to see if the fish flakes, which means the fish is done. The cooking time varies depending on the thickness of the fish. I find that it usually takes about 8 minutes.

Serve with lemon wedges, or perhaps with Caper Sauce (page 128) or a drop of Warm Horseradish Sauce (page 117).

WINE: Pinot Grigio or Pinot Bianco

Filetti di Trota con i Sapori dell'Orto

TROUT FILLETS WITH THE FLAVORS OF THE GARDEN

SERVES 4

I tasted this dish in a family home just outside Gemona. There everybody has a little plot of land, and the nearby rivers teem with trout. So it is no secret how this dish came about.

2 pounds / 900 g trout fillets

Juice of 2 lemons

3 tablespoons / 45 ml delicate extra virgin olive oil

1 onion, finely minced

1 garlic clove, green core removed, finely minced

8 ounces / 225 g baby zucchini, finely diced

8 ounces / 225 g yellow bell peppers, finely diced

Salt and freshly ground black pepper

8 ounces / 225 g plum tomatoes, cut in small chunks, with seeds and liquid set aside

1 tablespoon / 15 g fresh thyme, torn into small pieces

Unbleached all-purpose flour

3 tablespoons / 45 g unsalted butter

Caper Sauce (page 128), made with vegetable broth (optional)

Wash the trout fillets and dry with paper towels. Place them in a dish in a single layer. Pour on the lemon juice and cover the dish with plastic wrap. Refrigerate for 2 hours.

When you are ready to cook, prepare all of the vegetables. Heat the oil at medium temperature in a skillet (large enough to hold the trout fillets). Add the onion and garlic and sauté gently until the onion is translucent. Add the zucchini and peppers and sauté until they have softened but not become soggy. Season to taste with salt and pepper. Add the tomatoes and thyme and sauté for about 30 seconds. Transfer the vegetables to a bowl and cover to keep warm. Begin warming serving plates.

Dry the trout fillets with paper towels. Dip the fillets in flour to coat on both sides. Shake gently to remove any excess flour.

Melt the butter in the pan over medium-low heat. Add the fillets and sauté on both sides, just until they have turned a light gold color. Five minutes is an average cooking time, although this will vary according to the thickness of the fish you are using.

Place the trout fillets on individual warm plates and spoon a heap of vegetables next to them. Serve immediately. If you wish, you may serve this dish with Caper Sauce, as long as you have made the sauce with vegetable broth.

NOTE: You may also use yellow squash with green pepper. The goal is that you have a variety of color and texture.

WINE: Ribolla Gialla, Traminer, Pinot Bianco, or Riesling Italico

Coda di Rospo con Vinaigrette allo Zenzero

MONKFISH WITH GINGER VINAIGRETTE

SERVES 4 AS A
MAIN COURSE, 8
AS A SMALL PLATE

A delicate and delicious dish served at the Trattoria agli Amici in Godia, just outside Udine. The fish can be served either cool or tepid, although the sauce must be prepared 24 hours in advance.

FOR THE SAUCE:

Scant 5 tablespoons / 70 g peeled and grated
    fresh ginger, with its juice
4 teaspoons / 20 ml dry white wine
4 teaspoons / 20 ml freshly squeezed lemon juice
½ cup / 120 ml extra virgin olive oil
2 teaspoons / 10 g salt

FOR THE FISH:

2 monkfish fillets, about 1¼ pounds / 500 g each
3½ tablespoons / 35 g fresh dill leaves
4 teaspoons / 20 g fine sea salt
Pinch freshly ground black pepper
5 tablespoons / 75 ml delicate extra virgin olive oil
1 tablespoon / 15 ml white wine
3 tablespoons / 40 g fresh dill leaves, for the plates

The day before eating this dish, prepare the sauce. Combine the ginger in a bowl with the wine, lemon juice, oil, and salt. Cover the bowl with plastic wrap and refrigerate for 24 hours. Briefly blend to break up any large pieces of ginger and pass the sauce through a thin strainer. Set aside.

To prepare the fish, preheat the oven to 350°F / 180°C.

Wash the fish and carefully pat dry with paper towels. Cover the fillets with the dill, salt, and pepper. Using a little at a time, massage the oil into the fish. (Some of the dill, salt, and pepper may slightly penetrate the fish, which is fine.)

Combine the wine and 1 tablespoon / 15 ml cold water in an ovenproof baking dish (preferably of glass). Carefully place the fillets in the dish, cover, and bake for 10 minutes.

Remove the fish from the dish and let cool to tepid. Carefully flake the pieces of fish so that you have made medallions. Whether you choose to serve these tepid or let them cool, do not refrigerate the fish, which will tighten the flesh.

Casually distribute dill leaves around each individual plate. Decoratively place the monkfish medallions on each plate. Stir the sauce and brush lightly onto the fish. Put a few dots of the sauce elsewhere on the plate for color and additional bursts of taste.

WINE: Sauvignon Blanc

Pesse in Savòr

FISH IN TRIESTINE MARINADE

SERVES 6 AS A
MAIN COURSE,
10 TO 12 AS AN
APPETIZER

This is a classic preparation of the northern Adriatic. When you read about dishes such as sarde in saor and associate them with Venetian cooking, you probably do not realize that most historians believe that this preparation originally came from Trieste and Monfalcone in Venezia Giulia. We know this because it was a traditional preparation in this area when it was under the Roman Empire, more than four centuries before Venice would be born. The earliest mention of preserving fish this way was by Apicius, the world's first food writer.

The most traditional recipe uses the anchovies or sardines that once abounded in the waters near Trieste. Savòr is also used inland to preserve freshwater fish, such as trout, and you can consider it for other white-fleshed fish or, even, salmon. You should not use delicate prized fish, such as sole, as that would waste a precious commodity not suited to this recipe. Tuna, swordfish, and shark also do not take well to savòr.

The original intention of this marinade was to preserve fish that was caught in abundance. Now people eat it this way because it tastes so good.

FOR THE MARINADE:

1 tablespoon / 15 ml delicate extra virgin olive oil
2¼ pounds / 1 kg onions, sliced very thin
Salt and freshly ground black pepper
¾ cup / 175 ml white wine vinegar (see Note)
1 bay leaf

FOR THE FISH:

2¼ pounds / 1 kg fresh whole anchovies or sardines, cleaned and scaled (heads and tails may be left or removed as you prefer) (see Note)
Unbleached all-purpose flour
Delicate extra virgin olive oil

To make the marinade, swirl the oil in a broad deep pan so that the bottom is covered as much as possible. Add the onions and spread them out so they are evenly dispersed. Add the salt and pepper and cover the pan.

Place over medium heat and cook for 5 minutes. Remove the lid and continue cooking, stirring so that the onions do not stick to the bottom of the pan. If there is not much liquid in the pan, add 1 tablespoon / 15 ml tepid water. When the onions are translucent, add the vinegar and, if you have not used it before, the water. Add the bay leaf and raise the heat to high. When the sauce is just about to boil, turn the heat to low and simmer just until half of the liquid has evaporated.

Now prepare the fish. Rinse the fish in cold water and then pat dry with paper towels. Dip the fish in flour to cover completely, and then shake gently so that any extra flour falls away.

Pour just enough oil into a frying pan to lightly cover the bottom. Heat the oil over medium-high heat until hot (not crackling) and add the fish, a few at a time. Fry just until the fish are warmed through and slightly crunchy on the outside. Ideally, the fish should be soft rather than firm. If they cook too much, the fishy flavor will intensify with unpleasant results. Remove from the pan and set aside to cool. Repeat the process until all the fish are cooked and cooled.

Cover the bottom of a large square or rectangular glass dish with a layer of onions. Place the fish evenly across the onions, then pour the liquid part of the *savòr* over all of the fish. Top completely with another layer of onions. Marinate for at least 24 hours in the refrigerator. It will be much tastier after 48 hours and better still after 72. It is essential that the fish be served at room temperature, perhaps with some warm or cold white polenta (or yellow, if you don't have white).

NOTE: You can use other fried fishes, such as a small trout or a baby turbot. You can also substitute red wine vinegar for the white wine vinegar. The color of the pickled fish will be darker, but the flavor will be excellent.

VARIATION: Using Firm-Fleshed Fish: Use 2¼ pounds / 1 kg fish fillets, such as halibut, haddock, cod, or salmon. Steam until the fish is tender but not overcooked. (It is better still if the fish is slightly undercooked.) Let the fish cool and then slice into strips about ⅓ inch / .8 cm wide. Layer in a glass dish as above, taking care to make several layers of onions and fish with onions on top. Let marinate for at least 24 hours, and up to 48 hours.

WINE: Malvasia Istriana or Pinot Grigio

Boreto Graisan

SERVES 4 AS A
MAIN COURSE,
6 TO 8 AS A
SMALL PLATE

Livio Felluga is one of the grand old men of wine making in Friuli-Venezia Giulia. He is widely admired and much loved throughout the region, and his were among the first wines to be acclaimed beyond northeastern Italy. This is his version of the classic fish dish from Grado. Suitable fish for this stew include monkfish, grouper, shark, turbot, eel, halibut, cod, and Chilean sea bass (whose real, more evocative name is Patagonian toothfish). It is not a soupy stew, as you might expect, but one in which the fish absorbs the bracing flavors of vinegar and lots of black pepper. When we were preparing this in his kitchen, Livio kept insisting, "Ancora del pepe—non c'è ne abbastanza!" (Add more pepper—there's not nearly enough!) You should use a very free hand in adding pepper. Livio insists that this stew be served with red wine. I was lucky to have it with his marvelous barrel-aged Merlot called Sossò.

8 (¼-pound / 115-g) pieces of fish, preferably with skin on and bone in
(cut about 1½ inches / 3.75 cm thick)
Sunflower or delicate olive oil
3 garlic cloves
2 pinches coarse salt
A pepper mill filled with black peppercorns
¼ cup / 50 ml white wine vinegar

Rinse the fish in cold water and pat dry with paper towels. Into a large, heavy-bottomed skillet that will hold all of the fish comfortably, pour enough oil to just cover the bottom. Heat the oil over medium-high heat until hot and add the garlic cloves. Cook them until they are a very dark brown (much darker than one would normally want). Carefully remove the garlic with a slotted spoon and discard.

Add the fish to the hot oil with care (the oil will splatter), arranging the pieces so that there is room between them. The first contact of the fish with the oil should separate the skin from the fish. The skin will partially disintegrate during cooking, adding flavor and texture to the sauce. Note the time when you placed the fish in the pan.

Partially cover the pan and continue to cook over medium-high heat for 10 minutes. The important technique in this preparation is to never stir the ingredients. Use a flat spatula to lift or nudge the fish pieces so they do not stick to the pan. Every few minutes, remove the cover, lift the pan, and give it a shake to gently move the ingredients around.

After precisely 10 minutes add the coarse salt, set the cover aside, and continue cooking and shaking the pan every few minutes.

Five minutes after adding the salt, grind an abundant amount of black pepper from a pepper mill into the pan. Use much more than you would think to add. Keep cooking and shaking the pan every few minutes.

Five minutes after adding the pepper, add the vinegar, which is a flavor note. Cook for 2 minutes, then add a little boiling water from a ladle. Continue to add a little more (up to about 3 cups / 675 ml), just until the fish pieces are partially covered. Keep cooking and shaking the pan every few minutes. When the water reduces somewhat, add more black pepper, then add a little more water. You will not likely use all the water in the pot. The goal is to have about 2 tablespoons / 30 ml of pan liquid for each portion, and you should add just enough water (and more pepper) to achieve that aim.

After 30 minutes from the time the fish was added to the pan, check the sauce for flavor. There should be a pronounced pepper and fish flavor with echoes of vinegar and garlic. Push the pieces of fish toward the center of the pan, removing all the fish skin if possible. Also, where possible, lift the large bones out of the center of each piece of fish.

Cook for 5 more minutes, shaking the pan well and swirling the sauce about. Serve 2 pieces of fish per portion along with a generous amount of soft white polenta.

WINE: A well-structured Merlot or Pinot Nero

Brodetto alla Triestina

TRIESTINE SEAFOOD STEW

SERVES 6

While the stew from Grado uses only fish, in Trieste they use a combination of seafood plus delicate and oily fishes. The result is a more assertive flavor of the sea, as opposed to the peppery fire of the Grado stew. The rule is that there should be at least five different varieties of fish and seafood. Eel should definitely be part of the mix here if you want to be authentically Triestine. Sole and mullet often are used, as well as an oily fish such as mackerel or boned fresh sardines. Only use seafood with no shell attached (peeled shrimp, cuttlefish, squid, or large scallops are possibilities). All the pieces of fish and seafood should be more or less equal in size. Leave shrimp and scallops whole; cut the squid into rings of comparable size. Cut the cuttlefish into thin strips. Sole, mullet, mackerel, and eel pieces should be about the size of the shrimp or scallops. Sardines, heads and skeletons removed, should be halved lengthwise.

3 garlic cloves (2 cut in half, 1 minced)

Delicate extra virgin olive oil (from Trieste, Liguria, or Lake Garda, for example)

2¼ pounds / 1 kg assorted fish and seafood, washed, patted dry, and cut into pieces as noted above

Generous pinch coarse sea salt (or substitute fine sea salt)

3 to 4 grindings fresh black pepper

1 large yellow onion, minced

1 tablespoon / 15 g tomato paste

1 tablespoon / 15 ml white wine vinegar

2 tablespoons / 30 g unsalted butter

6 slices toasted or stale crusty bread

Rub the sides of a wide 4-quart / 4-l heavy-bottomed pot with one of the halves of garlic clove. Add ¼ inch / .6 cm olive oil. Heat the oil over medium-high heat. Take care that the oil does not splatter as you add the fish. Lower the heat to medium-low, and toss in the salt and pepper. Cook the fish, turning it occasionally so that it cooks almost through but does not brown.

Remove the fish, shaking off any oil, and transfer to a warm plate or dish and cover. Add the onion to the pot and sauté it in the same oil. After 1 minute, add the 4 garlic clove halves. Dissolve the tomato paste in the vinegar and add to the pot. Keep cooking until the onion is soft, stirring occasionally so it does not stick to the bottom of the pot.

Add 2 cups / 500 ml boiling water, cover, and simmer for 30 minutes. Then return the fish to the pot and simmer for 5 minutes.

Meanwhile, combine the butter and minced garlic clove in a large skillet and melt the butter over medium heat. Add the bread slices and fry on both sides until browned, 1 to 2 minutes per side.

Place a slice of bread in the middle of each serving bowl and add the stew. Serve immediately.

WINE: Malvasia Istriana or Pinot Grigio

Sardoni o Sardelle al Vapore

STEAMED ANCHOVIES OR SARDINES

SERVES 4 TO 6

I have sampled versions of this dish all along the Adriatic littoral from Capodistria and Muggia to Trieste, Monfalcone, Grado, and Lignano. In each place it is just a little bit different, so this recipe is an amalgamation of the best of each preparation. Use large fresh anchovies or sardines.

1 pound / 450 g fresh whole anchovies or sardines (or 4 sardines per serving)

4 tablespoons / ¼ cup / 60 ml freshly squeezed lemon juice

1 small garlic clove, the green core removed, finely minced

1 teaspoon / 5 g tiny capers (if they were packed in salt, rinse before using)

1 tablespoon / 10 g finely minced fresh parsley

1 teaspoon / 4 g finely minced fresh oregano, if available

8 tablespoons / ½ cup / 100 ml extra virgin olive oil

Clean the sardines, removing heads and tails and gutting the innards. Open each fish like a book, rinse very well with cold running water, and pat dry with paper towels. Place them carefully in a steamer basket and set the basket over a large pot of rapidly boiling water. If you do not have such a basket, put the fish in a metal colander or steamer and place it atop the pot of boiling water, covering it with a large lid. Let the fish steam for 7 to 8 minutes.

While the fish is cooking, pour the lemon juice into a cruet or a clean jar with a lid. Add the garlic, capers, parsley, and fresh oregano. Shake vigorously to combine all of the flavors. Set aside.

When the fish are cooked, carefully remove them from the basket or colander and place 4 on each serving plate. Fan them out prettily. Add the olive oil to the cruet or jar and shake very well so that you have thoroughly blended all of the ingredients. Pour some sauce at the base of the "fan" that you have created on each plate. Serve hot or tepid.

WINE: Malvasia Istriana or Pinot Grigio

Pedoci all' Anice

MUSSELS SCENTED WITH ANISE

SERVES 2 TO 4

I tasted this dish in Aquileia, close enough to the sea for the mussels to be fresh, yet drawing particular fragrance from the land. Pedoci *is the word in this region for mussels (in most of Italy, it is* cozze; *in Liguria, it is* muscoli).

1 tablespoon / 15 ml olive oil
½ cup / 125 ml Pinot Grigio or Malvasia Istriana
5 or 6 fresh anise leaves, wiped with paper towels (see Note)
1¼ pounds / 1 kg mussels, carefully scrubbed and beards removed

Add enough water to cover the bottom of a heavy broad skillet or a pot. Add the olive oil and wine and stir. Begin to heat the liquid over medium heat and add the anise leaves. Swirl for a couple of moments, add the mussels, cover.

Cook until the mussels have opened fully, approximately 5 minutes; discard any that have not opened.

NOTE: If you cannot locate fresh anise leaves, use 1 teaspoon / 5 g ground aniseeds.

WINE: Pinot Grigio or Malvasia Istriana

Calamaretti Grigliati

GRILLED BABY SQUID

SERVES 4 ON

SMALL PLATES

This is a recipe from Grazia Princic, wife of Sandro, who produces marvelous wines. Grazia is one of the top home cooks in the region, and her specialty is seafood. I learned a trick from her that I want to pass on to you. She takes a Moulinex-type hand grater for cheese and puts a peeled garlic clove and a few leaves of parsley inside. Then she grates this into olive oil, allowing the juices of garlic and parsley to drip in as well. She also grates this combination directly over cooked fish, which is marvelous.

The secret to successful grilled squid is that they be very thoroughly cleaned. If you do not want to attempt this, try to persuade your fishmonger to do so.

There are two ways to grill. Grazia uses a countertop grill that is plugged into her wall. There is another method, a little tricky, that is effective if you are adept and careful. This is to take two frying pans, one larger than the other. Be sure that the bottom of the smaller one is completely clean. Place the food (in this case squid) in the larger pan and then place the smaller pan on top of it. Press down so that the pressure will cause the food to grill equally on both sides.

Extra virgin olive oil
1 to 1½ pounds / 450 to 700 g baby squid,
    thoroughly cleaned and cut so they form flat sheets
1 garlic clove
Few leaves fresh flat-leaf parsley
Freshly ground black pepper

Add a couple of drops of olive oil (perhaps flavored with garlic and parsley as described above) to the grill (or the bottom of the larger pan). Place the sheets of squid on the grill (or in the slightly preheated pan) in 1 layer. Do not let them overlap. Close the grill (or place the small pan over) and cook for about 30 to 60 seconds, at medium-high heat, or until they are cooked through and slightly charred. Top with a little more flavored oil, grate some garlic and parsley over it, add a bit of freshly ground pepper, and serve immediately.

NOTE: It may take time to know how your grill works, but the goal is that the squid be tender and slightly charred.

WINE: Malvasia Istriana or Pinot Grigio

Cjâr

MEAT, POULTRY, AND GAME

People in this region select from a wide choice of meats and fish for their main courses, and often they make this decision based on what wine they wish to drink. Friuli-Venezia Giulia is one of the foremost game regions of Italy, and one can have venison, hare, goat, pheasant, wild duck, or goose. Excellent poultry and pork, and smaller amounts of beef and veal, form the foundations of many classic preparations.

All of these meats are often combined with various spices and flavorings, such as goat with nutmeg, veal with cinnamon, beef with paprika, and pork with horseradish. Many meats gain flavor and texture through slow-cooking in wine. High-quality wine vinegars are sometimes used in cooking fatty meats, such as sausage and ham, adding flavor and reducing grease.

It should be noted that—with the exception of the large platters of pork served in a Triestine buffet—one does not eat as much meat in a meal in Friuli-Venezia Giulia as might happen in Tuscany or Texas. As with so many dishes in the region, a small portion of meat provides the pleasurable concentration of flavor and fragrance that comes in many of these recipes. Combine meats with polenta, bread dumplings, or a barley dish and make this one plate in a larger meal or a hearty single-course meal with a glass of good wine.

Stinco di Vitello

SERVES 4 TO 6

Here is one of the iconic preparations of the Friuli-Venezia Giulia kitchen in a recipe provided to me by chef Stefano Fermanelli at La Subida in Cormons. No matter how many times I have dined there through the years, I always make sure someone at the table orders the stinco, *because I find it unthinkable to travel all that way and not taste it again. Once it is cooked, the* stinco *is rolled out on a trolley, where it is proudly sliced and served (the meat must be cut parallel to the bone). The meat on the shin can usually serve 4 to 6 persons, but we usually get a couple of pieces as part of a larger meal. My heart quietly breaks as the unsliced part of the* stinco *is wheeled away. Doggie bags don't exist in Italy.*

Whole veal shin (shank), 4 to 5 pounds / 1¾ to 2¼ kg

2 garlic cloves, peeled, cored, and cut in half

Fine sea salt and freshly ground black pepper

1 large white onion, coarsely chopped

1 large carrot, coarsely chopped

3 tablespoons / 45 ml extra virgin olive oil

3 tablespoons / 45 g unsalted butter, cut into ¼-inch / .6-cm pieces

2 ounces salt pork or pancetta, cut into ¼-inch / .6-cm dice

2 fresh sage leaves, wiped with paper towels and torn into pieces

1 tablespoon / 15 g dried marjoram

1½ cups / 350 ml veal or beef stock

Preheat the oven to 375°F/190°C. Place the rack in the middle of the oven.

Use spring water to carefully wash the surface of the veal shin. Then pat it dry with paper towels. Rub the garlic over the entire surface of the meat. Then season with sea salt and freshly ground pepper.

Put the onion and carrot in a heavy roasting pan, scattering them about. Place the veal in the middle of the pan. Drizzle the olive oil over the veal and, using your fingertips, spread it around. Then scatter the butter, salt pork (or pancetta), sage, and marjoram over the meat. Do not worry if much of these fall onto the carrots and onions.

Roast the veal for 30 minutes. It should be light gold in color. Turn it over and roast the other side for 30 minutes.

Lower the oven temperature to 300°F/150°C. Turn the veal over again and stir ½ cup/ 120 ml broth into the pan. Roast for 30 minutes more, turn again, and add ½ cup/120 ml. Roast for 30 minutes more, turn it again, and add the rest of the broth. Roast for 30 more minutes. At this point, the meat should be tender.

Let sit for 10 minutes, loosely covered with aluminum foil so the meat does not dry out. Then slice the meat parallel to the bone.

Serve with the vegetables and juices from the pan. You might want to skim some of the fat from the pan juices, but I discourage it. Enjoy this dish in all of its glory.

WINE: This dish calls for a grand red wine, and you should look for a big Pignolo, Merlot, Cabernet Sauvignon, or a blend from one of the great producers in Friuli-Venezia Giulia.

Sguazeto de Vedel

TRIESTINE VEAL STEW

SERVES 4 AS A MAIN
COURSE, UP TO 8
AS A SMALL PLATE *This is a very popular and traditional dish in Trieste. Sguazeto means stew in Triestine dialect, but it also implies a sauce or gravy. There is a recipe on page 123 for enhancing pan juices to make a delicious and spicy gravy.*

1¼ pounds / 500 g small veal chunks, relatively fatty

2 tablespoons / 30 ml olive oil (or 1 tablespoon / 15 g lard)

1 tablespoon / 15 g unsalted butter

1 small onion, cut into thin slices

1 garlic clove, minced

1 tablespoon / 15 g minced fresh parsley

Pinch salt

1 tablespoon / 15 g ground cinnamon

¾ cup / 150 ml white wine (Vitovska or Pinot Bianco)

In a large pot, combine the veal, olive oil, butter, onion, garlic, parsley, salt, and cinnamon over high heat. Cook, stirring actively, until the veal is browned on all sides. Add the wine and ¾ cup / 150 ml water, stir well, and reduce the heat to low. Simmer, uncovered, for about 1 to 1¼ hours, until the veal is tender and you have a nice dense sauce. If you feel that the sauce is becoming a little too thick, add judicious amounts of water during cooking. Serve hot with mashed potatoes, polenta, a barley dish, Stakalça (page 291), or Baked Onions with Cloves (page 294).

WINE: Vitovska or Pinot Bianco (or Terrano, if you prefer a red)

Gòlas

GOULASH

It is common to assume that goulash is Hungarian in origin, and that its name is gulyàs. As I learned when I traveled to Hungary as part of the research for this book, people there usually call this dish pörkölt, which means chunks of meat. The dish is usually called gòlas in Trieste and Gorizia, and gulasch in Italian. In Austria and much of the former Hapsburg domain, there is gulaschsuppe, which is more a soup with chunks of meat in it. There are, in fact, many kinds of goulash, all of which suggest a cooked soup or stew with a meat base (though you can find a vegetable goulash on page 289 and a potato goulash on page 290). Some are made with beef, others with veal, many others with pork, and still others have a combination of meats. In Vienna there is a restaurant called the Gulaschmuseum that has about twenty different preparations. While nationalist debates about goulash can go on endlessly, it does seem that Trieste contributed an important ingredient, the tomato, to the international style of goulash cookery.

This recipe is from Majda Cicigoj of the Trattoria da Majda in Gorizia. She is the daughter of a Friulian mother and a Slovenian father, and her goulash is widely regarded as traditional and exemplary. Majda told me that the quantities listed are for a family. She triples these to serve each day in her restaurant. It is generally agreed that goulash is much better when served reheated the day after it is cooked.

Safflower oil (or other seed oil)

2¼ pounds / 1 kg yellow onions, cut into sixths

2¼ pounds / 1 kg stewing beef, such as from rump, round, or chuck, cut into chunks

1 teaspoon / 5 g salt

½ teaspoon / 2.5 g rose paprika or dried red pepper flakes

1 small sprig fresh rosemary

2 teaspoons / 10 g dried oregano

1 tablespoon / 15 g all-purpose unbleached flour (or cornmeal)

1 tube (about 5 tablespoons / 75 g) triple-concentrate tomato paste

Cover the bottom of a 4-quart / 4-l pot with a very thin layer of oil. Heat ever so slightly over low heat. Top with the onions. Cook very gently for 2 minutes. On top of the onions, place the beef chunks. Add the salt, paprika, rosemary, and oregano. Turn the heat down as low as possible and partially cover the pot. Cook for 2½ hours.

The onions will fall apart and become a sauce. Check the pot periodically, especially after 90 minutes. If it seems the onions are sticking, add a little bit of water just to dislodge them.

After 2½ hours, dissolve the flour in 3 tablespoons / 45 ml very cold water. Add the tomato paste, flour mixture, and an additional ¾ cup / 175 ml cold water. Slowly bring the combination to a boil, stirring to combine all of the flavors. Then turn off the heat. Remove the rosemary sprig if it has not entirely decomposed.

The goulash is now ready to serve, but will be better reheated the following day. Serve with a bread dumpling (page 193), a wedge of polenta, or boiled potatoes.

WINE: Terrano, Refosco, or Merlot

Cevapcici

BEEF-PORK PATTIES

MAKES ABOUT

18 PATTIES

(SERVES 6 TO 9)

On Sunday afternoons, in the Carso it is typical to see families preparing mixed grills of meats, including sausages, pork chops, chicken, and cevapcici, *which are incredibly popular. It is usually thought that* cevapcici *and* pljescavica *(see page 8) are Slavic foods. In fact, they come out of the tradition of ground meat patties found in the Middle East. It is probable that these arrived in the Balkans from Turkey during an Ottoman occupation as lamb or beef patties, and local pork was added to the mix.* Cevapcici *are distinct, too, because they are customarily cooked on skewers, as kebabs are. They should be compact and can be either flat or egg-shaped.* Cevapcici *are quite small (at most 2 inches/5 cm long) and should be cooked quickly and eaten hot or quite warm.*

The first secret to the success of this recipe is that you have your butcher select high-quality meat for you that should be ground just before you use it. So buy the meat the day you use it. The second secret is that you not overwork the ingredients as you make the patties. Work quickly and think "delicate."

¾ pound/350 g fresh finely ground beef

¾ pound/350 g fresh finely ground pork

⅓ pound/150 g fresh finely ground veal

¼ teaspoon/1 g ground mace

1 teaspoon/5 g freshly ground black pepper

1 small onion (or ½ large), preferably red, coarsely chopped

Haivar Sauce (page 122)

Prepare a charcoal grill or a home grill to medium hot. Combine the beef, pork, and veal in a bowl with the mace, working nimbly. Then add the pepper, and work the meat just a bit more. Form into 18 small egg-shaped patties, 2 inches/5 cm in length at most. Place 6 on a skewer.

Grill over a flame until they are done medium well. Turn once while cooking. Remove from the skewer to serve. Top with chopped onion and serve with Haivar Sauce on the side.

WINE: Terrano or Vitovska

Pljescavica

LAMB-BEEF PATTIES

As with cevapcici, *the secret is in quality and care. You must use high-quality meat and take care to have it very finely ground just before you use it and then not overwork it as you make patties.*

⅔ pound / 300 g fresh finely ground lamb
⅔ pound / 300 g fresh finely ground beef
1 tablespoon / 15 g finely minced onion
1 small (or ½ large) garlic clove, finely minced
1 teaspoon / 5 ml red wine
Haivar Sauce (page 122) or Yogurt-Dill Sauce (page 126)

Combine the lamb, beef, onion, garlic, and red wine in a bowl and mix lightly. Form into 8 to 10 patties about 3 inches / 7.5 cm in diameter and no more than 1½ inches / 3.75 cm thick.

Prepare a medium-hot fire in a gas or charcoal grill or lightly butter a large cast-iron skillet and preheat. Cook the patties until well done, turning once. Serve hot or warm with a sauce of your liking, such as Haivar or perhaps one of yogurt and dill.

VARIATION: You can make the patties smaller, like *cevapcici* (see page 261), and grill them on skewers.

WINE: Terrano or Vitovska

Lamm Slawonisch

CROATIAN LAMB STEW

SERVES 4 TO 8   *This is a basic but tasty stew, a sort of lamb goulash, that I have tasted in Trieste, Istria, and Croatia. It is most delicate with chunks of spring lamb, and heartier with mutton in winter.*

2¼ pounds / 1 kg boneless lamb, cut into large chunks
2 red bell peppers, seeded and cut into strips
1 green bell pepper, seeded and cut into strips
2 onions, thinly sliced
2 large potatoes, peeled and sliced about ½ inch / 1.25 cm thick
2¼ pounds / 1 kg plum tomatoes, cut into chunks
1½ cups / 300 ml dry white wine
3 tablespoons / 45 ml extra virgin olive oil
Salt
Freshly ground black pepper

Combine the lamb, red and green peppers, onions, potatoes, tomatoes, wine, olive oil, and a little salt and pepper to taste in a deep, heavy-bottomed pot. Traditionally it will be entirely made of copper or at least be copper-clad, but use any pot you have that conducts heat evenly. Give the ingredients a gentle stir just to assure they are well blended.

The traditional preparation would have you stretch waxed paper across the top before covering it. If your pot has a cover that fits it tightly, then you are fine. Otherwise, consider the waxed paper under the lid. This tight seal permits the ingredients to cook together until they are tender.

Cook for 90 minutes over medium heat, never lifting the lid.

Serve hot.

WINE: Chardonnay or Ribolla Gialla

Persut col Asedo

SERVES 3

I learned this dish from Metoda Keber (her real first name is Kristina), the mother of Edi Keber, who produces one of the region's best Tocais and other excellent wines. Metoda is famous far and wide for this preparation, which is a classic of the local cuisine.

1½ tablespoons / 25 g unsalted butter

6 slices prosciutto di San Daniele, each 3 inches / 7.5 cm long and ½ inch / 1.25 cm thick

1 scant tablespoon / 12 g unbleached all-purpose flour

1½ tablespoons / 25 ml red or white wine vinegar

Melt the butter over low heat in a large skillet until golden. Add the ham slices in a single layer. If they all do not fit, cook 3 at a time. Cover, and cook over very low heat. After 2 minutes, turn the pieces over and cook for 1 minute. Transfer to a plate or pan that you can cover—it is important to keep the ham from drying out. If you are cooking more ham, do so now in the liquid already in the pan. Otherwise, proceed to the next step.

Dissolve the flour in 1 tablespoon / 15 to 17 ml water and stir so that there are no lumps. Add this to the pan liquid, then add the vinegar. Using a whisk, combine all of the ingredients in the pan to make a sauce. After 3 minutes, return the ham to the pan. Cover and cook over the lowest possible heat for 3 minutes.

Serve hot. It is traditional to accompany this dish with somewhat firm white polenta, although yellow polenta is fine too.

VARIATION: After removing the ham slices from the pan, Metoda gently broke 3 eggs into the pan and fried them sunny-side up for 4 to 5 minutes so that the whites were firm and the yolks runny. She placed a fried egg on some polenta, drizzled some pan liquid on the egg white, and served the ham on the side.

WINE: Tocai or a Collio white blend

About Vinegar

Vinegar in Friuli-Venezia Giulia is less acidic than what most of us find in our markets. I tend to add a little bit of wine to vinegar (3 parts vinegar to 1 part wine) to make it more traditional. A less desirable but acceptable alternative is 5 parts vinegar to 1 part water. For the amounts required in this recipe, you can use undiluted vinegar. For the ham, make sure your vendor cuts the pieces to your specifications. 🍇

The Pig in Trieste

In Trieste the local word for pork or pig should tell you everything about the city's relationship with this meat: *l'animel*. So primary is pork in Triestine cooking that it suffices to say "the animal" to know what you mean. It is a common mistake to say that Trieste's love of pork is due to the long years of Austrian influence. In fact, it was the Romans who introduced the roasting, boiling, and smoking of pork to Trieste, and I would imagine that they brought these traditions north when they founded Vienna (Vidibona) and other cities in central Europe. Trieste is one of the foremost pork-butchering cities in Europe. It seems that a lot of the Prague ham eaten in the Czech Republic and elsewhere actually comes from Trieste. The most famous pork producer is Principe, whose hams are widely exported.

If you enter any buffet, Trieste's typical dining institution, it is to eat some form or another of pork. A small amount can be sliced to put in a bun with mustard or fresh horse-radish, or you can sit down with a platter containing many cuts of pork, plus some sauer-kraut, rye bread, and condiments. The buffets, which also serve marvelous soups, all have devoted clients and maintain high quality to compete for new customers. When you visit Trieste, do not fail to visit the buffets for a slice of Triestine life and several slices of *porcina*.

First, I should note that *porcina* is very specifically the neck meat of the pig, but when you go to a buffet, you often get an assortment of meats that suit your fancy. Here is a list that you might see in a buffet:

Carrè di maiale: smoked meat, often from near the neckbone (or ask your butcher for
  smoked pork butt)
Cotechino: delicious minced sausage (called *muset* in Friuli)

Cragno or *cranio:* a pair of spicy pork sausages with little bits of fat in it. Many people think, because of the name, that this sausage is made from the cranium of the pig, but it is named for an old Hapsburg town called Krajna that made a similar sausage.

Lingua: tongue, usually of cow, often kept in brine

Lombo (also called *capocollo*): pork loin

Muso: the term means snout, but you will also find pork cheeks *(guanciale),* which are delicious, and *orecchie* (ears)

Pancetta: unsmoked bacon

Porcina: simple hacked pork from the neck

Prosciutto cotto: boiled ham

Salsiccia affumicata: smoked sausage

Spalla: freshly boiled pork shoulder that turns golden brown

Zampone: stuffed pig's trotter, boiled and sliced

Among the side dishes are:

Crauti: mild sauerkraut, sometimes with the addition of caraway seeds or juniper berries (see page 49; or Capuzi Garbi, page 287)

Cren (also *kren* or *rafano*): freshly grated horseradish (a perfect match with thinly sliced boiled ham)

Liptauer: a cheese spread for bread (see page 165)

Pane di segale: dark rye bread with caraway

Panini ai semi di papavero: pretzel-shaped bread with poppy seeds

Panini al sale: salt rolls

Senape: prepared mustard similar to Dusseldorf mustard

Porcina

This recipe is an adaptation for home use of the porcina *found in Triestine buffets. You might consider making* porcina, *that is, a combination of meats, for a casual dinner party or instead of a barbecue. The traditional drinks are either beer or Terrano wine, though I find that Riesling from Friuli-Venezia Giulia is also delicious.*

The first thing to do is become very friendly with your pork butcher. Ask him or her to prepare some of the cuts listed above and to clean them as necessary so they are ready to cook.

The secret to this preparation is that the meats are all cooked in the same water, although the cooking times are different. This way all the meats flavor one another. Ask your butcher if any of the products are uncooked and these are the ones you should cook first.

About ¾ pound / 250 g assorted meats per person,
  using a minimum of 5 pounds / 2¼ kg (see pages 265–266)

Fill a large pot (at least 8 quarts / 7 l) about one-half to two-thirds full with cold water and bring to a boil. When the water boils, add the uncooked meats (such as cotechino, *lombo, muso, porcina, zampone*) and boil for 30 minutes over very low heat. Then add cooked or smoked meats (*carrè, lingua,* pancetta, *prosciutto cotto, spalla*) and boil for 30 minutes. Then add uncooked sausages and boil for 10 minutes. Then add the smoked sausages and boil for 20 minutes. The total cooking time is 90 minutes.

You do not need to use all of these cuts, as a restaurant might. But try to have 3 or 4, for variety. Combine uncooked meat, smoked meat, *prosciutto cotto,* and sausages.

Remove the meats from the liquid, cut in slices, and serve on a large platter with sauerkraut, mustard, and freshly grated horseradish around the edges. Have breads and Liptauer cheese (page 165) available on the side.

Prosciutto in Crosta

HAM BAKED IN BREAD

FOR A LARGE
GROUP (UP TO 20
PERSONS) ON A
SPECIAL OCCASION
This marvelous preparation from Venezia Giulia always appears at Easter and may appear at other times as well. You may adapt the recipe to a smaller ham by not using all of the bread dough. This dish must always be served hot. It is great on a table as an appetizer and also makes a wonderful centerpiece for a meal. For best results, get an Italian boiled ham, which does not contain phosphates and other chemicals found in hams elsewhere. Principe, of Trieste, sells whole vacuum-packed boiled hams for export, and you should try to find one.

I learned this recipe at the wonderful Trattoria Cigui, south of Trieste and a stone's throw from Istria. When the ham in bread was triumphantly brought out to the tables in the garden, the son of the owner reached into the ground, pulled out a horseradish, wiped it off, and grated it to serve with the ham.

4⅓ cups / 1 kg unbleached all-purpose flour

2 pinches fine salt

3 tablespoons plus 1 teaspoon / 50 g active dry baking yeast

1 top-quality boiled ham, preferably from Trieste, weighing about 15 pounds / 7 to 8 kg

1 large sprig rosemary

Combine the flour and salt on a work surface and form a well in the middle. Dissolve the yeast in about 1½ cups / 357 ml tepid water and pour this mixture into the well. Wet your fingers in some more water and push the flour into the yeast, working the ingredients to form a dough. Judiciously add a few drops more of water to incorporate all the flour, but do not overdo it. Form a dough that is elastic and even. Place the dough in a large bowl, cover with a cloth, and set aside in a warm place for an hour. The dough will rise to almost double its original size.

Unwrap the ham, if you have purchased a whole boiled ham. Gently wipe it with paper towels, but do not cut away the fat. This will give the bread much of its flavor. After cleaning and drying your hands, roll the rosemary sprig in the palms of your hands and then massage the ham, keeping the sprig in one hand as you move around the surface. Discard the sprig after use.

Return the dough to the work surface and use a rolling pin to roll it out to about ½ inch/ 1.25 cm thick. This will take 5 to 6 minutes. The dough does not have to have a particular shape. It can be an irregular circle or square. The important thing is the thickness. Lift the ham and place it in the middle of the dough. Lift up the sides of the dough and join them in the middle. You may need to lightly moisten your fingers to seal the dough. Be sure you have enclosed the ham completely on all sides. If there is extra dough, pull it off in strips and use it to decorate the crust. Place the dough-enclosed ham on a large baking pan and let sit for 20 minutes.

Meanwhile, preheat the oven to 350°F/180°C. Place the tray inside and bake for 2 hours. Try to open the oven as seldom as possible. The result will be a light golden crust and an exquisitely fragrant dish.

Remove the ham from the oven and let sit for 5 minutes. Then break off the bread at one end (at the point that is most swollen) and munch on it while slicing ham. Break off more bread as you proceed, slice the ham, grate on some fresh horseradish, and eat immediately.

WINE: Malvasia Istriana is an unusual and interesting pairing with the sweetness of the ham and the sharpness of the horseradish. Tocai also goes very well.

Capretto con Noce Moscato

NUTMEG-SCENTED KID

SERVES 4 TO 6 *An unexpected combination of flavors that I have enjoyed in osterie in Udine. Kid (and goat) can be found in cities with Caribbean markets or any general meat purveyor of high quality. You need only ask.*

½ cup / 120 ml red wine vinegar

2¼ pounds / 1 kg kid, cut into chunks

¼ pound / 115 g pancetta, minced

2 tablespoons / 30 g unsalted butter

1 carrot, minced

½ onion, minced

2 teaspoons / 10 g freshly grated nutmeg, plus more for garnish

½ cup / 120 ml beef or vegetable broth

Salt and freshly ground black pepper

Combine the vinegar and 1 cup / 250 ml water in a large bowl. Add the kid and soak for 2 hours. Drain well.

Heat the pancetta and butter together in an ovenproof casserole over medium heat. Add the carrot, onion, and nutmeg. Sauté until the onion is translucent, then add the meat. Cook very gently over low heat for 20 minutes until the meat is browned on all sides.

Meanwhile, preheat the oven to 325°F / 170°C.

Add the broth and cover with aluminum foil. Place in the oven and bake for about 40 minutes. Check after 20 minutes and, if the broth has largely been absorbed, add more. Also add salt and pepper to taste.

The dish is done when you can easily cut a piece of meat with a fork and knife.

Serve with a dollop of hot polenta on a plate that is garnished with a little more ground nutmeg.

WINE: Cabernet Franc

Pollo al Tocai

CHICKEN COOKED IN TOCAI

SERVES 4

Here is simple Friulian home cooking. I like to serve Pollo al Tocai with buttered steamed carrots and barley.

1 young chicken, about 3 to 3¼ pounds / 1.5 kg, carefully cleaned and cut into 8 pieces,
    with the liver and giblets reserved for other uses
1 bottle Tocai
1 garlic clove, cut into 3 or 4 pieces
1 celery stalk, cut into several pieces
2 bay leaves
Salt and freshly ground black pepper
⅓ cup / 75 ml extra virgin olive oil
3 tablespoons / 45 g unsalted butter

Pat the chicken dry with paper towels. Place in a deep dish or casserole. Pour in the wine and add the garlic, celery, bay leaves, and salt and pepper to taste. Cover tightly and place in the refrigerator overnight.

When you are ready to cook the chicken, heat the olive oil and butter together over medium heat in a large skillet. Remove the chicken pieces from their marinade, let the excess liquid drip off, and add them to the pan. Brown the chicken evenly on all sides. Then, a little at a time, add the wine from the marinade, making sure to strain out the bay leaves, celery, and garlic. Once all the wine is added, cover the pan, and cook over low heat for about 30 to 40 minutes, or until the sauce is reduced, and the chicken is cooked through to the bone. Serve immediately.

WINE: Tocai from Friuli-Venezia Giulia, of course

Selecting and Handling Chicken

The most important thing to remember in making this dish is that you must exercise great care in handling the chicken. Try to get an organic or kosher chicken, and make sure that it is stored at a very cold temperature. If you buy cut chicken pieces, check that there is not much blood at the joints, and that the skin is an even color. When you clean the chicken, wash it thoroughly in several rinses of cold water. Remove and discard much of the fat under the skin. Make sure that whatever surface you place the chicken on is clean and dry. Afterwards, clean and sterilize those surfaces carefully before putting any other food on them. (I usually cook the liver and giblets separately and make a spread for toasts, or perhaps add them to soup for more flavor.) ❦

Pollo del Carso con Crauti

CARSO-STYLE CHICKEN WITH SAUERKRAUT

SERVES 4 TO 6

Here is marvelous country cooking found in farmhouses along the border between Venezia Giulia and Slovenia. Serve it with Patate in Tecia (Pan-cooked Potatoes, page 15) or boiled or roasted potatoes. Be sure to read about careful handling of chicken (page 272). The dish will be much better if you use a kosher or organic chicken.

3½-pound / 1.5-kg frying chicken, cut into pieces

Coarse sea salt

½ cup / 115 g lard or rendered bacon fat (see Note)

½ cup / 115 g chopped onion

1⅔ pounds / 750 g sauerkraut, drained, rinsed with several washes of cold water, then squeezed dry

½ teaspoon / 2.5 g black peppercorns

½ cup / 120 ml white wine, such as Vitovska, Malvasia Istriana, or Pinot Grigio

Carefully clean the chicken. Pat dry with paper towels, rub the pieces well with coarse salt, and set aside.

Heat a little more than half the fat in a large, heavy skillet over high heat until the fat is somewhat soft and translucent (or until the oil / butter mixture is hot but not splattering). Add some of the chicken pieces, skin side down, to the pan and cook them for a few minutes until golden in color. Then turn them over and repeat on the other side. Remove the browned chicken and add more pieces to the pan and continue until all the chicken pieces are golden brown. Set the chicken pieces aside, covered with a plate or aluminum foil.

Do not drain any of the liquid from the pan. Add the rest of the fat and heat until it combines with the liquid already in the pan. Add the onion and cook until translucent. Add the sauerkraut and peppercorns, reduce the heat to medium, and cook, uncovered, for about 8 minutes. Stir periodically to prevent the ingredients from sticking.

Place the chicken pieces evenly on top of the sauerkraut. Pour the wine over the chicken and continue to cook until the liquid reaches a boil. Then reduce the heat to low, cover the pan, and cook for 30 minutes. The chicken should be tender and cooked to the bone.

Serve immediately on a platter.

NOTE: Lard and bacon fat are the traditional cooking fats in this part of the Carso, and the flavor they give to the dish is unbeatable. If you wish to take a different path, try this:

heat 4 tablespoons / 60 ml delicate olive oil gently. Melt in 3 tablespoons / 45 g unsalted butter and toss in 1 tablespoon / 15 g very finely minced prosciutto di San Daniele or boiled ham. Once the butter has melted, stir the combination well and pour into a jar for use as needed.

WINE: The most traditional choice would be Vitovska, but use the wine that you cooked with.

Petto di Anatra al Aceto e Pepe Rosa

DUCK BREAST WITH VINEGAR AND PINK PEPPERCORNS

SERVES UP TO 4
AS A MAIN COURSE,
6 TO 8 AS AN
APPETIZER

This may sound like fancy restaurant cooking, but it was served to me in a farmhouse by a woman who has prepared it for years. It is exquisite when served with Sautéed Figs (page 315). It is important to note that in the United States duck usually means domestic duckling, whereas readers in other places might have access to wild duck. Duckling is more tender and delicate. If you are using flavorful wild duck breast, you may need to add more vinegar than the recipe calls for. It is important to note that the vinegar should be as consumed in Friuli-Venezia Giulia, which is to say less acidic than elsewhere. See page 10 for guidance on how to dilute vinegar.

2¼ pounds / 1 kg duck breast (1 or more depending on whether you are using
    domesticated duckling or wild duck)
4 tablespoons / 60 g unsalted butter
3 tablespoons / 45 ml top-quality red wine vinegar, or more as needed
1 teaspoon / 5 g pink peppercorns

Pat dry the duck with paper towels. Cut, if necessary, into pieces about ½ pound / 250 g each.

Melt the butter over medium heat in a large, deep pan. Add the duck and sauté vigorously for about 30 to 45 seconds. Turn the pieces over and sauté for 1 minute.

Add the vinegar around the sides of the pan (not on top of the duck!). Grab the handle, lift, and shake the pan so that the vinegar swirls with the butter and duck fat in the pan. Return the pan to the heat and toss in the peppercorns. Shake the pan well for a few seconds, then carefully turn over the pieces of duck. If you find that there is not much liquid in the pan, add a little more vinegar around the sides. Cook for another minute or so. The duck should be brown on the outside, but rare inside.

Using a sharp knife, cut the duck breasts into slices about 1 inch / 2.5 cm thick. It is wise to cut at a slight angle rather than straight down—the slices will be more even. Create portions on each plate and add some of the pan liquid on top. In addition to the sautéed figs, serve mashed turnips to make an unusual symphony of flavors and textures.

WINE: Merlot, Pignolo, or Cabernet Sauvignon

Fegatini con Salsa di Cipolla

CHICKEN LIVERS WITH ONION SAUCE

SERVES 4 TO 6

Using humble ingredients, Leda della Rovere of da Romea in Manzano has fashioned a marvelous dish that works well as a small plate or a larger course.

1 to 1½ pounds / 450 to 700 g chicken livers

1 to 2 cups / 240 to 475 ml white Friulian wine,
    such as Ribolla or Pinot Bianco

Peppercorns

1 bay leaf

2 tablespoons / 30 g unsalted butter

Pinch white pepper

½ teaspoon / 3 ml cognac

Hot soft yellow polenta, for serving

FOR THE SAUCE:

1 pound / 450 g small white boiling onions,
    peeled and trimmed

Pinch salt

1 cup / 240 ml hot vegetable broth or water

1 tablespoon / 15 g unsalted butter

Carefully wash and clean the livers, removing the fat and connective tissue. Cover with the white wine with a few peppercorns and a bay leaf and set aside to soak for 6 to 7 hours in the refrigerator.

Before cooking the livers, prepare the onion sauce. Place the onions and salt in a medium-size pot and cover with water. Cover the pot and boil over low heat until the onions fall apart. Drain thoroughly, place the onions in a blender or food processor, and puree. The puree should be smooth, without any chunks of onion. If necessary, strain to get rid of large pieces. Return the puree to the pot, and stir in some hot broth and the butter to make the sauce quite creamy. Use up to 1 cup / 250 ml of liquid, but no more. Keep warm.

Now cook the livers. Drain them well and discard the peppercorns and bay leaf. Melt the butter in a frying pan over medium-high heat. Add the livers and white pepper and sauté for 1 minute. Add the cognac and sauté for just 1 more minute. Thoroughly drain the liquid from the pan.

There are two ways to serve this dish. The first way is to put a dollop of soft yellow polenta on a plate. Burrow a hole in the middle (using a ladle), and pour in some onion sauce. Place a few livers on top of the sauce, and serve. The other way is to compose a plate with polenta to one side and a pool of sauce on the other, with the livers dotted in between.

WINE: Cabernet Franc or Merlot

Jerbum e Verdure

Many people who do not know better think that Friuli-Venezia Giulia, practically at the door of central and eastern Europe, does not have good vegetables. In fact, northeastern Italy is one of the places in Europe (including Nantes in France and a few parts of Spain and Italy) that grows and consumes a very broad range of vegetables. When one includes the many influences on the cuisine of this region, and the presence of spices, one finds many interesting dishes: onions studded with cloves; zucchini dusted with cinnamon; mashed turnips with cumin; and barley tossed with mushrooms, carrots, and grapes. These are but a few of the tantalizing specialties. The region also has many superb lettuces and leafy vegetables that make great salads and cooked cabbage dishes. Beets with sour cream and dill offer color and flavor. Turnips pickled in wine vinegar or in apple cider vinegar with pear juice have been a classic for 2,000 years.

The star vegetable is white asparagus. It makes a fleeting annual appearance, like a diva who returns to an opera house for a brief season each year—just enough to make you love her again and remember that there is no one else like her.

There are local flavors, such as hops, native green radicchio, *sclopit* (silene), and other herbs and grasses that are hard to find elsewhere, though some are approximated in this and other chapters.

Another local specialty is wild mushrooms. In addition to the famous porcini, the people in this region love *chiodini,* little nail-shaped mushrooms. The better ones are green-gray; less prized are the red ones. You might not be able to locate these, so substitute oyster or shiitake mushrooms instead.

There are very careful laws in Friuli-Venezia Giulia concerning mushroom picking. It is only permitted on even days of the calendar. A person may take only 3 kilos (6.6 pounds) each. Tourists visiting the region may purchase a weekly pass permitting them to collect every day or a monthly pass allowing picking every second day. To get a permit one must go to a town's city hall *(il palazzo del comune)*. Of the approximately 2,000 mushroom varieties in Friuli-Venezia Giulia, about 10 are lethal. The most common nonlethal variety is the *chiodino*. Other varieties are porcini and *ovuli,* also known as *amanita cesarea* (named for the Emperor Caesar, who enjoyed them). To determine if mushrooms are safe, there are several options. One is to inquire in city halls, where there is often an informed mycologist (mushroom expert). Many pharmacies have a trained person too, and some police officers in mountain zones can help you as well.

The best use of mushrooms is to sauté them in a little butter and then put them on top of Toc' in Braide (page 215) or another combination of polenta and cheese.

If you are reading this book in North America or the United Kingdom (and many other places), I strongly encourage you to purchase only vegetables that are "certified organic." It is a sad state of affairs that agriculture has been so invaded by science that we have to worry about everything we eat. Delicate baby vegetables and leafy greens are more likely to contain higher levels of sprays and chemicals. In purchasing certified organic foods you are not only benefiting the health of yourself and your family but also supporting the farmers and their families who bravely resist the overwhelming power of large agricultural business interests. Ask your grocer or supermarket to sell certified organic products, and then be sure to buy them so that your market will stock them again.

Ûs e Sparcs

ASPARAGUS WITH EGG SAUCE

SERVES 2 TO 6

This is one of the most divine dishes in the repertoire of the Friulian cook. For two months in the spring, when marvelous white asparagus are available, people feast on this dish as often as possible. I know of no better way to use white asparagus. You should eat this preparation only if white asparagus is available (see page 378 for suggestions), because green asparagus is not delicate enough. This is a lovely plate as part of a larger meal, or it can easily be the center attraction. You probably want to serve 4 or 5 asparagus as a single plate and 8 to 10 as a main course.

To successfully prepare this dish, you do not really need measuring equipment, but rather an attentive eye and a sensitive nose and mouth. The first thing to decide is whether you want the asparagus and eggs hot, tepid, or cool, although I don't think cold eggs are as good as hot or warm ones.

I find that hot asparagus with warm eggs works best for me because the sauce becomes creamy and the heat of the asparagus makes the sauce come alive.

Hard-boiled eggs (1 per person as an appetizer; 2 per person as a main course)
2¼ pounds / 1 kg white asparagus
Excellent-quality wine vinegar (white or balsamic is best)
Extra virgin olive oil
Salt and freshly ground black pepper

First, make hard-boiled eggs. See page 152 for hints.

Peel the bottom third of each asparagus stalk and cut off the base if it is tough. Boil the asparagus upright in lots of water (do not cover the tips with water) or steam them lying down in a pan in a little water. When you can stab the thickest part with a fork, the asparagus stalk is ready. Serve hot, warm, or cool on a platter or individual plates.

Whichever temperature at which you elect to serve the asparagus, have the boiled eggs available. Shell each egg and place 1 or 2 on every plate next to the asparagus. Cut each egg in half lengthwise before serving.

Present the plates to the diners and pass the vinegar and oil at the table, as well as the salt and pepper mill. The most traditional way to eat this is to mash the eggs with the tines of your fork and then pour on some vinegar and a few drops of oil. The dominant taste should be vinegar, and oil should make the combination smoother. But be stinting with the vinegar, too. Add a little salt and pepper and stir so that you have created an egg sauce that you can slather on the asparagus or use as a dip.

Some people do not mash the egg, but simply cut it in larger pieces and add drops of vinegar and oil and small amounts of salt and pepper. They scoop this up with a piece of asparagus. I encourage you to try the classic method.

WINE: Sauvignon Blanc is the classic match, although Pinot Bianco, Tocai, and Ribolla Gialla all work.

Asparagi Verdi con Salsa di Miele

GREEN ASPARAGUS WITH HONEY SAUCE

SERVES 4 TO 6 AS A
MAIN COURSE, 8 TO
12 AS A SMALL PLATE

If you do not have white asparagus for the previous recipe, use thick green stalks and make a honey-egg sauce. The honey goes very well with the more assertive green asparagus, but would overwhelm the white ones.

2 tablespoons / 30 ml top-quality honey

2 tablespoons / 30 ml white wine vinegar or balsamic vinegar

5 tablespoons / 75 ml delicate extra virgin olive oil

1 hard-boiled egg, cooled and shelled

1 tablespoon / 15 g finely minced fresh parsley

Pinch salt

Pinch freshly ground black pepper

3¼ pounds / 1.5 kg thick green asparagus

First, make the sauce. Combine the honey, vinegar, and oil in a large bowl and blend with a whisk until silken and uniform. Mash the egg in a separate bowl into tiny pieces. Add the parsley, salt, and pepper to the egg and combine thoroughly. Add the egg mixture to the honey mixture and carefully whisk until you have a creamy sauce. Cover with plastic wrap and set aside.

Peel the bottom third of each asparagus stalk, and cut off the base if it is tough. Boil the asparagus upright in lots of water (do not cover the tips with water) or steam them lying down in a pan in a little water. When you can stab a fork through the thickest part of the stalk, the asparagus is done. Drain well.

To serve, transfer the asparagus to a platter or individual plates. Quickly beat the sauce again and pour it on top of the asparagus. Serve immediately.

WINE: Tocai, Traminer, or Sauvignon Blanc

Insalata Triestina

SERVES 4 TO 6

When people learn a certain amount about particular cuisines, traditions, and products, it can be rewarding, of course, but can also lead to confusion. Say "radicchio" to someone in North America, northern Europe, or in the southern hemisphere, and he or she will understand this term as the round ball of streaky-leafed red and white lettuce that Italians call radicchio di Chioggia. *This lettuce is grown in the sandy soil of Chioggia, an ancient fishing port in the Venetian lagoon. Most Italians who eat red-leafed radicchio think of the head of lettuce shaped like romaine that is known variously as* radicchio di Treviso, radicchio trevigiano, *or* insalata trevigiana.

But in most of Italy, radicchio refers to small delicate greens that give character to a salad. In Liguria and Emilia-Romagna, radicchio is typically one type of mild local green. In Friuli-Venezia Giulia, when you say "radicchio," it does not refer to one single green, but a series of greens, each with its own season, that have soft leaves and long edible stems. Its principal characteristic is a mild, slightly buttery flavor. Among these are radicchio canarino, *which is somewhat yellow because it is planted in the summer and then covered in autumn so it grows in the dark;* salatina de primo taio, *baby lettuces picked just as they appear out of the ground;* radichietto *(baby chicory);* rucoletta *(baby arugula), and delicate cabbages.*

To evoke the spirit of this salad, you will want to use a local, fresh green that is available to you, such as baby spinach, lamb's quarters, mâche, limestone lettuce, Boston, bibb, or something similar.

In Trieste, the greens are the foundation of a salad that will also inevitably include red or brown beans, such as cranberry or pinto beans. One can also use kidney beans, although this is less common. The bean provides a fleshy sweetness that goes well with the buttery flavor of the radicchio. Beans are indispensable salad ingredients in Friuli-Venezia Giulia.

For this salad to be a success, all the ingredients must be in pristine condition, greens washed and thoroughly dried, and at room temperature.

1 cup / 250 g cooked cranberry, pinto, kidney, or other red or brown beans, at room temperature

   (if not available, use canned beans that have been well drained)

1 tablespoon / 15 g finely minced onion

1 tablespoon / 15 g dill leaves (no stems)

1 pound / 450 g radicchio or other comparable green (if the leaves are large, tear them into small pieces)

½ pound / 225 g savoy cabbage, cut into small pieces

½ cup / 125 g grated fresh carrot (use the sweetest you can find)

Salsa Triestina (page 124)

Combine the beans, onion, and dill and let sit for 1 hour.

To prepare the salad, you have two options. You can either combine all of the ingredients in a big bowl and toss, or you can make individual portions. With the former, put the greens, carrots, and beans in the bowl and toss. If you do the latter, make a bed of greens and chopped cabbage on each plate. Put a spoonful of beans in the middle and then decorate the whole plate with grated carrot. Serve dressing on the side.

WINE: This salad, when served with Salsa Triestina, goes well with a delicate white, such as Malvasia Istriana, Riesling Italico, or Pinot Bianco.

Insalata del Carso

CARSO SALAD

SERVES 2 AS A
MAIN COURSE, 4 AS
A SMALL PLATE, OR
6 AS A SIDE DISH

This salad differs from the Triestine Salad in a few ways. You may use larger and more varied lettuces, ranging in color from white to dark green with small amounts of red radicchio. Do not use strong-flavored greens, such as arugula or watercress. You may also add kernels of corn and, if you wish, hot sautéed bits of bacon or boiled ham. Beyond these cardinal ingredients you might wish to add a few pieces of chopped hard vegetables (carrot, celery, and fennel), but these should be small accents. The dressing for this salad is also distinct.

1 pound / 450 g mixed greens (including romaine, endive, red radicchio, bibb lettuce, limestone lettuce, and chicory), washed, dried, and torn into small pieces

½ cup / 115 g corn kernels, preferably freshly boiled

1 tablespoon / 15 g Pestât Furlan (page 129) or unsalted butter

½ cup / 115 g cubes of pancetta, bacon, speck, or *prosciutto crudo*

⅓ cup / 85 g finely chopped mixed hard vegetables (carrot, celery, fennel) (optional)

1 cup / 235 ml delicate extra virgin olive oil

¾ cup / 180 ml freshly squeezed lemon juice

1 tablespoon / 15 g minced fresh dill

½ cup / 115 g finely chopped fresh flat-leaf parsley

Toss the greens in a large bowl. Top with corn kernels.

Melt the *pestât* or butter over medium heat in a small skillet. Add the pancetta and sauté until the meat is browned. Toss the meat onto the salad, reserving the pan liquid (which you may use for other cooking). Add the chopped hard vegetables, if you are using them, to the salad.

Make the dressing by combining the oil, lemon juice, and dill in a cruet or jar and shaking vigorously until the ingredients are combined. Toss the salad with some of the dressing and add more if you think it is necessary. Do not overdress the salad.

Distribute minced parsley on the rim and base of individual plates. Place some salad on top and serve immediately.

WINE: Vitovska, Tocai, or Pinot Grigio

Involtini di Radicchio Rosso

CHEESE-STUFFED LEAVES OF RED RADICCHIO

SERVES 4 TO 8 *You may serve this delectable dish that I tried in Pordenone as an appetizer, a side dish to grilled meat, or as a course on its own (and even as a light meal).*

16 leaves red radicchio, washed and patted dry

1 pound / 450 g young Montasio (60 to 90 days) or latteria cheese,
    cut into 16 equal rectangular sticks

2 tablespoons / 30 g Pestât Furlan (page 129) or unsalted butter

Preheat the oven to 400°F / 200°C.

Break off the crunchy base of each radicchio leaf and reserve for other cooking uses (such as making broth). Place a stick of cheese at one edge of a leaf and then roll the leaf so that the cheese is entirely enclosed. Stab a toothpick through it so that it will hold. Prepare all 16 leaves this way.

Heat the *pestât* or butter over medium heat in a skillet and quickly sauté the rolls for about 1 minute. Then carefully transfer the rolls to a lightly buttered baking dish. Pour any pan liquid around the rolls. Bake for 2 or 3 minutes, just until the leaves soften a bit.

Serve hot with a bit of the pan juices.

WINE: Refosco, Merlot del Grave, or Ribolla Gialla

Verza al Tegame

SAUTÉED SAVOY CABBAGE

The first time I tasted this dish, in Trieste, I noted a new flavor that I had not encountered in combination with cabbage. It was cumin, and I found the pairing very provocative. The cabbage was served with hot boiled ham (which was enlivened by the cumin), but I have also enjoyed it as the first small taste in a meal to whet diners' appetites. In that context you can make 6 portions from this recipe.

1 pound / 450 g savoy cabbage
2 tablespoons / 30 ml extra virgin olive oil
1 tablespoon / 15 g unsalted butter
1 to 2 pinches ground cumin

Bring a large pot (at least 4 quarts / 4 l) of salted water to a boil. Separate the cabbage into individual leaves and wash them all with care. If any pieces are quite large, tear them into smaller ones. Boil the leaves for 5 minutes, then drain in a colander. It is not a problem if water remains attached to the leaves.

Heat the olive oil over medium heat in a large skillet, then add the cabbage. Sauté for about 20 minutes, moving the cabbage around so it does not stick. Create a hole in the center of the cabbage and add the butter. Let it melt, then top it with the cumin. Combine thoroughly so that all the leaves are scented with the cumin butter. Heat for another 5 minutes and then serve very hot.

WINE: Sauvignon Blanc or Tocai

Capuzi Garbi

SWEET AND SOUR CABBAGE

MAKES ABOUT 2
CUPS / 425 G

It is not quite accurate to refer to this dish as sauerkraut, which is simply cabbage that has been pre-served in vinegar. You may use the flavorings in this recipe combined with sauerkraut (which you should rinse to make less acidic) to approximate capuzi garbi, *but this is an easy recipe to make from scratch. It is a perfect match with all pork dishes, but I also like it with a plate of potatoes (perhaps potato goulash) or next to meat goulash on a cold winter's day.*

2 tablespoons / 30 g unsalted butter

1 tablespoon / 15 ml extra virgin olive oil

1 small onion, sliced into rings

6 ounces / 175 g speck, pancetta, or prosciutto di San Daniele, cut into very small cubes

2¼ pounds / 1 kg savoy or green cabbage, shredded

1 apple, peeled, cored, and sliced

2 tablespoons / 30 ml white wine vinegar

Salt

1 teaspoon / 5 g raisins

½ teaspoon / 2.5 g whole black peppercorns (optional)

In a medium to large nonreactive pot, gently heat the butter and oil together over medium-low heat. Once hot but not splattering, add the onion rings and speck. Sauté gently so that all the ingredients flavor one another but do not burn. After a few minutes, add the cabbage and apple and stir with a wooden spoon until the cabbage is heated through and has begun to reduce in size. Stir in the vinegar, add a pinch of salt, and lower the heat. Cook, partially covered, for 20 minutes.

Meanwhile, pour 1 tablespoon / 15 ml boiling water on the raisins. After 20 minutes, stir this mixture into the cabbage and cook for 5 minutes. Then, if you wish, add the pepper-corns, which will give the dish a last-minute kick. Cook for 5 more minutes. Serve hot.

NOTE: There should be enough liquid in this recipe, but if the ingredients in the pot seem dry during cooking, add a little broth or hot water that has been enlivened with a dash of vinegar. The final product should be moist, but not awash in liquid.

WINE: Drink the wine that goes with the meat you are serving. Three wines that always go well with *capuzi garbi* are Pinot Bianco, Refosco, and Terrano.

Zucchine in Tecia con Cannella

TRIESTINE PAN-COOKED ZUCCHINI WITH EGG AND CINNAMON

SERVES 6 TO 12

This is an ancient dish, and wonderful. Modern versions often omit the egg, but I like it in the old style. You may serve this as a small plate in a large meal; as a side dish to fish, poultry, or veal; or as an interesting main course for a lacto-ovo vegetarian. To be faithful to the original, you should use baby or medium zucchini—waterlogged giants will drown the delicate balance of this recipe. You will be surprised and pleased at how felicitous a flavoring cinnamon is with the other ingredients.

3 tablespoons / 45 ml extra virgin olive oil

2¼ pounds / 1 kg baby or medium-size zucchini (with top cut off), cut lengthwise into thin strips, maximum 2 inches / 5 cm long

Pinch salt

2 tablespoons / 30 g minced fresh flat-leaf parsley

1 large egg

2 teaspoons / 10 g ground cinnamon

Heat the oil over medium heat in a large casserole or heavy pan. When the oil is hot but not splattering, add the zucchini and salt. Sauté for 30 seconds, then add the parsley. Keep stirring until the zucchini is soft but not mushy. Break the egg into the pan and stir all the ingredients vigorously. The egg should break into tiny bits as it cooks. Once the egg pieces are cooked but not browned, remove the pan from the heat. Dust the top of the zucchini-egg combination with the cinnamon and serve immediately.

WINE: When serving with a main course, choose a wine that goes with the meat or fish. If you are eating this dish by itself, Tocai is wonderful.

Gulash Serba

SERBIAN GOULASH

Although the name would suggest that this is a meat dish, in fact it is essentially vegetarian with a hint of pork flavor from the bacon fat. To make the dish truly vegetarian, use unsalted butter instead.

5 large, thick green bell peppers

4 tomatoes

4 tablespoons / 60 g bacon drippings (or substitute 6 tablespoons / 90 g butter)

1 onion, finely chopped

1½ teaspoons / 8 g rose or sweet paprika

Salt

Core the green peppers and cut into rings. Dip the tomatoes briefly in boiling water; peel and slice them.

In a large skillet, heat the bacon drippings over medium heat. Add the onion and sauté until translucent. Add the paprika, green peppers, tomatoes, and salt to taste. Simmer covered until the peppers are tender.

This is a very good side dish. If sliced, cooked sausage is added to the goulash, it may be served for lunch with steamed potatoes on the side.

WINE: Sauvignon Blanc or to match whatever you are serving for your main course

Gòlas de Patate

POTATO GOULASH

SERVES 6 TO 8 *This is an old Venezia Giulia recipe that made a virtue of poverty. It was once a main course, being to some people what polenta was for the poor in Friuli. This is "goulash" for families that could not afford meat. Nowadays it is a side dish, and it could make a nice small plate in a multicourse meal.*

1 heaping tablespoon / 18 g lard or ⅓ cup / 80 ml extra virgin olive oil

1 large onion, sliced into rings

2¼ pounds / 1 kg small to medium waxy potatoes, cut into large bite-size pieces

2 tablespoons / 30 g rose paprika (or substitute any Hungarian paprika)

Salt

1 tablespoon / 15 ml thick tomato paste

Over medium heat, melt the lard or heat the oil in a wide pot. Add the onion and turn the heat way down. Cook the onion very gently for 30 minutes, until the onion is soft and fragrant. Remove the pot from the heat for a couple of minutes if the onion gets too hot and looks like it may burn (this is more likely to happen with oil). It may be necessary to add 1 to 2 tablespoons (15 to 30 ml) of tepid water to slow down the cooking process.

Add the potatoes and about three-quarters of the paprika. Stir well to combine the ingredients and add a pinch of salt. Add enough cool water to the pot to just cover the potatoes. Then stir in the tomato paste. Simmer (but do not boil) for about 15 to 20 minutes, just until the potatoes are tender and the liquid has reduced by about one-third to one-half. Stir in the rest of the paprika and serve hot, tepid, or cool.

WINE: Terrano is a classic match, although any light wine will go well. A simple Pinot Grigio is also a good pick.

Stakalça

SERVES 4 TO 8

This is country cooking from the Natisone Valleys and parts of Collio. It goes well as a side dish with meat or fish, or as a gratifying small plate on its own.

1 pound / 450 g waxy potatoes (suitable for boiling)

1 pound / 450 g fine fresh string beans (haricots verts), with tips cut off

2 tablespoons / 30 g lard (or slightly more unsalted butter)

1 large garlic clove, halved

2 tablespoons / 30 ml top-quality white or red wine vinegar

1 tablespoon / 15 g minced green onion or scallion (optional)

Boil the potatoes in a pot of lightly salted water just until you are able to stab one easily with a fork. Drain, then peel the potatoes when they are just cool enough to handle, and mash lightly.

In a separate pot, boil the string beans just until you can stab one with a fork. Drain, and chop the beans into 3 or 4 small pieces each. Add to the mashed potatoes and stir together.

Heat the lard over medium heat in a heavy frying pan. As the fat softens, add the garlic but be sure not to let it burn. After a minute, remove the garlic and discard. Add the potato-bean mixture and let it heat for a few moments. Then use a spoon or whisk to vigorously whip the ingredients until you have a soft mash. If you are cooking with lard (the classic ingredient) it will be absorbed into the vegetables and give them an incredible flavor. Once the potatoes are pretty soft, stir in the vinegar and green onion. Whip further and then spoon into a warm dish. Serve immediately.

WINE: Sauvignon Blanc, Tocai, Pinot Bianco, or whatever wine you have selected for a main dish

Patate in Tecia

PAN-COOKED POTATOES

SERVES 4 TO 8

This recipe, also called patate alla scjava, *or Slavic potatoes, is well liked throughout the region (especially in Venezia Giulia), but is so intimately linked with Trieste that someone in Udine enjoys it as if it were an exotic ethnic food. This is not simply potatoes and onions, like American home fries, but a dish made slowly and with loving care, a melting combination of potato and onion that has some crunchy bits blended with softer ingredients.*

In Trieste there is great discussion about when the Patate in Tecia is finally cooked. Some people like it softer inside, others prefer more crackle. I asked Dario Bassi, who is the chef at the very fine restaurant at the historic Duchi d'Aosta hotel on Trieste's main square, how he knows the potatoes are ready. "You know the dish will be perfect," he told me, "when the crust has the color of the sun-bronzed skin of a healthy Triestine woman." My translation is that the color is caramel gold, but I like Dario's image more.

2¼ pounds / 1 kg medium floury potatoes, such as Idaho

3 tablespoons / 45 g lard (or 4 tablespoons / 60 ml olive oil)

1 large onion, minced

¼ cup / 60 ml chicken broth or warm water (if necessary)

Coarse sea salt

Freshly ground black pepper

Boil the potatoes in water to cover until they can be penetrated easily with a fork. Drain them, let cool slightly, then peel. Place the potatoes in a terrine or bowl and smash them coarsely with the fork.

In a large, heavy skillet, heat the lard or oil over medium heat until hot but not smoky. Add the onions and lower the heat to a minimum. Stir very often so the onions do not stick. If they become dry, add a *little* broth or warm water. Traditional recipes say that the onions should be cooked for an hour, until they almost fall apart; they should be chestnut-colored, sweet, and very soft. You may get these results sooner, but if you have cooked the onions for less than 40 minutes then you have used too much heat, and the flavor will not be as sweet.

Spoon the potatoes gently on top of the onions, then add a pinch of coarse salt and a generous amount of black pepper (about 4 or 5 grindings of the mill). Leave the ingredients as they are for 5 minutes.

Then begin the process that makes this recipe distinct. Using a wooden spoon, slowly stir and stir and stir and then stir some more, always making small circles as you gradually break down the potatoes and incorporate them into the onions.

After 5 minutes of slow but steady stirring, leave the ingredients to cook in the pan for about 5 more minutes. Then return to more stirring, and do not be afraid to break up the crust that has begun to form at the bottom side of the potato-onion mixture. This crust will be incorporated into the softer part of the mixture and will give it texture, character, and flavor. You may need to use a fork to pull off pieces of crust from the bottom of the pan. Use the fork to break up any large pieces. Let the crust form again, and this time slide the whole thing out of the pan (using the wooden spoon to nudge it along, if necessary) and onto a large plate. Then hold the plate in one hand and place the inside of the pan over it (holding the handle of the pan with your other hand). Flip the whole thing over quickly and carefully and return it to the heat. Grind a little more pepper on top. Let the potato-onion mixture form a crust on the second side (no more stirring at this point), and then slide it out of the pan onto the plate. Cut and serve immediately.

Cipolle ai Chiodi di Garofano

BAKED ONIONS WITH CLOVES

SERVES 6

Imagine the combination of sweet onions with the slightly musky fragrance of the cloves, and you can see this is an ideal match for roast meats, especially those that have been cooked with fruit or have it as a garnish. According to Walter Filiputti, to whom I often give the last word on Friulian food and wine pairings, onions are hard to match with wine, but you should choose a very lean white. If you are serving this dish with meat, the wine that suits the meat is the one to use.

6 yellow onions, unpeeled
18 whole cloves
3 tablespoons / 45 ml good red wine vinegar
3 tablespoons / 45 ml extra virgin olive oil
Pinch salt (optional)
Freshly ground black pepper (optional)

Preheat the oven to 350° F / 180° C. Do not peel the onions. Rather, simply make 3 incisions, about ½ inch / 1.25 cm deep near the stem end of the onion. Carefully push 1 clove into each cut. Wrap each onion tightly in aluminum foil. Bake the onions on the middle shelf of the oven until they yield to the touch, 40 to 45 minutes.

Using oven mitts so that you do not burn yourself, unwrap each onion and place it in a serving dish with the clove side facing upward. Slip off the outer skin if desired.

Gently heat the vinegar over medium-low heat in a saucepan for a minute or so, then stir in the oil and add the optional salt and pepper. (Friulians add these; I find that the more direct flavors of onion, clove, and vinegar shine through more if salt and pepper are omitted). Pour over the onions and serve.

WINE: Pinot Grigio or Malvasia Istriana

Fagioli con l'Aceto

BEANS WITH VINEGAR SAUCE

Here is an easy and traditional dish that goes well with meats or with creamy frico and polenta. You should either soak dried beans the night before or purchase fresh ones from a trusted supplier.

1 pound / 450 g shelled fresh borlotti, cranberry, or cannellini (alone or in combination)

1 celery stalk, minced

Pinch salt

1 tablespoon / 15 g Pestât Furlan (page 129) or unsalted butter

¼ pound / 115 g pancetta, speck, or prosciutto di San Daniele, cut into small cubes

1 small onion, minced

¼ cup / 60 ml red wine vinegar (slightly diluted)

Boil the beans and celery in abundant salted water until tender. If you are using more than one type of bean, cook them in separate pots. Drain well.

Melt the *pestât* or butter in a small pan. Add the cubes of meat plus the minced onions and sauté until the meat is cooked through, but not browned, and the onions are soft.

Combine the beans with the meat, onions, and pan juices in a serving bowl. Add the vinegar, toss well, and serve immediately.

VARIATION: When fresh beans are unavailable, you can make this dish with dried beans. Soak 8 ounces / 225 g dried beans for at least 8 hours, up to overnight, in cold water, adding at least 4 inches / 10 cm water above the top of the beans. Drain thoroughly and transfer the beans to a large pot. Add the celery and cover with cold water, bring to a rapid boil, then reduce the heat to a simmer for 50 minutes. Drain well. Sauté the meat and onions and combine with the beans as above.

WINE: Merlot

About Beets

Many people avoid cooking beets because they associate it with lots of work and red fingertips. There are canned beets in most stores, but these are only a moderately acceptable substitute. A better choice is a product from France that is appearing in more international markets: vacuum-packed cooked beets. They are economical and delicious. See page 378 for details.

If you do cook beets from scratch, it is quite simple. Cut any tops off the beets (save for another use) and scrub the beets well under lots of cold water. Place the beets in a saucepan, cover with cold water, and simmer over medium-low heat. The beets will be cooked when you can easily stab them with a fork. Cooking time varies considerably, based on the size of the beets. They may be done after 30 minutes or may take more than an hour if the beets are large or older. Lift the cooked beets out of the saucepan with a slotted spoon and drain in a colander. (Reserve the pan liquid for another use.) When the beets are cool enough to handle, slip off the skins or, if they do not come off easily, peel the beets with a small knife. ❦

Barbabietole in Agrodolce

SWEET AND SOUR BEETS

SERVES 4

This is my adaptation of a dish I have tasted a couple of times at the Ristorante Roma in Tolmezzo. The interest in this preparation is in the interplay of sweet with sour and bitter. Note that these latter two sensations are not the same, as most people think. Sour might be a pleasant taste in citrus fruit or cherries or cream, while bitter is a sensation in a complex range of experiences we have in tasting chocolate, coffee, onions, and other foods we love.

4 cooked beets (total about 1 pound / 450 g
   or a little more)

3 tablespoons / 45 g unsalted butter

1 teaspoon / 5 g sugar

3 tablespoons / 45 ml red wine vinegar

1 white onion, sliced into thin rings

Begin with the cooked beets. If you have cooked them yourself and they are still hot, drain well and peel them. With a melon baller, create little beet balls. If you think it is too fussy to make beet balls, then cut your cooked beets into small squares and rectangles.

Melt the butter in a medium saucepan. Add the beets, sugar, vinegar, and 2 tablespoons / 30 ml cold water, and cook over very low heat for 5 minutes. Stir with care so you do not break the beets. Then remove from the heat.

Place the onion rings in the colander (which you should have rinsed if there were beets in it). Place the colander over boiling water and steam the onions for about 8 minutes.

Arrange the steamed onion rings prettily on individual serving dishes. Then, using a slotted spoon, place the beets on the bed of onions. Spoon 1 tablespoon / 15 ml pan liquid over the beets and serve.

VARIATION: If you are using precooked beets (such as those that are vacuum-packed), you will need 4 cooked beets (total 1 pound / 450 g). Set a large pot of water to boil. The width of the pot should be the proper dimension for you to place a metal colander above it. Once the water reaches a boil, place the cooked beets in the colander and place them atop the boiling water for about 5 minutes. Then remove the beets and form little balls with the melon baller or cut into small squares or rectangles. Do not spill out the boiling water—you will still need it. Proceed with the recipe as above.

WINE: Pinot Bianco or Pinot Grigio

Barbabietole di San Floriano

BEETS WITH SOUR CREAM, DILL, AND HORSERADISH

SERVES UP TO 8

I call these beets of San Floriano del Collio only because I have twice tasted them there and never seen them elsewhere. It may not be a strictly local preparation, but since San Floriano is such a delicious place (one of the prettiest in the whole region), this delicious and pretty dish is honored by the association. It is a wonderful match with roasted, braised, or boiled meats and game. I also think it is a perfect accompaniment to roast goose. The ideal grain to serve on the plate is cooked pearl barley.

2¼ pounds (about 3 cups)/1 kg beets
½ cup/125 ml sour cream
1 tablespoon/15 g fresh dill
Up to 1 tablespoon/15 g freshly grated horseradish
Up to 1 teaspoon/5 g caraway seeds (optional)

Cook the beets as directed on page 296 or use cooked beets. Cut the beets into round slices, julienne sticks, or cubes, as you prefer.

Combine the sour cream, dill, horseradish to taste, and caraway seeds to taste in the top of a double boiler set over boiling water. Heat and stir for about 30 seconds, and then carefully add the beets. Let cook gently, stirring occasionally, for about 5 minutes. The sauce should never bubble actively.

Serve hot.

VARIATION: If you wish, you can use 2¼ pounds/1 kg whole cooked beets, vacuum-packed or canned (if absolutely necessary). Slice, julienne, or cut into cubes and proceed with the recipe above.

WINE: Nice wines with this are Pinot Bianco, Collio Bianco, or Ribolla Gialla. It also goes wonderfully with any red wine that you serve with a meat.

Orzo

PEARL BARLEY

This recipe is for when you want barley as a side dish, or for adding to soup or other dishes. It is not to be used to make orzotto, which is really a variation of risotto.

1 cup / 225 g pearl barley

In a colander, rinse the barley under cold running water. Transfer to a large pot, add 3 cups / 700 ml cold water, cover, and cook over low heat, simmering for 35 to 40 minutes, until all the liquid is absorbed.

Serve as a side dish or tossed with other vegetables, as in the next two recipes.

VARIATION: If you prefer the barley to be fluffier, rinse it first as directed above. Then add it to the pot, add the water, and soak for 5 hours, covered. Then simmer over medium-low heat until all the water is absorbed—about 15 minutes.

Orzo con Funghi, Carote, e Uva

BARLEY WITH MUSHROOMS, CARROTS, AND GRAPES

This is a family recipe that I tasted at the home of wine producers in the Isonzo zone. The grandmother told me that the reason she likes this side dish so much is that it goes well with just about every imaginable meat and many types of fish. Her son told me that the dish is also versatile because it seems to match well with most any red or white wine. Use small, sweet carrots, and try to find red wine grapes. If this is not possible, then Concord grapes are the best option. Thompson or Red Flame grapes are your last resort.

1 cup / 225 g pearl barley

2 tablespoons / 30 g unsalted butter

2 teaspoons / 10 g very finely minced onion

8 ounces / 225 g fresh mushrooms, such as cremini, *chiodini,* or shiitake (or 2 ounces / 55 g dried porcini
  that have been soaked in water until they are reconstituted), chopped

⅓ cup / 80 g grated carrot

⅓ cup / 80 g red grapes, cut in half and seeded

In a colander, rinse the barley under cold running water. Transfer to a large pot, add 3 cups / 700 ml cold water, cover, and cook over low heat, simmering for 35 to 40 minutes, until all the liquid is absorbed.

About 5 minutes before the barley is done, melt the butter in a large skillet over medium heat and immediately add the onion. A few seconds later, add the mushrooms and cook them just until they yield some liquid. Add the carrot and grapes, stir rapidly for about 30 seconds, then remove the pan from the heat. The goal is to have a fair amount of liquid in the pan from the butter, mushrooms, onions, and grapes. Once the barley is ready, stir it into the skillet so that all the ingredients are thoroughly combined. Serve immediately.

WINE: Your choice of wine should be based on which meat or fish you are serving.

Orzo con le Barbabietole

SERVES 4 TO 6   *Often beets and barley are neighbors on a plate in Friuli-Venezia Giulia. But they also make a nice dish when combined.*

1 to 1¼ pounds / 500 g beets
1 cup / 225 g pearl barley
2 tablespoons / 30 g unsalted butter
1 teaspoon / 5 g grated orange zest
Tiny pinch ground ginger (optional)

Place the beets in a medium saucepan and cover with water. Bring to a boil, cover, reduce the heat to maintain a gentle boil, and cook until tender when pierced with a fork, 30 to 35 minutes for medium-size beets. Drain well. Peel when cool enough to handle. Once the beets are cooking, in a colander, rinse the barley under cold running water. Transfer to a large pot, add 3 cups / 700 ml cold water, cover, and cook over low heat, simmering for 35 to 40 minutes, until all the liquid is absorbed. Cut the beets into little cubes.

Melt the butter in a large pan, add the orange zest and ginger, and quickly swirl the ingredients. Add the beets and stir them with a spoon so they are covered with butter. Remove from heat and stir in the cooked barley. Combine thoroughly, and serve.

VARIATION: If you wish, use 1 to 1¼ pounds / 500 g whole cooked beets, vacuum-packed or canned (if absolutely necessary). Cut the beets into little cubes, cook the barley, and proceed with the recipe above.

WINE: Base your wine choice on the meat or fish you are serving with this dish.

Brovada

PICKLED TURNIPS

SERVES 6 TO 8

Brovada is certainly an acquired taste, but any book of the cuisine of Friuli-Venezia Giulia that does not have a recipe for it would be incomplete. I should note that there are many people who genuinely like the taste of brovada, so do not knock it until you have tried it. Pickled turnips were described by Apicius in his manuals of gastronomy, and it is known that a food of this type was enjoyed in ancient Aquileia.

This is one of the most famous examples, along with polenta, of the food of once upon a time that was meant for the subsistence of people who had nothing. Brovada is classically served with cotechino (a fatty pork sausage known as muset *in Friulano that is very delicious but too rich to eat very often). You can find cotechino at excellent Italian pork butchers in many parts of the world (often by special order), and you should seek instructions there how to cook it. Brovada can also be served with roasted or grilled pork.*

Traditional brovada is made with turnips that are pickled in fermented grape skins and seeds left over from wine making. The turnips are put in wooden vats in alternating layers with the skins and left for 40 days (water is added periodically), until the turnips acquire a rosy pink color. This recipe does not include grape skins, but instead is an adaptation of the preparation made nowadays by many family cooks in Carnia and elsewhere in the provinces of Udine and Pordenone. I have also incorporated the expert counsel of Lidia Bastianich who, in addition to all of the other wonderful endeavors she is engaged in, makes brovada in her home in New York.

FOR PICKLING THE TURNIPS:

3 pounds / 1300 g medium white turnips (3 to 4 inches / 7.5 to 10 cm wide), with violet-colored necks

6 cups / 1500 ml red wine, such as Merlot or Refosco from the Grave del Friuli

1 cup / 240 ml full-strength top-quality red wine vinegar (use the best vinegar you can locate)

FOR COOKING THE PICKLED TURNIPS:

3 tablespoons / 45 g Pestât Furlan (page 129) (or substitute 3 tablespoons / 45 g lard or butter combined with
  1 tablespoon / 15 g minced onion, 1 small minced garlic clove, 2 fresh sage leaves, wiped with paper towel
  and torn into bits, and 1 tablespoon / 15 g minced fresh parsley)

Salt and freshly ground black pepper

1 cup / 250 ml broth made from boiling sausages, pork butt, or cotechino
  (or, alternatively, chicken stock or low-sodium chicken broth)

To pickle the turnips, cut the stems and leaves from the turnips. Wash the turnips very well in cold water to remove all dirt. Place the turnips in a tall large glass or earthenware dish; you must have about 2 inches/5 cm of space above the turnips. Combine the wine and vinegar in a separate bowl and pour it over the turnips. Cover well and set aside for 30 days in a cool cellar or for 40 days in the refrigerator. When you are ready to open the dish, stand back! The first olfactory sensation can be quite overpowering.

To cook pickled turnips, lift the turnips from their dish, one at a time, and grate them against the coarsest side of a box grater. (In Carnia there are large wooden boards with grates in the middle that are specifically designed for grating pickled turnips.) Some preparations of this dish call for skinny, spaghetti-like strands of grated turnip; others prefer stubby flat pieces. Either is fine.

Heat the *pestât* over medium temperature in a heavy nonreactive pot. Once the fat is soft and slightly bubbling, add all of the grated turnips, a little salt and pepper, and ⅓ cup/ 80 ml broth. Reduce the heat to low, cover, and then lift the lid periodically to stir. If the turnips become dry, add a couple of tablespoons/15 to 30 ml of broth, taking care not to add too much. Cook for about 90 minutes, and perhaps longer. The turnips should be firm and moist rather than mushy and liquidy. Serve hot.

VARIATION: In Carnia grape skins were seldom available, so the traditional brovada there is different. Instead, pear cider that had turned was used to make brovada and it is much more delicate and palatable than grape skins. I have adapted this recipe and I think you will find it pleasing. For 3 pounds/1300 g turnips, stir 1½ cups/350 ml apple cider vinegar (better still, pear vinegar if you can find it) into 5 cups/1250 ml pear juice or nectar. Take one juicy pear, wash, peel, and core it, and then grate it into the vinegar/juice mixture. Stir well and use this liquid to make the brovada. After 50 days in the cellar or 60 days in the refrigerator, the turnips will be a nice golden color and will have a pleasing taste.

WINE: Your wine selection should be based on what meat is being served with the brovada. Good picks include a young Refosco or Merlot.

Ufiêj

MASHED TURNIPS

There are many uses for turnips in Carnia, the most famous being brovada *(pickled turnips). They are also used as a vegetable on their own, especially with roasted meats and game birds. Cumin is an optional spice that works very well. Here is a useful recipe.*

2¼ pounds / 1 kg small, firm turnips, with leaves removed

4 tablespoons / 60 g unsalted butter

3 tablespoons / 45 g granulated sugar

2 tablespoons / 30 ml white wine vinegar

2 teaspoons / 10 g ground cumin (optional, but recommended)

Boil the turnips, partially covered, in lots of salted water until they are cooked. You should be able to stab them with a fork, but they should not split. Drain the turnips, peel, and cut into bite-size pieces.

Melt the butter in a pot and then add the turnip pieces. Stir to break the pieces up, then add the sugar and vinegar and keep stirring until you have a thick mash. Stir in the cumin and serve hot.

WINE: Your wine selection depends on what you serve with the turnips. Good choices include Tocai, Riesling, and Cabernet Franc.

Meeting Giulia Cimenti

I had known of Giulia Cimenti for a very long time. Whenever I spoke with people in Carnia or elsewhere about certain custodians of the traditional ways of Carnia, they would name a couple of names, then certainly mention "Il Grande Gianni Cosetti" to acknowledge the widely admired chef who once ran the Ristorante Roma in Tolmezzo. And then people would add, with hushed tones, *"e poi c'è la Giulia."* And then there is Giulia. She was not mentioned as an afterthought, but rather as a revered and mythic figure who was almost unapproachable.

I had often called, discreetly, before even venturing to Tolmezzo, to see if the Hotel-Ristorante Cimenti was open. Usually I would hear a friendly male voice at the end of the line, informing me that the hotel and restaurant were open but that *la Signora Giulia è impegnata.* This last is a very particular word. It suggests engaged, involved, committed. Were this an office in Milan, *impegnata* would be that vaguely dishonest euphemism "in a meeting." Somehow I sensed that Giulia was not avoiding me but was, indeed, engaged in something important.

On trips to or through Tolmezzo, I would always walk by the Hotel Cimenti and peer in. If there were people there, I could never tell.

One Saturday, in 1998, I placed another of my usual calls, and instead of the male voice, I heard a firm but slightly faded female voice. *"È la signora Giulia?"* I asked hopefully.

"Chi parla, scusi?" she asked.

"My name is Federico," I said, and I was hoping to come to taste her cooking.

"Well, I don't really do much anymore. I am old."

I paused.

Giulia paused.

I won. "Come tomorrow, Federico. Lunch."

Of course, I never explained the reasons why I wanted to come, aside from my obvious desire to eat delicious food. I canceled all of my plans and sped from Cormons to Tolmezzo. I checked into a nearby hotel because I did not want to appear early and perhaps have Giulia change her mind. The next day, at the appointed time, I arrived at the restaurant. I was greeted by a very cordial man who turned out to be her son, Paolo. I was led to a table and watched as the restaurant filled with happy people.

This was not a day to watch my weight, so I decided to taste all kinds of dishes that issued from the kitchen. I ordered a bottle of 1997 Sturm Sauvignon Blanc from the Collio. It was nicely perfumed and, as it opened, showed lovely fruit. Here would be a wine to complement whatever I might eat.

First there was a beautiful little frico flower on a bed of green radicchio from the Alps (you could use baby spinach or lamb's quarters). In the flower was a bit of tepid creamy polenta with a bit of warm milk and grated smoked ricotta in the middle. This was *toc' in braide,* a dish that was once an entire meal in old Carnia, reduced to a tempting portion.

Then *salame con aceto,* soft sausage cooked in delicate vinegar. There were 4 slices, each about 1 inch/2.5 cm in diameter and ⅛ inch/.3 cm thick. They were placed on a small mound of milky yellow polenta with the pan liquid spooned on one side of the polenta.

Then came a tasting of pastas. A lovely raviolo with nettles. Then gnocchi made with just-gathered mountain herbs, dressed with a little butter. Then two exemplary *gnocchi di zucca,* pumpkin pillows with just a couple of drops of melted butter and a few strands of smoked ricotta. On top, almost invisible, were 3 or 4 minuscule bits of speck that had been gently heated.

Would I have room for the *sacchetino di funghi,* a crêpe filled with a wild mushroom cream and pulled up in the corners like a little pouch of gold? Yes, I would. I also could manage the one perfect *gnocco di susina,* a golf ball–size dumpling stuffed with a plum and dressed in sugar, butter, bread crumbs, smoked ricotta, and cinnamon.

And then out came 2 *cjarsòns.* They had fewer ingredients than, say, those that appear at the Hotel Salon in Arta Terme. They were notable for having large pieces of walnut inside, with just a few herbs (but prominently there was melissa, or lemon balm). And the same dressing as the plum gnocco.

Then, finally, on to what would officially be the second course. It was *mûset arrotolat,* boiled cotechino that is skinned and then wrapped in veal breast and roasted. The veal was tender and delicious; the cotechino perhaps cooler than I expected, but delicious all the same. It was served with hot creamy polenta.

Out came a small *frittata alle erbe,* absolutely packed with mountain herbs. Never had I tasted one of these that had such a large amount of herbs per egg. Perhaps there was but one egg in this frittata, and it formed a connective tissue in this crispy mouthful of the glories of the earth.

What could top all this? What came next ranks on my list of the greatest desserts I have ever had. It was called *sorbetto di mele,* apple sorbet, but this was a misnomer. It was really a thick pulpy apple sauce, caramel brown in color, that was frozen just enough to have a few ice crystals in it. In my notepad, with heavy underlining, is a word I seldom use: *Fabulous* (recipe on page 319).

The meal ended with a few small, perfectly fried fritters with pieces of mint leaf inside.

The entire meal was served to me by Giulia's son, who was also busy overseeing the service at other tables. I chose to idle over my wine, hoping that Giulia would emerge from somewhere and that I might at least see her and perhaps exchange a few words. She did not appear, and at a certain point, though I was the first to arrive, I was the last person left. I moved to the counter to pay my modest bill and chatted with Paolo about the area's food.

After a few minutes a small, old woman appeared. She wore an apron and the traditional cloth slippers preferred by the women of Carnia. She said hello to me politely. Her expression was serious, but there was great warmth in her eyes. I assumed that this was Giulia and ventured, "Thank you for the wonderful meal."

"Federico?"

"Si, Signora Giulia," I replied. Then, asked "May I ask you a few things about the food of the area?"

"Oh, but I am not a scholar. I only know what I do. . . ."

I jumped in. "I have heard that there are special blueberries here." And I received a lesson.

"Well, you know, blueberries in Carnia only began to be consumed in the late eighteenth century. The reason is that only those who went to the *malga* [a hut in the high mountains where cheese is made] got to eat them. They would gather them while the cows grazed. Down in the fields, people were too busy to devote long periods to gathering blueberries. In the past, blueberries were too precious to eat. They were boiled and the water was medicinal. We would drink this water to benefit our eyes. Scientists are talking about blueberries and the eyes as if that were the latest discovery. We always knew that. Those berries usually required sugar to eat with them, and sugar was precious, like salt and coffee. So we did not eat them. Blueberries required too much time and expense to make them a staple, even if they were sitting there on the bushes. Even as recently as the 1930s sugar, salt, and coffee were too precious to waste. Same with butter, most of which we sold. Calves were not to be eaten. We sold them to earn money."

I realized that Giulia, born in 1918, at the end of the First World War that had so ravaged this area, was a vital link to the vanishing traditions of Carnia. Indeed, this was not about scholarship, but about a way of life that was all she knew. As a small child after the war, she and her family lived with what the land gave them. This taught her about seasons, planting, growing cycles, agriculture, butchering, food preservation, and identifying herbs and greens that grow in land that many modern people blithely walk over.

Her knowledge of local cooking came from the women who surrounded her, and has nothing to do with aspiring to be a chef. She opened a restaurant in 1946 as a means of supporting her family.

"Carnia equals Woman. Remember that. There are two reasons for this. Our men lived abroad to work, and they wasted nothing so that they could bring more money home. So it was the women who populated Carnia. And we built it. We raised children and animals and worked the land. Remember, Carnia and Friuli don't have much in common. We in Carnia have a character that can be a little hard. Maybe not the *carnici* of today, they are softer, but those of once upon a time. They had to be. Remember, with nothing we had to build our houses, we had to build everything. But there was nothing to use."

As I wrote down what she told me, I noticed that she had beseeched me three times to remember.

"We in Carnia are a people made hard by work. When I married in 1947, the way to get water was from a well. That is all we had, so we women had to carry buckets full of water from the wells to our homes. When Paolo was born in 1953, that was the first time we got running water. Before then, we washed from buckets, first plates, then food, then ourselves. In the winter, water froze, so we had to heat it.

"We used to say that for a family to survive there had to be one cow in the shed for each member of the family. The milk and cheese could feed us, and we would sell what was left. When a calf was born, that was sold too. When I got married in 1947, there were eight cows in the shed, so we were fortunate. And I milked them all, twice a day, every day. There were also horses, and they were used for work in the field. To feed my three children, I raised crops, gathered herbs from the pastures, and cooked." *Impegnata* indeed.

Part of why I was so eager to talk to Giulia was because almost no one from outside Friuli-Venezia Giulia could envision that life within living memory had been so hard in this part of Europe, somewhere between Venice and Vienna. In fact, most young people in the region do not have a sense of what life was like not so long ago. Friuli-Venezia Giulia has made such economic strides that older people are viewed as *simpatico*, folkloric, but out of touch. And here was Giulia, whose whole sense of purpose was so deeply tied to work.

Before her marriage, she opened a little eating place to earn some extra money. "In 1946, there was *miseria* you could cut with a knife. I began by cooking what little I could find: eggs and herbs to make a frittata; if a rabbit was caught, I cooked that. I picked apples from trees and made my *sorbetto*. It was always better to gather the foods I used. Remember, if you rely on prepared ingredients from the store, you have less control of the final product."

What herbs were in the gnocchi and the frittata I had tasted today? "Herbs change every day. The land gives you what it gives you. We should be grateful. Today there were some chopped greens combined with dill, valerian, a little bit of wild celery, and melissa. Always melissa [lemon balm]—it is the best of the mints, delicate and sweet. Melissa also calms nerves and is good for the stomach. It is a woman's secret. Perhaps men don't like it." We do.

With her late husband, Ettore, and her children, they saved what money they could with the idea of opening a hotel. The Hotel Cimenti is a brick structure that does not especially announce itself as a place of lodging but, once you enter, you find it warmed by the people who own it. "Our work is the work of a family. It is about hospitality always. It should be that you not only remember the food but that you remember who made it. Our motto is *A Casa Cimenti, saremmo contenti* [In the Cimenti house we shall be pleased]."

They are now building a new hotel that, Giulia says, "I hope will be the home for all of my children.

"To realize a dream, you have to work. I do not believe in shortcuts. I do not trust them. I taught my children to work from the time they were small. Why are children unemployed today and bored? In part because they are not taught, when they are small, to do things, to make things. I breast-fed each child for eleven months, worked all the time, washed diapers, and never had help. But this is what gave me pleasure." Then she smiled, briefly, and said, "Work is good for you. We should tell men that." And suddenly she turned serious again, "One cannot teach if one does not know how to work."

I found it interesting that many of the old tools that Giulia once used to work the land or prepare food are now in the front room of the restaurant, like a personal ethnographic museum. There was a very old *grat,* a turnip grater she used to prepare brovada. She showed me a wooden cheese grater that had been in her family for more than a century. And there were several pair of the traditional Carnic slippers most local women wear. They are made from every little piece of material a woman could locate—nothing should be wasted.

I asked her whether this was an exhibit of her life for diners to see. "No, no. These tools are here because I am used to them. I understand them. And I want my children to see the tools that got the food and money to feed and house them with. These are the tools of life."

When Giulia spoke of her life and her ideas, there was no air of studied autobiography in her telling. This was no spiel. Instead, she seemed to be presenting herself as living proof that it was probably a good idea that she paid close attention to what she had been taught.

Although I met Giulia very late in the course of my research for this book, she looms as a pivotal and representative figure. She acknowledges modernity and embraces it to some degree, but also finds her sense of proportion in seeing things that are the product of her own work rather than that which money can buy.

"There is false security in wealth. Some money is necessary for the needs of modern life, but that is not what is important. If we ruin the land, no amount of money can change that. If we do not love our children, no amount of money can fix that. Remember, waste nothing: not time, not resources, not energy."

Typically, you are told that the people of the region, and especially Carnia, are a bit cold and forbidding. My experience had been so entirely the contrary that I thought that this was a bit of exaggerated myth. But I discovered what people meant with Giulia Cimenti. She was earnest, honest, and accorded me, who was half her age, a remarkable degree of respect. Yet this was also someone who understood that time not working was, for her, time lost. And she had not changed with age. "In our time, we did a lot and created a lot. Yet I think that there is still so much I have in my head that I want to do. But I am old."

I knew that it was time for me to move on. She took a jar of her apple jam with fresh mint, opened the palm of my hand, pressed the jar in, and folded my fingers over it. "This is what I am. Go, Federico. And remember."

Frutam

Al tempo de l'ua e al tempo del figo
se desmentiga anca l'amigo

When it is time for the grape and time for the fig,
you can even forget your friends

—TRADITIONAL FRIULIAN PROVERB

Friuli-Venezia Giulia is blessed with extraordinary fruit. It is so good that eating it can make you forget almost everything else. I can report this as someone who, perhaps, prizes fruit above all other categories of food. My second favorite category is dairy products, which are sensational the world over when combined with great fruit. Think of Gorgonzola and pears, Camembert and apples, fresh peach ice cream, guava paste with soft white cheese, and bananas and sour cream.

There are several factors that have conspired to give this region such magnificent fruit. First, of course, is that the people are such devoted stewards of the land. They recognize that particular microclimates are well suited to certain fruits. Then it must be remembered that there are so many diverse terrains and climates in this small region that the possibilities are virtually endless. Finally, there is a tradition in this region, more than in any other in Italy, of using fruit in cookery. So it has to be good. Whether it is gnocchi filled with fruit (page 186), fruit omelets (page 153), or fruit combined with meat, there is a knowledge of the properties of fruits that is much greater than elsewhere.

Let us start with cherries, one of my favorite fruits. In the border area of Cormons and Slovenia, there were once many varieties of cherries and, I am told, there did not exist a Slovenian word in this zone for cherry, but instead different words that were used to express different kinds of cherry. As the zone was given over to viticulture in the 1960s and 1970s, cherry trees were cut down to make room for grapes. The cherries of Collio (before there was an Italian/Slovenian border) were once famous all over Europe. Since the rise of world-class wine making, cherries became less valuable to farmers.

Many chefs, wine makers, and farmers in the region have sought to revive old, almost-extinct varieties of fruit, vegetables, and grapes for wine. They have become seed savers and have literally salvaged fruits that were on the brink of extinction. In some cases, the old names are indeed lost, replaced by geographic designations. So now a cherry may be from Rosazzo or Cormons and be indicated as such. The alert taster can discern and appreciate the differences among these varieties.

One of the world's great honeys is produced in the Carso in a very short season. Bees are let loose among the cherry blossoms, and the honey they make is truly ambrosial. To people in this zone it is not cherry honey, but simply their everyday honey. Not much of it is produced, and it is almost all consumed between Trieste and Monfalcone.

Cormons was a prime growing zone not only for cherries and grapes, but also figs, apricots, and plums. They were so fragrant and succulent that they were considered among the best in the whole Austro-Hungarian empire. Most of the fruit went to Vienna until 1918 and gave extra character to local cooking. Many of these varieties were planted in Styria and elsewhere in southern Austria, where they grow today. The apricots (known to Austrians as *marillen*) grew well, but the plums cannot compare. Near Cormons plums and apricots are intoxicatingly fragrant, and their flesh is rich and complex.

There is a fascinating story about the fruit of Cormons (in two senses of the word fruit). In my numerous visits to the area, I met many older people (all born before 1918) who told me that they were Austrian citizens and enjoyed full benefits of pensions and protection from Austria. They were also Italian citizens and enjoyed that, too. In those long ago days, when a young woman of Cormons was in her seventh month of pregnancy, she was allowed to journey to Vienna with as much fruit as she could transport. She would sell the fruit in the Naschmarkt, Vienna's principal outdoor market. The money she earned would support her as she lived in the Austrian capital, where she re-ceived excellent prenatal care, and then she and her baby received two months of care after it was born. Only then would she return to Cormons with a new little Austrian bundled in her arms. The legacy of this tradition is a strong affection for Austria in the small towns around Cormons. In one, Giassico, the birthday of Emperor Franz Josef is celebrated every August.

Apples and pears are the preferred fruit in Carnia. Pears appear in gnocchi, as a sauce, and in salads with cheese and herbs. Apple cider vinegar appears in the alpine cuisine in place of wine vinegar. Apples become sauces, desserts, and have even appeared in frico. You should select the most fragrant apples and pears you can find, because it is these that will most closely reproduce the sensations you have in eating the fruit of Carnia.

This alpine region is also famous for berries that appear in few other places. In the hills and plains, bushes provide berries that give sweetness and color to sauces and desserts and once, in a clumsy phase of nouvelle cuisine that swept Europe, would flavor risotto.

All the berries, pears, apricots, plums, and other divine fruit of this region are granted near-immortal status when they are used to create distillates. The most popular is probably Slivovitz, made from local plums, which has been produced in Friuli, Slovenia, Serbia, Austria, and Hungary for a long time. While many small producers in the region make pleasing, if rustic, distillates from various fruits, those made by the Nonino family are stunning. If I were to single out those made of pear and cherry as my favorites, it is not meant as a negative judgment of all the others. Not only are they delicious, but you can happily inhale their perfume for hours before ever taking a sip.

Sad to say, the fruit you have available to you may not compare to that which you can find in Friuli-Venezia Giulia. For that reason, it may be necessary to enhance them by adding some fruit preserves. There are two producers whose products will impart authentic fruit flavor and fragrance. One is the D'Arbo brand from Austria; the other is Fiordifrutta, a company in the Veneto that makes organic fruit spreads. The plum and apricot conserves from D'Arbo taste very much like those from Venezia Giulia. The Fiordifrutta spreads have a bright Italian taste to them and the great advantage of being sweetened only with fruit juice. Of course, these cannot replace fresh fruit, but the advantage of these brands (both increasingly available in stores) is that the fruit grows in land that borders Friuli-Venezia Giulia, and has a taste closer to the real thing. So adding a little bit of Austrian apricot jam to boost your fresh apricots is fully acceptable in your attempt to reproduce the touchstone flavor of perfect Friuli-Venezia Giulia fruit, which is only to be eaten when Mother Nature and Father Time say so.

Fichi al Merlot

FIGS COOKED IN MERLOT

SERVES 4 TO 6

This dish is one of the rewards for the backbreaking work of the harvest each September and early October. Succulent figs are in profusion then, and this is an ideal way to use them.

12 fresh figs (green or black), peeled
1⅓ cups / 325 ml Friulian Merlot
1 tablespoon / 15 g sugar
2 tablespoons / 30 g fresh raspberries (optional)

Place the figs in a broad saucepan, large enough to give each fig room to cook without touching. Add the wine, sugar, and raspberries. Cover and cook over medium heat for 5 minutes.

Using a slotted spoon, carefully remove the cooked figs and place 2 or 3 on each dessert plate. Cut them in half vertically and let cool.

Continue heating the sauce until it boils and begins to thicken. When it forms a light syrup, pour over the figs and serve.

Fichi Saltati

SAUTÉED FIGS

1 FIG PER PORTION   *What a sensational recipe this is! I tasted it in the home of a farm family in the Bassa Friulana. It is the kind of thing one would expect to find in chic restaurants in Paris or New York, but in this context it was the simplest act of exalting a beautiful fruit. One could serve this as a lovely dessert, but I had it as a side dish with slices of duck breast that had been quickly sautéed with a touch of red wine vinegar, a few pink peppercorns, and butter (see page 275).*

A couple of notes about the ingredients: The figs you use should be firm, even slightly under-ripe, so that they do not fall apart when cooked. If you use balsamic vinegar as a flavoring, be sure that you are using Aceto Balsamico Tradizionale that is produced in either Modena or Reggio Emilia in Emilia-Romagna. This is not the stuff that comes in large bottles and has a few drops of balsamic in lots of regular vinegar. Traditional balsamic comes in little bottles and you dose it out with an eye dropper or some other similarly stingy measure. In Friuli they have begun to make balsamic vinegars that are quite promising, but until they come onto the market and can be compared to the classic ones, I encourage you to stick to the traditional version.

Large firm green or black figs
1 tablespoon / 15 g unsalted butter per fig
Balsamic vinegar or top-quality red wine vinegar

Wash and thoroughly dry each fig and stand it upright. Slice just a little bit of peel off two opposite sides of each fig. Then, cutting vertically, cut each fig into 3 or 4 slices at least ½ inch / 1.25 cm thick.

Melt the butter over medium-low heat in a small saucepan, just big enough to hold all the pieces of fig. Add a scant ¼ teaspoon / 1 ml of vinegar per fig. Swirl the vinegar and butter together until the butter is foamy. Then add the slices of fig, increase the heat to medium-high, and sauté them until they have absorbed much of the butter and become hot. Halfway through the cooking, turn them gently. Serve hot.

Fichi con le Mandorle

SERVES 6 TO 10   *I have tasted versions of this all over the Carso and in Trieste. It is a little labor-intensive, and you need to work delicately, but the results are gratifying.*

2¼ pounds / 1 kg firm green or black figs

1 unsalted blanched almond for each fig

1½ cups / 400 g sugar

⅞ cup / 200 ml white wine (Pinot Grigio or Pinot Bianco are good)

4 whole cloves

Wash and carefully peel each fig and place standing up in a large, broad pot. Insert 1 almond into each fig by pushing it through the top. Then pinch the top shut. Top with the sugar, making sure that most of it falls in the crevices between the figs. Cook over the lowest possible heat, moving the figs with great delicacy to prevent them from sticking to the pan. Partially cover the pan and let cook for 1 hour, checking every few minutes. Gradually the sugar should become somewhat golden as it combines with the juice from the figs.

Add the wine and the cloves. Cook for another hour, stirring periodically with great gentleness. The result should be figs in syrup.

Remove the cloves if they are still whole and discard. Cover and let cool.

Serve the figs as they are or with a little vanilla ice cream. I also like the figs hot when served with ice cream, with the syrup drizzled over everything.

If you have leftover figs, they will last for a couple of days covered in the refrigerator. I recommend warming them, in the top of a double boiler set over simmering water, before serving.

Lòps ta Spòngje

The apple is a fruit that transcends cultures and climates as few others do. In ancient Greek and in Sumerian, the word for apple and the word for fruit were the same. In many languages and traditions, the apple is a symbol of the fertility of the land, and the sustenance of apples, like bread, is considered life-giving.

The apple is a fundamental food in Carnia because it can be transformed and preserved as a sauce, a juice, or a flavor in a dish. In its simplest form, it is sliced and cooked in butter, as in this recipe. In Carnia apples are called lòps; *elsewhere I have heard them referred to as* melus. *Slivers of apple find their way into frico, along with potatoes and onion. It also is the preferred filling in strudel, which is one of the most popular desserts in Friuli-Venezia Giulia.*

This recipe probably began as a dessert when people in Carnia had few ingredients. It is now used in different ways, particularly as a side dish to cooked pork. I like to combine these apples on a plate, still hot, with wedges of young Montasio or the freshest young ricotta you can find (preferably still warm, if possible). I make this pairing also when I use quince, pears, or a combination of the fruits, as described in the variations below.

The success of this recipe is based on two things. First, of course, is that you use the most flavorful apples you can locate. So-called Delicious apples are boring and will give you a pallid outcome. Second, you must have a good basic knife technique. This means working quickly and carefully, discarding the unneeded parts of the apple and then slicing the rest with speed so that the fruit does not oxidize. Other apple recipes recommend squeezing lemon juice on the sliced fruit, but in this recipe that would distort the flavor.

4 flavorful, fragrant apples

½ cup / 1 stick / 120 g unsalted butter

1 teaspoon / 5 ml (or more) grappa or distillate of quince (called *mela cotogna*) (optional)

½ cup / 100 g sugar

Peel the apples and then insert a knife in each so that you cut away the core and seeds. Lay the apples on their side on a clean work surface and slice them into rings about ¼ inch / .6 cm thick.

Cut the butter into chunks and melt them in a pan over medium heat. Add the grappa or quince distillate and swirl it in the pan.

Add the apples and the sugar and cook over medium-high heat for about 10 minutes. Serve hot or warm.

VARIATIONS: You may make the identical preparation with either quince or pears, although the pear slices should be thicker than the apple or quince slices. As to the alcohol you add, I would still use grappa or quince distillate. Something like pear distillate or Calvados is too aggressive. I have also made this using 2 apples, 1 pear, and 1 quince together and it was sublime. I had not seen this done in Friuli-Venezia Giulia, but perhaps they should consider it.

WINE: If you are serving this as a dessert or with a mild cheese, Moscato Rosa is a nice match. If you are using this as a side dish, it will match with most any wine that you are serving.

Sorbetto di Mele

GIULIA CIMENTI'S APPLE "SORBET"

Our food memories are often refracted through experiences other than what was in the dish before us. Were we happy at the moment we tasted something extraordinary? Were we alone or in company? Did we like a particular food because it so exceeded our expectations? In the case of this chilled compote of apples, I was taken aback because I expected a smooth, neat little ball of yellow-green sorbet, but received a martini glass full of glorious, caramel-colored slush. It arrived toward the end of a great meal prepared by Giulia Cimenti (page 305). I was surprised by its simplicity and rusticity, and then dazzled by its flavor and texture. Of course, as always, the secret to your success is to use the best fruit available.

FOR THE SYRUP:

1½ to 1¾ cups / 350 to 375 gs sugar (see Note)
1 teaspoon / 5 ml freshly squeezed lemon juice

FOR THE FRUIT:

Cold water with a few ice cubes
4 tablespoons / 60 ml freshly squeezed lemon juice
4 pounds / 1.75 kg apple
2 tablespoons / 30 ml grappa

First make the syrup. Combine the sugar, 2 cups / 475 ml cold water, and the lemon juice in a saucepan, and gradually bring to a slow boil, stirring continuously. Chill, covered, in the refrigerator either in the pan or in a glass or metal bowl for at least 2 hours. The syrup must be quite cold before you may use it.

When you are ready to prepare the sorbet, take a very large metal or glass bowl and fill it half to two-thirds full with cold water. If your tap water tastes of chemicals or is treated with chlorine, you may want to consider using distilled or spring water. Add a few ice cubes and then stir in the lemon juice.

Peel and core the apples, and then chop them into chunks. Toss the chunks into the water. Once all the chunks are done, spill out the water. (Note: In the spirit of wasting nothing, I have often saved this water and find it pleasant for drinking.) You will be left with a cold bowl filled with 4 pounds / 1.75 kg apple chunks.

With an egg beater, break up the apple chunks to the extent that you can, but they should still be recognizable pieces. Add the grappa and stir with a wooden spoon. Then spoon in the syrup and stir to incorporate completely. Cover the bowl with aluminum foil and place in the freezer for 30 minutes.

Remove the bowl from the freezer and beat the combination with the egg beater to form a bit of a slush. Return the bowl to the freezer for 30 minutes, then beat again. Return the bowl to the freezer for 30 minutes, then beat again. Return the bowl to the freezer for 30 more minutes. Now the "sorbet" should be ready. Your goal is that it be more like a very chilled chunky fruit sauce than an icy sorbet.

Serve in chilled glass bowls or, if you have them, martini glasses. Giulia Cimenti sometimes tops the sorbet with a bit of freshly whipped cream, but it is just fine without.

NOTE: The original recipe calls for the greater amount of sugar. My personal preference is to make it slightly less sweet.

VARIATION: Using paper towels, wipe the leaves of melissa (lemon balm) or some other mint, tear them coarsely, and add to the ice water. The apple-mint combination is sublime. Use up to 3½ ounces/100 g mint.

Sorbetti di Frutta alla Cimenti

FRUIT SORBETS AS GIULIA CIMENTI PREPARES THEM

SERVES 12
GENEROUSLY

The procedure for making other fruit sorbets alla Cimenti *is very similar to her apple sorbet. Variations occur according to the type of fruit you use.*

FOR THE SYRUP:

1½ to 1¾ cups / 350 to 375 g sugar (see Note)

1 teaspoon / 5 ml freshly squeezed lemon juice

FOR THE FRUIT:

Cold water with a few ice cubes

Freshly squeezed lemon juice (amounts vary depending on the fruit used)

4 pounds / 1.75 kg fruit (see below)

2 tablespoons / 30 ml grappa or other spirit (depending on the fruit used, see notes below)

First make the syrup. Combine the sugar, 2 cups / 475 ml cold water, and the lemon juice in a saucepan, and gradually bring to a slow boil, stirring continuously. Chill, covered, in the refrigerator either in the pan or in a glass or metal bowl for at least 2 hours. The syrup must be quite cold before you may use it.

When you are ready to prepare the sorbet, take a very large metal or glass bowl and fill it half to two-thirds full with cold water. If your tap water tastes of chemicals or is treated with chlorine, you may want to consider using distilled or spring water. Add a few ice cubes and then stir in the amount of lemon juice required

Add the fruit, according to instructions for each fruit. Spill out the water. (Note: In the spirit of wasting nothing, I have often saved this water and find it pleasant for drinking.) You will be left with a cold bowl filled with fresh fruit.

If you have chunks of fruit (such as apples, pears, quince, nectarine, apricot, peach, plum, prune), break them up somewhat with an egg beater. There should still be recognizable pieces of fruit. Add the grappa or other spirit and stir with a wooden spoon. Then spoon in the syrup and stir to incorporate completely. Cover the bowl with aluminum foil and place in the freezer for 30 minutes.

Remove the bowl from the freezer and beat the combination with the egg beater to form a bit of a slush. Return the bowl to the freezer for 30 minutes, then beat again. Return the bowl to the freezer for 30 minutes, then beat again. Return the bowl to the freezer for 30 more minutes. Now the "sorbet" should be ready. Your goal is that it be more like a very chilled chunky fruit sauce than an icy sorbet.

Serve in chilled glass bowls or, if you have them, martini glasses.

NOTE: The original recipe calls for the greater amount of sugar. My personal preference is to make it slightly less sweet. Only quince requires a generous amount of sugar.

Instructions for Different Types of Sorbets

The main variations in preparing these sorbets come in whether you are using whole fruit (such as berries and figs) or ones that you have cut. Some require more lemon juice in the water than others. Some need active crushing with an egg beater; others do not. In most cases, the grappa or distillate you use will vary according to the fruit you are using.

Apricots and Plums: The question here is the degree of ripeness. If the fruit is firm and can be easily cut, then wash them and cut them into chunks and add to the water, discarding the pits. Use 2 tablespoons / 30 ml lemon juice in the water. The distillate for the apricots is a delicate grappa, while for plums it is plum distillate or Slivovitz. Crush the fruit with the egg beater before adding syrup. Then continue crushing every 30 minutes, as in the basic recipe.

If you are using apricots or plums that are soft and pulpy, then you will not need a bowl of water. Instead, you should place your bowl in the freezer until just before it is needed. Wash the fruit carefully and cut it into large chunks, discarding the pits. Place the fruit chunks in the bowl. Add 1 tablespoon / 15 g sugar, 1 tablespoon / 15 ml lemon juice, and the spirit (a delicate grappa for apricots; a plum distillate or Slivovitz for plums). Let macerate for 10 minutes before adding the fruit syrup. Then continue with the procedure as above, but stir and lightly crush the fruit rather than beat it. You must use your judgment here. The result should be pulpy, not smooth.

Berries: Use whole blackberries, blueberries, boysenberries, currants, gooseberries, loganberries, and raspberries. One tablespoon / 15 ml of lemon juice in the water is sufficient. If you are working with strawberries, leave small ones whole. Hull larger ones and cut in half. I find that the best way to make a berry sorbet is to use mixed berries. The most successful ones served on their own are blackberries, boysenberries, and raspberries. When you combine the berries with the syrup, crush them only very slightly and, when you remove the sorbet periodically from the freezer, stir with a spoon rather than beat with an egg beater. The preferred alcohol is either grappa or raspberry distillate (sometimes called framboise).

Cherries: Remove and discard the stems from the cherries. If you have a cherry pitter (or olive pitter), use it to pit each cherry (to then be tossed in the water). Otherwise, cut each cherry in half and toss it into the ice water. You need to use only 1 tablespoon/15 ml lemon juice in the water. Crush the cherries only slightly with the egg beater, enough to yield some cherry juice. The alcohol of choice is cherry distillate (sometimes called Kirsch).

Figs: You do not need a large bowl of water. Instead, place your bowl in the freezer until just before it is needed. Peel the figs, cut them in half, and toss them into the bowl. Use 2 tablespoons/30 ml lemon juice. The alcohol of choice is cherry distillate. When you have added the juice and distillate, also add 1 tablespoon/15 g sugar, stir thoroughly, and let macerate for 10 minutes before adding the syrup. Crush the figs gently with the egg beater or a wooden spoon before adding the syrup. Continue according to the recipe, using either an egg beater or a spoon to crush and stir the fruit.

Peaches or Nectarines: Wash and peel the fruit. Discard the pits. Cut into chunks and toss into the cold water, to which you have added 1 tablespoon/15 ml lemon juice. The alcohol of choice is a delicate grappa. Use an egg beater or a wooden spoon to crush the fruit, depending on whether the fruit is firm or slightly mushy.

Pears or Quince: The procedure is almost identical to that for apples. One difference is that you should use pear distillate with pears and grappa with quince. Use more sugar with the quince, which might be rather tart.

Prunes: Because prunes are dried, this procedure is a bit different. Cut the prunes into chunks, discarding any pits. You need only 1 tablespoon/15 ml lemon juice for the water. Soak the prunes for 15 minutes before tossing out the water. The alcohol of choice is a plum distillate or Slivovitz. You might choose to use 3 tablespoons/45 ml instead of the usual 2. Depending on the size of the prune chunks you make, you should use either an egg beater or a wooden spoon. Follow the traditional procedure to make the sorbet. I once served a tiny glass of this next to some just-cooked foie gras. The combination was sublime.

Budin di Pirus

Although this is a very basic recipe, it results in a marvelous dessert that I have served with great success to conclude fancy dinners. At its heart it is a simple preparation made with basic ingredients. It is not a pudding in the American sense, which would have cream and cornstarch. Rather, its name derives more from the British sense of the word to suggest what Americans call dessert. This version, typical of northern Friuli, uses pears. They use special pudding molds to make this dish, and that is fine if you have one. I have often used a fluted ceramic tart or quiche dish. You may also use a 9-inch by 9-inch (23-cm by 23-cm) baking dish.

2¼ pounds / 1 kg pears, grated (discard peel, stem, core, seeds)

4 large eggs, separated

5 tablespoons / 75 g sugar

1 tablespoon / 15 g ground cinnamon

1 tablespoon / 15 g freshly grated lemon zest

Unsalted butter

Plain fresh bread crumbs

Preheat the oven to 400°F / 200°C.

Prepare the pears and then cover with plastic wrap to prevent oxidation. Beat the egg yolks with the sugar and cinnamon in a large bowl. Fold in the fruit, then fold in the lemon zest.

Beat the egg whites until they are just short of firm. Fold them into the fruit mixture. Butter the bottom and sides of a pudding mold (or quiche pan). Lightly sprinkle a layer of bread crumbs on the bottom and sides. Spoon in the fruit mixture and even it with a spatula.

Place the pan in a bain-marie or a larger pan half-filled with hot water. Bake for about 20 minutes. The pudding should be somewhere between custardy and firm, depending on your taste.

Serve cool or cold.

NOTE: Certain fruits give off a fair amount of juice as this dessert bakes, including pears. Drain it carefully before you let the baked pudding cool. What you may want to do with the pear liquor is cook it gently (do not let boil) in a saucepan to reduce it until it is almost a syrup. It is divine when served with this pudding. This also works well with apples, cherries, and some peaches and apricots.

VARIATIONS: Budin di Frutta (Fruit Pudding). Select quince, apples, plums, apricots, peaches, or nectarines. You can also make this with cherries, with the proviso that you pass them through a food mill after removing the pits. But it is sublime with cherries. As always, you want the freshest, most fragrant fruit at the peak of its season. The dominant flavor should be fruit; sugar is a relatively minor note in this recipe. Note, however, that a tart fruit (as quince sometimes are) may require more sugar to suit your taste.

You will want about 4½ to 5 cups / 1200 g fruit after it has been peeled and grated. You need to drain off liquid from juicier fruits (and reserve it for other uses; see Note). The fruit you use for this recipe should, in effect, be pulp. Proceed with the recipe above.

To prepare the fruit, grate quince and apples; mill apricots, peaches, nectarines, and cherries. If you are using a juicier fruit than pears the pudding may take more than 20 minutes to set. Test this by inserting a toothpick and seeing if it comes out clean.

Pere al Ramandolo (o Verduzzo)

SERVES 4

Pears poached in wine is a classic Italian dessert. In most of the country, red wine is used. In Piedmont, the choice is either red wine or sparkling Moscato d'Asti. In Friuli-Venezia Giulia, they use their somewhat sweet Ramandolo or Verduzzo wine, sometimes with additional flavorings, although I think it best to omit these (you will see them here listed as optional). Once, in a fit of profligate extravagance, I poached pears in Picolit (with no added flavors). It was too delicious for words, but I think that Picolit is better used for meditative sipping.

4 of the ripest, most fragrant pears you can find, about ¼ pound / 125 g each
    (among the varieties are Williams, Kaiser, and Bosc)
2¾ cups / 700 ml Ramandolo or Verduzzo
3 tablespoons / 45 g sugar
1 cinnamon stick (optional)
1 tablespoon / 15 g grated lemon zest (optional)
2 to 3 cloves (optional)

Peel the pears, leaving on the stem. Using a spoon or corer, remove the core and seeds from the pear, working through the bottom so that there is a hole there to absorb the flavors in the pot.

In a large, broad-bottomed pot, simmer the wine, sugar, and optional ingredients over low heat. Carefully place the pears in the pot, stems up, cover the pot, and cook for 15 minutes. Then check for doneness by sticking a fork into the upper part of one of the pears. If it penetrates easily, they are done. If not, cook for just a couple of minutes more.

Using a slotted spoon, carefully remove the pears to a platter or individual dishes. Filter any matter out of the sauce through a fine mesh strainer, and then simmer further in a saucepan, stirring continuously, until it has become syrupy. Pour a little around each pear and then serve warm or cool. Do not chill these pears.

Another way to serve this dish is to let the pears cool somewhat and then slice them vertically. Arrange them fan-like on each plate, and then prepare the syrup. Pour the hot syrup over the pears and serve immediately.

Pesche con la Marmellata e Miele

SERVES 6

I tasted this as a dessert one hot summer day at the home of a wine maker who wanted to show off a ripe, luscious Pinot Bianco. It was a happy combination—a dessert wine would have been overkill.

6 large, ripe peaches
¾ cup / 175 g high-quality apricot or plum preserves
5 tablespoons / 75 ml high-quality honey

Bring 4 quarts / 4 l water to a boil in a large pot. Lower each peach in with a slotted spoon, one at a time. Boil for 2 minutes, remove with the spoon, and slip off the skin. Repeat the procedure with each peach.

Cut each peach in half, remove the pit, and place 1 tablespoon / 15 ml preserves in the hollow of each peach.

Combine 1 cup / 250 ml cold water and the honey in a small saucepan. Bring to a boil over high heat, then reduce the heat, and stir more or less continuously for about 10 minutes, until you have a syrup.

Drizzle the syrup over the peaches and serve.

WINE: Pinot Bianco

Sugoli

"CUSTARD" OF WINE GRAPES

SERVES 4 TO 6

This is a very old preparation that is as tasty as it is elemental. No one has been able to tell me what the name means. I tasted sugoli *in Cormons at the annual Sagra dell'Uva, the grape festival that takes place on the second Sunday in September.*

The secret to making this is to have high-quality wine grapes at your disposal. If you live in a grape-growing zone, you have an embarrassment of riches. Elsewhere, you might find Concord grapes. If all else fails, consider high-quality grape juice, such as Kedem brand (a kosher juice found in the United States). But if at all possible, use wine grapes. You need enough grapes to make about 33 ounces (1 l) of juice. This varies depending on which grapes you use. Tiny grapes have less juice than fatter grapes.

6½ pounds / 3 kg wine grapes, or 33 ounces / 1 l fresh grape juice (plus a few more tablespoons' worth)
2 tablespoons / 30 g sugar
4 tablespoons / 60 g unbleached all-purpose flour

Wash and dry the grapes and squeeze them through a sieve, letting the juice pass through while eliminating the skins and pips. Your aim is to produce about 33 ounces / 1 l of grape juice. Pour 33 ounces / 1 l juice into a saucepan and add the sugar. Place over low heat and let it come to a boil.

While the juice is heating, place the flour in a bowl and add a little more fresh grape juice. Stir so that the flour dissolves and you have a thick grape-colored sludge.

When the juice comes to a boil, stir in the flour, and decrease the heat to the lowest possible. Stir as the combination heats and becomes thick. This should take about 5 minutes.

Pour the mixture into a pretty serving dish that has high sides. Let cool, and then serve it either sliced like polenta (if possible) or by the spoonful as you might with a custard or soft polenta.

Fritulis di Frutta

FRUIT FRITTERS

MAKES ABOUT

40 FRITTERS

In Carnia the most commonly used fruit in fritters are apples, but I have also tasted fritters with pears, apricots, plums, peaches, and nectarines. In every case, the fruit being used is cut into a slice or chunk and then dipped in batter.

3 large egg yolks (reserve the whites for other uses)

4 tablespoons / 60 g sugar, plus additional sugar for sprinkling (see Note)

¾ cup / 150 ml whole milk

3 tablespoons / 45 ml grappa

Grated zest of ½ lemon (preferably organic and unsprayed)

2 tablespoons / 30 g sultana raisins (optional)

Approximately 10 tablespoons / 150 g unbleached all-purpose flour

3 cups / 750 g sliced apples or other fruit

Oil, such as canola, corn, peanut, or a delicate olive oil, for deep-frying

To make the batter, combine the yolks and 4 tablespoons / 60 g sugar in a medium bowl. Add the milk, then the grappa, then the lemon zest, and the sultanas. Stir with a wooden spoon and gradually add the flour until you achieve a consistency that is creamy and uniform. The amount of flour is approximate, but your result should be a light- to medium-weight batter. Let it sit, covered, for at least 2 hours, or up to 3.

Wash, peel, and cut the fruit into slices (apples, pears, quince) or chunks (nectarine, peach, plum—it is not necessary to peel these fruits).

In a deep, wide pot, heat at least 3 inches / 7.5 cm oil until hot but not smoky. Toss a few pieces of fruit in the batter. With a wooden spoon, gather each batter-clad piece of fruit and add it to the oil. Fry until golden brown, but not darker. Fish the fritters out with a slotted spoon and drain briefly on paper towels. Serve immediately with a few grains of sugar sprinkled on top.

NOTE: If you use quince in the fritters, use 6 tablespoons / 90 g sugar.

VARIATION: Once I tasted something wholly un-Friulian, but quite delicious: pineapple chunks (totally drained of liquid), covered with batter and fried. This is really good if some fresh mint is added to the batter. Before the pineapple is dipped into the batter, make sure that fresh mint leaves have been wiped with paper towels, torn to bits, and folded in. Try it.

Altri Dolci

Friuli-Venezia Giulia has a formidable baking tradition, combining local rural traditions with influences from Vienna, Budapest, Venice, and elsewhere. In most cities, but especially Trieste and Gorizia, bakeries offer most of the complicated specialties that are part of the tradition. Except on holidays, most people in the region do not have cake to conclude a meal at home. They much prefer the wonderful fruit of their region. However, there are some homey cakes and preparations that you can make without being a world-class baker, and some of these recipes appear in these pages.

Probably the most famous cake in the region is *gubana,* which is quite labor-intensive. Since very good *gubanas* are commercially baked for home use and for export (see "Baked Goods," page 378), almost no one makes them at home anymore.

Cugelhopf

This is the version of the famed Austro-Hungarian cake (spelled with a K in Vienna) that I have enjoyed in Trieste and Gorizia.

5 large eggs, separated
¾ to 1 cup / 180 to 200 g sugar (according to your preference)
1 tablespoon / 15 ml lemon juice
1 teaspoon / 5 ml vanilla extract
¾ cup / 180 g all-purpose flour
½ cup / 1 stick / 115 g unsalted butter, melted and cooled
¼ cup / 60 g raisins
Vanilla-flavored confectioners' sugar or Chocolate Glaze (page 339)

Preheat the oven to 350°F / 180°C. Butter and flour an 8- to 9-inch / 20- to 23-cm kugelhopf form or Bundt pan.

Beat the egg whites until stiff; gradually add one-third of the sugar and mix until they are fluffy and rise to a peak.

In a separate bowl, combine the egg yolks, remaining sugar, lemon juice, and vanilla and beat until thick and yellow. Carefully fold in the egg whites alternating with the flour. Gently fold in the butter and raisins.

Pour into the pan and bake for 15 minutes. Lower the heat to 300°F / 150°C and bake for another 35 to 45 minutes. Test for doneness by inserting a needle or a toothpick near the center to see if it comes out clean.

Cool on a wire rack and turn onto a platter. Sprinkle generously with vanilla-flavored confectioners' sugar or let cool and cover with glaze.

Palacinche

There are numerous spellings for this word, depending on whether you are in Austria, Hungary, Romania, Istria, or Friuli-Venezia Giulia. In effect, these are delicate pancakes or crêpes that are filled with different flavorings and served at the end of a meal. Occasionally, savory ingredients such as vegetables or hard cheeses are used with palacinche, *making a nice appetizer or small plate.*

2 large eggs
2 cups / 475 ml whole milk
¼ cup / 60 g sugar
½ cup / 115 ml club soda
1 teaspoon / 5 ml vanilla extract
½ tablespoon / 8 ml rum or plum distillate (Slivovitz)
1 tablespoon / 15 g grated lemon zest (preferably organic)
6 tablespoons / 90 g unsalted butter, melted and cooled
2 cups / 450 g unbleached all-purpose flour, sifted
Vegetable oil

Using a whisk, beat the eggs in a large bowl. Add the milk and whisk again. Then add the sugar and whisk until it begins to dissolve. Add, at once, the club soda, vanilla extract, rum, and lemon zest. Whisk in the melted butter. Add the flour, a little at a time, and keep whisking until you have a thick, creamy batter with no lumps.

You will make each *palacinca* individually, using a 6- to 7-inch / 15- to 17.5-cm crêpe pan. For each one, heat 1 tablespoon / 15 ml vegetable oil over medium to high heat, coating the surface of the pan. Spill the extra oil into a dish for later use. Lift the pan from the heat, tilt it slightly, and add about 2 tablespoons / 30 ml of batter to the higher end of the pan. Twist your wrist so that the batter lightly covers the surface of the pan. The *palacinca* should be very thin.

Decrease the heat to medium, place the pan over the heat, and cook for 30 seconds. Then use a spatula to carefully turn the *palacinca* over and cook the second side for another 30 seconds. Slide the *palacinca* out of the pan and onto a warm plate. Repeat the process until you have used all the batter. Note that the pan should not be re-oiled after every pancake, but only as needed.

There are various ways to serve the *palacinche*. Here are some suggestions.

Jam-Filled Palacinche: After making all of the *palacinche,* place 1 tablespoon/15 g jam in the middle of each, spreading it out so the surface of the *palacinca* is covered. Fold in half and then in half again. Serve 2 or 3 per portion, perhaps topped with a little confectioners' sugar. Among the jam flavors to try are plum, apricot, cherry, raspberry, and rosehip.

Cheese-Filled Palacinche: Use farmer cheese or ricotta that you have softened by stirring it well to make creamy. You might want to flavor the cheese with a judicious amount of grated lemon zest or a drop of orange water. You might add a few poppy seeds as well when using these citrus flavorings. An unusual and delicious addition to the cheese, used in Collio (based on Slovenian tradition), is a little minced tarragon (omit the lemon, orange, and poppy seeds if you do this). When filling with cheese, use about 1 tablespoon/15 g and spread it around the *palacinca* and then fold in half and in half again.

WINE: Verduzzo or a dry sparkling wine

Pita di Mele

SERVES 6 TO 10

There are versions of this cake, which can also be made with pears, throughout the region. I have made this recipe with grated carrots instead of apples, with magnificent results. This version of apple cake is one that I have often tasted in Udine. Your cake will be as good or bad as the quality of fruit you use, so try to get the most fragrant and flavorful apples you can locate. Insipid mass-produced Delicious or Macintosh apples will prove disappointing. Try Northern Spy, Rome, Gala, or other more distinct varieties.

FOR THE DOUGH:

2 cups / 225 g unbleached all-purpose flour

½ cup / 1 stick / 115 g unsalted butter,
    at room temperature

½ cup / 115 g sugar

2 tablespoons / 30 ml whole milk

1 tablespoon / 15 ml grappa

Grated zest of 1 lemon (be sure to use organic,
    untreated lemons)

1 teaspoon / 5 g baking soda

FOR THE FILLING:

4 tablespoons / 60 g raisins

½ cup / 115 g sugar

1 tablespoon / 15 ml grappa

1 pound / 450 g apples

¾ cup / 175 g finely chopped or pounded walnut meats

1 tablespoon / 15 g ground cinnamon

TO FINISH:

¼ cup / 60 g confectioners' sugar

Ice cream (optional)

Cinnamon, ginger, poppy seeds, cardamom, white
    pepper, or star anise (optional)

Place the flour on a clean, empty work surface (a wood or marble board, for example). Make a well in the middle of the flour and add the butter, sugar, milk, grappa, and lemon zest. Briefly beat these ingredients with a fork and then start to work them into the flour with your hands until the liquid ingredients are loosely incorporated. Sprinkle the baking soda on top of the dough and keep kneading just until all the ingredients are combined. Do not overwork the dough. Wrap it in a clean dish towel and store in a cool place for 1 hour.

Combine the raisins, sugar, and grappa in a large mixing bowl and stir so that all the ingredients are well mixed. Peel and core the apples and grate coarsely directly into the bowl. Combine all the ingredients well, cover tightly with plastic wrap, and set aside.

When you are ready to work with the dough, cut the dough into 2 pieces with a sharp knife. Make one piece twice the size of the other (in other words, one piece will be two-thirds and one piece one-third of the dough). Place a piece of plastic wrap on your work surface and flatten the large piece of dough with a rolling pin. Once flat, place another large piece of plastic wrap on top of the dough. Continue rolling until the flattened dough is 12 inches/30.5 cm in diameter and, at most, ½ inch/1.25 cm thick. Carefully place this plastic-wrapped dough in the refrigerator.

Repeat the process with the smaller piece of dough, rolling it out in a similar way until it is 10 inches/25.5 cm in diameter.

Preheat the oven to 375°F/190°C.

Lightly butter a baking dish that is 10 inches/25.5 cm in diameter and at least 1½ inches/3.75 cm deep.

Remove the top layer of plastic from the larger round of dough and carefully flip the dough over into the pan. Gently position the dough and press it down so that about 1 inch/2.5 cm hangs evenly around the perimeter of the pan.

Add the walnuts and cinnamon to the fruit mixture and combine thoroughly. Spoon this mixture into the pan and then smooth it gently.

Take one sheet of plastic off the small piece of dough and then flip the dough carefully on top of the filling. Fold the flaps from the larger piece of dough over the smaller one and gently press so that they merge. Remove the other piece of plastic. Take a fork and prick the top piece of dough a few times, forming a pretty pattern if you wish.

Bake for 30 minutes, remove from the oven, and let cool for 1 hour. Then decorate with confectioners' sugar. If you feel creative, take a paper doily and place it over the cake. Top with the confectioners' sugar and then lift the doily so that a pattern remains.

Cut into squares or wedges.

Serve with a small scoop of ice cream flavored with a spice, such as cinnamon, ginger, poppy seeds, cardamom, white pepper, or star anise. If you live in the eastern United States, look for Berkshire Farms ginger ice cream, made with organic milk and fresh ginger. If you cannot find spice-flavored ice cream, get a top-quality vanilla and let it soften slightly. Then stir in the spice of your choice and serve a scoop with each portion of cake.

VARIATIONS: To make a Pear Cake, substitute pears for the apples and proceed with the recipe above. You should seek out the juiciest, most fragrant pears around. To make a Carrot Cake, substitute carrots for the apples and substitute 1 teaspoon/5 g ground ginger for the cinnamon. Use organic carrots that you have washed, peeled, and coarsely grated.

Wine: Picolit, Verduzzo, or wooded Pinot Bianco

Pinza

This is a famous Triestine Easter cake representing the sponge that was used to wipe Christ's brow. When hot, pinza is delicious with a slice of boiled ham or dipped in melted chocolate.

FOR THE SPONGE:

1 envelope (¼ ounce / 7 g) active dry baking yeast

1 cup / 225 g unbleached all-purpose flour

FOR THE CAKE:

3 cups / 675 g unbleached all-purpose flour

1 teaspoon / 5 g salt

3 large eggs, beaten

1 egg white

¾ cup / 175 g sugar

⅔ cup / 150 ml warm whole milk

½ cup / 1 stick / 115 g unsalted butter, melted

1 teaspoon / 5 ml vanilla extract

2 tablespoons / 30 ml rum

Additional melted butter for brushing

First, make a sponge by dissolving the yeast in ⅔ cup / 150 ml tepid water in a large bowl and then adding the flour. Thoroughly combine, using a wooden spoon. Cover with a cloth and let stand in a warm place until the sponge doubles in volume, about 30 to 45 minutes.

In a large bowl, combine the flour, salt, eggs, and the egg white. Combine the sugar and milk well and add to the flour and egg mixture. Then fold in the melted butter, vanilla, and rum. Stir until all the ingredients are thoroughly combined.

Add the sponge, mix all of the ingredients, and then cover loosely with a clean cloth. Allow the dough to rise to double its volume, about 30 to 45 minutes.

Preheat the oven to 350°F / 180°C. Butter and lightly flour a 9-inch / 22-cm round baking pan with 4-inch / 10-cm sides. When the dough has risen, stir it so that it sinks a bit. Pour the batter into the pan. Brush with melted butter.

Bake for 40 minutes, until golden brown and firm to the touch. You only need to cool on a rack for 5 minutes, though you may cool it longer.

Serve hot, warm, or cool.

Torta di Semi di Papavero alla Carsolina

CARSO-STYLE POPPY SEED CAKE

SERVES 8

This is an adaptation of versions of this cake that were served to me by families all over the hinterland above Trieste. It is delicious, homey, and easy to make.

4 large eggs

2 tablespoons / 30 g unbleached all-purpose flour

2 tablespoons / 30 ml heavy cream

1½ teaspoons / 8 g grated lemon zest (unsprayed and organic, if at all possible)

½ teaspoon / 2.5 g ground cinnamon

¼ teaspoon / 1 to 2 g ground cloves

Tiny pinch fine salt

⅓ cup / 75 g sugar

1 cup / 225 g poppy seeds, ground or pounded with a pestle

Chocolate Glaze, optional (page 339)

Grappa-Scented Whipped Heavy Cream, optional (page 338)

Preheat the oven to 300°F / 150°C. Butter or oil a 7-inch / 17- to 18-cm tube pan.

Separate the eggs, putting the yolks in a large mixing bowl and the whites in a smaller chilled bowl. Beat the yolks just until they are broken and combined. Use a whisk and gradually add the flour and then the cream. Add the lemon zest, cinnamon, and cloves. Do not overwork the mixture.

Using an egg beater, beat the whites with salt until they are frothy. Beat in the sugar a little at a time. Using a rubber spatula, spoon the whites into the yolk mixture and combine gently. Again, take care not to overwork the mixture. Using the spatula, blend in the poppy seeds and combine well. Pour the mixture into the cake pan.

Bake for about 45 minutes, or until golden on top. A toothpick inserted near the center should come out clean.

Let cool for 10 minutes on a rack. Carefully turn the pan over and let the cake gently land on a wire rack or cake plate. Let cool completely. Frost, if desired. Serve with grappa-flavored whipped cream, if desired.

Panna Montata al Profumo di Grappa

GRAPPA-SCENTED WHIPPED HEAVY CREAM

SERVES 4 TO 6

This is a wonderful accompaniment to many cakes.

Heavy cream
Top-quality grappa

For every 1 cup/225 ml heavy cream that you use for whipping, add 1 teaspoon/5 ml top-quality grappa. Pour the cream and grappa into a chilled bowl and whip until frothy using an egg beater. If you do not intend to use the cream right away, cover it with plastic wrap and place in the refrigerator. Use within 2 hours.

Chocolate Glaze

This is the glaze I learned in Trieste, where delicate olive oil is available. If you cannot locate Triestine oil, then those from Liguria or Lake Garda are the only acceptable alternatives. Tuscan and Umbrian oils are much too heavy. Opt instead for canola oil.

8 to 10 ounces / 225 to 275 g semisweet chocolate
2 to 3 tablespoons / 30 to 45 ml light, fresh extra virgin olive oil

Melt the chocolate in the top of a double boiler set over simmering water. Slowly add the oil, stirring until blended. The chocolate should be of a good consistency to pour over a cake. Pour the frosting slowly and evenly over cake, letting the frosting spread itself. If necessary, use a spatula to smooth the frosting over the sides, but try not to touch the glaze on top so that it remains shiny and beautiful.

Caffè

COFFEE

To most serious coffee drinkers, Italy is the nation whose coffee tradition is the one to be used as the gold standard. Of course, coffee is not grown there, but it is the nation that seems to roast and brew the most delicious coffee and has created some of the most beguiling places in which to drink it.

Neapolitans often insist that the true *caffè all'italiana* can only be found in their city. In Naples there is a wonderfully direct and inky dark espresso, but this can also be tasted elsewhere. Turin can stake a claim to coffee preeminence, too. The city has the excellent century-old Lavazza, Italy's largest coffee company, and some outstanding historic *caffès* to visit. Standards in Turin are remarkably high. Rome, Florence, Bologna, Venice, and Milan all have long coffee traditions. In fact, you can get a good cup of coffee just about anywhere in Italy.

Yet I feel that I stand on very firm ground in asserting that Trieste is without question the coffee capital of Italy and, by extension, Friuli-Venezia Giulia can claim to be the nation's top coffee region. There are several reasons for this, all based in history.

The earliest evidence of coffee (and of Homo sapiens, for that matter) appears to be in central East Africa, in what is now Ethiopia. The coffee plant grew wild in a place called Kaffa, though coffee historians assert that the name of the drink comes from another source: the Arabic word *qahwa,* meaning a drink made from plants. In fact it was the Arabs who discovered, around the year 1000, that an infusion could be made of boiling water and green (unroasted) coffee beans. Only later were coffee beans roasted and ground before brewing.

From Africa, the coffee plant arrived in the Arabian peninsula (where one type of bean got the name *arabica;* the other type is known as *robusta*). By the fourteenth century, the Arabs were cultivating the plant and often brought it along on invasions. It reached lands occupied by Arab invasions through the centuries: North Africa, Iberia, Persia, India, and, most notably, Turkey.

There is some debate as to how coffee then got to the rest of Europe. Some people believe that Venetian traders brought it as early as 1615. *Caffès* in Venice, including Florian and Quadri, opened to serve this delicious beverage. In Venice, coffee was also used for medicinal purposes. But as Venetian economic power declined in the seventeenth century (as trade routes shifted to the Atlantic and the Americas), the city was forced to compete for the coffee trade with other European ports.

Most experts acknowledge that wherever the Turks went they brought coffee with them. It was likely in the Balkans during the fifteenth and sixteenth centuries, as well as in Hungary. The Turks made several attempts to seize Vienna and were repulsed definitively in 1683. As the Turks retreated, they left sacks of coffee behind. The Viennese quickly put the coffee to good use and began inventing pastries to serve with it.

Coffee made its way to other parts of Europe, but in 1700, it was most popular in Venice, Vienna, Budapest, Amsterdam, and Paris. The Dutch later brought the coffee plant to their colonies in East Asia (especially Java and Sumatra). The French (who grew coffee plants in the hothouses of Versailles) brought the plant to Martinique in the Caribbean, from which it would reach Colombia and Brazil, the two nations that are now the world's leading producers. It also reached other Caribbean islands (Jamaica, Hispaniola, and so on) and Central American countries, such as Costa Rica and Honduras. The English, those famous tea drinkers, also traded in coffee and are thought to have brought it to West Africa. Curiously, after a group of rebellious Bostonians refused to pay a heavy tax on tea and threw it into their harbor, North America became a coffee-drinking zone.

As coffee circled the globe, Trieste came to occupy a crucial position in coffee's growth as Europe's preferred beverage. When the city became a free port (with no duties on imported products) for Austria in 1717, it stole a lot of business from the Venetian importers. By that time, Venice was in serious decline and Trieste was growing. Almost all the coffee imported for the vast Hapsburg empire arrived in Trieste. The city also usurped Venice's role as the chief port of entry for northeastern Italy (Genoa, the peninsula's largest port, served the area that is now northwestern Italy, while Naples and other ports served the south). But it was Trieste, which served the huge zone of central Europe, that drank the most coffee. Trieste also became one of the most important spice ports.

When coffee and spices arrived in Trieste, port agents for importers would often repack the products before sending them to Vienna or elsewhere. Gradually, many of these people set up their own firms to import coffee and spices to their offices in Trieste and then resell them elsewhere. These goods penetrated what is now Friuli-Venezia Giulia and became part of the local tradition and cuisine.

The next step was for coffee-roasting firms to open in Trieste. As competition grew, quality rose as each roaster strove to make the best product. They also geared their roasting to different preferences, so that the coffee that went to Vienna was stronger than that which would go to Munich, and the coffee for Budapest was stronger still. *Caffès* opened in Trieste that served coffee to the local population as well as to the many foreigners who lived in the city. A tradition grew among the Triestines of distinguishing among many local roasts and establishing preferences. This made their coffee palates among the most sophisticated anywhere.

While most other cities in Italy may have one or two prominent roasters who set the tone for local taste, Trieste has always had many different ones who compete for customer loyalty. Trieste's most famous brand nowadays is surely Illy, although brands such as Hausbrandt, Cremcaffè, and Perlanera also have many local admirers. Each bar in the city only sells one brand (though perhaps in many blends and roasts), and all vie for faithful clients by making the coffee as fresh and delicious as possible and serving lovely pastries with it. In Trieste you will also find bars selling coffee from Udine, Gorizia, and Pordenone, plus brands from outside the region, such as Bologna's Segafredo and Turin's Lavazza.

While Venice may have two or three historic *caffès* and Turin a half dozen, Trieste is full of places geared to drinking excellent coffee in a beautiful setting. The most famous are the Tommaseo (favored by political types), the San Marco (probably the greatest literary *caffè* in Italy), the Specchi, the Pirona (favored by James Joyce), La Colombiana, Stella Polare, and Tergesteo. For many *triestini,* the best coffee in town is at Cremcaffè on Piazza Goldoni. Yet there are many more wonderful spots in town for a perfect cup of coffee. In the rest of Friuli-Venezia Giulia the quality of the coffee is almost as high as in Trieste.

As in Vienna, the *caffè* in Trieste was the second home for its habitués. Many *caffès* closed during World War I, never to reopen. *Caffè* life rebounded a bit in the 1920s and 1930s, and again in the 1950s. Nowadays, people in Trieste are making a special effort to restore the *caffè* tradition. In the San Marco, one of my favorites, there are nights with debates, others with music or poetry readings, and others where chess players take over. The writer Claudio Magris has a table where he likes to work for a few hours each day. He is a nationally admired figure, yet people in Trieste are very careful to let him work rather than engage him in discussions.

In the twentieth century, the two companies that did the most to improve the quality of coffee in Italy and to bring Italian coffee to the world are Lavazza and Trieste's Illycaffè. Lavazza claims to roast one-sixth of the world's coffee, and they do a very good job. Illy is more of a boutique item, but with an intensely loyal following. Five million persons around the world drink Illy every day. Illy is probably Italy's most expensive major brand, and many coffee drinkers consider it the best. If this is so, much of the credit should go to Ernesto Illy.

Dr. Illy is one of that group of highly original thinkers who have changed the destiny and economy of Friuli-Venezia Giulia. At this writing, at the turn of the century, he is in his eighties and continues to astonish all who meet him. He is first and foremost a chemist, one who understands the makeup of coffee (whose flavor, texture, and fragrance have more than eight hundred components). He told me that "chemistry is the science of complexity. If you learn chemistry, you learn to deal with complex things."

He is also an innovative engineer who has invented many machines to roast, pack, and store coffee, along with creating machines that improve coffee making. He says that "if you follow an unusual path, you have to do it alone." To that end, his goal is to analyze every stage of the process that leads to an ideal cup of coffee: growing the plant and the beans, harvesting, drying, shipping to Trieste, sorting, chemical analysis, roasting, and packing. Then there is the whole procedure to make the cup of coffee: grinding the beans, selecting the right machine, the best water, and then brewing everything correctly.

In packing coffee, most companies vacuum-pack. Illy has a machine that withdraws all air and then pressurizes the package with nitrogen. Dr. Illy believes this is the best way to preserve the freshness and flavor of coffee. He thinks that coffee should be aged before being put on sale. "Everybody tries to sell their coffee as fresh as possible. We want to age it one month. Ideally you will drink it two months after roasting. We put a date on the can and guarantee quality for three years."

He told me that there are five key components in a perfect cup of espresso coffee: the temperature at which it is brewed ($194°F/90°C$ is ideal), the total brewing time (25 to 30 seconds is correct), the correct grind of the beans, the dose of coffee (1 heaping teaspoon/ 7 g per cup), and a little more than 1 ounce/30 to 35 ml of fresh good water that is not laden with chemicals or minerals. He said that Panna mineral water from Tuscany has the right makeup for a good cup.

Dr. Illy told me that his notion of what the ideal cup of coffee is came from more than thirty years of feedback from customers. He said that the qualities of a classic cup of espresso have not changed through the years since. The liquid will fill the espresso cup halfway. It will have a dark orange *crema* (sort of a coffee-flavored foam) on top. In many, though not all, coffee brands, the *crema* is derived from the addition of some *robusta* coffee to the blend, which gives structure and produces the *crema*. *Arabica* coffee provides that almost wine-like flavor, and adds color and personality to the blend. Yet many brands in

Trieste and elsewhere are 100 percent *arabica,* and they yield a nice *crema,* too. The perfect *crema* will have a nice balance of bitterness and acidity, with a hint of natural sweetness and many fragrance and flavor elements.

No matter how you make your perfect espresso, that is only the beginning. In Trieste (and all of Italy) *un caffè* is an espresso of the type I described above. A *caffè macchiato* has a dash of steamed milk poured into it (*macchiare* means "to stain"). A *latte macchiato* is a glass of warm milk "stained" with some espresso. A *caffè corretto* is an espresso to which an alcoholic spirit such as brandy or grappa is added. In Trieste, an order of *un cappuccino* or *un cappo* will get you a cup of espresso with the froth of steamed milk on top, and often a little fresh whipped cream on the side. If you want cappuccino as served in the rest of Italy, you need to ask for *un cappuccino grande.* But if you go to Udine or just about anywhere else in Friuli-Venezia Giulia, an order of a cappuccino will get you the drink you are used to, while requesting a *cappuccino triestino* will get you the espresso with the steamed milk froth on top. In Trieste, a *cappuccino viennese* is a cappuccino topped with fresh whipped cream and cocoa powder.

In Trieste and all of Italy, an espresso is a sort of period or exclamation point at the end of a meal. It is also a beverage to be taken standing at a bar with friends or acquaintances in a brief restorative pause in the middle of a busy day. Under no circumstances should you ever serve a lemon zest with an espresso. This is an affectation that arrived in America at a time when good coffee was too expensive, and Italian immigrants attempted to correct the taste of their bad coffee with the lemon. But it is never done in Italy, and you should immediately lose the habit. If you frequent espresso bars or restaurants near your home that use lemon zest with coffee, ask them to desist and then spend what money they are saving on lemons to buy a better brand of coffee.

If you become a serious espresso drinker, consider investing in a home espresso maker. I strongly urge you to choose an Italian brand (such as Gaggia, Faema, or Pavoni) for the simple reason that they are designed to make espresso as consumed in Italy. Famous brands from Germany, Switzerland, France, and America make more generic espresso that only approximates the genuine article. For everything you need to know about selecting, buying, storing, and brewing coffee, read *The Joy of Coffee* by Corby Kummer (Houghton Mifflin, 1997).

Caffè al Cardamomo

CARDAMOM-SCENTED COFFEE

SERVES 4

I tasted this coffee in Trieste, where it is an old preparation. Unlike many coffee preparations found in places like Seattle, which are flavored with nut oils and berries, this one is more classical. Spices are essential to the Triestine flavor palate, and cardamom is an unusual and highly congenial companion to good coffee. You may drink this straight or with a small drop of whipped cream.

10 teaspoons / 50 g freshly ground Italian espresso coffee
4 teaspoons / 20 g sugar
3 cardamom seeds, lightly ground

Combine the coffee, sugar, and 1½ cups / 350 ml cold water in a small saucepan over medium heat until it starts to boil and a small orange-brown foam forms. Remove the saucepan from the heat and stir with a spoon all the way to the base of the pot.

Return the saucepan to the heat and remove it again just when the foam forms. Stir again and add the cardamom.

Return the saucepan to the heat and let the liquid just come to a boil. Pour the coffee into espresso cups (or into a thermos if you wish) very gently so that the grounds remain in the saucepan. Serve at once.

VARIATION: What you see above is the recipe as served in Trieste. In using my drip coffeemaker at home, I sometimes stir some ground cardamom into my ground coffee before brewing. The idea is the same, although the result is different. I do not add sugar, so the cardamom flavor is actually more pronounced.

Sgnape

If you know grappa as a fancy product high in alcohol, but with a distinct forward flavor of glorious wine grapes, you may not know the humble history behind it. Conversely, if in your youth you tasted a firewater called grappa that made you gasp from the kick, then you surely do not know what this libation has become.

Grappa is a high-alcohol distilled drink from northeastern Italy (it is found in lesser amounts farther west in Lombardy and Piedmont) that was originally made with the assorted grape skins that remained following wine making. Similar distilled drinks made with cherries, pears, raspberries, plums, and other *whole* fruit are known as fruit distillates.

People in the Veneto, the Trentino-Alto Adige, and Friuli-Venezia Giulia will probably insist that grappa was born in their specific regions. All three make an excellent product, but I think it is fair to say that the best and most famous grappa now comes from the region that is the subject of this book.

It seems that distillation of food products to make a beverage dates back to ancient Egypt. Documentation of grappa-like drinks in Italy exists from the eleventh and twelfth centuries, although these seem more like herb-infused alcoholic drinks whose purpose was primarily medicinal. Grappa as it is now defined seems to date back to the end of the eighteenth century.

There is some confusion about a certain term: *acquavite.* The usual interpretation is that this is a distillation of a fruit or plant, and it is usually translated as "water of life." In Italian, the confusion is furthered because *vite* does not mean "life" but rather either "grapevine" or the plural noun "lives." So *acquavite* in Italian can mean "water of the vine," and the implication is usually of a distillation of a product of grapes, hence grappa. By contrast, distillates in Friuli-Venezia Giulia are almost always made of whole fruit or other products, as we will discuss later, while *acquavite* elsewhere connotes a very wide range of potent potables.

In the past, in Udine, Trieste, and other cities, grappa was consumed by laborers and the working classes against the winter's cold. It was inevitably a harsh drink whose purpose was to provide relief from the miseries of cold and privation. Grappa came in rather conventional square-shouldered bottles with labels that were almost clinical in presentation. Grappa was utilitarian, not something that could be perceived as a pleasure, save for the warmth and cheap inebriation it provided.

Until the late 1960s, grappa was a beverage—a food, really—of the poor. It provided warmth and calories to nearly destitute farmers, who sold their meager yields to survive. If they were working the lands of overlords, the product of that land was given to the landowners. Grapes were pressed to make wine for landowners or for sale, and then the pomace (skins, stems, and pits) went to the poor. These people subsisted on polenta, grappa, butter or lard, the occasional egg, and what little they could pull from the ground (such as herbs) that was not intended for sale.

The process of distilling grappa has changed little over the years. Once the pomace is delivered, the first step in the process is to remove the stems and then to allow fermentation with the skins (and sometimes pits). During this process, sugars are transformed to alcohol. The product is put in alembics, wooden vats with copper interiors, where the distillation takes place. The resulting libation has a typical alcohol content of 40 to 50 percent. It is usually stored in glass bottles for at least 6 months before sale.

Nowadays, most top producers distill from the end of August, with the arrival of the first pomace of white grapes and then, as they arrive, other whites and then red grapes. For 3 months, they distill 7 days a week, until early December. To assure maximum fragrance, flavor, and persistence in the grappa, the goal is to have the pomace within 10 to 12 hours after the grapes were pressed. The average yield per 100 kilograms (220 pounds) for most grappa producers is 9 to 11 liters of finished product.

*T*he first boom in grappa consumption beyond northeastern Italy began in the 1960s as people elsewhere found it a strong and warming postdinner drink or something to add to coffee. Quality had certainly risen by then among leading grappa makers, and the product became somewhat fashionable. But it still tasted like an amalgam of grape skins and was sold in plain bottles.

The whole world of grappa changed thanks to one person, Giannola Nonino, one of the trailblazing pioneers I described in this book's introduction. She felt that although grappa was experiencing commercial growth, it would never be taken seriously at fine restaurants and by people with refined taste.

The Nonino distillery, located in Percoto in the province of Udine, produced its first grappa in 1897 and was a small family business that made a grappa that was surely as good as the standard for the time, and probably somewhat better. Giannola was (and is) a restless person for whom these accomplishments were not enough. Just as one person came along and looked at a world that others saw as flat and called it round, Giannola Nonino saw that grappa could be much more than a drink made from the leavings of the wine-making process.

Until this time, most people who made even the best grappa took pomace, stored it, and gradually distilled it to make the harsh final product. In this, there was no difference from high-proof alcoholic beverages the world over, whether they were derived from wheat, rye, potatoes, barley, sugarcane, or other sources that were meant to make the drinker drunk. In Friuli-Venezia Giulia, wine makers would deliver truckloads of pomace to distillers once all wine making was done. Typically all the skins and other materials were combined whether they came from red or white grapes.

Giannola asked herself whether a grappa could be different and more pleasing if it were derived from a single grape instead of a haphazard mélange. In 1973, Benito and Giannola Nonino did the first distillation of a grappa made entirely from the skins of one grape variety, Picolit. Because this is one of the most extraordinary grapes in Italy, it promised great things for the grappa.

Bringing about this change would not be easy. As a Friulian woman who felt great solidarity with others, as the mother of three girls, and in a period when the first rumblings of the feminist movement were heard in Italy, Giannola sought to make her idea work for women. She contacted the wives of men who grew grapes and asked them to set aside the skins of Picolit grapes. She offered ten times the price usually paid for skins, and many women got involved because it was an incentive to have money apart from their husbands'.

And thus the Noninos made the first grappa derived from the skins of one grape variety. It had a subtle taste and even more subtle aroma, and this marked the beginning of connoisseurship in grappa. But it was not an easy trail to blaze. The 1973 production went entirely unsold. Prices were thought to be too high for a drink with historic peasant connotations. Giannola gave away all the Picolit grappa to journalists, restaurateurs, sommeliers, and others. She explained her concept to each. She asked to serve her grappa at important dinners and went from table to table, pouring and describing. Slowly, her work and personality created a following.

After the Picolit grappa began to acquire a following, the Noninos looked at other grapes for single-variety grappa. In Italian, the term *monovitigno* means single-grape variety. It is widely believed that the Noninos invented this word or, at the very least, introduced it into common usage. Among the *monovitigno* grappas they make as of this writing are Chardonnay, Fragolino, Merlot, Müller Thurgau, Picolit, Refosco del Peduncolo Rosso, Ribolla Gialla, Sauvignon Blanc, Schioppettino, Tazzelenghe, Terrano, Tocai, and Verduzzo.

The creation of *monovitigno* grappas had an important corollary benefit. Because they were eager to have the highest-quality skins to make their grappa, the Noninos did all they could to encourge the improvement in the quality of grapes in Friuli-Venezia Giulia. Italy's largest grape nursery, in Rauscedo (UD), became a locus for this activity. And some wine-making families, notably the Dorigos, did all they could to improve the way grapes grew in the vineyard.

The Noninos and other grappa producers benefited from a change in wine making in the region. In the past, when wine grapes were heavily crushed to extract juices for wine, the remaining pomace produced a harsh product. Since the 1970s the trend has been to more gentle pressing of grapes, so that what remains for grappa has more fragrance and character.

These developments gave this little region's wine an incredible qualitative boost so that it would stand shoulder to shoulder with Tuscany and Piedmont as the national leaders. But Friuli-Venezia Giulia would have no rivals in terms of the diversification and innovation in wine making.

In the past, grape skins were typically stored in wood vats that were put aside so that grappa could be made in the winter. Benito Nonino realized that skins left this way would ferment and deteriorate, producing a grappa that would be harsh and inferior. After all, isn't wine made as soon as grapes are picked (and isn't oil made with newly picked olives)? He decided that grappa should be made as soon as the skins arrive at the distillery. The final product was more flavorful and aromatic, setting new standards in elegance.

In 1981, the Noninos visited Alsace to observe the distillation of many fruits with the idea of doing that in Friuli. Giannola realized that *whole* grapes could be distilled as a fruit (rather than using only grape skins, a by-product of wine making, to make grappa). By becoming an additional market for excellent grapes, the Noninos provided further impetus to the regional desire to improve quality.

Because distilling whole grapes was a new idea, and Italy is a famously bureaucratic country, approval had to come from the Ministry of Agriculture before this new product could be created. This required a great deal of charm and persuasiveness, which Giannola amply supplied. In 1984, the Italian government finally granted its permission. The Noninos were the first to do this and named the line Uè, which means grape in Friulano.

Among these are delicious Malvasia Istriana, spicy Moscato, fiery complex Müller Thurgau, unusual Traminer (grown in Caviola, near Grado by the Adriatic, and different from the usual Traminer taste), Cabernet Franc from Grave, and Uva Fragola (similar to Concord grape). All of these distillates evoke the flavor and fragrance qualities of the grapes, and it is intriguing to discover the grapes this way and then taste them as wines.

In 1984, the Noninos made a Picolit distillate that was aged in three types of wood barrels (sherry casks, Limousin oak, and Nevers oak), called Uè Invecchiata. It was released in 1997 in honor of the company's centennial. Typically grappas and distillates are bottled once ready, so that barrel-aging is unusual as well. Uè Invecchiata has a golden sherry color and a remarkably complex flavor. They made only 600 bottles, each by Riedel. In years since, the family used a grape that they consider outstanding in each vintage for aging in wood.

In 1985, the year following the production of the first grape distillates, the Noninos began to distill superb Friulian fruit as well. My two favorites are cherry and pear, but the others (apricot, blackberry, peach, plum, raspberry, and strawberry) are excellent, too. This has taken what was once a seasonal business (grappa making occurred during and immediately after the grape harvest) to one that works most of the year, depending upon when certain fruits are at their peak.

In most of Italy, people drink something called *amaro,* which means bitter, but in fact is a postmeal drink thought to favor digestion. The recipe for *amaro* varies from producer to producer, but most include alcohol plus the flavorings of herbs, some fruits, and occasionally spices. In Abruzzo, a famous brand is Centerbe, which means "100 herbs." One of my favorites, and one of the most popular in Italy, is Sicily's Averna. The Noninos make one simply called Amaro Nonino, which contains 33 herbs and flavor ingredients, including orange and licorice. It is very fine.

Despite all of this growth, the Noninos have always kept their operation smaller than those of major distilleries, believing that industrial products can reach a good consistent level but will seldom reach the heights achieved when things are done in an artisanal fashion.

Giannola has made staggering innovations in marketing her superb products that are written about by students in business schools and emulated everywhere. The functional and austere bottles that grappa used to be sold in had to go, she said. As Giannola created new products, they had to be sold in special bottles. Drawing inspiration from apothecaries of old and the proximity of the famous glassworks near Venice, she used bottles that looked as though they held health-giving elixirs rather than booze. The bottles resemble those that hold perfume, and this is very much in keeping with such a delicately fragrant libation. The *monovitigno* grappas are in broad-bottomed, slope-shouldered bottles, while grape and fruit distillates come in bottles that have a rounder more feminine aspect. You will notice on all Nonino labels an approximation of the universal female symbol, the circle with the plus sign attached to it. Most Italian grappas now come in exaggeratedly tall or design-conscious bottles, but few have the elegant simplicity of Giannola's classic shapes.

Many Nonino products are quite expensive, because they are made with great care with fine ingredients. Yet their influence has yielded an across-the-board increase in quality, especially in Friuli-Venezia Giulia, so that if you acquire other grappas from this region you will probably be very pleased.

Some Grappas to Look for from Friuli-Venezia Giulia

I must warn you that it is essential that you only drink grappa from established producers. In Italy you are sometimes offered homemade grappa *(grappa fatta in casa),* which you should politely refuse. It is often high in methanol and can cause harm.

Distilleria di Aquileia. Founded in the 1960s, this firm produces well-regarded distillates, including Grappa Flavia (made of skins of Traminer and barrel-aged), La Centenara (from white wine grape skins), Le Vinaceis (from Cabernet, Verduzzo, and Sauvignon Blanc), and La Livia (from Picolit).

Distillerie Buiese, in Martignacco (UD).

Distillerie Camel, Via della Roggia 2, Marsure di Sotto (near Povoletto, province of Udine); tel: 0432 / 664144. Closed in the first three weeks of August. Following the lead of the Nonino family, this firm produces excellent grappas and distillates (here called Most) derived from single-grape varieties. Many of the bottles are labeled with the name Bepi Tosolini, in honor of the firm's founder.

Distillerie Ceschi in Nimis (UD) is also an excellent producer. I especially like their grappa di Ramandolo.

Distillerie Domenis in Cividale del Friuli (UD).

Distillerie Nonino, Via Aquileia 104, località Percoto (near Pavia di Udine); tel: 0432 / 676331. www.nonino.it. Closed Saturday and Sunday.

Distillerie Pagura in Castions di Zoppola (PN) began production in 1879 and is one of the finest small producers in the region. They follow old traditions and have endeavored to maintain quality by making small quantities. If you go to the distillery, you can purchase grappa with your name written on the bottle, as was once done with all clients of the firm.

Tenuta Villanova in Villanova di Farra (GO).

For a complete list of grappa producers who are members of the consortium of Friuli-Venezia Giulia, contact the Consorzio per la Tutela della Grappa Friulana, Via Poscolle 6, 33100 Udine; tel: 0432/509394.

TASTING GRAPPA AND DISTILLATES

If you are going to spend good money on these products, it is important that you know how to drink them. Unlike wine and beer, which spend a brief time in the mouth being savored before they are swallowed, grappa and distillates should be slowly consumed in small sips that evaporate in the mouth.

The beverage should be served in a small amount in a small glass that you hold by the stem. Swirl the liquid in the glass, then bring it to your nose to enjoy. This fragrance will open your senses for what is to come.

Swirl the liquid again and then take a small sip on the tip of your tongue. Lift your tongue to the roof of your mouth in such way that the liquid permeates your palate. Keep your tongue up for a few extra moments so that the warmth will evaporate some of the liquid. The flavor and fragrance will spread to your mouth, throat, and nasal passages, all of which will allow you to perceive the beverage in a different way. Let this sip disappear (with the remaining liquid sliding down your throat).

Focus meditatively on the sensations you feel and then note the *ritorno,* the flavor that comes back in your mouth a few minutes later. This is how you will tell the true quality of a grappa. A good one will have its best flavors come back up; a bad one will return with its worst flavors.

After savoring the *ritorno,* wait a couple of minutes and then take another small sip and repeat the process.

When you walk into a bar or fine restaurant in Italy and elsewhere, it is typical to see a display of brilliant bottles of after-dinner libations on a shelf or a trolley. This leads many people to believe that this is how grappa and distillates should be stored. But it is important to remember that these bottles are consumed rather quickly, so that their precious contents will not suffer the ravages caused by light and exposure.

You should store your grappas and distillates in a cool, dark place, such as a cabinet or a closet. Here they can last for several years, although there inevitably will be some evaporation. Will they change as they age? Some producers say no, but one very experienced grappa maker told me that the more aromatic ones—usually made from white grapes—become rounder and lose some of their fragrance as they age. Fruit distillates will lose some of their perfume, although the flavor will last considerably longer.

Discovering the Outstanding Wines of Friuli-Venezia Giulia

One can devote several lifetimes to discovering the wines of this region. Although it is small in terms of wine produced, it is one of the great zones of the world for top-quality wine full of surprises and pleasures. If you are traveling in Friuli-Venezia Giulia, consider visiting the *enotecas,* where many of the region's wines are available to purchase in one place. Similarly, the region's marvelous *osterias* offer long lists of wines by the glass, served by knowledgeable proprietors who also make traditional dishes.

This chapter includes a subjective list of top producers in the region. Many are quite famous, while some are little known. You will quickly recognize some of my favorites, but I have tried to report fairly on the strengths and weaknesses of every producer I have mentioned. This list contains most every winery of note. Because I hope this book will be read in many countries, some readers will have more access to these wines than others.

No matter where you live, you should develop a close working relationship with your wine seller and, when possible, the owners of restaurants you really like. Discuss wine with them; encourage them to bring in some of the wines that are of interest to you. (Show him or her this chapter and then select wines that are enticing.) These people will have access to importers and will know how to get their hands on bottles that you may not be able to locate easily. Then, of course, you should support their efforts on your behalf by becoming a devoted customer. This will help bring the wines of Friuli-Venezia Giulia to you.

There are numerous organizations and consortiums that regulate and promote the quality of wine making in Friuli-Venezia Giulia. The most important is Un Vigneto Chiamato Friuli, ERSA (Servizio della Vitivinicoltura, Casa del Vino, Via Poscolle 6, 33100 Udine; tel: 0432/297068 or 506097; fax: 0432/510180). This is the regional office for promotion of all agricultural products of the region, including wine. There are wonderful informational materials and tasting classes offered for restaurateurs and wine professionals. This should be the first place to contact, especially if you are a wine professional, for guidance about the region's wine. This office was an important resource for me as I conducted research for this book. It is also the seat for two smaller consortiums: Consorzio DOC Friuli-Latisana and Consorzio DOC Friuli-Annia.

ADDRESSES FOR CONSORTIUMS

CONSORZIO DOC AQUILEIA DEL FRIULI
Via Carso 1, Scodovacca, 33052 Cervignano (UD)
tel: 0431/34010

CONSORZIO DOC CARSO CCIA,
Piazza della Borsa, 34123 Trieste;
tel: 040/200761

CONSORZIO DOC COLLIO
Via Sauro 9, 34071 Cormons (GO)
tel: 0481/630303

CONSORZIO DOC COLLI ORIENTALI DEL FRIULI (COF)
Via Candotti 1, 33043 Cividale del Friuli (UD)
tel: 0432/730129

CONSORZIO DOC FRIULI-GRAVE
Via Oberdan 26, 33170 Pordenone
tel: 0434/523654

CONSORZIO DOC ISONZO
Via Sauro 9, 34071 Cormons (GO)
tel: 0481/61833

ENOTECAS WORTH KNOWING

ENOTECA REGIONALE DEL FRIULI-VENEZIA GIULIA "LA SERENISSIMA"
Via Battisti, Gradisca d'Isonzo
tel/fax: 0481/99528
(Open 10h-14h, 16h-24h; closed Monday)
In the beautiful town of Gradisca is the foremost *enoteca* in the region. It opened in 1965 and was one of the earliest initiatives to promote the wines of Friuli-Venezia Giulia. Many of the top producers have wines for sale here. Some can be had by the glass at very fair prices, and you can buy bottles or cases to take away. There are light snacks, too. Note that the people who sell here cannot and do not endorse one wine rather than another, but this is a place for you to explore and sample to gain an education.

ENOTECA DI CORMONS
Palazzo Locatelli, Piazza 24 Maggio 21, tel: 0481/630371
Open Wednesday, 17h-22h (24h in summer); Thursday through Monday, 11h-13h, 17h-22h (24h in summer)
This lovely spot in the middle of Cormons has several purposes. It is the tourist office, with very good informational materials. You may sample wines by the glass of many Cormons and Capriva producers. There is good light food. Upstairs, producers meet and plan policy on how to improve their already outstanding wines.

ENOTECA GRUPPO VITICOLTORI DI CORNO DI ROSAZZO
Via Aquileia 68, Località Quattroventi
Corno di Rosazzo (UD); tel: 0432/753220
(Open 8h-24h; closed Tuesday.)
The place to sample and purchase many of the marvelous wines of the Colli Orientali del Friuli (COF).

Some Notable Wine Producers of Friuli-Venezia Giulia

AZIENDA AGRICOLA AITA
Via Dante 9, 34071 Cormons (GO)
tel: 0481/61555
Boris and Rosi Aita live a few steps from the Collio consortium office and wine bar, and their animated presence makes it a fun place to visit. In their own home, Boris produces nice typical Collio wines—particularly Tocai—and Rosi, who is from Styria in Austria, prepares outstanding dishes that combine the various culinary traditions of this part of the world. Boris's job in the kitchen, and he does it perfectly, is to slice the leg of famous prosciutto made by their neighbor Gigi d'Osvaldo.

TENUTA DI ANGORIS
Località Angoris, 34071 Cormons (GO)
tel: 0481/60923
Angoris was the first producer in the modern era of wine making in Friuli-Venezia Giulia to intentionally create a blend. In the past, farmers and small wine makers would blend grapes together indiscriminately. But at Angoris, in 1970, the goal was to make a special and meaningful wine combining different grapes in a deliberate way. Mont Quarin Blanc was made of Pinot Bianco, Tocai, and Traminer. Mont Quarin Ros combined Merlot and Cabernet Franc. Nowadays, the red blend is called Ravòst and combines Schioppettino and Refosco. But their best-regarded whites are now single-grape: Pinot Bianco and Sauvignon Blanc. There is a nice spumante made from Pinot Nero, with a little Chardonnay and Pinot Bianco.

ASCEVI
Via Uclanzi 24, 34070 San Floriano del Collio (GO)
tel: 0481/884140
This winery has two vineyards, the original one and the newly acquired one named Luwa (for the Pintar family children, Luana and Walter). You will find nice typical Collio whites here, including Chardonnay, Pinot Grigio, Ribolla Gialla, Sauvignon Blanc, and Tocai. For the moment, the Luwa wines are less interesting than the original vineyard wines, but they will surely grow in stature. There are three appeal-

ing blends: the Col Martin Luwa includes Pinot Grigio, Sauvignon Blanc, and Tocai. The Vigna Verdana is Chardonnay, Ribolla Gialla, and Sauvignon Blanc. Grappoli Shaden is more unusual, containing Moscato Bianco, Riesling, and Sauvignon Blanc. It has a cool flavor and interesting acidity.

BASTIANI
Via Savaian 36, 34071 Cormons (GO)
tel: 0481/60725
Although this is a small producer, it is interesting for the fact that it emphasizes natural fertilizers and what one might call minimum interference with nature. Also, it has vineyards in both the Collio and Isonzo zones, so that the same grapes grown in different vineyards may have different characteristics. I particularly like their Pinot Bianco.

BASTIANICH CASALI OTTELIO, FRAZIONE PREMARIACCO, BUTTRIO
(all correspondence should go to Viale Grado 4, 33050 Lauzacco-Pavia di Udine (UD); tel/fax: 0432/675612).
For information in North America, call 212-473-7998
This is a new winery (first harvest 1998), but one with great credentials and potential. It is owned by Joseph Bastianich, the highly successful New York restaurateur and son of Lidia Matticchio Bastianich, the foremost exponent of the food of Friuli-Venezia Giulia in North America. They have acquired prime terrain in Buttrio and have begun to produce white wines. These include Pinot Bianco, Pinot Grigio, Tocai, and a blend including 85 percent regular Tocai and 15 percent late-harvest Tocai. Then there is a white blend called Vespa (45 percent Chardonnay, 45 percent Sauvignon Blanc, and 10 percent late-harvest Picolit).

TENUTA BELTRAME
Loc. Antonini 6/8, Frazione Privano
33050 Bagnària Arsa (UD)
tel: 0432/923670
A good producer in the Aquileia zone. The Pinot Bianco and Sauvignon Blanc are appealing, and all of their wines are of interest.

TENUTA DI BLASIG
Via Roma 63, 34077 Ronchi dei Legionari (GO)
tel: 0481/475480
Elisabetta Bortolotto Sarcinelli is now in charge of this old family winery in Isonzo. Her white blend, Falconetto Bianco, is an interesting combination of Chardonnay, Malvasia Istriana, and Tocai that has a lot of fragrance plus round fruit taste. She also makes a nice sparkling wine, simply called Vino Spumante Brut.

BORGO CONVENTI
Strada Colombara 13, 34070 Farra d'Isonzo (GO)
tel: 0481/888004
This winery, with terrain in both Isonzo and Collio, has many admirers, especially outside the region, because of the more international perspective of its owner, Gianni Vescovo. This is most evident in the red blend called Braida Nuova, which recalls Bordeaux more than a wine of Friuli-Venezia Giulia. There are three different Chardonnays. The one from Collio is rather crisp and European. The Isonzo one, called I Fiori, is more herbal than tart. The Chardonnay Colle Russian will appeal more to drinkers who like California style. Vescovo produces a balanced, medium-weight Refosco dal Peduncolo Nero. The Isonzo Cabernet Sauvignon and Collio Merlot merit consideration. I would also point you to the two Pinot Grigios (one from Collio, the other from Isonzo) and a lovely Collio Pinot Bianco.

BORGO DEL TIGLIO
Via San Giorgio 71, fraz. Brazzano
34070 Cormons (GO)
tel: 0481/62166
Nicola Monferrari is part of the generation of producers who came of age in the late 1980s and sought to distinguish themselves from the grand old men. He began with an outstanding Tocai and some interesting reds. Through the years he has continued to express himself through his wines, with the result that some people consider him a genius and others a bit of a heretic. I would generalize by saying that his wines have unusually long persistence of fragrance and flavor, lingering in your nose, mouth, and thought long after other wines would wane. His Collio Rosso and Bianco blends merit your attention.

BORGO LOTESSA
Località Giasbana 23, 34070 San Floriano del Collio (GO)
tel: 0481/390302
Giasbana is one of the loveliest little areas in the San Floriano zone, and the vineyards here have a dreamy beauty. This winery makes appealing wines, including an Isonzo Cabernet Sauvignon, a very fine Collio Pinot Bianco, and a Pinot Grigio with delightful flavors of pear and apple. The Poggio Crus Soli is a red blend that includes Merlot grown in Collio and a small amount of Cabernets from Isonzo. They also produce a light, but lovely Picolit.

BORGO SAN DANIELE
Via San Daniele 16, 34071 Cormons (GO)
tel: 0481/60552
The Mauri family makes one of the best Tocais around, abundant in fragrance and flavor of fruit. I also like the Arbis Bianco, which is a blend of Müller Thurgau, Sauvignon Blanc, and Tocai. The Arbis Rosso is a blend of Cabernet Franc and Cabernet Sauvignon. The Merlot, called Lucky Red, is aged *in barrique.*

ROSA BOSCO
Via Abate Colonna 20, 33044 Oleis di Manzano (UD)
tel/fax: 0432/751522
Prior to her divorce she was known as Rosetta Dorigo and, together with her husband Girolamo, made some of the best wines in Italy. She returned to her maiden name and was forced to go it alone under rough conditions. Without land, a *cantina,* or resources, it seemed that Rosa's formidable natural ability to make great wine would go to waste. But taking grapes away from her would be like taking a paintbrush from Michelangelo, and many friends and fellow wine makers in the region were eager to see her back at work. She had many offers to work for other wineries, but wanted to make her own wine. At the time, a young female wine maker said to me of Rosa that "he or she who is a guide does not need to be led by others. She is so knowledgeable and has such a developed palate and nose that she can go her own way and rely entirely on her own talents."

The oenologist at Dorigo, Donato Lanati, decided to leave that winery to work with Rosa, whose vision was more like his. Ultimately Rosa decided to start over by making one white and one red. The year 1998 was a difficult one for many producers because of bad weather. After careful work Rosa decided that her red (COF Merlot) and white (COF Sauvignon Blanc) met her high standards. Both wines were met with universal acclaim and lots of press attention throughout Italy. They are marvels, full of fruit, fragrance, texture, and personality. They drink well now, and can probably last for a number of years and still be special. Rosa had ten times as many orders for the Sauvignon as she had wine.

The year 1999 was a great one for wine making throughout the region, and Rosa bottled excellent Merlot (called Boscorosso) and Sauvignon Blanc. The future looks bright for her, which means that there will be more outstanding wine for Rosa Bosco's many admirers to drink.

BUZZINELLI
Località Pradis, 22/bis, 34071 Cormons (GO)
tel: 0481/62272
Brothers Boris and David make a delicious Pinot Bianco and very nice examples of Tocai and Merlot.

PAOLO CACCESE
Località Pradis 6, 34071 Cormons (GO)
tel: 0481/61062
Good Pinot Bianco, Pinot Grigio, Cabernet Franc, Merlot, and, especially, Malvasia Istriana.

CA' DI BON
Via Casali Gallo 1, 33040 Corno di Rosazzo (UD)
tel: 0432/759316
Gianni and Ameris Bon grow grapes in the COF and Grave. The Grave Sauvignon Blanc and Cabernet Franc are pleasing, and the COF Merlot, Refosco dal Peduncolo Rosso, Pinot Grigio, and Tocai are all nice.

ALFIERI CANTARUTTI
Via Ronchi 9, 33048 San Giovanni al Natisone (UD)
tel: 0432/756317
This winery, with terrain in Grave and COF, offers a good quality/price ratio for ever-improving wines. I especially like the red blend, COF Rosso Poema, which combines Cabernet Franc, Merlot, Schioppettino, and Tazzelenghe. This is a big wine, but one with very local flavor, thanks to the two native grapes. The COF Bianco Solivo is also unusual. It takes Pinot Bianco that has been fermented and aged *in barrique*

and blends it with Riesling and Tocai that have been made in stainless steel. The result is creamy, acidic, fruity, and fragrant all at once. They also make good single-grape wines, although they are not up to the level of the blends.

CANTINA PRODUTTORI DI CORMONS
Via Vino della Pace 31, 34071 Cormons (GO)
tel: 0481/60579
I heartily commend the Cantina to you because it represents the best of the spirit of the region. With an address called "Street of the Wine of Peace," this is a cooperative effort by many producers to make wines that appear under a collective label. In cooperatives in other parts of the world, quality is often middling. Here, you find some excellent wines. The Chardonnay is lush and lovely, as is the Collio Pinot Grigio. (Note that there are some growers in Isonzo, and the Cantina also makes an Isonzo Pinot Grigio.) I also enjoy the Collio Pinot Bianco and Ribolla Gialla, plus dessert wines Picolit, Passito di Cormons, and the Isonzo Vendemmia Tardiva Vino degli Angeli. The one red of note is an Isonzo Refosco del Peduncolo Rosso.

CASA ZULIANI
Via Gradisca 23, 34070 Farra d'Isonzo (GO)
tel: 0481/888506
Bruna Zuliani has vineyards in both Isonzo and Collio and is dedicated to careful maintenance of grapes. The results can be appreciated in the glass, with a Sauvignon Blanc from Isonzo and a range of wines from Collio: Pinot Bianco, Pinot Grigio, Sauvignon Blanc, Tocai, Cabernet Franc, and Merlot. A white blend, called Swing, combines *barrique*-aged Chardonnay with Sauvignon and Tocai. A wine called Merlot Gospel is partly aged *in barrique,* and a Cabernet Franc Habanera is aged in oak casks. These music wines are very appealing, but I shudder to think what a rap or technomusic wine would taste like.

LA CASTELLADA
Frazione Oslavia 1, 34170 Oslavia (GO)
tel: 0481/33670
This winery is probably most famous for its outstanding Ribolla Gialla, which is like drinking creamy fruit. Yet there are also good Chardonnay, Sauvignon Blanc, and Tocai, plus two very impressive blends. Bianco della Castellada combines

Pinot Grigio, Ribolla Gialla, Sauvignon Blanc, and Tocai and is fermented *in barrique*. Rosso della Castellada is big and beautiful and made from Cabernet Sauvignon and Merlot.

CASTELLO DI SPESSA

Via Spessa 1, 34070 Capriva del Friuli (GO)
tel: 0481 / 639914
Loretto Pali, the owner, and Patrizia Stekar, the guiding spirit and arbiter of taste in all things, have created a special winery on land where grapes have grown for many centuries. Their Pinot Bianco is outstanding, the red blend (Rosso di Conte di Spessa) is excellent, and so is the Pinot Grigio. They also own and operate the nearby La Boatina winery (tel: 0481 / 60445), turning out delicious and highly drinkable wines good for quaffing or combining with food. The Pinot Bianco is my favorite. Both wineries have lovely accommodations for travelers in the region.

CASTELVECCHIO

Via Castelnuovo 2, 34078 Sagrado (GO)
tel: 0481 / 99742
This winery is almost unknown outside of Friuli-Venezia Giulia and many people in the region have never heard of it or tasted their product. Part of the reason is its location in Carso very close to the Slovenian border. It is off the beaten path for many wine routes. Also, Castelvecchio has developed a particular strength in reds, and many people look to this region for whites. The Cabernet Sauvignon is outstanding, with richness and balance. The Cabernet Franc is almost as good. I also like the Terrano, the most popular red of the Carso zone. The very fine red blend, called Carso Rosso Turmino, combines 70 percent Terrano with 30 percent Cabernet Sauvignon. Whites are also made here, and I think the best is Malvasia Istriana.

CENCIG

Via Sottomonte 171, 33044 Manzano (UD)
A small estate that eschews technology where possible. There is nice Sauvignon Blanc and Tocai, and the Verduzzo is also very appealing.

COLLAVINI

Via della Ribolla Gialla, 33040 Corno di Rosazzo (UD)
tel: 0432 / 753222
Since 1896, Collavini has been a well-known producer in the region and among the first to export wines. Their peachy Pinot Grigio is very popular, and they make a sparkling wine (vino spumante) that meets great favor. The light-bodied Refosco dal Peduncolo Rosso is a very pleasing and drinkable red wine.

COLMELLO DI GROTTA

Via Gorizia 133, Frazione Villanova,
34070 Farra d'Isonzo (GO)
tel: 0481 / 888445
Lucia Bennati has grapes planted in both Collio and Isonzo. In the former is a white blend called Bianco Rondon that combines Chardonnay, Pinot Grigio, and Sauvignon Blanc to produce a rich and appealing wine. She also uses these grapes to make three individual Collio wines, and uses the same grapes from her Isonzo vineyards to make three additional wines. She also produces a very nice Collio Tocai.

PAOLINO COMELLI

Via della Chiesa, Località Colloredo, 33040 Faedis (UD)
tel: 0432 / 711226
This producer is at the western extreme of the COF, almost at the Grave zone. The Chardonnay and Pinot Grigio are well regarded. The Tocai has a bewitching fragrance that is more imposing than its subdued flavor. The Sauvignon Blanc Superiore is intense and interesting. Among reds, there is Cabernet Sauvignon, Schioppettino, and a blend called Rosso Suffumbergo, which is mostly Cabernet Sauvignon and Merlot.

DARIO COOS

Via Ramandolo 15, 33045 Nimis (UD)
tel: 0432 / 790320
Coos is perhaps the most famous producer of Ramandolo, and his wine must be tasted to understand the potential and special characteristics of this grape. He produces two wines. The one simply labeled Ramandolo is fermented and aged *in barrique*. His Ramandolo Longhino is unoaked. I like both very much and commend them heartily.

DAL FARI

Via Darnazacco, 33043 Cividale del Friuli (UD)

tel: 0432 / 731219

This house, with well-regarded oenologist Fabio Coser, makes good single-grape wines and very interesting COF blends. The white, called Bianco delle Grazie, is made of Chardonnay, Riesling, Sauvignon Blanc, and Tocai. I like the acidity in this wine, which goes well with food that has some fat in it. The red, called Rosso d'Orsone, is made with Cabernet Franc, Cabernet Sauvignon, Merlot, and Schioppettino. It is aged *in barrique,* which takes some of the edge off the high tannin content.

MARINA DANIELI

Via Beltrame 77, 33042 Buttrio (UD)

tel: 0432 / 673283

One is immediately struck by Marina Danieli's beauty (she resembles Candice Bergen), and soon discovers that it is not at all skin-deep. She is a person of great sensitivity who injects this quality into everything she does. Marina is one of four daughters from one of the leading industrial families of the region. Each sister paved a distinct path, and Marina was drawn to the land and to hospitality. She has some of the most prized vineyards in the COF and produces wines that are tasty, affordable, and widely available. She also has devoted herself to organic farming; the products of this endeavor may be discovered at her agritourism, Scacciapensieri, and in the restaurant of the Locanda alle Officine, her hotel on S.S.56, in Buttrio.

CONTE D'ATTIMIS-MANIAGO

Via Sottomonte 21, 33042 Buttrio (UD)

tel: 0432 / 674027

One of the oldest producers in the COF, and always reliable. Count Gianfranco D'Attimis-Maniago began bottling wine in 1932. They make a white blend, Vignariccio, that combines Chardonnay and Pinot Bianco. It is aged *in barrique* and would appeal to those who like California-style whites. The red Vignariccio combines Cabernet Sauvignon, Merlot, and Schioppettino, is aged *in barrique,* and has notes of spice and plum. I like this wine with game.

MASSIMO DI LENARDO

Via Battisti 1, Frazione Ontagnano, 33050 Gonars (UD)

tel: 0432 / 928633

This producer in the Grave makes some nice wines, ones that will appeal particularly to drinkers who like their whites to have contact with wood as they mature. In fact, one is even called Chardonnay Woody, lest there be any doubt. I am more drawn to the Pinot Grigio, Pinot Bianco, and Tocai. The red blend, Ronco Nolè, combines Cabernet Franc, Cabernet Sauvignon, and Merlot.

GIROLAMO DORIGO

Via del Pozzo 5, 33042 Buttrio (UD)

tel: 0432 / 674268

I knew and enjoyed Dorigo wines long before I met Girolamo and his wife, Rosetta, and their children, Alessandra and Alessio. Their Pignolo was my favorite red wine in all the region, if not all of Italy, and wines such as Sauvignon Blanc, Chardonnay, Ribolla Gialla, and a red blend called Montsclapade were outstanding. The Picolit was the best I knew. All the other wines, including Pinot Grigio, Tocai, and Schioppettino, were laudable.

As a family they built a superb reputation for wine making. The parents were equal protagonists in the winery, and the finished product was the fruit of both of their efforts. Girolamo was known for his love of books and research, and Rosetta was universally loved as one of the great personalities and palates in Italian wine. An important component in this equation was their oenologist, Donato Lanati, who vigilantly maintained quality and transformed the Dorigos' special outlook into wine. So it was sad for many reasons when Girolamo decided to leave Rosetta in the late 1990s, having previously arranged things so that the winery would rest entirely in his hands. Alessio continues to work with his father. Lanati chose not to work there anymore.

I did thorough tastings of available wines from the 1997 and 1998 vintages produced by father and son. Obviously, a long tradition of tending fine grapes and transforming them into good wine was not forgotten. Yet I found that while all the wines were technically impressive, some lacked soul, which was what Dorigo wines had in the past. Missing were Rosetta's nose, palate, and character, and perhaps some of Lanati's skill. As long as the Dorigo men do not change their approach (say, by boosting yields or being less attentive to grape quality), this winery will remain among the best-regarded in the region, though ultimately lacking some qualities that made it, in my view, the very best. Now, I believe, other top producers can match them in a one-on-one tasting for individual grapes such as Pignolo, Sauvignon Blanc, Chardonnay, Tocai, and Ribolla Gialla.

GIOVANNI DRI
Ramandolo di Nimis
tel: 0432/478211
Dri began growing Ramandolo on a tiny property, producing only 600 bottles in 1968, his first vintage. It is now justifiably famous, so much so that people fail to acknowledge the good Picolit, Sauvignon Blanc, and Refosco.

(LE) DUE TERRE
Via Roma 68B, 33040 Prepotto (UD)
tel: 0432/713189
I was so very impressed during my visit to Le Due Terre with the work that Flavio and Silvana Basilicata are doing. Their vineyards are gorgeous, and they use as few chemicals as possible both in growing grapes (which they are proud to harvest entirely by hand) and then vinifying them. Silvana said to me that "a wine must have great character, like music or a person. It must cause you great emotion." These wines do.

The Basilicatas have decided to make a limited range, but make them well. Their Sacrisassi is a red blend that combines the 100 percent Friulian grapes Refosco and Schioppettino. Its color is lovely and the flavor extraordinary—aristocratic, elegant, feminine. They produce very few bottles each year. They also produce a very fine Pinot Nero, a grape that is not seen very often in this region. Their white wine is the Sacrisassi Bianco, combining Ribolla Gialla, Sauvignon Blanc, and Tocai. They also produce a lovely Picolit, called Implicito. One of the most devoted customers of this winery is the European Parliament, which has its pick of every winery on the continent.

ERMACORA
Via Solzaredo 9, Frazione Ipplis, 33040 Premariacco (UD)
tel: 0432/716250
Brothers Dario and Luciano Ermacora produce impressive COF wines, and the stars are all white. The Pinot Grigio is one of the best you will try, and you will also be pleased with the Pinot Bianco, Sauvignon Blanc, Tocai, and Verduzzo.

FANTINEL
Via Cussignacco 80, 33040 Pradamano (UD)
tel: 0432/670444
This winery has made slow progress toward establishing a name for quality. In the past, they focused more on quantity and that reputation has clung for quite a while. They make a sparkling wine, Fantinel Brut, that is pleasant, and the Grave Cabernet Sauvignon is nice, too.

FEIGL
Località Lenzuolo Bianco 1, 34170 Oslavia (GO)
tel: 0481/31072
This Collio winery is run by three brothers—Alessio, Giuseppe, and Rinaldo. All of their single-grape wines—Chardonnay, Pinot Bianco, Pinot Grigio, Ribolla Gialla, Sauvignon Blanc, Tocai, and Merlot—are of equal high quality. I also like their blends. The white, called Leopold Cuvée Blanc, contains Pinot Bianco, Ribolla, Sauvignon Blanc, and Tocai. Leopold Rosso is 80 percent Merlot and 20 percent Cabernet Franc.

LIVIO FELLUGA
Via Risorgimento 1, Frazione Brazzano,
34071 Cormons (GO)
tel: 0481/60203
Livio Felluga is one of the best loved of the grand old men of oenology in Friuli-Venezia Giulia. His labels, with their beautiful old maps, are immediately recognizable and suggest a history that he has played a large part in forming. Part of the reason he put maps on his labels was that before DOC laws existed, nothing on a wine label gave a sense of place or history.

Felluga makes several lines of wines. Economical wines of quality are labeled Esperto, and they are all reliable. He also makes top single-grape wines from his terrain in Rosazzo in the COF (including Pinot Grigio, Sauvignon Blanc, Tocai, and Refosco dal Peduncolo Rosso). His Sossò is anything but so-so. This is one of the best Merlot wines you will ever taste. And the COF Terre Alte (a blend of Pinot Bianco, Sauvignon Blanc, and Tocai) is one of region's top white wines. Livio also produces a delicious Picolit. Note that although

Livio resides in what is technically the Collio, most of his vineyards are just over the border in the COF.

MARCO FELLUGA

Via Gorizia 121, 34072 Gradisca d'Isonzo (GO)
tel: 0481/99164

In addition to his Russiz Superiore winery (see page 371), Marco Felluga produces wines in Gradisca under his own name. At Russiz, the wines are more classical and intense, while here they are varied and interesting in their effort to express the qualities of individual grapes. All of them are fermented entirely in stainless steel. My favorite is the yummy Moscato Rosa, a pink dessert wine that is one of the most distinctive and pleasing I know in Italy. Other wines, including Chardonnay, Pinot Bianco, Pinot Grigio, Ribolla Gialla, Tocai, and Merlot, are all good. The red blend, called Carantan, combines Cabernet Franc, Cabernet Sauvignon, and Merlot. The white blend, Molamatta, is made of Pinot Bianco, Ribolla Gialla, and Tocai.

WALTER FILIPUTTI

Piazza dell'Abbazia 15,
Località Rosazzo, 33044 Manzano (UD)
tel: 0432/759429

If Noël Coward were to look for a couple in Friuli-Venezia Giulia who could fit into one of his plays or social events, he would surely select beautiful Patrizia Filiputti and her handsome husband Walter. Living in a converted abbey and surrounded by a collection of ancient glass and centuries-old books, Missoni-swathed Patrizia and Walter are marvelous, witty hosts. Trieste-born Patrizia is one of the best cooks I know in the whole region and prepares food that makes Walter's wines even more delicious than they already are. They lease the land from the Curia of Udine to produce singular wines from old vines.

The Pignolo is one of the finest reds you will taste. One red blend, called Broili di Filip, combines Merlot with smaller amounts of Cabernet Franc, Cabernet Sauvignon, and Refosco. The fabulous Ronco dei Domenicani is 80 percent Cabernet Sauvignon, the rest being Franconia, Tazzelenghe, and Refosco. The Riserva dei Benedettini is almost a pure Merlot, and it is wonderful. The Poesis Bianco is a blend of Chardonnay, Pinot Bianco, Tocai, and a small amount of Picolit—it is immensely appealing and rich. Another white blend, called COF Bianco Ronco del Monastero, combines Malvasia, Ribolla Gialla, and Tocai. It is softer than the Poesis, but just as good. A third white blend is the Ronco degli Agostiniani, largely Chardonnay, with a fair amount of Pinot Bianco and a small percentage of Tocai. It is very special. There are also single-grape whites: Pinot Grigio, Ribolla Gialla, and Sauvignon Blanc. The Ribolla will make you think of peaches and apples—it is a love.

FORCHIR

Via Ciasutis 1, Frazione Provesano,
33095 San Giorgio della Richinvelda (PN)
tel: 0427/96037

This is a very large winery in terms of land and production. It is among the leading brands in Grave and makes some good wines, though quantity is often given more weight in some decisions. By that I do not mean that quality is reduced, but that decisions are made to emphasize taste and other factors that appeal to a broader range of consumers. So you find good grape characteristics rather than personality. Nonetheless, the Cabernet Sauvignon, Chardonnay, and Sauvignon Blanc have their strengths. I also recommend the Bianco del Martin Pescatore, which combines Chardonnay, Riesling, and Traminer into a very appealing white wine.

CONTE FORMENTINI

Via Oslavia 5, 34070 San Floriano del Collio (GO)
tel: 0481/884131

This famous estate was founded in 1520 and occupies a glorious spot with incredible views. On a clear day you can see across vineyards, down hills, and all the way to the Adriatic some 15 to 20 miles (25 to 32 km) away. There is a famous wine museum here and a huge cellar. The Chardonnay Torre di Tramontana is of golden color, with a fragrance of musk, almond, and apple. It has a clean taste of almond and apple. Very sexy. The Ribolla Gialla is just as good, and they also produce likable Cabernet Franc, Pinot Grigio, Sauvignon Blanc, and Tocai.

AZIENDA AGRIVITICOLA FURLAN CASTELCOSA

Via Palazzo 1, Frazione Cosa,
33095 S. Giorgio della Richinvelda (PN)
tel: 0427/96134

Alessandro Furlan, son of the founder, is a very forward-looking and pragmatic producer of quality Grave wines, much of which he exports. He spent a lot of time in America as a young man, which influenced his outlook on wine and the selling of it. His approach is to carefully analyze the quality of the grapes each year and then decide how to best use them. While he will typically produce a Pinot Grigio, Tocai, and Chardonnay among his whites, he also makes a blend called Tai di Castelcosa. In most years it contains some Tocai, but beyond that it will only include white grapes that he thinks will make an outstanding wine. One year Tai may have Chardonnay, Riesling, and Sauvignon Blanc, and the next will be Malvasia, Pinot Grigio, and Tocai. He refers to this wine as an evolving mosaic, adding that "we don't look for continuity of flavor, but of quality." He also produces small quantities of Ribolla Gialla and Picolit. Reds include Merlot, Cabernet Franc, Refosco, and a small amount of Schioppettino. He is proud of the Pinot Nero, which he only makes in years when he believes the grapes are good enough. They come from a vineyard called Campo di Nappa. This last word refers in Friulano to someone who has a large bulbous nose thanks in part to imbibing. It was the nickname of the former owner of the land.

LUCIA GALASSO

Strada di Planez 32, Fraz. Spessa,
33043 Cividale del Friuli (UD)
tel: 0432/730292

In what one must assume to be an act of love, Lucia Galasso named two of her wines "Don Giovanni" after her husband, Giovanni Crosato. The white is made with Pinot Bianco, Sauvignon Blanc, and Tocai, and is a loving gesture indeed. The *rosso* has a bit of everything: Cabernet Franc, Cabernet Sauvignon, Merlot, Refosco, and Schioppettino. It is rich in fruit and, one assumes, passion. Lucia also makes a COF Rosso which is 80 percent Merlot and 20 percent Refosco.

ADRIANO GIGANTE

Via Rocca Bernarda 3, 33040 Corno di Rosazzo (UD)
tel: 0432/755835

This winery produces a broad range of COF wines, including very good Chardonnay, Pinot Grigio, Picolit, Tocai, and Verduzzo. Among reds, the Refosco is noteworthy.

JOSKO GRAVNER

Località Lenzuolo Bianco 9, 34170 Oslavia (GO)
tel: 0481/30882

No wine producer in Friuli-Venezia Giulia, and perhaps all of Italy, arouses more debate and controversy than Josko Gravner. Many of the region's top wine makers think Gravner is the only genius they have. Many other people consider him a heretic or, worse, a lunatic or a fake. Gravner is quite reclusive and has very little contact with people he does not know. I have had the occasion to visit him twice. He has the air of a genuine believer who is unshakable in his values, much like Pope John Paul II. He has a powerful gaze and a facial expression that indicates that his mind is far off in thought, most certainly about wine. Gravner devotes himself to his grapes and wines with maniacal intensity that can seem genuinely frightening. He once said to me that his chief goal was to make a wine that would have his late father's approval. Given that he can never really know if he has earned the approval, Gravner will remain on this elusive quest for as long as he makes wine.

In recent years, he has decided to revert to the oldest methods of wine making. He has studied the traditions of ancient Greece and Rome, and one year buried a terra-cotta container full of Ribolla Gialla. Supposedly this recalled a lost method that, in effect, returned the wine to the earth where it could best evolve. Word has it that the terra-cotta cracked and all the wine was lost. He uses only wood in wine making (unlike the stainless steel now used in almost every winery) and has eschewed almost all machinery in favor of manual labor. He is, in fact, a hero to many young wine makers in Venezia Giulia who wish they could be as "heretical" as their idol.

The overwhelming opinion of Gravner wines is that they are extraordinary. They are also very expensive. The Chardonnays he made in the 1980s are still drinking well, and those from the early 1990s are fascinating. His older Ribolla Giallas and Sauvignon Blancs are compelling. It is still too soon to determine how his more recent wines have come out, because almost no one has had the chance to taste them.

AZIENDA AGRICOLA ISOLA AUGUSTA
Strada Statale 14, 33050 Palazzolo dello Stella (UD)
Just off the road is this farm that includes a winery and crops. There is a restaurant that serves simple, delicious food accompanied by wines made here. The whites and reds are pleasing and the *rosato* (rosé) is delightful. This kind of farm attracts many passing travelers on the road between Venice and Trieste, who pick up a case of moderately priced wine for everyday drinking. The wine made here is part of the Latisana DOC. It will never achieve the heights of the region's great wines, but is notable because it is well made and enjoyable with food.

VINNAIOLI JERMANN
Via Monte Fortino 21, Frazione Villanova,
34070 Farra d'Isonzo
tel: 0481/888080
There are many wine writers who consider Silvio Jermann the genius of Friulian oenology and rate his wines the best the region has to offer. Jermann wines are also notable for their stratospheric prices. I admire them but find that they are not always congenial with food. The house's famous Vintage Tunina (made of Chardonnay and Sauvignon Blanc) has many interesting characteristics, not the least of which is its ability to age for years and develop intensity. But this is more a wine for meditation than pairing with food. Vinnae (made from Ribolla Gialla, Riesling, and some Malvasia) is in some ways more appealing. The Capo Martino is another white blend of some interest. Many people were crazy about a white blend once called Dreams that is now called Were Dreams, Now It's Just Wine!, but I find it a meditation wine more than one I could find a food match for. Jermann's Chardonnay, Pinot Bianco, Pinot Grigio, and Riesling are pretty good, but many producers do a better job and sell their wines at a lower price. I think very highly of what is called the Venezia Giulia Sauvignon Blanc, which combines fruit, acid, and a mineral taste that speaks of the soil in which it is grown—this is a venerable wine.

EDI KANTE
Località Prepotto 3, Frazione San Pelagio,
34011 Duino-Aurisina (TS)
Edi Kante is probably the best-known wine maker in the province of Trieste. My lasting memory of him, from my first visit to his winery in 1993, was of man versus nature. The Carso, where he lives, is named for the hard red rock known in English and German as karst. When I arrived, Edi was pushing boulders around and cursing in a language I could not decipher. He greeted me warmly and then returned to pushing rocks. He did not speak to me again until I rolled up my sleeves to push rocks as well. I think this rock pushing had as much to do with self-flagellating virtue as grape growing. But Edi, who is a disciple of Josko Gravner (see page 364), must be doing something right, because his winery has acquired deserved respect. The Chardonnay and Sauvignon Blanc are consistently fine, leaner than those from Isonzo, Collio, or COF, but benefiting from distinct fruit flavor. Edi probably makes the best Vitovska around, using the Carso white grape to make a creamy, complex, and fragrant wine. His Carso Terrano is a fine example of the typical light red wine so beloved in Trieste.

EDI KEBER
Località Zegla 17, 34071 Cormons (GO)
tel: 0481/61184
Following in the footsteps of his father, Pepi, Edi Keber has become one of the most revered of the newer generation of Collio wine makers. What is notable is that, as far as I can tell, he has done almost no campaigning to acquire this esteem. I have visited him in his home, cooked with his mother, and can attest to his humility and, indeed, his shyness.

What has garnered Edi's acclaim is that his wines are marvelous examples of the properties of his grapes and soil. His Tocai is one of the best, with clean flavors of apple and citrus. His blends, Collio Bianco (Malvasia, Pinot Bianco, Ribolla Gialla, and Tocai) and Collio Rosso (Cabernet Franc and Merlot) are scrumptious. His Merlot is splendid. Edi lives a stone's throw from the Slovenian border, and his family has strong ties to the other side. I expect that as Slovenian wine making improves, Edi will play an important role.

KURTIN

Località Novali 9, 34071 Cormons (GO)

tel: 0481/60685

Pleasing whites are made at one of the oldest Collio wineries (founded in 1903).

LA RAJADE

Località Restocina 12, 34070 Dolegna del Collio (GO)

tel: 0481 /639897

This small estate, right at the Slovenian border, produces some attractive Collio wines. The Sauvignon Blanc and Tocai are very pleasing, and the white blend, called Caprizzi di Marceline, brings together Malvasia, Ribolla Gialla, Sauvignon Blanc, Tocai, and Verduzzo. There is a Cabernet Franc, and the red blend, called Stratin, combines Cabernet Sauvignon with Merlot.

LA VIARTE

Via Novacuzzo 50, 33040 Prepotto (UD)

tel: 0432/759458

The name of this winery means "spring" in Friulano. I think the Siùm ("dream") is a divine dessert wine that I find wonderful for pairing with fruit-filled gnocchi. It is a blend of Verduzzo and Picolit, fermented *in barrique.* The white blend, called Bianco Liendge ("legend") combines Pinot Bianco, Riesling, Sauvignon Blanc, Tocai, and a dash of Ribolla Gialla. It is beautiful and ages well for several years. The red blend, Roi, combines Merlot with Cabernet Sauvignon and is *barrique*-aged. The single-grape whites—Pinot Bianco, Pinot Grigio, Ribolla Gialla, Sauvignon Blanc, and Tocai—are all very good to excellent. There are also good examples of native Friulian red varietals, such as Schioppettino and Tazzelenghe.

LE MONDE

Via Garibaldi 2, Località Le Monde,

33080 Prata di Pordenone (PN)

tel: 0434/626096

The name of this Grave winery refers not to the Parisian newspaper, but to the clay soils in which the grapes are grown. Reds are the stars here, including a Refosco dal Peduncolo Rosso, Cabernet Franc, and two Cabernet Sauvignons. The red blend is called Querceto and combines the two Cabernets. It is rich and spicy.

LIS NERIS-PECORARI

Via Gavinana 10, 34070 San Lorenzo Isontino (GO)

tel: 0481/80105

I first met Alvaro Pecorari, the owner of Lis Neris, when he was a very young wine maker about whom many good things were being said. He worked his land diligently and studied everything he could find to learn how to make his grapes better. He never went for big yields, but focused on quality even when it must have been a struggle as an unknown to sell his wine. Through intelligence, patience, and great effort, Alvaro has become a star and his wines appear on top lists in America, Italy, and, especially, London. Yet he is still the earnest person he always was, much more in awe of nature than of his own success.

His Sauvignon Blanc Dom Picòl is spectacular, with remarkable fragrance, flavor, and finish. The Chardonnay St. Jurosa is just as good. He also makes one of the region's best Pinot Grigios, and his Verduzzo (called Tal Lûc) is one of the best dessert wines. A white blend, Confini, is largely Pinot Grigio and is remarkably perfumed. A red blend, Isonzo Rosso Lis Neris, combines Cabernet Sauvignon and Merlot with generous results.

Alvaro recently built a new *cantina,* but his hallmark is slow deliberate growth that continues to provide a comfortable life for his parents, wife, and daughters while responding to his own passion to produce extraordinary wine.

LIVON

Via Montarezza 33, Frazione Dolegnano,

33048 San Giovanni al Natisone (UD)

tel: 0432/757173

There is a broad range of opinion about this winery. Some producers, chefs, and wine writers consider Livon among the region's best, yet others are left totally cold by these wines. What this means is that Livon has a definite viewpoint and approach that thrills only some tasters. In a word, it is wood—some of these wines bear as much imprint of the barrel as of the grape. Certainly, the white blend, called Braide Alte, is a very important wine. It combines Chardonnay, Moscato Giallo, Picolit, and Sauvignon Blanc. The grapes are harvested late, when they are loaded with sugar. The wine is aged for a long time *in barrique,* and this sugar (and therefore high alcohol content) combined with wood is very provocative. The wine is incredibly aromatic, but the taste elicits divided opinions. I like this wine in combination with rich, tangy cheeses. Another major wine is the COF Verduzzo Casali Godia, which also spends a long time *in barrique* and has a honeyed taste. Single-grape wines are mostly from Collio: the Chardonnay, Pinot Bianco, Sauvignon Blanc, and Tocai are all very interesting. The Merlot is also notable, but it will not appeal to all tastes.

More than a few people have observed that while the winery strives to make great wine, they are periodically careless and inattentive when precision is required. The Livon winery recently acquired the Villa Chiopris estate, located in Grave. I like the Tocai very much and also the Cabernet Sauvignon and Merlot from this estate.

LORENZON

Via Ca' del Bosco 6, Località Pieris,
34075 San Canzian d'Isonzo (GO)
tel: 0481/76445
A large winery, one of whose large terrains, I Feudi di Romans, produces most of the significant wines of this estate. The top is probably the white blend, called Alfiere Bianco, which is made up of Chardonnay, Malvasia Istriana, Pinot Bianco, and Tocai. There are also nice single-grape wines made with these grapes. The notable reds are Cabernet Franc, Merlot, and Refosco.

MAGNÀS

Via Corona 47, 34071 Cormons (GO)
tel: 0481/60991
A small winery owned by Luciano Visintin and his son Andrea. They produce agreeable Collio Pinot Bianco, but I am more fond of their rich Chardonnay made from grapes grown in the Isonzo.

MANGILLI

Via Tre Avieri 2, Frazione Flumignano,
33030 Talmassons (UD)
tel: 0432/766248
This company is primarily a distillery, but I call it to your attention for its COF Ramandolo. Their other wines come from holdings in Collio, COF, and Grave and are not standouts.

GIORGIO MAREGA

Via Valerisce 4, 33070 San Floriano del Collio (GO)
tel: 0481/884058
This small Collio winery makes a very impressive red blend called Holbar Rosso. It is mostly Merlot, with Cabernet and Gamay added. It has strong notes of plum and raspberry and very concentrated flavor. The Holbar Bianco, mostly Riesling Renano with Chardonnay, is a mixture of citrus and almond in the nose and has a straightforward, pleasing flavor. I also like the very herbal Tocai. These wines are expressions of a point of view and are done with seriousness of purpose rather than a desire to meet some perceived niche in the market.

DAVINO MEROI

Via Stretta del Parco 1, 33042 Buttrio (UD)
tel: 0432/674025
Dominin is an appealing red blend that combines Cabernet Sauvignon, Merlot, and Refosco dal Peduncolo Rosso. I enjoy their Picolit, golden in color and rich in fig, pear, and almond flavors. There is also a nice Ribolla Gialla. These wines can be tasted at the family's Trattoria al Parco, at the same address.

MIANI

Via Peruzzi 10, 33042 Buttrio (UD)
tel: 0432/674327
Now one of the region's top producers in terms of quality, under Enzo Pontoni the Miani winery has acquired almost cult status. The amount of wine made is limited, and most is sold in the region or to top restaurants in Italy. Therefore, you will probably have to make a journey to taste these wines. The red and white blends are wonderful, complex, and gratifying to the senses. The COF Bianco is made with Chardonnay, Pinot Grigio, and Riesling. The COF Rosso is made with Cabernet Franc, Cabernet Sauvignon, Merlot, and Tazzelenghe. Single-grape wines, including Tocai, Sauvignon Blanc, Ribolla Gialla, and Merlot, are all excellent.

MIDOLINI

Via Udine 40, 33044 Manzano (UD)
tel: 0432/754555
Lovely vineyards in the COF zone between Manzano and Buttrio provide grapes for making single-grape wines,

including Cabernet Franc; rich, fruity Merlot; delicious Refosco dal Peduncolo Rosso; Chardonnay; Pinot Grigio; good, typical Sauvignon Blanc; and Tocai. In addition, there is a nice Picolit. This family also produces Asperum, a balsamic sauce made of grapes with skins and seeds removed (see page 384).

MULINO DELLE TOLLE
Via Roma 29, Loc. Sevegliano,
33050 Bagnària Arsa (UD)
tel: 0432 / 928113
An Aquileia producer of nice reds, including Cabernet Franc, Merlot, and Refosco. They also make a good Malvasia.

MUZIC
Località Bivio 4, 34070 San Floriano del Collio (GO)
tel: 0481 / 884201
Cabernet Franc and Cabernet Sauvignon are well made here—the former from Isonzo and the latter from Collio. All whites come from Collio, including Chardonnay, Pinot Grigio (quite fine), Ribolla Gialla, Sauvignon Blanc, and an excellent Tocai.

PIERPAOLO PECORARI
Via Tommaseo 36C, 34070 San Lorenzo Isontino (GO)
tel: 0481 / 808775
Many people confuse this producer with Alvaro Pecorari of Lis Neris (page 366). This is not surprising given that they have the same name and are from the same town. Pierpaolo's signature is his love of intense fragrance and flavors. His wines are for those looking for big impact in the glass, but it is a little hard to pair some of them with food.

The Sauvignon Blanc Kolàus is outstanding, and I am fascinated by the Pratoscuro, an Isonzo white blend that combines Müller Thurgau made in stainless steel with Riesling that has had contact with oak. There are so many flavors and textures in this wine, all exhilarating. The single-grape Isonzo whites—Chardonnay, Malvasia Istriana, Pinot Bianco, Pinot Grigio, Sauvignon Blanc, and Tocai—are all interesting though I expect that they will appeal more to some drinkers than others.

AZIENDA AGRICOLA LA PERGOLA
Località Beligna 4, 33051 Aquileia (UD)
tel: 0431 / 91306
This is not a winery you will find mentioned when the grand wines of the region are discussed. But I like it because it is typical of many small, hard-working producers throughout the region who don't have the resources for famous oenologists or fancy marketing plans. Yet there is an honesty about these wines that is endlessly appealing. You will find Chardonnay, Malvasia, Müller Thurgau, Pinot Grigio, Sauvignon Blanc, Tocai, and Traminer among the whites. There is a local rosé wine called Rosato Aquileia, and reds include Cabernet Franc and Refosco dal Peduncolo Rosso. The wines of La Pergola turn up in many local *osterias* and trattorias in the Aquileia zone, and are nice partners with homey food.

TERESA PERUSINI
Via Torrione 13, Località Gramogliano,
33040 Corno di Rosazzo (UD)
tel: 0432 / 675018
The most famous and distinctive wine here is the Ribolla Gialla, which may taste a bit immature when young, but takes on richness, shape, and character as it matures. The Merlot Nero (the label is black, not the grape) is similarly imposing. You may also enjoy the Pinot Grigio and Picolit.

LINA AND PAOLO PETRUCCO
Via Morpurgo 12, 33042 Buttrio (UD)
tel: 0432 / 674387
A good producer from the Buttrio zone in COF, with notable Chardonnay, Ribolla Gialla, Cabernet Franc, and Merlot.

PETRUSSA
Via Albana 49, 33040 Prepotto (UD)
tel: 0432 / 713192
A good producer of COF reds, Petrussa makes a Cabernet that is spicy and complex, and their Rosso Petrussa is a Merlot full of fruit and structure. The Bianco Petrussa, a white blend, combines Chardonnay, Pinot Bianco, Sauvignon Blanc, and Tocai into a wine of great depth and variety. The Pinot Bianco and Tocai are also used to make single-grape wines. Finally, there is Penisero, an excellent Verduzzo, for dessert.

ROBERTO PICECH
Località Pradis 11, 34071 Cormons (GO)
tel: 0481/60347

A small winery with outstanding wines, Picech makes a Malvasia Istriana that is lean, fruity, and dry. This grape is also used to make a splendid dessert wine called Passito di Pradis that tastes like dried fruits with hints of cream and chocolate. It is very unusual. Tocai here has a distinct apple flavor with a hint of honey. The very nice white blend, Collio Bianco, combines Malvasia, Ribolla Gialla, and Tocai. Forty percent of the wine is fermented *in barrique* and then blended with the rest of the wine, so that it is rich, round, and fragrant. Among reds, the Cabernet Sauvignon and Merlot are quite fine.

PIGHIN
Viale Grado 1, Frazione Risano,
33050 Pavia di Udine (UD)
tel: 0432/675444

Pighin is one of the largest producers in the region, with significant exportation of its wines. They have vast holdings in Grave and some terrain in Collio. Pighin makes good basic versions of wine from all the popular grapes of the region. They are notable for their experimentation with root stock in the vineyard and point the way toward developments at other wineries.

VIGNETI PIETRO PITTARO
Via Udine 67, Zompicchia, 33033 Codroipo (UD)
tel: 0432/904726

Pietro Pittaro is a leading personality in the panorama of the region's wines and has been active in various world wine organizations, including the Union International des Enologues, of which he was president. He has amassed a notable collection of wine-making artifacts, which is now in a museum on the property and merits a visit if you are in the area (call first). About 60 percent of Pittaro's wines are exported, mostly to other countries in Europe.

PLOZNER
Via delle Prese 19, Frazione Barbeano,
33097 Spilimbergo (PN)
tel: 0427/2902

Valeria Plozner runs one of the foremost Grave wineries, producing fragrant, elegant wines that go very well with food. Whites include Chardonnay, Pinot Bianco, Sauvignon Blanc, Tocai, and Traminer Aromatico. There is a good Cabernet Sauvignon, plus a Merlot, among the reds.

ISIDORO POLENCIC
Località Plessiva 12, 34071 Cormons (GO)
tel: 0481/60655

This producer has most of his vineyards in Collio, with a few in Isonzo. There are nice examples of all the typical white grapes (especially Pinot Bianco), plus a very good blend called Oblin Blanc, made with Chardonnay, Ribolla Gialla, and Sauvignon Blanc. These grapes ferment and age in small oak barrels. This is a lovely family that knows good food, so they produce wine with cuisine in mind.

FLAVIO PONTONI
Via Peruzzi 8, 33042 Buttrio (UD)
tel: 0432/674352

The Braidès Bianco is a blend made largely of Chardonnay. The Picolit is quite appealing, and all the whites are likable, as is the Merlot.

MARKO PRIMOSIC
Via Madonnina di Oslavia 3, 34170 Oslavia (GO)
tel: 0481/535153

This winery produces high-quality wines, all but two of which have the name Gmajne on the label for the vineyard where they are grown. The Ribolla Gialla and Chardonnay are carefully aged in oak and still taste more of grape than wood. The Pinot Grigio and Sauvignon Blanc are also nice. Klin is a *barrique*-aged blend that combines Chardonnay, Ribolla Gialla, and Tocai. The Collio Merlot Riserva is rich and tasty.

ALESSANDRO PRINCIC
Loc. Pradis 5, 34071 Cormons (GO)
tel: 0481/60723

For a long time the winery was named for Alessandro's father, Doro, a wonderful man who in recent years has aged and turned over the running of the estate to his son, known to all as Sandro. This is a delightful family and the cooking here—in the warm and capable hands of Sandro's wife, Grazia—is among the best I know anywhere in the region, especially for seafood.

Sandro makes a lovely Tocai that is almondy and dry. I have implored him to continue making his Malvasia Istriana, one of the finest I have tasted, though he seems to think it is no longer viable. It is the perfect complement to mussels. The Pinot Bianco, Pinot Grigio, Sauvignon Blanc, and Merlot are all excellent. This is a winery that people in the region admire, but it is not nearly as touted abroad as it should be.

PUIATTI
Via Aquileia 30, 34070 Capriva del Friuli (GO)
tel: 0481 / 809922
Vittorio Puiatti is one of the post–World War II generation of pioneers. He took his degree in oenology in 1948 and has since dedicated his life to the improvement of his region's wines and image. He bottles wine under his own name (produced in Farra d'Isonzo) and also produces good wines at fair prices under the Enofriulia name (in Capriva), which are easily found abroad. The hallmark of Vittorio Puiatti's wines is their freshness and concentrated flavor. He is one producer who has militantly avoided using wood with his wines, and believes that their freshness is due to the fact that he vinifies them and stores them in temperature-controlled stainless steel. The range of whites he makes is very nice, and you should also note his Pinot Nero. Giovanni Puiatti, his son, has ventured out on his own and makes a lovely Pinot Grigio, rich in spice and fruit, and a nice Chardonnay, a fragrant Cabernet Franc, and a pleasant Merlot.

DARIO RACCARO
Via San Giovanni 87B, 34071 Cormons (GO)
tel: 0481 / 61425
The three wines of note here are the Malvasia and Tocai, produced in Collio, and the Cabernet Franc from Isonzo.

TERESA RAIZ
Via della Roggia 22, Località Marsure di Sotto, 33040 Povoletto (UD)
tel: 0432 / 664144
This winery has vineyards in Grave and COF. I particularly enjoy the COF Ribolla Gialla, which is rich in flavor, with a pleasing acid finish. Also note the Refosco dal Peduncolo Rosso from the Grave.

ROCCA BERNARDA
Via Rocca Bernarda 27, Frazione Ipplis, 33040 Premariacco (UD)
tel: 0432 / 716273
Named for the sixteenth-century fortress above the vines, this COF winery is well regarded. I am a big fan of the Merlot Centis, a big, delicious complex wine. The Pinot Grigio and Tocai are also very nice. Pay attention to the outstanding Picolit, which seems to be native to this very zone.

PAOLO RODARO
Via Cormons 8, Fraz. Spessa, 33043 Cividale del Friuli (UD)
tel: 0432 / 716066
This winery makes very special whites, led by a superb Tocai. There is the "basic" Tocai, which is meant to suggest traditionally made, but it is a very sensuous glass of wine. The Tocai Bosc Romain has a higher alcohol content and even more concentrated flavor. I also think very highly of Rodaro's Ribolla Gialla. His Verduzzo Friulano Pra Zenâr and Picolit are wonderful dessert wines.

RONCHI DI CIALLA
Frazione Cialla 47, 33040 Prepotto (UD)
tel: 0432 / 731679
This is one of the most important and historic wineries in the region. The Rapuzzi family were among the first to dedicate themselves to saving the traditional and native grape varieties of the region. You will only find wines made of native grapes here. In terms of wine-making innovation, they were the first producers in Italy to use *barriques* for aging their red wines, and later the very first in Italy to use them for white wines. There is a long tradition here of making single-grape wines using Refosco dal Peduncolo Rosso and Schioppettino. These grapes are combined to make Ciallarosso, the house red blend. Ciallabianco combines Picolit, Ribolla Gialla, and Verduzzo to make a compellingly rich white. In addition, there is a very good Picolit dessert wine.

RONCHI DI MANZANO
Via Orsaria 42, 33044 Manzano (UD)
tel: 0432 / 740718
Roberta Borghese has achieved a lot of recognition for her work to make this a top winery and seems to have had particular success with her COF reds. The Merlot Ronc di

Subule is one of the best, and her Cabernet Sauvignon is excellent, too. I can also commend Le Zuccule, a red blend combining the Merlot and Cabernet. The Chardonnay, Pinot Grigio, and Tocai are all solid whites. She also makes very fine dessert wines: Rosazzo Picolit and Verduzzo Ronc di Rosazzo.

RONCO DEI TASSI
Località Monte 38, 34071 Cormons (GO)
tel: 0481/60155
Wines produced here by Fabio Coser are quite distinctive expressions of a modern Collio style that favors blending of grapes to balance body, acidity, sugar, and fragrance. The Collio Bianco Fosarin combines Malvasia Istriana, Pinot Bianco, Ribolla Gialla, and Tocai. The velvety Rosso Cjarandon has a notable presence of Cabernet Sauvignon. Don't overlook the Pinot Grigio or Tocai, both excellent. Coser also produces wine under the Vigna del Lauro label. These grapes are grown on an estate in San Floriano del Collio; the Merlot, Pinot Bianco, Pinot Grigio, Sauvignon Blanc, and Tocai are all notable.

RONCO DEL GELSO
Via Isonzo 117, 34071 Cormons (GO)
tel: 0481/61310
This winery, with vineyards in Isonzo, produces some of the most admired wines in the region. The Tocai and Merlot are exceptional; the Sauvignon Blanc and Cabernet Franc are almost as good. The Bianco Làtimis (Chardonnay and Tocai) is superb, with a long, fruity finish.

RONCO DEL GNEMIZ
Via Ronchi 5, 33048 San Giovanni al Natisone (UD)
tel: 0432/756238
Serena and Gabriele Palazzolo work with great seriousness and talent, and the result is that their wines are first-rate. Chardonnay may be the outstanding wine here, but I would quickly add praise for the Müller Thurgau, Pinot Grigio, Sauvignon Blanc, and Tocai among the whites. The COF Schioppettino is one of the region's best, and I also like the red blend, Rosso del Gnemiz, which combines Cabernet Sauvignon and Merlot. This also happens to be an unusually special family, with three great young boys, and I feel that their positive approach to life reflects in the care and quality that is lavished on the wines.

RONCO DELLE BETULLE
Via A. Colonna 24, Località Rosazzo, 33044 Manzano (UD)
tel: 0432/740547
The most famous wine of this house is the red blend called Narciso, which is mostly *barrique*-aged Cabernet Sauvignon with some Merlot added. It is a big, complex red that is the pride of Ivana Adami, who runs this winery. Another unusual red of note is Franconia, based on a rare local grape. The Pinot Grigio and Tocai are formidable, and I can also recommend the Pinot Bianco, Ribolla Gialla, and Sauvignon Blanc. The Rosazzo Picolit is also very special.

RONCO DI ZEGLA
Località Zegla 12, 34071 Cormons (GO)
tel: 0481/61155
A promising new winery run by Maurizio Princic, nephew of Sandro Princic (page 369). I particularly enjoyed tasting the Ribolla Gialla.

RONCÙS
Via Mazzini 26, 34070 Capriva del Friuli (GO)
tel: 0481/809349
Owner Marco Perco is part of the new generation of Collio wine makers who follows his own instinct and palate. I respect his evident talent and dedication. I have tasted some of his whites and particularly admire the Pinot Bianco, the Tocai, and his blend made with Malvasia, Pinot Bianco, and Ribolla Gialla. His Merlot is really wonderful. (In my tasting notes, I wrote that "this wine sings to me like a mermaid.") People I trust admire his other reds as well.

RUSSIZ SUPERIORE
Via Russiz 7, 34070 Capriva del Friuli (GO)
tel: 0481/80328
Founded by Marco Felluga and now guided to a large extent by his daughter, Patrizia, this is one of the most famous and outstanding wineries in the region. Wines here combine fermentation in steel and wood. Although they produce a wide range of wines from many grapes, the quality does not suffer in any way. The Rosso Riserva degli Orzoni, made

largely of Cabernet Sauvignon, is a big, wonderful, complex wine. Among reds, I also point you toward the Cabernet Franc and the Merlot. The whites are all worth knowing, especially the Sauvignon Blanc.

SCARBOLO-LE FREDIS
Viale Grado 4, Frazione Lauzacco,
33050 Pavia di Udine (UD)
tel: 0432/675612
Walter Scarbolo is a busy man, what with raising pigs for outstanding pork products, running his excellent La Frasca restaurant on the same property, and producing wine. Yet he seems to manage, and he produces some nice Grave wines, especially Merlot, but also Chardonnay, Pinot Grigio, and Tocai.

MARIO SCHIOPETTO
Via Palazzo Arcivescovile 1, 34070 Capriva del Friuli (GO)
tel: 0481/80332
One of the pioneers of modern wine making in Friuli-Venezia Giulia, Mario Schiopetto was one of the first people to put the region on the world map of wines. He reintroduced native varieties, refined techniques in the vineyard and the *cantina,* and, along with Livio Felluga and a few others, brought the wines of this region to the attention of taste-makers in Italy and then beyond. By the time I met him in the early 1990s he was hobbled by various illnesses but worked with steely determination to maintain the high standards he had set. Inevitably, there was doubt in some quarters that he could do this. But his children have learned well from him, combining his wisdom with their own preferences (especially regarding the use of wood with white wines) to point the winery forward with confidence in the twenty-first century.

All of the white wines are excellent. They produce one of my favorite Pinot Biancos (called Amrità), and the Pinot Grigio, Sauvignon Blanc, and Tocai all deserve praise. The Merlot and the Rivarossa (a red blend) are also very fine.

ROBERTO SCUBLA
Via Rocca Bernarda 22, Frazione Ipplis,
33040 Premariacco (UD)
tel: 0432/716258
This winery is most noted for two COF white blends. One is Bianco Pomédes, combining Pinot Bianco, Tocai, and Riesling grapes that are dried somewhat to intensify the sugar before making the wine. The other is Bianco Speziale (meaning Spicy White), which includes late-harvested Pinot Bianco with Sauvignon Blanc and Tocai.

LEONARDO SPECOGNA
Via Rocca Bernarda 4, 33040 Corno di Rosazzo (UD)
tel: 0432/755840
Signor Specogna makes good whites (try the Verduzzo), but I am especially taken with his reds: Cabernet, Merlot, and Refosco dal Peduncolo Rosso.

OSCAR STURM
Località Zegla 1, 34071 Cormons (GO)
tel: 0481/60720
This Collio winery distinguishes itself by its big, powerful white wines, some with a high alcohol content and all with intense fruit. The Chardonnay Andritz, Sauvignon Blanc, and Tocai are all quite dramatic. The Bianco Andritz is a compelling blend of Chardonnay, Pinot Grigio, and Sauvignon Blanc. The Refosco dal Peduncolo Rosso is a lush red with big flavors of raspberry and blackberry.

SUBIDA DI MONTE
Località Monte 9, 34071 Cormons (GO)
tel: 0481/61011
Very good reds and whites come from this Collio winery. The Cabernet Franc Riserva and Merlot Riserva are long-lasting and powerful, and the nonreserve Cabernet Franc is just as impressive. The Chardonnay Vigna delle Acacie and the Tocai are also worth knowing. Particularly appealing is the white blend, called Bianco Sotrari, which uses Riesling, Sauvignon Blanc, and Traminer.

MATIJAZ TERCIC

Via Bukuje 9, 34070 San Floriano del Collio (GO)
tel: 0481/884193

Tercic is a young producer in Collio who is making notable strides. His Vino degli Orti is a fruity and ingratiating white blend of Malvasia Istriana, Riesling, and Tocai. There is also good Chardonnay, Pinot Grigio, Sauvignon Blanc, and Merlot.

FRANCO TERPIN

Località Valerisce 6A, 34070 San Floriano del Collio (GO)
tel: 0481/884215

A Collio winery producing single-grape white wines of ever-increasing quality, Terpin makes Chardonnay, Pinot Grigio, Ribolla Gialla, Sauvignon Blanc, and Tocai.

FRANCO TORÒS

Località Novali 12, 34071 Cormons (GO)
tel: 0481/61327

This Collio producer makes distinctive Merlot, Chardonnay, Pinot Grigio, Sauvignon Blanc, and Tocai.

TORRE ROSAZZA

Località Poggiobello 12, 33044 Manzano (UD)
tel: 0432/750180

Nice whites include Ribolla Gialla and Tocai. The Pinot Bianco Ronco delle Magnolie has contact with barrique, giving it a touch of vanilla that is intriguing, but some may find overbearing. The Verduzzo is also very appealing. Among reds, the COF Ronco della Torre Cabernet Sauvignon is rich and balanced, and the Altromerlot is impressive, if somewhat tannic.

VENICA & VENICA

Via Mernico 42, Località Cerò,
34070 Dolegna del Collio (GO)
tel: 0481/60177

What a lovely family are the Venicas! Brothers Gianni and Giorgio, their wives, and children run this top-notch Collio winery with all hands working in perfect synchronicity. You will not go wrong with any Venica wine you select, as all the wines are laudable. The Ronco delle Mele Sauvignon Blanc has a divine fragrance and lovely flavor. Other fine whites are the Pinot Bianco, followed by the Chardonnay and Ribolla Gialla. There is a white blend, Vignis, made of Chardonnay, Sauvignon Blanc, and Tocai. Another white, called Prime Note, is a lovely blend of Tocai and Chardonnay with a few drops of Sauvignon and Ribolla. Their Perilla Merlot is the most notable red. But you should also try their Bottaz, a cherry-flavored Refosco with wonderful balance and character. There are a few rooms that make nice accommodations for travelers.

VICENTINI ORGNANI

Via Sottplovia 1, Frazione Valeriano,
33090 Pinzano al Tagliamento (PN)
tel: 0432/950107

Alessandro Vicentini Orgnani owns a fine Grave winery. He makes a Tocai that has citrus and pineapple notes in the nose and mouth and is very appealing. Some wines are labeled Braide Cjase, and these are partially aged in barrique. The best of these are the Pinot Bianco and Merlot. The unwooded line includes a delicious Merlot and nice Pinot Grigio, Sauvignon Blanc, and Tocai.

VIDUSSI

Via Spessa 16, 34070 Capriva del Friuli (GO)
tel: 0481/80072

A good, small winery in Collio with some nice whites and notable reds, including a Refosco and Ronc dal Rol, a red blend combining Cabernet Franc, Cabernet Sauvignon, and Merlot.

VIE DI ROMANS

Località Vie di Romans 1, 34070 Mariano del Friuli (GO)
tel: 0481/69600

This Isonzo winery is one of the most consistently top-rated producers in the region. All wines of note are white, some very delicate and some big enough to stand with foods where red wine is traditionally indicated. The star is the Bianco Flors di Uis, which combines Chardonnay, Malvasia, and Riesling into a wine of intense fruit and fragrance, with proper acid and great freshness. The name means, more or less, floral scent, and you notice that straightaway. There are two Sauvignon Blancs: the Piere has no contact with oak (and it is a fresh marvel), while the Vieris has more complex fragrance deriving from the wood. The Pinot Grigio and Chardonnay also have contact with wood and will particularly please drinkers who favor that style.

LE VIGNE DI ZAMÒ
Via Abate Corrado 55, Località Rosazzo,
33044 Manzano (UD)
tel: 0432/759693

It would be too complicated to explain how wines produced under various names, including Vigne dal Leon, Zamò e Zamò, Zamò e Palazzolo, Ronco dei Roseti, and Abbazia di Rosazzo, evolved to become Le Vigne di Zamò. If you encounter older wines under any of these names, I can assure you of their quality. By the time this book is published, almost all of these estates will be under the name Le Vigne di Zamò, with the whole operation in the capable hands of Barbara Maniacco. You should know that the vineyards that surround the Abbazia di Rosazzo, where Walter Filiputti (page 363) lives, still provide grapes—many to Filiputti, and some to Zamò. These are among the best grapes in the entire region. Because so many different wines fall under this one listing, at least for the first few years of the twenty-first century, suffice it to say that all are very fine, and that the Pignolo, the red blend called Ronco dei Roseti, the white blend called Ronco delle Acacie, and the Picolit are among the best wines you will taste from the COF. The Zamò COF Bianco TreVigne, combining Chardonnay, Sauvignon Blanc, and Tocai and aged in oak, is also very fine. The Vigne dal Leon line produced delicious Malvasia Istriana, Pinot Bianco, and Schioppettino. Look for Le Vigne di Zamò to get even better in years to come.

TENUTA VILLANOVA
Via Contessa Beretta 29, Frazione Villanova,
34070 Farra d'Isonzo (GO)
tel: 0481/888593

Wine has been produced here for more than five centuries. The wines are traditional and appealing, though not old-fashioned. Three good whites, all labeled as Collio Monte Cucco, are the Ribolla Gialla, Sauvignon Blanc, and an unusually fruity Chardonnay. The Collio Pinot Grigio and, especially, Tocai are quite nice. Menj Bianco is a lemony blend of Malvasia Istriana, Pinot Bianco, and Tocai. The berry-like Menj Rosso combines Cabernet Franc, Cabernet Sauvignon, Merlot, and the little-seen Petit Verdot.

VILLA RUSSIZ
Via Russiz 6, 34070 Capriva del Friuli (GO)
tel: 0481/80047

Not to be confused with Russiz Superiore (page 371), this winery enjoys a great reputation especially for its two "de la Tour" series of wines—a Sauvignon Blanc and a Merlot that might have better been called "tour de force." The Pinot Bianco, Pinot Grigio, Ribolla Gialla, and Tocai are all excellent, too, and I want to single out their very special Malvasia Istriana, a combination of fruit and flowers.

ANDREA VISINTINI
Via Gramogliano 27, 33040 Corno di Rosazzo (UD)
tel: 0432/755813

Straddling the border between COF and Collio, this winery produces in both zones. Both reds, Cabernet Franc and a nice Merlot, are from COF. There is a wider range of whites. The Collio Pinot Bianco, Pinot Grigio, and Tocai all merit your attention. Among the COF whites, the best is probably the Sauvignon Blanc, but you should also look at the Pinot Grigio, Ribolla Gialla, Tocai, and, especially, the Traminer Aromatico.

VISTORTA
Via Vistorta 87, 33077 Sacile (PN)
tel: 0434/71135

Brandino and Marie Brandolini D'Adda have an estate in the westernmost part of Friuli and live much of the time in Venice. In a way, they are re-creating a time when this zone was the agricultural backyard for the Venetian Republic. They have decided to focus their attention on Merlot, and they produce a very appealing example of this wine.

VOLPE PASINI
Via Cividale 16, Frazione Togliano,
33040 Torreano di Cividale (UD)
tel: 0432/715151

This historic and esteemed COF winery went adrift some years ago and was sold to a new owner, Emilio Rotolo. He has brought energy, boldness, and big infusions of cash to see that Volpe Pasini returns to its earlier stature. There are two lines: the Zuc di Volpe has white wines that are aged (to some extent) in oak. The Villa Volpe wines are unoaked. Chardonnay, Pinot Bianco, Pinot Grigio, Ribolla Gialla, Sauvignon Blanc, and Tocai all merit investigation. I like the Moscato Rosa dessert wine, which is very good, though not at the level of the one made by Marco Felluga.

ZOF
Via Giovanni XXIII 32A, 33040 Corno di Rosazzo (UD)
tel: 0432 / 759673
Father Alberto and son Daniele make interesting COF wines that are good to excellent expressions of local taste and tradition. The Pinot Grigio, Sauvignon Blanc, and Tocai lead the way among whites, and you should also sample the Merlot and Schioppettino. The best red, though, is the blend called Va' Pensiero, made primarily from Cabernet Franc and Merlot, with a dash of Cabernet Sauvignon. It is named for the most famous piece of choral music in Italian, from Verdi's opera *Nabucco*. This chorus is the unofficial Italian national anthem and is a rare expression of patriotism in this very regionalized country.

AZ. AGR. LIVIO ZORZETTIG
Via del Collio 14, Ipplis di Premariacco (UD)
tel: 0432 / 716030; fax: 0432 / 716494
I have tasted and admired their Sauvignon Blanc; garnet-colored, fruity Cabernet Franc; and a very special saffron-colored Picolit, with complex and complete fragrance and flavor.

Sources for Ingredients

You already know that you are what you eat. To that I would add that you are what you eat eats. The feed given to poultry, pigs, and cattle affects the flavor and health of the animal. Needless to say, any animal injected with hormones and antibiotics, or raised on feed that has been treated with chemicals, will pass these on to you. Agribusiness has aggressively forced genetically altered seeds and crops on farmers (especially in the USA), and there simply is not enough proof that these foods will not have a long-term negative effect on the soil, on animals that eat them, and especially on humans.

So my strongest exhortation is that you seek out certified organic products as often as possible and do all you can to support the farmers and stores that make the extra effort to get them to you. It might make a huge difference in your health and in the well-being of the earth. And these foods also taste much better. Every product from Friuli-Venezia Giulia that I list below is pure.

In these pages you will find suggestions and recommendations for acquiring ingredients and products needed to prepare some of the recipes in this book.

The listings in this chapter are intended for two different readers. First, and primarily, the listings are for those readers who can't find needed ingredients in local markets. The lists are also for food sellers and importers who want to know how to acquire products for retail sale. I also encourage you to visit www.madeinfriuli.com where you can research products and tourism in the region, particularly in Friuli.

Note: For contacting Italy from abroad, the country code is 39. Do not omit the zero that starts the area code. So, for example, to call Trieste from North America, dial 011-39-040, and then the number. From most of Europe, dial 00-39-040, and then the number.

AMARO

An *amaro,* in most of Italy, is an herb-based digestive drink. Many were born as pharmaceutical preparations and evolved into tasty drinks that were both bitter *(amaro)* and somewhat sweet. The Nonino distillery makes an excellent *amaro* that adheres to modern tastes. In Udine there is an old-style *amaro* that really is bitter and is sold by the pharmacy where it has been produced since 1846. It does have a pleasing taste, especially if diluted with a little water, and can offer relief, if you have gastric distress, and pleasure, if you do not.

AMARO DI UDINE
Farmacia Colutta, Via Battisti 14, 33100 Udine
tel: 0432/506126

ASPARAGUS

Friuli-Venezia Giulia is famous for its white asparagus, which is exported to many places. Most of it is consumed in the region from March to May in an infinite variety of preparations. The best is probably white asparagus that is steamed carefully and served with chopped boiled egg that has been blended with delicate vinegar. Fresh white asparagus can be found in specialty markets in early spring.

AGRICOOP ASPARAGI
Via dell'Asilo 1, 33010 Tavagnacco (UD)
tel: 0432/650054
The leading source for white asparagus is this cooperative of growers based in Tavagnacco, north of Udine.

GIGI AND ANNA MARSONI
Via Levata 6, Varmo (UD)
tel: 0432/778178
Devote immense care to their asparagus

BAKED GOODS

GIUDITTA TERESA
Località Ponte San Quirino 1,
San Pietro al Natisone (Udine)
tel: 0432/727585
(closed Monday)
This firm makes one of the better packaged *gubanas,* the divine snail-shaped yeast cake filled with raisins, nuts, plum brandy, and other ingredients. It can be packed for export, and is preserved only by the alcohol—there are no additives.

CONSORZIO PER LA TUTELA
DEL MARCHIO GUBANA
c/o Unione Artigiani del Friuli Viale Libertà 50,
33043 Cividale del Friuli.
For information about other producers, contact the Consorzio per la Tutela del Marchio Gubana.

BEETS

There is a wonderful product for people who want to avoid the nuisance of cooking and peeling beets. You can purchase vacuum-packed, ready-to-eat cooked beets (4 to the package, no additives or preservatives, and quite inexpensive) that are grown in France.

ROCAL
45730 St Benoit/Loire, France
tel: 3835-7470; fax: 3835-7044
(The country code for France is 33.)

CHAIRS AND FURNITURE

The famous "Triangolo della Sedia" or Chair Triangle is centered around Manzano, south of Udine. Its promoters kick around all kinds of figures about the production of chairs, but it is generally agreed that at least 40 percent of the chairs produced in the world come from this one little area. This is also one of the foremost areas for the production of

baby cribs and many other kinds of furniture. If you own a
restaurant, you might as well have your guests sit on Friulian
chairs. The annual exhibition of the area's new creations is
held each September in Udine. For information, contact:

PROMOSEDIA
Via Trieste 9/6, 33044 Manzano (UD)
tel: 0432/745611; fax: 0432/755316
promosedia@promosedia.it
www.madeinfriuli.com, then press the link to Promosedia.

CHEESES

I have listed below the contact information for the cooperatives that produce and sell most of the Montasio in the
region. They make an excellent basic product, but you
should also do all you can to support the efforts of small,
independent cheesemakers throughout the region, whose
cheeses are an expression of the land that fed the cows,
which in turn gave milk to a cheesemaker who expresses
himself. I encourage grocers who read this book to seek
out smoked ricotta from Friuli-Venezia Giulia. It is delicious, travels and stores well, and is a cardinal food from
this region.

Remember that the cheeses of Friuli are often described
by the generic term "latteria," and then are given a geographic designation. Also bear in mind that almost every
cheese produced in the region (except fresh ricotta and
smoked ricotta *affumicata*) is described by its age. Young
cheese is good for melting, semi-young cheese (about 4
months old) is ideal for making frico, and older cheese is
good for grating. All, of course, are good for eating.

The Consorzio Cooperativo Latterie Friulane is the
largest producer of Montasio in Friuli-Venezia Giulia and
the one best equipped for exporting its products.

CONSORZIO COOPERATIVO LATTERIE FRIULANE
Via Pietro Zorutti 98, 33030 Campoformido (UD)
tel: 0432/653911; fax: 0432/653965
www.infotech.it/latterie-friulane (Web site in Italian and
English); e-mail: latterie-friulane@ud.nettuno.it

CONSORZIO PER LA TUTELA DEL
FORMAGGIO MONTASIO
Strada Statale Napoleonica, 33030 Rivolto di Codroipo (UD)
tel: 0432/905317

Also www.esperya.com has an excellent selection of
cheeses.

CHERRIES

Many recipes from Friuli-Venezia Giulia use cherries. When
fresh cherries are not in season, use dried cherries that have
not been sulphured to preserve them. Or, use a whole fruit
preserve, such as D'Arbo from Austria or Fiordifrutta from
the Veneto. Both approximate the flavor you would find in
Friuli-Venezia Giulia. Or purchase the lovely dried cherries
from the American Spoon Foods, Inc. or the Baker's Catalogue (see mail-order sources in North America, page 384).

CHICKEN

It has been years since I have permitted myself to eat an
industrial chicken. I encourage you to invest in either a
kosher or organic chicken. Both are handled with much
more care and have more flavor than factory-raised birds.
One very good brand that is free of chemicals is Murray's,
which is available in parts of the northeastern United
States and perhaps elsewhere. Nonetheless, wherever
your chicken comes from you must handle it with great
care (page 272).

COFFEE

Trieste has long been the most important city in Italy for
roasting and importing coffee. Although coffee certainly
arrives in ports, such as Genoa, Naples, and Bari, there is
not the long tradition of so many brands that one finds in
Trieste. This city was the chief port of the Hapsburg

empire, a community of 50 million souls that included the coffee-loving nations of Austria and Hungary. Each roaster in Trieste sent beans to different markets throughout central Europe.

Illy ranks among the most prized and expensive coffees in the world. The Illy family has operated in Trieste since 1933 and, led by Dr. Ernesto Illy, has pioneered techniques in roasting, packing, and selling. Illy and Turin's Lavazza are the two most famous Italian brands and regularly compete nationally and internationally. I am a great admirer—and consumer—of both.

Although Illy is the most famous Triestine brand, there are many smaller ones that merit your attention. They are not found much abroad, but importers should consider them. Among my favorites are Cremcaffè and Hausbrandt, both of which are the daily cup for many people in Venezia Giulia. The excellent Caffè Udinese and Grosmi are among the most popular in Udine.

CREMCAFFÈ
Via Pigafetta 6/1; Trieste
tel: 040/820747 or 040/380777; fax: 040/810351
www.cremcaffe.it

TORREFAZIONE DEMAR CAFFÈ
Viale Palmanova 415, 33100 Udine
tel: 0432/601277 or 0432/523330; fax: 0432/520737

GROSMI CAFFÈ DI FRANCESCUT ENNIO & ANGELO SNC.
Via Rialto, 6/A, 33100 Udine
tel: 0432/506411

CAFFÈ HAUSBRANDT
Via del Cerreto 4/A, Trieste
tel: 040/43104; fax: 040/43619

ILLYCAFFÈ S.P.A
Via Flavia 110, 34147 Trieste
tel: 040/389-0320; fax: 040/389-0492
info@illy.com

ILLYCAFFÈ ESPRESSO OF THE AMERICAS
200 Clearbrook Road, Elmsford, NY 10523 USA
tel: 914/784-0500; fax: 914/784-0580
illyus@worldnet.att.net

TORREFAZIONE DEL CAFFÈ MATTIONI
Via Terza Armata 133, 34170 Gorizia
tel: 0481/521444

CAFFÈ PERLANERA
Via Piccardi 22, Trieste
tel: 040/397310
(closed Saturday and Sunday)
Perlanera (black pearl) is a very new coffee roaster and quite good. There is a fragrant bar blend and a milder one for family use. Both are good, though I prefer the former.

CAFFÈ UDINESE DEGUSTAZIONE
Via Rialto 5, 33100 Udine
tel: 0432/504080

ZAGO ALIMENTAZIONE
Via Einaudi 18, 33080 Prata di Pordenone (PN)
tel: 0434/621583; fax: 0434/610222
zago@zago.it
Various *arabica* blends, flavorful and well-chosen. My favorite is called Tarrazu and comes from Costa Rica.

GOOSE PRODUCTS

AZIENDA AGRICOLA JOLANDA DE COLÒ
Via Mameli 6, Località Joannis
tel: 0432/997733

GRAPPA AND DISTILLATES

For information on all the grappa producers in the region, contact:

CONSORZIO PER LA TUTELA
DELLA GRAPPA FRIULANA
Via Poscolle 6, 33100 Udine
tel: 0432/509394

MEATS (SPECIALTY)

WILD S.R.L.
Via Isonzo 21/A, 34070 Mossa (GO)
tel: 0481/809611; fax: 0481/809665
Wild (pronounced VILLD) offers an excellent line of products made mostly of game, wild birds, as well as beef, pork, lamb, turkey, and snails. These meats might be air-cured as a sort of prosciutto, or made into ragùs (sauces for pasta, polenta, or toasts), pâtés, salamis, or sausages. Wild exports to much of Europe, and some of their products probably can be imported to North America and Japan. These traditional flavors of Friuli-Venezia Giulia may be exotic for some diners but ambrosia for others. Among the animals they work with are cow (*bovino*), chamois (*camoscio*), duck (*anatra*), elk (*alce*), fallow deer (*daino*), goat (*capra*), goose (*oca*), hare (*lepre*), horse (*cavallo*), lamb (*agnello*), partridge (*pernice*), pheasant (*fagiano*), pig (*maiale*), red deer (*cervo*), roe deer (*capriolo*), snails (*lumache*), turkey (*tacchino*), wild boar (*cinghiale*), wild goose (*oca selvatica*), and wood pigeon (*colombaccio*). Wild uses no preservatives or food colorings. The wild animals graze freely and are caught. The domestic animals they use are fed organic diets.

SALUMIFICIO WOLF
Via Dante Volvlan 88, Sauris (UD)
tel: 0433/86054
(closed Christmas, New Year's, and Easter)
Smoked pork products and cheeses of distinction, including excellent speck (bacon).

MINERAL WATER

The leading water bottled in Friuli is Goccia di Carnia (Drop of Carnia). The source is at Fleons, 4,521 feet/1,370 meters up in the central Carnic Alps. It is sold in three versions: *naturale* (still), *leggermente frizzante* (lightly sparkling), and *frizzante* (sparkling).

OLIVE OIL

Olives have come back from near extinction in Friuli-Venezia Giulia, which is often said to be the northernmost place in the world where they are grown. The town of Oleis, not far from Cividale, means "place of the olive" in Friulano. Olive oil was produced in the region until two frosts in the 1920s destroyed nearly all of the trees. Replanting only began in very recent years. There are not many bottles of oil now made in the region, although it is slowly rebounding. Most of the planted hectares are in the province of Udine, but the most common olive is a native of the province of Trieste, the Bianchera. It is found on Monte Usello, near Trieste, on hills that also bloom with lavender and rosemary. Varieties from Tuscany (the Leccino, Maurino, Moraiolo, and Pendolino) and from Lake Garda (Grignano, Casaliva, Favarol) are also found in the region. Listed below are some leading producers.

BRUNO CASAGRANDE
Fiaschetti di Caneva (PN)
tel: 0434/77476

IL MELOGRANO
Coop. Agricola di Solidarietà Sociale
Rizzolo di Reana del Roiale (UD)
tel: 0432/857169

ROBERTO OTA
Loc. Bagnoli della Rosandra 357
San Dorligo della Valle (TS)
tel: 040/227019

VITJAN SANCIN
Loc. Bagnoli della Rosandra 360
San Dorligo della Valle (TS)
tel: 040/228870

DANILO STAREC
(one of the historic producers)
Loc. Bagnoli della Rosandra 375
San Dorligo della Valle (TS)
tel: 040/228827

AZIENDA AGRICOLA RONC DAI ULIVS
(owner Achille Stefanelli)
Via San Rocco 27, Campeglio di Faedis (UD)
tel: 0432/711363 or 0432/46930

AZIENDA AGRICOLA DOMENICO TAVERNA
Castello d'Arcano, Riva D'Arcano (UD)
tel: 0432/809018

PORK

One of the sins of focus groups and marketing is that if consumers can be persuaded that they want something, even if it is mediocre or bad, they ask for it instead of the excellent product that it is replacing. Such has been the case with pork in the United States. When the word "fat" became a universal source of panic, rather than a food to be eaten in moderation, many products attempted to become fat-free. In the case of packaged cereals and baked goods, when the fat came out, more sugar was added. Most American pigs are now bred on factory farms, en masse, being fed a controlled diet laced with hormones. The result is that the pigs are bloated with water; when the meat is cooked, the water runs out, leaving meat that is dry and tasteless. The meat is now white because focus groups think it is healthier than red or pink meat. Someone should remind marketing people that fat is white. Fortunately, a slow backlash has begun that endorses quality, flavor, and more environmentally friendly farming techniques (pig farms in North Carolina and parts of the Midwest have created a major environmental disaster by not providing for safe disposal of waste).

There are two American brands worth looking at that appear in some stores.

Niman Ranch (which also makes fine beef) raises pigs in an environmentally friendly way and with good feed. The result is a succulent, delicious product that is more expensive than mass-produced pork, but worth it. This is as close to the beautiful American pork of once upon a time that I have found. If you eat organic, as I do as often as possible, there is pork sold under the Valley's Family label that is certified organic. It does not have the richness of the Niman Ranch brand, but it is far superior to commercial American pork. Ask for both of these brands at fine markets.

PROSCIUTTO

Prosciutto di San Daniele is now available in fine stores all over the world, making it easy for you to use the genuine article rather than some pretender. You must make sure that your grocer or butcher slices the ham to your specifications.

For information about this ham and where to buy it, you may also contact the consortium of producers, the Consorzio del Prosciutto di San Daniele, which represents all the producers of prosciutto di San Daniele. They can provide information to importers about how to acquire this divine ham. I have tasted and enjoyed hams from all the producers, and you will appreciate the differences when you savor them. Large producers, such as Brendolan and Principe, make a tasty and reliable product, and they have led the way in exporting around the world. Because certain nations, including the United States and Japan, require different handling of hams (removal of the trotter and, often, removal of the bone), these larger firms have set aside separate butchering, salting, and aging space for these countries' hams.

If you are traveling in the area, you might wish to visit smaller producers who still do much of the work by hand. Their products are less often exported beyond Europe.

CONSORZIO DEL PROSCIUTTO DI SAN DANIELE
Via Andreuzzi 8, 33038 San Daniele (UD)
tel: 0432/95751
http://www.madeinfriuli.com/online/prosc_on.htm

CORADAZZI
Viale Kennedy 102
tel: 0432 / 957582

GIOVANNI PROLONGO
Viale Trento e Trieste 117
tel: 0432 / 957161

SAUERKRAUT

The sauerkraut used in Italy to serve with pork or to add
to *jota* is not nearly as sour as that found in North America.
A very good canned Italian brand, if you can locate it, is
Zuccato. New Yorkers can go to Fairway market to purchase
wonderful Alsatian sauerkraut that is sold from a large bin.
There are a couple of good organic sauerkrauts available in
North America that I recommend. One is Cascadian Farm
(Rockport, WA 98283 USA), which is relatively delicate. The
other is Hill Farm of Vermont, sold in markets, but which
you can also have delivered by UPS in 1-gallon buckets (tel:
802 / 426-3234). Hill Farm is crunchier and tangier than what
one would eat in Trieste, so use a little less of it or heat it
slightly longer to soften the texture and flavor.

SPICES AND FLAVORINGS

FRATELLI BAUER
Casella Postale 260, 34100 Trieste
tel: 040 / 816256 or 816209; fax: 040 / 381290
Since 1884 Fratelli Bauer has been a leading importer and
exporter of spices, medicinal and aromatic herbs, dried fruits
and vegetables, and fragrances for vermouth and other
liqueurs. This classic family company has weathered wars,
revolutions, changes in borders and national allegiances
within the city of Trieste, not to mention the mercurial
characteristics of the international spice trade, to survive
into the twenty-first century.

My other Triestine source for spices and lots of wonderful foods is Gerbini on Via Cesare Battisti 29. I do not believe
they do mail order, so on your next visit to Trieste stock up
at this superb store and then repair to the Caffè San Marco
across the street to relax.

TABLE DECORATIONS

ADRIANA BEGNIS-CORTINOVIS
La Gazza Ladra, Viale Lombardia 7
33037 Colloredo di Prato (UD)
tel: 0432 / 652030; fax: 0432 / 652003
It really does not do Adriana Begnis-Cortinovis justice to
describe her work as table decorations. She is a singular
artist who has the ability to transform dried flowers, fruit,
plants, and other natural materials into stunning center-
pieces and decorations. Her work graces fine tables in restaurants and homes all over Europe, and merit discovery
in North America. To me, what she does is an extension
of the local knowledge of the land and all that it provides.
When I dine in restaurants in Friuli-Venezia Giulia that
have especially beautiful appointments, I almost always
am told, *"È di Adriana."*

TROUT

Friuli-Venezia Giulia produces and consumes more trout
than any Italian region. It is prepared in traditional and
delicious ways when fresh. In recent years, smoked and
cured trout products have appeared on the market. They
are delicious in antipasto, and even as a replacement for
prosciutto in certain pasta preparations.

FRIULTROTA DI PIGHIN
Via Aonedis 10, 33038 San Daniele (UD)
tel: 0432 / 956560
(closed Saturday, Sunday, and mid–August)
Friultrota di Pighin produces delicious Friulian trout in
many forms. The most delectable is *fil di fumo,* cooked
smoked trout. This firm also markets tasty trout eggs as
a caviar.

VINEGAR

Many wine producers in Friuli-Venezia Giulia also make vinegar for home use and a few of them bottle and sell it. As you come to notice the different flavors of wine grapes used in Friuli-Venezia Giulia, you may be able to detect and appreciate the different flavors as they appear in vinegar. The important thing to recall is that the vinegar used in the region is slightly less acidic than that used in many other places. In using vinegar for cooking, you should use one that has interesting flavor but lower acidity. If you cannot get vinegar from the region, use a very good white or red vinegar from elsewhere. Add a few drops of wine to it, or just a couple of drops of water to diminish the acidic impact.

There is another interesting grape product in the region, known generically as *mosto cotto,* or cooked must. In ancient Aquileia, the Romans and locals who lived there had three products: *caroenum, defrutum,* and *sapa.* These are bittersweet condiments of different concentrations made when grape musts were cooked down and formed a liquid by turns sour, bitter, and sweet. It was used with raw and cooked fish, meats, and fruit.

In parts of Italy, *sapa* (also called *saba*) still exists today. In Emilia-Romagna, for example, it is made primarily of Trebbiano grapes. In Friuli-Venezia Giulia one can occasionally see it, but there is another product of even more interest.

Asperum is produced by the Midolini winery in the Colli Orientali. They use Tocai, Chardonnay, Pinot Bianco, Pinot Grigio, and Sauvignon Blanc. The grapes are crushed and cooked with their skins at 194°F/90°C for 45 to 50 hours until they are reduced to an intense dark liquid. This is then poured into small barrels and aged for many years. Each year, the liquid goes into a different barrel, and a new wood is used. Among these are acacia, ash, cherry, chestnut, oak, and juniper. This last imparts a special fragrance to the condiment. The procedure is not unlike that used to make balsamic vinegar in Emilia-Romagna, but the taste is not the same. Asperum is thinner, more aromatic, and is good on food of this region: fish of all types, beans (especially in soup), and foie gras.

AZIENDA AGRICOLA MIDOLINI
Via Udine 40, 33044 Manzano (UD)
tel: 0432/754555; fax: 0432/21574

MAIL-ORDER PURVEYORS AND SPECIALTY FOOD STORES IN NORTH AMERICA

AMERICAN SPOON FOODS, INC.
P.O. Box 566 Petoskey, Michigan 49770-0566
tel: 231/347-9030 or 888/735-6700; fax: 800/647-2512
www.spoon.com and information@spoon.com
An excellent option for flavorful fruit, many of which are dried or preserved. Cherries, berries, and apples are especially recommended.

THE BAKER'S CATALOGUE
P.O. Box 876, RR 2, Box 56, Norwich, VT 05055
tel: 800/827-6836
A wide selection of flours plus imported cornmeal and polenta. The King Arthur unbleached flour is an excellent product. This catalogue is also a good source for caraway seeds, aniseeds, and poppy seeds. They sell unusual spice measuring spoons that are ideal for inserting into narrow-mouthed spice jars. And there are delicious dried fruits that you can use in cookery, especially to fill gnocchi. Finally, they have excellent fresh crushed ginger that you can use in gnocchi with pears or stir into polenta.

BALDUCCI'S
424 Sixth Avenue, New York, NY 10011
tel: 800/225-3822; fax: 516/843-0383
www.balducci.com
An excellent selection of food products from Italy, including polenta, pasta, produce, spices, prosciutto di San Daniele, and a wide selection of cheeses.

CONVITO ITALIANO
1515 Sheridan Road, Willmette, IL 60091
tel: 847/251-3654; fax: 847/251-0123
A good supplier of Italian products.

CORTI BROTHERS
5810 Folsom Boulevard, Sacramento, CA 95819
tel: 800/509-3663
Carefully chosen foods from Italy, including good Ligurian olive oil that will work well in recipes in this book.

DAIRY FRESH CANDIES
57 Salem Street, Boston, MA 02113
tel: 800/336-5536; fax: 617/742-9828
Candied and dried fruits.

DEAN AND DELUCA
560 Broadway, New York, NY 10012
tel: 800/221-7714
Polenta, pasta, cheeses, prosciutto di San Daniele.

WWW.ESPERYA.COM
This is an excellent new Web site to purchase products from Italy, especially cheeses.

FAIRWAY MARKET
2127 Broadway (at 74th Street), New York, NY 10023
tel: 212/595-1888 and 2328 12th Avenue (133rd Street)
tel: 212/234-3883
I know of no more complete food store in North America. Most of the products you need for this book are here. Fairway is run with great spirit and community awareness and features outstanding food items from all over the world at very fair prices. The knowledgeable staff is ready to help. To order via the World Wide Web, visit an excellent site called www.starchefs.com and then go to the Fairway link.

GIUSTO'S
344 Littlefield Avenue, South San Francisco, CA 94080
tel: 888/873-6566; fax: 650/873-2826
Polenta and other grains and flours.

IL CIBO DI LIDIA
P.O. Box 4461, Grand Central Station, New York, NY 10163
tel: 800/480-2426; fax: 212/935-7687
Lidia Matticchio Bastianich, when she is not running restaurants, appearing on her excellent series of cooking programs, teaching cooking classes, leading a tour group to Italy, writing a cookbook, being a mentor to young people interested in the food business, or being a mother and a grandmother, also finds time to select and import quality food items, many from Friuli-Venezia Giulia.

JAMISON FARM
171 Jamison Lane, Latrobe, PA 15650
tel: 800/237-5262
www.jamisonfarm.com
Top-quality lamb (free-range and without antibiotics or hormones), shipped fresh or frozen.

LARCHMONT VILLAGE WINE AND CHEESE
223 N. Larchmont Blvd., Los Angeles, CA 90004
tel: 323/856-8699
A source in Los Angeles for wine and cheese.

MOZZARELLA COMPANY
2944 Elm Street, Dallas, TX 75226
tel: 800/798-2954 or 214/741-4072
www.foodwine.com (then click on Mozzarella).
Famous for mozzarella, but you can also acquire good handmade ricotta if you do not have access to ricotta from Italy.

MURRAY'S CHEESE
257 Bleecker Street, New York, NY 10014
tel: 212/243-3289; fax: 212/243-5001
www.murrayscheese.com
Outstanding cheeses, carefully selected and lovingly tended to. Call for their catalogue.

SUMMERFIELD FARM
10044 James Monroe Highway, Culpepper, VA 22701
tel: 800/898-3276
www.summerfieldfarm.com
Excellent veal.

TODARO BROTHERS
557 Second Avenue, New York, NY 10016
tel: 212/679-7766
A classic old Italian food store that happens to be in a neighborhood that has long had a small but consistent Friulian presence.

VIVANDE
2125 Fillmore Street, San Francisco, CA 94115
tel: 415/346-4430
Their catalogue lists many useful products.

WALLY'S
2107 Westwood Blvd., Westwood, CA 90025
tel: 310/475-0606
Cheese and other products at this Southern California shop.

WAR EAGLE MILL
Route 5, Box 411, Rogers, AR 72756
tel: 501/789-5343
www.wareaglemill.com
Stone-ground certified organic flours and grains.

WILLIAMS-SONOMA CATALOGUE
P.O. Box 7465, San Francisco, CA 94120
tel: 800/541-2233; fax: 415/421-5153

ZABAR'S
2245 Broadway, New York, NY 10024
tel: 212/787-2000
Prosciutto di San Daniele, D'Arbo and Fiordifrutta preserves, and there is always good Montasio cheese on hand.

ZINGERMAN'S
422 Detroit Street, Ann Arbor, MI 48104
tel: 734/769-1625 or 888/636-8162; fax: 734/769-1260
www.zingermans.com
An excellent and friendly supplier of many good products. They are especially attuned to finding and importing items before other stores, so this may be one of the first to sell many of the products you read about in this book.

Traveling in Friuli–Venezia Giulia

There really is no useful guidebook in English devoted solely to Friuli-Venezia Giulia, primarily because the region is so unexplored. The standard guidebooks to Italy have a few pages on Trieste, Udine, Cividale, and perhaps Aquileia. The most complete listings I know happen to be in a book that I wrote, called *Italy for the Gourmet Traveler,* published in North America by Little, Brown and in Britain by Kyle Cathie. There is a whole chapter dedicated to Friuli-Venezia Giulia. Note that chef Dario Bassi in Trieste is no longer at Hostaria Bellavista but has moved to Harry's Grill, the restaurant of the Hotel Duchi d'Aosta.

Also note that when calling within Italy one must now dial the entire number, including the area code. To call from North America, dial 01139 and then the entire number. To call from the UK and the rest of Europe, dial 0039 and then the entire number.

To reach the region by air from Italy, Alitalia has flights from Rome, Milan, Genoa, and, occasionally, from Sardinia to Trieste. From abroad, you can fly Alitalia or other airlines to Rome or Milan and then connect. If you are flying from New York City or the eastern United States, Delta Airlines has nonstop service to Venice, whose airport is about 30 minutes from Friuli-Venezia Giulia. Trieste airport is served by British Airways from Gatwick airport (London) and by Lufthansa from Munich. Ryanair, www.ryanair.com, has inexpensive flights from London-Stanstead to Treviso, within easy reach of western Friuli.

The region's airport is very convenient for most of the population of Friuli-Venezia Giulia. It is near the town of Ronchi dei Legionari, just outside Monfalcone and Redipuglia. It is 23 km from Gorizia, 33 km from Trieste, and 39 km from Udine. The exit from the A4 autostrada is Redipuglia. The airport's main telephone number is 0481/7731. Information is available by calling 0481/773224 or 773225. Its excellent Web site, in Italian and English, is www.aeroporto.fvg.it. You may find the latest flight information on this site. For taxis at the airport, call 0481/779193.

Rail service reaches the region from Venice's two key stations, Santa Lucia in the city center and Mestre on the mainland. From Venice, there are trains for the 2-hour trip to Trieste. There are also trains that head north through Pordenone and on to Udine (also 2 hours). Udine and Trieste are connected by a train that also stops in Gorizia and Cormons. There are also trains (usually originating in Rome or Venice) that go from Udine up through Tarvisio and on to Vienna.

For complete information about Italian train schedules, here is a useful Web site: http://www.fs-on-line.com/eng/index.htm. When you are traveling in Italy, it is useful to buy a lightweight train schedule, called an *orario,* at newsstands in train stations. There are a few different versions, more or less of equal quality, and typically they have a yellow cover.

Bus service is decent in this region, except on Sundays. There are important stations in Trieste, Udine, Gorizia, Tolmezzo, and other smaller towns.

TOURIST INFORMATION IN FRIULI-VENEZIA GIULIA

For regional tourist information, contact the Azienda Regionale per la Promozione Turistica, Via Rossini 6, Trieste; tel: 040/60336.

The government of the region has a Web site that may be of interest: www.regionefriuli-ve-giulia. You may also wish to visit http://www.fvgpromo.

The promotional site for Friulian products also has an interesting tourism page with numerous links. Go to www.madeinfriuli.com/turcul/tur_cult.htm.

Each of the four provincial capitals (Gorizia, Pordenone, Trieste, and Udine) has an office for information on all the destinations of interest in their provinces, including the capital cities. In some cases, towns that receive many visitors often have their own tourist offices. Some of these are indicated below. Note, too, that Trieste has a city tourist office that is distinct from the provincial and regional offices.

Aquileia. Ufficio informazioni di Aquileia; call 0431/919491 or get information from the provincial office in Udine or the regional office in Trieste.

Aviano. A.P.T. Aviano, Piazza Duomo, 34081 Aviano (PN), Italia; tel: 0434/651888; fax: 0434/660348.

Carnia. A.P.T. Carnia, Via Umberto I, 15, 33022 Arta Terme (UD); tel: 0433/929290; fax: 0433/92104. This office is well stocked with information on all of Carnia.

Cividale. A.P.T. Cividale del Friuli, Largo Boiani 4, 33043 Cividale del Friuli; tel/fax: 0432/731398.

Cormons and the Collio. Enoteca di Cormons, Palazzo Locatelli, Piazza 24 Maggio 21; tel: 0481/630371. Open Thursday through Monday, 11h–13h; 17h–22h (24h in summer); Wednesday, 17h–22h (24h). Closed Tuesday and for two weeks in January or February.

Gorizia and its province. A.P.T. Gorizia; Via Diaz, 16, 34170 Gorizia, Italia; tel/fax: 0481/533870. Note that Grado has its own tourist office, and the *enoteca* in Cormons has information about that part of the Collio wine zone.

Grado. A.P.T. Grado, Viale Dante Alighieri 72, 34073 Grado (GO), Italia; tel: 0431/899111; fax: 0431/899278.

Lignano. A.P.T. Lignano Sabbiadoro, Via Latisana, 42, 33054 Lignano Sabbiadoro (UD); tel: 0431/71821; fax: 0431/70449; Ufficio informazioni di Lignano Pineta; tel: 0431/422169. These are the region's largest beach resorts, and the water and sand are marvelously clean.

Pordenone and its province. Corso Vittorio Emanuele 58, 33170 Pordenone; tel: 0434/21912; fax: 0434/523814.

Tarvisio and its zone. Consorzio Servizi Turistici del Tarvisiano e di Sella Nevea, Via Roma 10; tel: 0428/2392; fax: 0428/2306. http://www.tarvisiano.org/consorzio; consorzio@tarvisiano.org. This area has its own very well-run tourist information office. It can be helpful in all seasons, but should be especially considered in winter, when there is excellent Olympic-quality skiing nearby.

Trieste (information about tourism in the city). Azienda di Promozione Turistica di Trieste, Via San Niccolò 20, 34121 Trieste; tel: 040/6796111; fax: 040/6796299. There is also a smaller tourist office at the train station, which is stocked with informative materials; tel: 040/420182.

Trieste (information about its province).   Provincia di Trieste; Assessorato al turismo, Viale Miramare 19, 34135 Trieste; tel: 040/3771111; fax: 040/3775791.

Udine and its province.   A.P.T. di Udine, Piazza I Maggio, 7, 33100 Udine; tel: 0432/295972 or 504743; fax: 0432/504743. This office has good information about many events and destinations throughout the large province of Udine, as well as for the city itself. Also, see listings for Carnia, Cividale, Lignano, and Tarvisio.

AGRITOURISM AND FARM HOLIDAYS

For information: Agriturist Comitato Regionale, Via Savorgnana 26, 33100 Udine; tel: 0432/297068.

CYCLING TRIPS IN FRIULI-VENEZIA GIULIA

The varied terrain of the region offers many possibilities for cyclists. The lagoon and the Bassa Friulana are perfect for beginners. The Carso, Collio, and Colli Orientali zones are beautiful and present more of a challenge. For advanced cyclists, Carnia, the Valcanale, and the Alps above Pordenone are exciting. At this writing, a company called Ciclismo Classico is planning an itinerary to offer the best of Friuli-Venezia Giulia to groups of cyclists. Given all the great food and wine you will consume, cycling is probably the best means of staying trim!

CICLISMO CLASSICO
30 Marathon Street, Arlington, MA 02474 USA
tel: 800/866-7314
www.ciclismoclassico.com; info@ciclismoclassico.com

VISITING CASTLES

Friuli-Venezia Giulia has more old and historic castles than most Italian regions. Some are private residences, some are hotels, some contain restaurants, and others are public property. To protect them, an organization has been created that gathers funds to restore castles in disrepair, and occasionally organizes tours to some of the most impressive ones (102 at this writing). Typically, there must be a group of at least 20 persons to organize a castle visit.

LELLA STRASSOLDO
Consorzio per la Salvaguardia dei Castelli
Storici del Friuli-Venezia Giulia
tel: 0431/93217

HOTELS

Hotels in Friuli-Venezia Giulia, for the most part, tend to be modest and familial, making up in courtesy what may be lacking in luxury. In general, hotel prices in much of the region are lower than in most of the rest of Italy. Consult standard travel books (I use the red Michelin guide) for suggestions on hotels. Also, both of the organizations listed below represent small hotels in the region. I include these for your reference, but cannot recommend all of the hotels for the simple reason that I have not stayed in them all.

CONSORZIO FRIULALBERGHI
Via XXIV Maggio 1/C, 33072 Casarsa della Delizia (PN)
tel: 0434/869452; fax: 0434/86173

CORALB HOTELS
(Consorzio Regionale Albergatori Friuli-Venezia Giulia),
Viale Ledra 24, 33100 Udine
tel: 0432/505091; fax: 0432/509070

WINE TOURISM

Among Italian regions, Friuli-Venezia Giulia probably ranks
with Tuscany as the best for wine tourism. At certain times
of the year, some wineries open their doors for tasting and
purchasing of wines. A few wineries, such as Venica and
Castello di Spessa, also have lovely rooms for rent, and it is
sometimes possible to dine with the families. Much of my
education in the region's food and wine came from many
mornings in the vineyard, afternoons in the kitchen, and
evenings at the table with wine-producing families. While
it is true that I had greater access because I was conducting
research for this book, even a night or two spent with one
family can open new worlds for you.

MOVIMENTO DEL TURISMO DEL VINO
Sede Regionale del Friuli-Venezia Giulia,
Casa del Vino, Via Poscolle 6, 33100 Udine
tel: 0432/509394; fax: 0432/510180

For information about *enotecas* worth visiting, see page 356.

TRAVEL AGENTS AND TOUR ORGANIZERS

WANDA S. RADETTI, TASTEFUL JOURNEYS
32–84 45th Street, Astoria, NY 11103
tel/fax: 718/932-6893
tastetours@aol.com
Wanda Radetti was born in Istria and has lived in America
for many years. She specializes in travel to Istria and Friuli-
Venezia Giulia, especially food and wine vacations, as the
name of her company would suggest.

**SUZANNE CAMPION-TITTOTO,
CAMPIONI ITALIANI DI VENETO**
50B Peninsula Center Drive, Suite 153
Rolling Hills Estates, CA 90274
tel: 310/373-2226; fax: 310/791-0817
Suzanne@campioni-italiani.com
Also in Italy at Via Campo Sportivo 37
31011 Asolo (TV), Italia
tel/fax: 0423/952350
Suzanne Campion began by specializing in the Veneto, but
as interest in the food, wine, and culture of Friuli-Venezia
Giulia grew, she expanded into the neighboring region with
organized tours to several towns and to places of interest to
food and wine lovers. She also imports Friulian wines into
the western United States.

MARJORIE SHAW'S INSIDER'S ITALY®
PMB 891, 41 Schermerhorn Street, Brooklyn, NY 11201
tel: 718/855-3878; fax: 718/855-3687
e-mail: INSIDERSIT@aol.com
http://members.aol.com/insidersit
Marjorie Shaw, born in Italy of American parents, operates
Insider's Italy, a special service designed to create personal-
ized visits for discerning travelers. Her firm offers specialized
assistance with itinerary planning, accommodation bookings,
transportation planning, and means of enjoying all manner
of good Italian food and wine. For a fee, Insider's Italy custom-
designs itineraries based on the client's budget and interests.
Insider's Italy is not a travel agency per se; they do not book
air or rail tickets, but they will plan the trip you describe
rather than fitting you into a preplanned group tour. For
more information, visit the firm's Web site and complete
their no-obligation travel-planning questionnaire.

ESPERIENZE ITALIANE TRAVEL
243 E. 58th Street, New York, NY 10022
tel: 800/480-2426 or 212/758-1488; fax: 212/935-7687
or contact Shelly Burgess at www.lidiasitaly.com or
shelly@lidiasitaly.com
Lidia Monticchio Bastianich, who holds high the banner of
the foods of Istria and Friuli-Venezia Giulia in her restaurants, cookbooks, and television programs, also oversees
guided tours to Italy that have a strong food and wine orien-
tation. One tour, to northeastern Italy, also includes Friuli-
Venezia Giulia.

FRIULIANI AROUND THE WORLD

If you are of Friulian background, there is an organization in Udine that you should know about. It is called Friuli nel Mondo. Under the longtime presidency of Mario Toros and a devoted staff, this organization has kept links with the huge Friulian émigré communities in Argentina, Australia, Canada, Germany, France, Belgium, and Austria, along with small groups found in places throughout the world. They send out a newsletter, in Friulian language, about the region and its customs. They also promote instruction of the language abroad, with the belief that as long as there is a language there will be the Friulian people. There is a link to them on the Web site www.madeinfriuli.com. Even if you are not Friulano, local chapters of the organization can be a window into the region and its members can introduce you to the region as you prepare to go there.

FRIULI NEL MONDO
Via del Sale 9, 33100 Udine
tel: 0432 / 504970

Bibliography

As I began my research on this book, I found it remarkable how little there is written in English about Friuli-Venezia Giulia. Most of what you will find in our language are interesting recollections of wartime exploits. In addition, there are some remembrances tucked into letters of artists and writers such as Joyce, Hemingway, Wagner, and Rilke. In terms of publications about food and wine in English, there is almost nothing, so I have endeavored to make this volume the book that this marvelous place deserves. A few American magazines that specialize in wine and food printed articles about the region as I was completing this book that are so riddled with mistakes that to cite them here would only encourage acceptance of the misinformation they contain.

Books by Magris, Saba, Svevo, and Pasolini that you can find in translation will provide a meaningful window into Friuli-Venezia Giulia. If you can read Italian, there are numerous books about the region, its people, wine, and food.

Alberti, Giorgio, et. al. *Maria Teresa, Trieste e il Porto.* Trieste, Istituto per L'Enciclopedia del Friuli Venezia Giulia, 1980.

Angelico Benvenuto, Gianfranco, ed. *Cucina e Vini Friulani nel Mondo.* Codroipo (UD), Gianfranco Angelico Benvenuto Editore, 1992.

Apih, Elio. *Mostra Storica della Risiera di San Sabba.* Trieste, Comune di Trieste-Civici Musei di Storia ed Arte, 1983.

———. *Trieste.* Bari, Laterza, 1988.

Ara, Angelo, and Claudio Magris. *Trieste: Identità di Una Città Frontiera.* 1982.

Arneri, Glauco. *Trieste: Breve Storia della Città.* Trieste, Lint, 1998.

Ascoli Vitali-Norsa, Giuliana. *La Cucina nella Tradizione Ebraica.* Padova, Adei Wizo, 1984.

Attridge, Derek, ed. *The Cambridge Companion to James Joyce.* Cambridge, Cambridge University Press, 1990.

Au Fiore, Lella. *La Gubana Goriziana.* Mariano del Friuli (GO), Edizioni della Laguna, 1973.

Barbina, Guido. "La Centralità di Udine nel Sistema Insediativo Friulano: Analisi di Un Processo."
In *Udin: Milagn tal cûr Friûl,* ed. Gian Carlo Menis, pp. 43–49, 60n Congress, 25 Sept 1983, Societât
Filologjche Furlane. Udine, Società Filologica Friulana, 1983.

Behr, Edward. "In the Vineyards of Friuli," *The Art of Eating,* issue #28, Peachum, Vermont, Fall 1993.

Benedetti, Andrea. *Storia di Pordenone.* Pordenone, Il Noncello, 1964.

Bergamini, Giuseppe, and Ottorino Burelli. *Friulani: I Grandi Uomini di un Piccolo Popolo.* Tavagnacco
(UD), Arti Grafiche Friulane, 1996.

———. *Vivere in Friuli.* Tavagnacco (UD), Arti Grafiche Friulane, 1993.

Bosio, Luciano. *Le Strade Romane della Venetia e dell'Histria.* Padova, Editoriale Programma, 1991.

Buseghin, Maria Luciana, ed. *Buon Vino, Favola Lunga: Vite e Vino nei Proverbi delle Regioni Italiane.*
Perugia, Electa, 1992.

Camporesi, Piero. *Alimentazione Folklore Società.* Le Forme del Discorso no. 20. Parma, Pratiche, 1988.

———. *Il Paese della Fame.* Saggi no. 178. Bologna, Il Mulino, 1978.

———. *Il Pane Selvaggio.* Saggi no. 195. Bologna, Il Mulino, 1980.

Canetti, Elias. *Crowds and Power,* trans. Carol Stewart. New York, Continuum, 1981.

Caputo, Fulvio, and Roberto Masiero. *Trieste e l'Impero: La Formazione di Una Città Europea.* Venezia,
Marsilio, 1988.

Cary, Joseph. *A Ghost in Trieste.* Chicago, University of Chicago Press, 1993.

Cassin, Danilo. *Vecchi Mestieri in Friuli Occidentale.* Pordenone, Edizioni Concordia Sette, 1997.

Chiaradia, Giosue. *La Provincia di Pordenone.* Novara, De Agostini, 1987.

Colomba, Giulio, ed. *Friuli Venezia Giulia.* Roma, Gambero Rosso Editore, 1996.

Colombini, Paola. *Trentino-Alto Adige e Friuli Venezia Giulia.* Milano, Touring Club Italiano, 1995.

Contini, Mila. *Friuli e Trieste in Cucina.* Santarcangelo di Romagna, Edizioni Gulliver, 1998.

Corbellini, Roberta, ed. *Interni di Famiglia.* Tavagnacco (UD), Arti Grafiche Friulane, 1994.

Cox, Sir Geoffrey. *The Race for Trieste 1945.* London, William Kimber, 1977.

Dassovich, Mario. *Dopoguerra a Trieste: L'Esperienza e la Testimonianza di un "Optante" Fiumano
(1949–1996).* Udine, Del Bianco Editore, 1996.

de Grassi, Marino, and Alessandro Felluga, eds. *La Cucina di Grado.* Mariano del Friuli (GO), Edizioni
della Laguna, 1994.

del Fabro, Adriano. *Le Ricette della Tradizione Friulana.* Bussolengo (VR), Edizioni La Libreria di
Demetra, 1994.

del Piero, F., ed. *Il Friuli Venezia Giulia più Tipico.* Feletto Umberto (UD), Arti Grafiche Friulane, 1997.

del Savio, Elena, ed. *Friuli-Venezia Giulia.* Milano, Guida d'Italia del Touring Club Italiano, 1982.

De Matteis, Luigi. *Case Contadine nella Carnia e nel Friuli Montano.* Torino, Priuli & Verlacca, 1989.

Dercsényi, Balázs. *Budapest.* Budapest, Magyar Képek & Merhávia, 1993.

de Santa, Fulvio. *Carnia La Mia Terra.* Mestre, Controcampo, 1995.

de Vonderweid, Iolanda. *Ricette Triestine Istriane e Dalmate.* Trieste, Lint, 1972.

Ellero, Gianfranco, and Guido Barbina, eds. *Tarvis.* Udine, Societât Filologjche Furlane, 1991.

Fast, Mady. *Mangiare Triestino.* Padova, Franco Muzzio Editore, 1993.

Ferrari, Giovanni. *Il Friuli: La Popolazione dalla Conquista Veneta ad Oggi.* Udine, Camera di Comercio-
Industria-Agricoltura, 1963.

Filiputti, Walter. *ll Friuli Venezia Giulia e i Suoi Grandi Vini.* Feletto Umberto (UD), Arti Grafiche
Friulane, 1997.

Fonda, Cesare. *Cucina Carsolina di Ieri e di Oggi.* Trieste, Edizioni Italo Svevo, 1997.

————. *Cucina Triestina*. Trieste, Edizioni Italo Svevo, 1997.

Gallarotti, Antonella. *Dolci Ebraici della Mitteleuropa*. Mariano del Friuli (GO), Edizioni della Laguna, 1997.

Ganzer, Gilberto. *The Treasures of Gemona Cathedral,* trans. Benita de' Grassi di Pianura. Udine, Arti Grafiche Friulane, 1985.

Gatt-Rutter. *Italo Svevo: A Double Life*. Oxford, Clarendon Press, 1988.

Giannatasio, Giovanna Ludovico, ed. *Come Mangiavamo*. Mariano del Friuli (GO), Edizioni della Laguna, 1996.

Gillespie, Michael Patrick. *James Joyce's Trieste*. Harry Ransom Humanities Research Center.

Ginzburg, Carlo. *The Night Battles: Witchcraft and Agrarian Cults in the Sixteenth and Seventeenth Centuries* (originally called *I Benandanti*), trans. John and Anne Tedeschi. London, Routledge and Paul, 1983.

Giurcin, Rosanna T., and Stefano de Francheschi. *Mangiamoci L'Istria*. Trieste, MGS Press, 1996.

Godoli, Elio. *Trieste*. Roma, Laterza, 1984.

Grassani, Silvana Bergamaschi. *La Selvaggina (a Modo Mio)*. Feletto Umberto (UD), Missio, 1988.

Grassi, Livio. *Trieste Venezia Giulia, 1943–1945: dall'8 Settembre al Ritorno all'Italia*. Trieste, Edizioni Italo Svevo, 1990.

Gundel, Károly. *Gundel's Hungarian Cookbook*. Budapest, Kossuth, 1988.

Hemingway, Ernest. *A Farewell to Arms*. New York, Scribner, 1995.

Illy, Andrea, and Rinantonio Viani, eds. *Espresso Coffee: The Chemistry of Quality*. London, Academic Press, 1995.

Illy, Francesco and Riccardo. *From Coffee to Espresso*. Milano, Mondadori, 1989.

Jenkins, Steven. *Cheese Primer*. New York, Workman, 1996.

Joyce, James. *Letters,* 3 vol. London, Faber, 1957–1966.

Kalla, Kálmán. *Gundel New Hungarian Cookbook*. Budapest, Pallas Stúdió, 1998.

Keegan, John. *The First World War*. New York, Alfred A. Knopf, 1999.

Lackenberger, Anita, and Thomas A. Aichmair. *Geschichten und Rezepte aus dem kaiserlichen Wien*. Wien, Modul, 1997.

Lazzari, Graziella. *Ricettario della Cucina Istriana, #2, #3*. Trieste, Edizioni Zenit, 1991.

Leghissa, Adolfo. *Trieste Che Passa: 1884–1914*. Trieste, Edizioni Italo Svevo, 1971.

Lihovay, Eva, ed. *The Historic Ghetto of Pest*. Budapest, Seriart Studio, no date.

Londero, Bruno. *Carducci e il Friuli*. Udine, Doretti, 1995.

Luzzani, Sandra, and Enrica Caimi, eds. *Il Calendario Lunare per il Giardino, l'Orto e il Frutteto con le Tavole delle Fasi Lunari*. Novara, Il Mosaico, 1998.

Magris, Claudio. *Microcosmi*. Cernusco (MI), Garzanti, 1997.

Maldini, Sergio. *La casa a Nord-Est*. Venezia, Marsilio, 1991.

Maniacco, Tito. *Breve Storia del Friuli dalle Origini ai Giorni Nostri*. Roma, Tascabili Economici Newton, 1996.

————. *Breve Storia di Udine*. Pordenone, Edizioni Biblioteca dell'Imagine, 1998.

Martin, Timothy. *Joyce and Wagner: A Study of Influence*. Cambridge, Cambridge University Press, 1990.

Mauriès, Patrick. *Quelques Cafés Italiens*. Paris, Quai Voltaire, 1997.

Menis, Gian Carlo. *History of Friuli: The Formation of a People,* trans. Marisa A. Caruso. Pordenone, GEAP, 1988.

Miloradovich, Milo. Cooking with Herbs and Spices. Garden City, Doubleday, 1950.

Muir, Edward. *Mad Blood Stirring: Vendetta and Factions in Friuli During the Renaissance*. Baltimore, Johns Hopkins University Press, 1993.

Nazzi, Gianni and Luca. *Dizionario Friulano-Italiano.* Cernusco (MI), A. Vallardi, 1997.

Paoli, Luisella. *Magnari Bisiachi.* Mariano del Friuli, Edizioni della Laguna, 1998.

Pilastro, Giorgio, and Gavino Isoni. *Miramare: The Castle of Maximillian and Charlotte.* Trieste, Fachin, 1984.

Plotkin, Fred. *The Authentic Pasta Book.* New York, Simon & Schuster, 1986.

———. *Italy for the Gourmet Traveler.* New York, Little, Brown, 1996 (and London, Kyle Cathie, 1998).

Potter, Timothy W. *Roman Italy.* London, Guild Publishing, 1987.

Potts, Willard, ed. *Portraits of the Artist in Exile: Recollections of James Joyce by Europeans.* Portmarnock, Wolfhound Press, 1979.

Powell, Nicolas. *Travellers to Trieste: A History of the City.* London, Faber, 1977.

Rabel, Roberto Giorgio. *Between East and West: Trieste, the United States, and the Cold War 1941–1954.* Durham, Duke University Press, 1988.

Rebellato, Pier Luigi, and Enzo Santese. *San Daniele dal Persutto al Prosciutto.* Vigonza (PD), Biblioteca Cominiana, 1993.

Rebora, Giovanni. *La Cucina Medievale Italiana tra Oriente ed Occidente.* Genova, Brigati Glauco, 1996.

Romanelli, Giandomenico. *Il Mondo di Giacomo Casanova: Un Veneziano in Europa 1725–1798.* Venezia, Marsilio, 1998.

Ruaro, Giuliapaola. *Passeggiando per Trieste.* Trieste, Fachin, 1988.

Saba, Umberto. *Tutte le Poesie.* Milano, Mondadori, 1988.

Saccari, Claudio. *Trieste: Una Città Così.* Trieste, Edizioni Italo Svevo, 1976.

Sachau, Susanne, and Vitko Kogoj. *Istria.* Novara, DeAgostini, 1997.

Scarel, Silvia Blason. *Aquileia: A Tavola con gli Antichi Romani.* Feletto Umberto (UD), Missio, 1992.

Spinosa, Antonio. *Il Poeta Armato.* Milano, Mondadori, 1987.

Squecco, Giovanna. *La Carnia in Cucina.* Pillinini Editore, 1997.

Stavroulakis, Nicholas. *Cookbook of the Jews of Greece.* Athens, Lycabettus Press, 1990.

Stuparich, Giani. *Trieste Nei Miei Ricordi.* Milano, 1988.

Svevo, Italo. *Scritti du Joyce.* Parma, Pratiche, 1986.

Tentori, Francesco. *Udine.* Roma, Laterza, 1988.

Tessitori, Antonio. *Gemona: Breve Recensione Storico Descrittive Compilato per Uso dei Visitatori.* Gemona, Società Vincoli d'Arte, 1905 (reprint 1998).

Torossi, Ermanno. *Ristoranti, Osterie e Frasche del Friuli-Venezia Giulia.* Colognola ai Colli (VR), La Libreria di Demetra, 1997.

Ulmer, Christoph. *Die Villen des Friaul.* München, Prestel, 1994.

Valli, Emilia. *La Cucina Friulana.* Padova, Franco Muzzio Editore, 1992.

Vinci, Stelio. *Al Caffè San Marco: Storia, Arte e Lettere di un Caffè Triestino.* Trieste, Lint, 1995.

Vizváry, Mariska. *Hungarian Cuisine.* Szeged, Corvina, 1994.

Wagner, Richard. *Selected Letters.* London, Dent, 1987.

Weiss, Beno. *Italo Svevo.* Boston, Twayne, 1987.

Wiskemann, Elizabeth. *Europe of the Dictators 1919–1945.* Ithaca, Cornell University Press, 1966.

Index